European Literatures of Military Occupation

Shared Experience, Shifting Boundaries, and Aesthetic Affections

European Literatures of Military Occupation

Shared Experience, Shifting Boundaries, and Aesthetic Affections

Edited by
Matthias Buschmeier and Jeanne E. Glesener

LEUVEN UNIVERSITY PRESS

Published with the support of the KU Leuven Fund for Fair Open Access, Universität Bielefeld, and Universität Luxemburg

Published in 2024 by Leuven University Press / Presses Universitaires de Louvain / Universitaire Pers Leuven. Minderbroedersstraat 4, B-3000 Leuven (Belgium).

ISBN 978 94 6270 407 7 (Paperback)
ISBN 978 94 6166 554 6 (ePDF)
ISBN 978 94 6166 591 1 (ePub)
https://doi.org/10.11116/9789461665546
D/2024/1869/22
NUR: 617
Layout: Crius Group
Cover design: Jason Anscomb
Cover illustration: Mit offenen Augen durch Belgien. Herausgegeben von der Propaganda Abteilung Belgien beim Militärbefehlshaber für Belgien und Nordfrankreich. Brüssel: Druckerei Steenlandt, 1942. Scan: Matthias Buschmeier

Table of Contents

PART 2
CULTURAL SPACES OF OCCUPATION

PART 3
WRITING UNDER/AGAINST OCCUPATION: STRATEGIES OF RESISTANCE AND PROPAGANDA

PART 4
REMEMBERING OCCUPATION

Acknowledgments

This volume is the result of a collaborative effort of scholars from different disciplines and countries who share a common interest in the topic of the literature of military occupations. It has grown out of discussions of a conference that took place at the Villa Vigoni, Italy in April 2022, which was generously funded by the MIS—Migration and Inclusive Societies research unit at the University of Luxembourg. At the top of Lake Como, the conference provided a stimulating environment for fruitful discussions and exchanges among the participants, who contributed to this volume with original and insightful chapters.

We are grateful to our home institutions, Bielefeld University and the University of Luxembourg, for their continuous support and encouragement for this project. We would also like to thank the Villa Vigoni for hosting us in their beautiful premises and for facilitating our work with their excellent services. We are indebted to all the contributors for their intellectual engagement and their willingness to rewrite their papers into coherent chapters of a book. We appreciate the work of Laura M. Rosell, who did a perfect and proficient language editing of the entire manuscript. We would not have been able to assemble this multilingual book as quickly and efficiently. This appraisal also extends to our student assistants at Bielefeld University, Florian Stühlmeyer and Malina Busse, who helped preparing the manuscript for print. Finally, we are thankful to Leuven University Press for accepting this volume for review, and for their professional and efficient handling of the publication process.

We hope that this volume will contribute to the ongoing academic debate on military occupations in history and present times, and that it will inspire further research and dialogue on this important and timely issue.

General Remark on Translations

We aimed to reach a broad audience, so we chose American English as the language for all articles in this volume. We acknowledged the translators at the end of each chapter if they were different from the authors. We also asked the authors to translate any quotes or use existing translations of the cited works to improve readability. For longer quotes, the authors could include the original texts in the endnotes. We formatted the titles of any literary and non-literary works in italics, followed by the translations in brackets. If the translation was from a published source, we also italicized the title. Otherwise, we used quotation marks for the translated title. If there is no published translation of a work in the reference section, it means that the quotes were translated by the authors themselves or the chapter translators.

Matthias Buschmeier and Jeanne E. Glesener
Bielefeld/Luxembourg, February 2024

European Literatures of Military Occupation

An Introduction to the Topic and Terminology of the Genre

MATTHIAS BUSCHMEIER

Europe–A History of Occupations

The experience of military occupation has fundamentally shaped communities and their members throughout Europe. Almost every European citizen has been affected by it. As Europeans, we have lived and still live in an "implicated community" (Morris-Suzuki 2005, 25–27), and we are entangled in a long-standing history of violence. These experiences, even if unconsciously, "live on into the present, and lodge themselves in the minds" (Morris-Suzuki 2005, 27) of Europeans. Occupation literature, however, shines a sweeping light on the heterogeneous yet still conjointly experienced "painful learning process" (Habermas 2001, 21) of Europe's "Europeanization." As a political and social entity, Europe is deeply connected to *and by* the experience of occupation. But as experience is both collective and individual, it is impossible to sum these experiences up into a single integrative concept of identity—although such a concept is perennially attempted on the battlefield of contested pasts.

In this volume, we propose that instead of trying to base a European identity on some set of (humanistic) common values (cf. Fortunati and Lamberti 2008, 131)—values that contrast so starkly with the bloodlands of European history (Synder 2010)—we should acknowledge that the experience of mutual violence, benevolence, friendship, love, or any kind of business relationship, particularly in the forms that are typical to military occupation, creates a web of guilty entanglements that Europeans cannot easily escape (Biess and Moeller 2010).[1] The literature of occupation weaves this web by displaying, remembering, and reconfiguring the workings of such a disconcerting life as that experienced under such conditions.

This book is the outcome of a common enterprise that emerged from an intensive four-day conference at the prestigious German–Italian Center for European Dialogue, the Villa Vigoni at Lake Como, in April 2022. When we first scheduled this conference, the starting point of this book, we could not be aware that our topic would turn out to be not only of historic but also of immediate relevance: suddenly, we were witnessing a military occupation within spitting distance, after Russia invaded Ukraine on February 24, 2022. It is not only Europe's history, especially in the 20th century—called 'the age of extremes' (cf. Hobsbawm 1995)—that has been deeply marked by the experience of military occupation during and after horrific wars; it is now again our very present. This book attempts to contribute to the understanding of the impact of Europe's 20th-century occupations by shedding light on the literary representations of such experiences.

Living under occupation means finding oneself in a situation of accelerated historical change and heightened social pressure. It seems obvious that such life conditions have effects on their literary representation. Literature both affects and is affected by this process in very different ways. It can provide heroic narratives of resistance; condemn collaboration and complicity; give insight into the often-complex, tragic, and desperate situations of persecuted groups and individuals—but it can also place itself in the shoes of the occupiers, sometimes even in a humanizing way. In short, occupation literature can portray human encounters in inhuman situations.

Jeroen Olyslaegers, author of *Wil* (*WILL*), a World War II occupation novel set in Belgium, writes in his opening chapter of this volume:

> World War II will never be over, because of its moral ambiguity that keeps haunting one generation after the next—although one must admit that literature, movies, and television series each play their part, and not all of them focus on the moral questions involved but rather indulge in story lines that can be described as exploitative.

Imagining life under occupation, in literature, often challenges or fortifies widespread assumptions about a nation's identity and its collective cultural memory; at other times, occupation is simply reduced to the backdrop for some adventurous story. What is more, and what has often been dismissed, is that the European literature on occupation also displays the occupation of European *minds*, with their history comprising a bundle of interwoven, rather than separated and separating, stories.

French historian Henry Rousso, in his famous book *Le syndrome de Vichy 1944–1987 (The Vichy Syndrome)* (published in 1987), as well as with Eric Conan in 1994 (Conan and Rousso 1994), argued that the French, for instance, remained obsessed with the era of German occupation as a means to avoid engaging with their country's present-day ethnic-political conflicts.[2] Rousso saw the expulsion of memory in the 1960s, in order to retain national unity and identity, as a healthy (if delayed) reaction by the body of the French People to the excesses of the *épuration* that had happened right after the war (Rousso [1987] 1991). The returning obsession with Vichy in the 1980s and 1990s, as he saw it, was the revenant of a sick national memory that was hiding away from current cultural and political conflicts. In this regard, Rousso presents a very identity-based view on the impact of occupation. Moreover, this view also focuses solely on France and its aspiration to resurrect as a great nation. Nonetheless, perhaps Rousso's core idea can be applied to other memory landscapes in Europe. Does the commemoration of occupation in contemporary European literature serve as a distraction from the challenges faced by the notion of a transnational European identity (at least in many European regions)? Or, conversely, do literary explorations of Europe's occupations facilitate and promote such a shared experience, by deconstructing the myths of national unity and identity that underlie the self-concept of many of the nation states that were reestablished after the two world wars and after 1989 (Lagrou 2019)?

Europe's 20th-century history has been described as a history of wars, or as Timothy Snyder (2010) has notably named it, a territory of "bloodlands." The continent's political landscape, as we see it today, was significantly shaped in the aftermath of World War I. Its territory went through a process of political reordering and restructuring. In light of the extensive character of this development, it is worth noting that the new structuring of the European landscape was hardly accompanied by the enduring presence of massive alien military forces—with the exceptions of the French and Belgian occupation of the Rhineland and the Ruhr to secure claims of reparations according to the Peace Treaty of Versailles, and at the edge of the continent in regions where national independence was soon destroyed through Soviet occupation and annexation (in Georgia, for instance).[3] That said, the history of military occupation in Europe is by no means restricted to the 20th century. Peter Stirk, distinguishing 'conquest' from 'occupation,' argued that its modern story started during the French Revolution and the Napoleonic Wars in the late 18th century (cf. Stirk 2016), even though after the Franco-Prussian War from 1870 to 1871, Central Europe did not experience any other major occupation by force again until the 20th century. World War I and its aftermath then confronted many Europeans with the reality of military occupations anew, although the occupations spawned by World War I can barely be compared with one another, having remained mainly regional and arisen out of special circumstances in each respective place.

This situation radically changed with Germany's attempt at subjugating almost every European country during World War II. In 1938, Czechoslovakia was destroyed under German pressure through the Munich Agreement, and Germany annexed the so-called Sudetenland. Poland was occupied by Germans and Soviets in 1939. The Hitler–Stalin treaty also paved the way for the Soviets to occupy Estonia, Latvia, and Lithuania. Hungary had lost parts of its territory to Nazi-Germany in 1938 and, after turning away from the Axis powers, was completely occupied by German forces in 1944. Albania was occupied by the Italians from 1939 to 1943, followed by the Germans, and became a satellite state of the Soviets from 1945 to 1946. The German ally Bulgaria was invaded by German troops on their way to occupy the Kingdom of Yugoslavia and Greece in 1941, and, in return, by the Red Army in 1944. The story in Romania was similar: after the regime's support of the German invasion of the Soviet Union, helping to kill and deport the local Jewish population, it fell prey to Stalin's imperialistic expansion. To make a long and sad story short: in East and Central Europe, people ultimately found themselves in a protracted scramble of diverse and changing regimes that, at least in some places, resulted in decades of occupation.

The northwestern theater in World War II was different but can also be described by a protracted and shifting occupation experience. France, Holland, Belgium, Luxembourg, Denmark, and Norway were all occupied by German troops. Later, Italy experienced German and Allied occupation, as did, of course, Germany and Austria themselves become occupied by the Allies after the war. It was only Switzerland, Sweden, Portugal, Great Britain, Spain, and (to a certain degree) Finland that did not have to bear alien occupiers during World War II.

After the Thirty Years' War and the Napoleonic Wars, Hitler's expansive imperial policy confronted millions of European citizens with the experience of an enduring occupation, forcing states and individuals into everyday ethical dilemmas over where and how to position themselves along the broad spectrum between collaboration and resistance. This experience of occupation continued after the war in many parts of Europe, even if the post-war occupation regimes differed enormously in character from Germany's wartime occupation practices. It is no exaggeration to claim that it is the experience of occupation, rather than the combat operations themselves, that most shaped Europe's history in the 20th century.

Historical Research on Military Occupation—Desiderata for Literary Studies

For a very long time, historians have investigated the history of occupations during World War II within the history of nation states and with respect to their impact on a sense of "national experience" (Stirk 2016, 1). Moreover, everyday experience under occupation has mainly been researched within the (often oversimplified) framework of the collaboration–resistance dichotomy. The historiography of occupation, thus, often partook of national narratives that were supposed to foster national identities. In the German case, for instance, a generation of perpetrator–historians sought to diminish the role of the *Wehrmacht* and its entanglement in massive war crimes, including the Shoah. It was not before the early 1990s that historians and social scientists from all over Europe gathered in an EU-sponsored project (Benz, Houwing ten Cate, and Otto 1996–2001; Bähr and Banken 2005) to research the national histories of occupation during World War II through a comparative perspective and to overcome national resentments and political taboos in the field. Historians, on the one hand, were able to pinpoint the very specific and shifting policies of Nazi Germany in its campaigns in various countries; on the other hand, they opened up a new perspective beyond the investigation of national cases. The state of occupation revealed itself as an experience that was, to a certain degree, common to almost all European societies at the time, and one that should, thus, be compared.[4]

Most recently, therefore, historians have argued that life under occupation escapes any easy dichotomy, such as the perpetrator–victim or the collaboration-resistance narratives. Historian Harald Führner persuasively argued that societies under occupation cannot be adequately described by loaded moral binaries, such as collaboration and resistance (see Führner 2007). Such simplifications do not adequately represent the everyday experience in these societies (Dieckmann, Tönsmeyer, and Quinkert 2003; Tönsmeyer 2014, 2015). Tatjana Tönsmeyer, in particular, criticized that this binary, which stems from the self-presentations of many post-occupied societies, merely reproduces their historical imaginations of separate perpetrator–victim communities that mirror the occupier–occupied dichotomy, rather than offering a corrective view on it. She coined the term "*Besatzungsgesellschaften*," that is, occupation societies.

Indeed, in contrast to their radical opposition on the battlegrounds, the experiences of occupiers and those occupied are necessarily far more intertwined and complex, considering the lasting temporal character of the occupations in Europe in the 20th century. Each occupation opened a "contact zone" (Pratt 1991, 1992) that also forced exchange and ongoing communication, transforming the military front into a selectively permeable membrane of contact. Stephanie Wodianka recently argued that such a contact zone is characterized by "interrelations between and the staging of control, unpredictability and improvisation" (Wodianka 2017, 8), which is also a very appropriate description of the occupation scenario. This is to say, occupation is—and became for many across Europe in the 20th century—a "social process of everyday life" (Długoborski 1996, 15), not limited to battle or to overt political conflict. For instance, historian and Auschwitz survivor Wacław Długoborski (1996, 14) criticized that much of the historical research on the German occupation in Eastern Europe was done from the perspective of the genocidal conduct of war in its *last* phase. To Długoborski, such a perspective ignores the fact that, in the beginning, in some regions, the German invasion was met with positive expectations; troops were welcomed as 'liberators' or 'protectors' from the Bolshevist regime (as in some Baltic States, Ukraine, and Romania for instance; see Bartusevičius et al. 2003; Feldmanis 2005; Dieckmann 2011). There was also support from fascist, Germanophile, or nationalistic groups in the Netherlands, Luxembourg, Norway, Croatia, then-Soviet Ukraine, Slovenia, Finland, and Romania. Such "long-denied histories of collaboration in the territories of former Nazi-occupied Europe" (Biess 2010, 2) have even continued to repress the perception of occupation as an experience that cannot be reduced to either resistance or collaboration after collaboration became acknowledged and researched within international Holocaust Studies.

Under the threat of latent or concrete violence, life under occupation also necessitated the continuation or reestablishment of a sort of normalcy: to visit sporting events, go dancing, fall in love—even with occupiers—and things alike. But this seeming normalcy was not accessible to everyone, and it differed enormously among the occupied territories. According to Tönsmeyer, these occupation societies were characterized by a highly complex and fluid web of relationships between occupiers and occupied: a dynamic situation marked by the omnipresence of potential or actual violence, amid ever-changing opportunities for action and participation in power structures.[5] In this sense, many Europeans, as occupiers and even as occupied, were indeed "implicated subjects" in Rothberg's (2019) terms. The subject position between the occupier and the occupied is strongly relational; it depends on the dynamics of power, privilege, and concrete historical circumstances, and escapes a static victim–perpetrator relationship. The implicated subject navigates a complex moral terrain.

This might be one of the reasons why the memory of occupation is so contested to the present day; individuals and communities that, beyond doubt, suffered under occupation and its aftermath are necessarily exposed to the idea that they or their ancestors helped "to propagate the legacies of historical violence and prop up the structures of inequality that mar the present" (Rothberg 2019, 1) in a similar way as the occupiers themselves did—an imposition indeed. To live under occupation means to experience the restructuring of political, social, moral, and cultural orders in everyday situations (Tönsmeyer 2015). In the same way as the implicated subject's connection to historical violence or injustice can range from passive complicity to more active, albeit possibly indirect, involvement, its temporal or spatial connection to the events may not be immediate or direct. In Rothberg's understanding, the concept thus expands beyond the individual's concrete experience of the events; instead, history's myriad possible subject positions spawn into a multiplicity of narratives and memories that coexist, interplay, and intersect.

We suggest that the complexity within occupied societies paved the way for very different moralities. Furthermore, we suppose that the multiplicity of moral positions under occupation could no longer be accepted after the war, and that this personal discomfort led to certain myths about widespread resistance, as well as to the idea of, for instance, a need for *épuration* in France or similar movements in formerly German-occupied countries. The ethical complexity under occupation is also a nuisance on a political level; it poses challenges for official memory politics in many European countries today, most prominently Poland, Hungary, and Romania. Although the role of literature in such discourses can be ambiguous, it bears noting that literature can, all the same, be instrumentalized as an expression of national identity and a tool of national-identity politics (cf. Momčilović's chapter in this volume). Such a perspective, however, ignores the fact that literature under occupation operates under the same moral plurality as people do in their everyday lives and follows very different rhetorical functions and strands of discourse for the collective memory of Europe (cf. Andersen and Törnquist-Plewa 2017). Literature can be instrumentalized as an expression of national identity and as a tool of national-identity politics; however, upon closer inspection, one tends to see that the narratives of heroism, victimhood, and perpetration that such literature presents are, in fact, very poriferous.

While historical research has led to an extensive analysis of the political, military, and social realities of occupation, the cultural and (more specifically) literary responses to this experience have, interestingly, not yet come under scholarly consideration in quite the same manner. Certainly, we see an immense research output on specific *aspects* of literature, as well as on individual literary texts within their national contexts. Among these research foci, it is no exaggeration to assume that the French literature of occupation has attracted more intensive research than other European literatures of occupation: from 2006 to 2010, Margaret Atack and Christopher Lloyd, at the universities of Leeds and Durham, respectively—along with their colleagues—identified more than 2,000 novels published since the war's outbreak and into the 21st century that deal with the period of occupation in World War II France (for an overview, see Atack and Lloyd 2012). It is clear that many more could be added for the last 10 years or so. In Germany, however, although quite a few authors who wrote about life in occupied territories were themselves employed in the *Wehrmacht* and participated in these occupations, the corpus that resulted out of this experience has rarely been examined systematically (for an exception, see O'Keeffe 2013). Furthermore, research that investigates the literary impact of post-war Germany's experience of occupation under the Allies has just taken off. It still seems true, as Christopher Lloyd suspected, that "the vast production of cultural material stimulated by World War II [...] makes it a phenomenon both remarkable and often unexplored" (Lloyd 2003, 4).

Henceforth, we also need to discuss the function of the enormous *continued* or *renewed* output of literary narratives of occupation depicting the years from 1938 to 1955. These narratives render possible a new imagination of the occupations, one that allows for viewing the broad complexity of life in that era with the moral dilemmas they posed, the new opportunities they opened, and the omnipresent threat of violence and death. Indeed, the 'new' literatures of occupation do a disservice to any identity politics that have historically tried to build on the occupation; in most cases, today's literature of occupation distinctly *opposes* national identity politics, as many examples in this volume demonstrate.

Meanwhile, in many other European countries, especially in Eastern and Southeastern Europe, the German and Soviet occupations are highly contested in their character from a historiographic perspective—but comparing one to the other is often seen as taboo (as Benedikts Kalnačs' chapter in this volume argues for the Baltic States). Unlike national historiographies, though, the literature of occupation cares little for such taboos; in representing the very complex and shifting realities under occupation, it often broke and still breaks taboos required for the post-war rebuilding of national identities. Literature imposes fewer limits on itself, so to speak, and thus allows us to access comparative perspectives that other disciplines either cannot or have been reluctant to offer.

As cultural artifact, occupation literature works on and within Europe's collective memories (cf. Erll 2011; Fortunati and Lamberti 2008, 2009), and beyond the long-discussed relationship between memory and nationhood. This relationship was (and sometimes still is) crucial to many European states in the process of redefining their national and cultural identities after World War II (cf. Lebow, Kansteiner, and Fogu 2006). Evidentially, one could argue that the idea of a communally shared memory of Europe is still a mere fantasy. We need to think of it as an "'open' and 'dynamic'" (Fortunati and Lamberti 2008, 131) narrative rather than as a monolithic entity. Furthermore, we do need to remember that our foggy European identities are influenced by a much longer history of European wars since the Thirty Years' War, and by Europe's colonial subjugations of major parts of the world since the 16th century—at least. European minds are largely imprinted by the continent's imperial experiences. Still, the literature of military occupation referring to World War II and the new order after 1945 reflects these events as a matter of 'Europeanness'—eliding the fact that these matters did not merely affect Europe alone. That said, the majority of Europeans never *experienced* the non-European theaters of war, nor the massive impact of colonialism on the colonized. By contrast, even if hundreds of books and newspaper and magazine reports, fictional and nonfictional, mediated the colonial enterprise for a large European audience, the literature of occupation speaks to an experience that *directly affects* European generations on a very concrete level and to which they relate in a very different way than to colonialism.

This—besides our dyed-in-the-wool Western racism—might be one of the reasons why Europeans today sympathize more with the victims of the Russian aggression in Ukraine than with those from any of the many wars inflicted by European colonialism on other continents. It might also be true that this is one reason why some African, Asian, and South American states do not join the US–European coalition against Russia; far too often, people outside of the US and Europe have seen that wars and occupations on their own continents did not lead to similar attention, as long as industrialized, wealthy, Western power interests were not severely touched by them. For Europe, however, it can be bluntly put: for a very long time, occupation has been an experience with which almost any European family is intimately implicated, whereas colonialism has not been in a similar manner. Nonetheless, it has been argued that the long-lasting experience of occupation, especially in Eastern Europe, has had dynamics and effects similar to colonialism. As Epp Annus writes, and Benedikts Kalnačs quotes him in his chapter:

> If the occupation does not end by expelling the occupiers from the country, then the relationship of domination in the occupied areas acquires features of colonialism: the occupiers settle in the occupied territory, and their ideology starts to change how the occupied people relate to the world. The oppressed country can still be called an occupied country, yet the economic, social and cultural models at work become those of the colonial enterprise. (Annus 2012, 37)

The relationship between occupation and colonialism is an intricate and debatable matter, as our forthcoming discussion of terminology (in the subsequent section) will reveal.

Our current debates on the aftermath of colonialism, which only now begin to transcend the academic sphere, indicate that the debate on how Europeans are affected by their history of colonialism is subject to change. Correspondingly, the notion of 'Europeanness' has undergone significant transformations as a result of the diverse and dynamic societies that constitute Europe today. It is neither accurate nor desirable, therefore, to equate 'Europeanness' with 'whiteness,' as doing so ignores the complex and intertwined histories of colonialism that shape both European and non-European communities. In fact, the legacies and repercussions of colonialism are as salient and relevant as those of occupation in contemporary Europe, although they may play different roles in the collective memory and identity of these communities.[6]

Occupation Literature—The Making of Psychogeographical Spaces

Our book features case studies and major narratives from a variety of European theaters of military occupation—Belgium, Bohemia, England, Estonia, France, Greece, Georgia, Germany, Italy, Latvia, Luxembourg, Moravia, the Netherlands, Norway, Poland, Serbia, and Romania—to examine how the transnational experience of military occupations from 1938–1955 is represented and memorialized in literary texts from wartime to the present.

In recent years, and as described above, occupation has been a topic of intensive historical research, and to some degree also in our field of literary scholarship. This book, as we believe, is distinct from other publications on the literature of occupation in five important ways.

First, the book approaches occupation as a phenomenon that *transcends political caesuras*, such as the end of World War II in 1945. As we have mentioned above, many European regions had already suffered from occupations before the war officially started in September 1939. Likewise, after the German occupation regimes collapsed in 1944–1945, this did not spell an end to the experience of occupation altogether (cf. Erlichman and Knowles 2018). On the contrary, Europe continued to transform dramatically under the changing regime of the new Allied occupiers, in Germany and elsewhere in Europe, especially in the East. This series of changes generated confusing role reversals in these incessantly occupied settings—an "age of metamorphosis," as Erlichman and Streicher recently characterized it (cf. Erlichman and Streicher 2022). We therefore seek to understand the wartime and post-war periods as not fundamentally separate from each other; indeed, the literature of occupation starkly reveals the periods' interconnectedness.

Second, we do not pursue a national focus in our investigations, since such a methodological decision runs the risk of perpetuating the same (national) identity politics that it claims to scrutinize. On the contrary, the chapters and parts, as read alongside each other, constitute a comparative perspective. Beyond the comparative view, we apply innovative methodological thinking to these case studies in the literature of occupation that attempts to supersede the oft-applied national foci.

Third, by this systematic approach, the book attempts to cast occupation literature as a *genre* rather than as a set of common thematic features. Moreover, as this is a genre that strongly relates to a specific historical moment, the question arises as to how it relates to its counterparts in factual literature (wherever a given work of occupation literature is fictional) or in other historical sources (wherever it is a work of non-fiction).

Fourth, the book offers the reader an integrative perspective on very distinct texts by understanding them as the articulation of, simultaneously, an individual and a collective experience of *European* citizens. Indeed, we suggest that stories play a major role in negotiating the meaning of the experience of occupation individually but also collectively. The literature of occupation reflects, in a nutshell, the proximity and interconnectedness of occupiers and the occupied.

Fifth and finally, our volume integrates new approaches that seek to understand the affective nature of the experience of occupation. The intricate narrative structures, symbolic overdeterminations, unreliable narrators, confusion about layers of time, and the material and symbolic reconfiguration and resemantization of space in occupation literature align with the multifaceted realities of life under occupation. This is especially true for spatial delineations between war and non-war with respect to gender. Cynthia Enloe, in her pioneering study of the gendering of war narratives, exposed the ideological strategies at play in the military's constant redefinition of war and its spaces "as wherever 'women' are not" (Enloe 1983, 15). Furthermore, Chris Cuomo and Miriam Cooke have queried the extent to which spatial boundaries between "war" and "non-war," combat zones and safe zones, relate to the experiences of women. Cuomo critiques that "the spatial metaphors used to refer to war as a separate, bounded sphere indicate assumptions that war is a realm of human activity vastly removed from normal human life" (Cuomo 1996, 30), and Cooke (1996) rejects the idea of a binary polarization between (male) war zones and (female) non-war zones.

This last element of the book's approach bears expanding upon, as it is also a good argument in favor of differentiating occupation literature from war stories. As we argue, the genres are not the same, since, in times of occupation, clear boundaries or delineations between militarized and civilian spaces get blurred. Moreover, in her argument, Cooke holds on to the binary between war and peacetime. The time of occupation, though, as we define it, is neither a time of combat nor of peace; instead, we see it as a time of constant threat and latent violence overlaid atop the continuation of daily routines. One could possibly discuss Cooke's conclusion that, for women, "the violence of war is not so different from the violence of peace" (1996, 43). We would argue that, in World War II, women and adolescent girls living under occupation were especially forced to make difficult choices in the midst of moral dilemmas, in order to secure their own and their families' lives, given that men—either deployed, displaced for forced labor, or imprisoned—were often absent. The European literatures of military occupation display such (en)gendered spaces as a reality that affects women in particular ways (as Buschmeier, Siess, Laffin, Mamatsashvili, and Schumacher show in their chapters of this volume). We argue that this situation cannot be easily compared with the peacetime experience, as the politics of sex, love, eating, and inhabiting (among other fundamental human needs) operate differently under occupation.[7] The majority of this book's chapters explore how occupation literature maps what, in reference to Guy Debord, Jeroen Olyslaegers calls the "psychogeographical space" of the European mental landscape in his chapter, and these spaces are experienced differently by the sexes.

As mentioned earlier, we argue that the complex and interconnected effects of different occupying regimes in Europe during and after World War II cannot be easily separated along political caesuras. Moreover, the literature of occupation is often sensitive to the transgenerational effects of the occupation experience. To illustrate this point with special respect to a gendered perspective, I shall briefly discuss—digressively but importantly—a contemporary example: Trude Teige's 2015 Norwegian novel, *Mormor danset i regnet*[8] ("Granny Dancing in the Rain"). This novel showcases many features of our genre in question; namely, Teige's plot shows how occupation creates transnational and gendered spaces that persist as 'psychogeographical spaces' across generations. I will summarize here the main events of the novel (spoiler alert!) and discuss how they reveal the heavily gendered moral dilemmas and challenges faced by women under occupation.

The plot is centered on the protagonist Juni's search for her family history, in her attempt to understand the pain and dysfunction so evident in her maternal line. It becomes quickly evident that the inherited chain of traumas begins with the titular character, Juni's "Mormor" (Granny), a woman named Tekla. No synopsis can do justice to the many nuances that Teige's novel portrays regarding the gendered affronts suffered by women and girls in times of occupation, but for the sake of extreme brevity, suffice it to say that Tekla personally suffers, witnesses, and/or becomes otherwise implicated with more than a few of these injustices.

First is the fact that Tekla is cast as a disgrace by her family, community, and country for the fact that she falls in love with a German soldier, Otto, during the Nazi occupation. Then, she loses her Norwegian citizenship on account of their relationship—and when Tekla later tries to recover it, her family refuses to cooperate. Once the Nazi occupation ends, she and Otto (now married) go back to his hometown of Demmin[9] in Germany, where Soviets have requisitioned his family home; food insecurity is rampant; and women, including the women of Otto's household, have been raped en masse. Tekla 'agrees' to carry on a sexual relationship with a local Soviet Commander (whose own wife was raped during the Nazi occupation of Russia) in an effort to avoid the same overtly violent fate as so many other women—as well as simply to survive amidst a time when food is so scarce. This latter development is a sort of double-injury to Tekla's psyche; not only have the unnatural circumstances of the occupation pressed her into submitting to a sexual relationship that, obviously, cannot be called entirely consensual, but this arrangement now also leaves Tekla to contend with a burden of guilt for being unfaithful to the husband whom she loves so much that she has already sacrificed home, country, and reputation.

Eventually, hoping to flee the Soviet zone before it can be turned into a satellite communist state, Tekla and Otto decide to go to Hannover, in the British zone of occupation. Instead, they are intercepted by a Russian patrol, who murders Otto and then gang-rapes Tekla. This is how Tekla becomes pregnant with her daughter Lilla, the protagonist Juni's mother.

Yet the gendered travails of occupation *still* do not end for her: stateless, widowed, traumatized, and pregnant, she now tries to reach Berlin to reacquire her Norwegian citizenship. The endeavor is ultimately fruitless, but, in Berlin, she witnesses how the American occupation is imposing its own gendered violations onto the crumbled city's women and girls, and how the local women and girls, in turn, are pushed by their own fear and starvation to acquiesce to unwanted sexual liaisons, too.

When Tekla then meets and marries a Norwegian man named Konrad (resigning herself to a future in which she never lives in Norway again) Konrad is willing to accept Lilla, despite knowing that he is not the biological father; indeed, Tekla forever hides the secret of how Lilla was conceived. But Tekla's marriage to Konrad is not a happy ending—because the *intergenerational* aspect of Tekla's occupation trauma is just beginning: while Tekla suffers from anxiety and depression through the rest of her life, Lilla suffers under the stigma, even decades later, of being the daughter of a *tyskertøs* (a derogatory term for Norwegian women and girls who had liaisons with occupying Germans) and falls into alcoholism as a result. Meanwhile, the protagonist Juni, raised by an alcoholic mother, falls into a marriage with an abusive man. It is only when Juni herself becomes pregnant (by her abuser) that she decides to investigate the missing puzzle pieces of her family history, to understand her female forebears better and, it is hoped, forge a healthier home life for her own unborn child.

Through this plot, Teige masterfully illustrates a vast breadth of gendered traumas under occupation, as well as their intergenerational effects. Simultaneously, she incorporates a helpful device that bridges the occupations' affective realities with their historical ones: she includes two historian characters to help Juni with her family history search.[10] While one of these characters, Georg, becomes Juni's love interest and ultimately welcomes her unborn child (much like Konrad did for Tekla and her daughter Lilla), one can surmise that Teige wrote him as a historian largely for the reader's benefit (i.e., to complement the narrative with historical exposition in an organic and engaging way).

In the end, the reader understands that Juni's child will be raised in a still-implicated but now-enlightened family, as her newfound insights into the complex transgenerational and transnational history of the experience and effects of occupation finally allow her to accept all her positive memories of her mother and grandmother, and to start anew with Georg and her child.

Mormor danset i regnet highlights how occupation is a gendered phenomenon: women had to negotiate their roles as mothers, daughters, lovers, citizens, and survivors in a hostile environment, but they also enacted agency and resistance in their own ways. Teige's book also shows how occupation transcends national borders and temporal bounds.[11] Moreover, as do many other examples discussed in our volume, her novel ultimately explores how occupation affects individuals and societies on many levels at once: political, social, cultural, psychological, emotional, ethical, and even physical—the *affective* realities of occupation, as we would like to name them.

Our book argues that the literature of occupation can serve as a model for investigating such affective realities of occupation. Furthermore, it contends that, unhampered by the constraints of traditional historiography, the literature of occupation contributes a much-needed, more emotionally impactful portrait of this particular chapter of European history.

Terminology and Material

Having already presented a very characteristic example of our genre, we need to reconsider some terminology used throughout the volume. As we propose to shed new light on the literary and cultural representation of occupation as a European experience, we suggest forming a European corpus that, until now, has never even been considered a corpus at all. How we define the term 'occupation' has direct implications for the scope of our corpus. In this section, thus, we will propose some definitions for different types of occupation and provide a working definition for what we mean by 'occupation literature.'

Occupation

In this book, we focus on the concept of military occupation as a specific mode of transforming the political geography of a territory. We do not address other forms of changing the boundaries or affiliations of states, such as referendums for secession or voluntary integration with another state. We also exclude cases where states redraw their borders through diplomatic negotiations, even though such policies may sometimes trigger further conflicts and subsequent military occupations.

The *Hague Convention (IV) of 1907*, as a result of a series of multilateral conferences that began in 1899, provides a legal framework for the rights and obligations of occupying powers and the protection of the civilians and property of the occupied territory. According to Article 42, a territory "is considered occupied when it is actually placed under the authority of the hostile army. The occupation extends only to the territory where such authority has been established and can be exercised" (*Hague Conventions of 1907*). In other words, military occupation occurs when an invading force takes control of an enemy territory and establishes authority over it. Following the contents of Article 43, the *Hague Conventions* go on to explain *how* the occupying power should govern the occupied territory, maintain order and security there, and enforce its own laws, while respecting the existing laws and customs of the occupied population. Literally, this means that the authority of the invaded state is exercised by the occupying forces (Stirk 2009, 37), whose own actions are (at least in theory) restricted by international humanitarian law, which prohibits acts of violence, looting, and destruction, and requires the provision of essential services and medical care to the civilian population. The occupying power must do everything it can to ensure safety and public order, and it is expected to respect the laws already in force within the occupied country. To summarize, three fundamental principles govern the international law of occupation:

> (a) sovereignty and title to an occupied territory are not vested in the occupying power; (b) the occupying power is entrusted with the management of public order and civil life in the territory under control; (c) occupation is temporary and may be neither permanent nor indefinite. (Gross 2017, 3)

The concept of military occupation remains highly contested, reflecting differing interpretations of international law and the political dynamics of conflict situations (cf. Gross 2017, 1–16). The history of World War II's occupations, as well as examples from more recent times, has challenged the humanitarian intent of international law to the point that one must question whether international law regarding occupation has even been helpful. On the contrary, applying the existing law of an occupied state by way of an occupying power may also be problematic, especially if the legal system of the occupied state was one of the factors that triggered the invasion; such a scenario could create conflicts of interest and undermine the legitimacy and credibility of the occupying power's actions in the eyes of the people who suffered under the old juridical system. The Allied forces in Germany, for example, did not consider the Nazi regime and its laws to be legitimate and thus refused to comply with the regime's racist and antisemitic policies—even though the Allies' refusal to implement Nazi policies in post-war Germany might technically have represented a violation of the *Hague Conventions'* Article 43.

One of the reasons why the concept of military occupation in international law is contested is that it involves a power dynamic in which a dominant state exerts control over a subordinate state that has been defeated or is unable to resist. This raises issues of sovereignty and the right to self-determination, as well as the potential for abuses of power and violations of human rights. Gross (2017), as do other scholars of international law, argues for a normative understanding of the term that restricts occupation regimes to the three principles mentioned above. If one decides, rather, to look into the realities of occupation though, the legal definition of military occupation seems not always clear-cut. This fact leads to disagreement among states and legal scholars about whether certain forms of intervention constitute legitimate occupation or not.[12]

The *Hague Conventions* define occupation exclusively as a relationship between nation states, which raises the question of whether territories that do not belong to any nation state and have no sovereign government can technically be referred to as 'occupied.' Eyal Benvenisti points out that, since the term "occupation"

> was meant to safeguard national sovereignty, it could not apply to regions whose sovereignty was not recognized. The prevailing view among the mainly European powers was that sovereignty, as a 'gift of civilization,' did not extend beyond the circle of self-defined 'civilized,' mainly Christian nations. For the European theater in the 20th century, this might be a negligible question. (Benvenisti 2008, 647)

We suggest a definition of the term with a slight, but important, variation: in our understanding, 'occupation' is an enduring presence of military forces in a territory that technically belongs to *an external political entity*—and not always necessarily a state.[13] This definition differs from the common usage of the term, which often implies a violation of international law or human rights. We argue that our definition is more precise and objective, as it does not depend on the legal or moral status of the occupying power, nor of the occupied population. Rather, it focuses on the factual and spatial aspects of occupation.

One of the terms we avoid using in our definition is 'foreign,' as this word implies a radical difference between occupiers and occupied. When such a binary opposition is invoked, it might be a rhetorical strategy. For instance, in a conflict between neighboring countries, such as Ukraine and Russia, the word 'foreign' can be used to create clear-cut boundaries, rather than to acknowledge the complex ties of proximity. Furthermore, we use the term 'political entities' instead of 'nation states,' as the latter might disqualify imperial aggressions on communities that do not conform to the Western concept of the 'nation state' from being considered occupations (as some scholars have argued for Asia; cf. Baillargeon and Taylor 2022, 2).[14]

This is not to suggest that military occupation and colonization are identical in character. Stirk, for example, contends that occupation and colonization employ different modes of exercising power with respect to sovereignty. One important distinction is that occupation should be understood as a temporary phenomenon (based on the definition of occupation given in the *Hague Conventions*); by contrast, colonization is generally understood as indefinite. In this view, the occupier exercises absolute authority over the occupied territory, but it *does not possess sovereignty* over it. In contrast, under colonization, "imperial powers asserted sovereignty over the territories they claimed as colonial possessions. Indeed, they often justified their assertion of sovereignty on the grounds that there were no sovereign authorities in the territories they claimed" (Stirk 2016, 5; see also Stirk 2009, 43). Thus, Stirk warns against hastily equating "military occupation and colonialism" (Stirk 2016, 5). He acknowledges, however, that the term occupation has been widely used in the context of colonial enterprises, "but with the very different purpose of asserting title to sovereignty" (Stirk 2016, 6).

During World War II, Nazi Germany employed different strategies for occupying various European countries. Some countries, such as the Balkan states or Italy, were occupied mainly for military advantage. Others, such as the Netherlands or Norway, were regarded as '*Brüdervölker*' (sister nations) according to the Nazis' racist ideology and were supposed to have puppet regimes loyal to Berlin. Still others were targeted for annexation into the Reich based on the concept of '*Lebensraum*' (living space), which Hitler and Nazi foreign policy used to justify the colonialist exploitation of Eastern Europe.

Some commentators, thus, prefer the term 'belligerent occupation,' in continuation of the Roman idea of *occupatio bellica*. This term refers to the occupation of enemy territory during an armed conflict when a belligerent actor is in control of some of its adversary's territory and is directly responsible for administering that territory. The *British Manual of the Law of Armed Conflict*, for instance, includes the occupation of neutral territory during wartime as an example of belligerent occupation, but it excludes situations wherein another military has entered a territory in order to liberate it from a belligerent actor or wherein a territory is being administered by an international organization such as the United Nations (Stirk 2009, 37). As Stirk points out, the various core meanings that can be ascribed to any given occupation affects the range of *types* of occupation that exist; in other words, military occupation suggests a wider range than belligerent occupation does (Stirk 2009, 37).

One might question the usefulness of distinguishing between occupation and colonization in this context. As Stirk argues, the historical actors may have assigned different meanings to these terms, but that does not necessarily imply that we, as scholars, should adopt their terms as analytical categories. In fact, when

we examine the social and political realities of occupied and conquered societies, we may find more similarities than differences, as Knowles recently suggests.[15] Within short course, the reality of occupation for a '*Brudervolk*,' despite
the ostensibly fraternal reasons for the occupation to have arisen, were liable to
turn quickly into sheer brutality during World War II. We also remind that occupation was already a daily threat to life for local Jews and other groups who
were considered 'hostile' to the 'Aryan' race, even during the earlier, less broadly
violent days within the *Brudervolk* territories.

Ultimately, we argue for a wider application of the term 'occupation' than international lawyers and scholars such as Stirk propose: we believe that 'occupation' should not only refer to the legal or governmental status of a territory under
foreign control, but also to the social and psychological effects of living under
such conditions. At the same time, we still want to distinguish between various
types of military occupation. By no means are all occupations the same. It may
matter, to emphasize just one point, whether the occupiers intend to incorporate
or associate the occupied territories with their own state. On the basis of this
criterion, we can distinguish at least five different variants of occupation, with
respectively distinct possible consequences for occupied populations.

1. Forces invade a territory of another political entity for certain ends and aims
   (for instance, to prevent greater harm to their own populations, to enforce
   reparation duties, to reeducate the population, or to implement or forestall
   bi- or multilateral agreements) but *without* the intention to annex it. Examples: the French and Belgian invasion of the '*Ruhrgebiet*' after World War I,
   or the Allied occupation in Germany after World War II.

2. Forces invade a territory of another political entity *with* the intention to annex it, and the occupier is willing to incorporate the alien population as
   long as it obeys the new rulers. Colonial regimes of 'indirect rule,' as well as
   the German attempts to establish so-called '*Aufsichtsverwaltungen*' ('super-
   visory administrations') in the occupied territories of World War II (e.g.,
   Finland, Norway), are examples of such an occupation policy. The Soviet
   occupation in the Baltic States and elsewhere also seems to belong to this
   category.

3. Forces invade a territory of another political entity *with* the intention to annex it, and the occupier is *not* willing to incorporate the alien population,
   but instead pursues the population's displacement, relocation, or extinction.
   Examples can be drawn from many cases of ethnic cleansing during World
   War II and beyond.

4. Forces invade a territory of another political entity *with* the intention to annex it, and the occupier is willing to incorporate major groups of the alien
   population for certain economic needs. However, at the same time, the new

rulers pursue the displacement, relocation, enslavement, or extinction of other groups considered hostile, racially distinct, or simply 'not useful' in the eyes of the intruders. The German occupation regime in Eastern Europe, especially in Poland and the Soviet Union during World War II, is the most horrific example.

5. Forces are accepted or even invited by another regime or political group to move in and act without restrictions within its territory, since these forces are considered an ally. Most likely, the 'host' of such an occupation has depended on the occupier's power to obtain its own power position. Short-term regimes such as in Croatia, Slovakia, Romania, and, to a certain extent, in Italy and Vichy-France during World War II would be examples of this sort. Occupation that received the consent of the sovereign can also be termed 'pacific occupation' (Benvenisti 2009).

As a matter of course, these policies can intermingle, interlock, or blend into one another over time. Regardless of the type, belligerent or pacific, any occupying power, beyond military intervention and suppression, requires political, administrative, and cultural actions that, to a certain degree, need to involve and are dependent upon parts of the occupied population. In other words: complicity and collaboration are inherent consequences of the definition of occupation because the application of the term requires the substitution of authority for that of the ousted regime.[16]

Literature of Occupation: Concept and Periodization

One of the aims of occupying forces is to control the landscape of the occupied territory. To achieve this, they establish a military presence and create new orders in administration, law, executive power, and the economy. However, occupiers often face a central challenge: their resources are limited or needed elsewhere. Therefore, they seek to reduce resistance and increase collaboration and complicity among the occupied population.

During World War II, occupiers used various strategies to create an atmosphere of complicity, such as restricting food supply, creating competition for living space, or manipulating other basic needs. Furthermore, cultural intervention and adoption became techniques by which not only the Germans but also the Allies after invading German controlled territories tried to change local attitudes toward the occupiers. Therefore, a history of the literature of occupation must also examine the cultural life within occupied territories, by analyzing the socioeconomic conditions of producing "cultural goods" under occupation (see, for German cultural politics in various occupied countries: Benz, Otto, and Weismann 1998; for the French situation under occupation, the following groundbreaking books: Sapiro 1999 and Cantier 2019).

This brings us to the main question that we intend to explore with the term 'literature of occupation.' How do we define our corpus? We propose that any literary work should be primarily regarded as 'occupation literature' if:

(a) it includes episodes located in occupied territories, and

(b) it depicts any form of interaction between occupiers and occupied.

In addition to this very basic definition, a couple of further characteristics can (but do not necessarily need to) appear. Namely:

(c) the absence of actual battlefield fighting (the possibility for this absence being what separates 'occupation literature' from mere 'war literature')

(d) instead, the representation of everyday life under occupation

(e) the portrayal of situations of ethical dilemma that can lead either to complicit or antagonistic behavior among the occupied, and, hence, represent the complex living conditions in occupied communities.

This definition, and the chapters in this book, thus, transcend Molasky's proposal in his study on the literary representation of the American occupation of Japan in Japanese Literature. Molasky focuses only on literature published after the occupation ended, and hence, on the question: "How has Japan's experience of the occupation been recreated when filtered through the literary imagination?" (Molasky 1999, 1). He chooses literary works "that depict interaction between the American occupiers and the occupied populace" (Molasky 1999, 3) in order to distinguish his coining of the term "occupation literature" from a broader definition in the sense of "literature under occupation" (the latter of which includes works written during but not about the occupation).[17]

We adhere to this notion of his approach that highlights the representation of the social interactions between occupiers and occupied. All being said, where we differ is the question of how an author relates to the events in space and time. Molasky's focus in his inquiry is not on whether the events that a work narrates are autobiographical or fictional. Rather, he is interested in how these stories represent the experience of living under foreign occupation, how they connect with other stories on the same topic, how they contribute to the wider discourses on the war and post-war periods, and how they reveal the relationships between the occupiers and the occupied. Our volume contains many chapters that address similar questions, but we contend that an author's relationship to the narrated events matters for determining the cultural position of a text in the discourse on occupation. We use the term "relationship" to encompass both the temporal and the spatial distance between the author and the events, as well as the author's perspective and attitude toward them. By examining how different authors relate to their subjects, we can better understand how they construct and communicate their views on occupation over time. In light of the previous discussion on the various possible types of occupation regimes, we suggest a more nuanced approach to the problem: rather than treating all cases as equivalent, we argue that it is necessary to distinguish between different types and degrees of complexity. This would allow us to develop more specific and effective solutions for each scenario. Hence, we differentiate between texts as follows:

(a) written under the experience of occupation, whether authored by occupiers or the occupied,

(b) written after the occupation ended, authored by those who had experienced it (as occupiers or occupied), or

(c) written after the occupation by authors who did not live under nor participate in the occupation, but rather who return to it by means of historical documentation, fictional imagination, and generational tradition. These texts, intentionally or not, take part in memory politics and are often contested within their national contexts.

Molasky contrasts the lived experience of occupation with its post-war memory, implying a clear distinction between the war and post-war periods. Such a model suggests that, for the European theater, the timeframe of 1938–1945 corresponds to the German occupation regimes established throughout Europe—albeit heterogeneous in character. However, this approach does not account for the complexities and continuities of occupation and its aftermath. Specifically, the second occupation period—the post-war period spanning from 1945 to 1955—was marked by several significant events that shaped the political and social landscape of Germany and Europe overall. These events included: the presence of Allied forces in Germany and other European countries after World War II; the plans of some neighboring countries, such as the Netherlands, Belgium, and Luxembourg, to annex parts of German territory; the establishment of two separate German states in 1949, namely the Federal Republic of Germany (FRG) and the German Democratic Republic (GDR); the occupation of Eastern European countries by the Soviet Union; the death of Stalin in 1953, which led to some changes in the Soviet occupation regime in the Baltic States; and finally, the official end of the occupation period in West Germany through the signing of the General Treaty (also known as the Bonn–Paris conventions) in 1952 and 1955.

The experience of occupation varied greatly across and within these periods, and a major part of our work is to illuminate the specificities of each. While we argue for a fundamental difference between the German and Allied occupation regimes, we do not suggest that we should view this transition in occupations as a temporal rupture. People and their attitudes did not change overnight. Moreover, our case studies in this volume demonstrate that there was no *Stunde Null* (zero hour), neither specifically in the German nor in the broader 'European Literature of Military Occupation.' Rather, it seems that when we shift our focus from the war novel as a genre to the 'Literature of Military Occupation' as a genre, we are faced with the question of how the time periods are, in fact, intimately connected, as could be seen in the example of Teige's novel that I discussed earlier. 'Occupation literature,' in other words, is a genre that precludes the fantasy of a fresh start, since it constantly confronts everyone with the ethical dilemma of having lived or of still living under occupation, to name just one salient issue. Our volume deliberates how this connection is established and how this passage of time is constituted, by aesthetic and narrative means.

For many Europeans, the experience of occupation did not stop with the end of the war. Of course, for most Europeans and for some Germans, the war's end did mean a liberation from the hated Nazi occupiers. Liberation by the Allies was indeed the end of the dehumanizing imperial politics of Nazi Germany. Still, the American landing in southern Italy, for instance, has been portrayed as an occupation in Italian literature (cf. Glynn 2015; Ninno 2023; and Laffin's chapter in this volume). Furthermore, the beginning of the East–West divide and of the so-called Cold War led to a situation in which the liberators (including *but not only* the soldiers of the Red Army) were also considered new occupiers. (In this volume, see Bogdal's chapter on the British and Schell's chapter on the Americans as occupiers; I have also discussed Trude Teige's novel as a striking example of this.). The Allies called their administered territories 'occupied zones' (*Besatzungszonen*), and they meant for the territories to be handled as such.

Meanwhile, in the cases of the Netherlands and France, the former occupied parties reassumed the role of occupiers in some of their own colonial territories. Do colonial occupation practices and their representations change after the colonizer has had the experience of being occupied? This is highly discussed in the French context, especially with respect to the occupation of Algeria and its War of Independence (see, for the Netherlands and Indonesia: Romijn 2022). And if colonial occupation practices *do* change in response to the experience of the colonizer having been occupied, can theories of postcolonialism be applied to occupation? Benedikts Kalnačs, for instance, argues in his chapter in this volume that the Soviets attempted to transform the Baltic states from states under occupation into colonies of some sort, by strategies with which we are familiar through European imperialism and colonialism—and, thus, according to Kalnačs, could be described with terminologies from postcolonial studies.

In Eastern Europe, the renewed presence of the Red Army and the population's involuntary integration into the Soviet Union or the Warsaw Pact were perceived as a continuation—sometimes even a fortification—of the occupation during World War II. The history of occupation in Eastern Europe is also complex because, in some territories, such as Georgia (see Mamatsashvili's chapter) or the Baltic States (see Kalnačs' chapter), people experienced a swift transition from Soviet to German occupation and back. This situation forced many authors into exile, and strangely enough, as they fled from the Soviets into Western Europe (especially into France) prior to World War II, some eventually found themselves in occupied countries once again. As a consequence, their writing mirrors the experience of different occupations tumbling into one another, producing 'kaleidoscopic' mental spaces of individual and collective remembrance. In the Baltic States in particular, the German and Soviet occupations paved the way for national identity narratives, which are commemorated very differently in each of the three states (Velmet 2011). This reminds us that the term 'occupation' itself is not only a 'scientific' term (so to speak) for describing a certain historical situation but rather is also an interpretive formula; in the interpretive sense, 'occupation' becomes conceptualized as a situation whereby individual agents and groups intervene in the realm of another people's cultural politics.

In summary, the history of Europe's World War II occupation literature should not be divided into compartmentalized time periods, but instead should consider occupation and its representation as a continuous and shared experience across political caesuras. This approach would allow for a more nuanced and comprehensive understanding of how different writers from different countries and contexts responded to the moral ambiguities of living under domination during and after the war.

Occupation Literature: From "Affected Realities" to "Affective Realism"

As a genre that strongly relates to a specific historical moment, the question arises of how the fictional literature of occupation relates to its counterparts in factual literature – that is, sources that historians usually trust to access historical realities. It would be naïve to think of fiction as the representation of historical truth. Nor can fiction be treated the same way as ego documents, for instance, which have become a central source in Occupation Studies (see also Siess in this volume). Simply put, literature, even the in the most realistic vein, is not a clean window into history. Granted, probably no serious historian would make such a claim about her sources anyway, especially in the field of the history of experience. Instead, fictional occupation literature can be regarded as a subgenre of the historical novel—at least for texts that belong to categories b) and c) as defined above—and it must, to some extent, reflect the historical past as we conceive it. Otherwise, readers would despise such texts as inauthentic—pure imagination, conjecture, or fabrication—and thus incapable of informing our understanding of the past. This sort of dismissal even happens with factual texts that merely *appear* to be fictional; consider, for example, how the British public dismissed shocking contemporary occupation literature—factual included—as "propaganda" (see Rzepa's chapter). Thus, realism is a crucial element of fictional occupation literature if the author intends for the work to be illustrative of a concrete historical past and received as such. In this sense, occupation literature emerges as a subgenre of realism.

Realism, as a mode of representation rather than a specific literary period in the 19th century, can be achieved in two fundamental ways. First, a literary text can attempt to mimic the world as accurately as possible by portraying it in common and familiar terms. It is this resemblance to our perception of reality that makes a literary text 'realistic.' This conception of realistic literature led Plato to denounce the poet as a liar, arguing that poetry presents something as real that is not. Realistic literature, in this sense, is concerned with the level of the story, *histoire* in Todorov's terms, or what is narrated. It must conform to our understanding and experience of the world. Thus, in realism, the same fundamental laws and logic that govern our world must also apply to the fictional world, and if that logical order were disrupted, it would need to be explained by some psychological phenomenon, such as dreams or trauma intrusion.

The second mode of 'realistic literature' does not depend on the level of *histoire*, which is the content or events of the narrative, but on the level of *discours*, which is the way the signifiers construct the diegetic world. Hence, realism is an effect of literary technique, not necessarily a reflection of reality (which, of course, it could still be). In his recent book *Populärer Realismus* ("Popular Realism"), Moritz Baßler defines realism of this sort as a way of writing that "makes itself invisible, so to speak, and which—while reading—transports us directly to the level that is most important here, the level of the story" (Baßler 2022, 19). According to this definition, readers are not especially concerned with the signifiers, the rhetoric, or the aesthetic qualities of a text. Rather, they are immersed in the diegetic world created by the text (which may or may not be realistic according to the first mode). As readers, "we are close to the characters and their emotions and thoughts, and we are able to identify with them" (Baßler 2022, 19). Realistic literature, in this sense, seeks to make readers forget that they are reading a text composed of arbitrary signs, by using these signs in a conventional way. As Christoph Bode (1988, 148) relatedly argues, conventionalism creates the impression of closeness to reality. Baßler (2022, 46) contends that most contemporary literature is realistic in this sense, because it offers quick and easy reading, which is essential for economic success on a globalized book market. Realistic literature is thus "accessible" in every sense of the word (Baßler 2022, 46).

Realism is a common feature of many contemporary texts that depict World War II occupations; this use of a realistic style bridges the gap between the reader's present-day and the otherness of historical reality, largely because realism allows authors to employ certain strategies to convey the occupation experience more vividly and effectively. Since most readers have not lived through occupation, they may find it difficult to relate to a historical novel that portrays a reality very different from their own, especially under the conditions of a global book market with a huge diversity of readers. De Groot calls this phenomenon a kind of "double othering" (2010, 94), which occurs when readers are confronted with a history that not only is not their own, but is not part of their "imagined communities" either (Anderson 2006). To address this challenge, contemporary authors have adopted a form of 'popular realism' that uses familiar schemes of perception and linguistic expression to make the situation of a specific military occupation more accessible and less alienating for an international readership. This allows the reader to empathize with the characters and their fate, and to 'experience' occupation imaginatively, even if the fictional world and their own are quite dissimilar. In such a manner, the contemporary European Literature of Military Occupation indeed "address(es) a transnational community" (de Groot 2010, 97). It is evident that such realistic writing calls for an ethical conduct of writing, as readers easily suffer authentic fallacy due to this aesthetic form.

Teige's aforementioned *Mormor danset i regnet* is a very good example of such a kind of realism; although the story is challenging, complex, and spans three generations, the reader is always oriented and never confused about times or locations. The novel's German edition gives extra hints by using different typefaces, depending on whether a chapter is set in the present (Juni's story) or the past (Tekla's). Furthermore, we have two historian characters within the novel who explain the historical context. (It seems their explanations are directed more often to readers than to the protagonist.) The language is not very complex; large parts of the novel are written in easy-to-follow, quoted, direct speech. Finally, readers have insight into the characters' emotional responses to the story's events and can easily comprehend the actions resulting from them.

Christopher Lloyd, in his book on literary *Collaboration and Resistance in Occupied France*, asserts that the popularity of French Resistance novels published in the years right after the war resulted from their aesthetic simplicity and "crude Manicheism in ideological [...] terms" (Lloyd 2003, 158). The same is probably true for its German counterpart, the *Landser* novel. As pulp genres, both serve as an imaginative projection of the war experience: one depicts the myth of a people who joined the resistance movement, while the other portrays the image of a brave and honorable German soldier who fought a war that was ostensibly unconnected to the crimes of Nazi-elite perpetrators in the *SS* or *SD* (see also Meid's chapter in this volume on Kästner's very popular Greece travelogues, which transported such views into the post-war period). These genres tend to simplify the historical complexity into a clear-cut binary of good and evil, while their simplified ideological plots find their equivalent in a correspondingly simplistic aesthetic form.

In contrast, when things are not presented in such binary terms, the complexity of occupied societies and their memories requires more aesthetic sophistication than simple "clichéd adventure stories" (Lloyd 2003, 3) or even the popular realism of Teige's kind. Therefore, an author who wants to highlight the awkwardness and strangeness of a historical experience may choose to do so not only through the content of the story but also through the use of unconventional language and through a form that deviates from realism's norms. Very often, these novels use some kind of metafictional approach for the display of history.

Since postmodernism, metafictional narrative means have pointed toward the delicate relationship between history and fiction. As radically as they questioned this relationship in the 1970s, 1980s, and 1990s, they have become mainstream and popular since quite some time now. De Groot argues that "techniques of historical fiction *necessarily* imply a form that is self-conscious, complex, and questioning" (de Groot 2010, 100, emphasis in the original). In fact, some examples discussed in this volume seem to support this argument. Jeroen Olyslaegers in *Wil*, for example, employs a complex metafictional structure in order to transcend the historical plot and interlock it across three generations of family, up to the present (see Olyslaegers' chapter). Such form of aesthetic distancing, however, does not necessarily reduce the sense of reality that the text creates. It can rather enhance it by complementing the unfamiliarity or complexity of the historical experience with the perspective and style of the literary text.

The historical novel, however, not only reconceptualizes the relationship between past and present (de Groot 2010, 102). It also reconceptualizes the relationships between those who lived through this history, and even their relationship to those who are implicated with the history still today, whether this link across time remains alive by means of transmitted, transgenerational family memory or any other form. By avoiding conventional schemes and expressions, by deconstructing narrative stability and trust in the narrative voice—and thus rendering the historical experience less accessible—a text may draw attention to its own 'remarkableness.' This strategy, too, has its value; the challenges it presents for a reader might prompt critical thinking on a level that a more 'accessible' text might not. Namely, as Hutcheon (1988) pointed out, historiographic metafiction in postmodernism produces alternative versions of history that urge us to rethink the factual 'standard version.' This procedure not only appeals to the reader's imagination (as in popular realism) but also challenges the reader's cognitive abilities to comprehend the 'irritation' imposed by such a reading experience.

The reader is confronted with a text that resists easy interpretation and demands active engagement. This irritation is both a source of frustration and a stimulus for curiosity. Indeed, postmodern narrative techniques can often be perceived in contemporary occupation literature. To claim, however, as de Groot does, that they "are fundamental to the historical novel as a phenomenon or format" (2010, 108) neglects the fact that many examples of our genre subscribe straightforwardly to popular realism, which does *not* bother the reader with metafictional tricks. Furthermore, in this genre, postmodern narrative techniques (if applied) do not necessarily destabilize the relationship between the diegetic and historical world in the first place; on the contrary, they seem paradoxically to mimic the amplified complexity of social relations and instability of everyday life that exist under occupation. That is to say: aesthetic complexity can also be considered, if not as a means of authenticity in regard to factual truth, then rather as a means of portraying the authentic *affective* reality experienced under occupation.

Lloyd suggests that certain aspects of occupation "can be understood only through works that attempt to convey subjective experience" (Lloyd 2003, 5). Historians of the everyday history of occupation also seek to understand the affective nature of this experience, by turning to sources that (at least for a certain strain of historians) were long considered to be without much merit. Historians such as Nicholas Stargardt (2006) or Maren Röger (2015) have explicitly argued for incorporating into history scholarship the very subjective perspectives of people, such as through ego documents, in order to realize the full emotional, ethical, psychological, and physical impacts of occupation. Indeed, literary imagination seems to be an even better medium for capturing and conveying these dimensions of human experience. One possible way to understand the literary imagination of occupation is to consider it a form of double subjectivity. On the one hand, it involves an individual's representation of occupation by way of fictional characters that the reader accepts as real for the duration of reading, even if they are constructed in a complex and distanced manner. On the other hand, it involves the use of distancing narrative techniques that require and elicit an individual reader's response.

Perhaps this emphasis on the transmission of subjective experience is among the reasons why many contemporary novels on occupation ultimately do conform to the genre of popular realism. The European memory culture of World War II has relied heavily on the idea of testimony. For such a concept, it is crucial that readers can relate to 'real' victims through their literary counterparts, and aesthetic disruptions may hinder such identification.[18]

If one wants to learn in any detail about the experience of torture, the motivation of collaborators, the callousness of bureaucrats, the survival skills needed to be a clandestine agent, the attractiveness or brutality of Germans, one needs to turn to autobiographical writing and fiction, though all these examples are obviously central to any understanding of the effects of occupation. (Lloyd 2003, 5)

Fictional literature eventually shapes our perception of the past; it can create, reinforce, or challenge certain historical narratives through its aesthetic and affective potentials. One might even say that literature can capture the complexity of historical experience more accurately than any single factual source viewed in isolation.

Klaus-Michael Bogdal (2015) argues that war literature works through the omnipresent threat of violence and death by articulating emotional responses to these threats that result from the destruction of normalcy. Such a working-up is deeply marked by anxiety that can, of course, also disguise itself in displays of heroism or fantasies of supremacy. Bogdal contends that anxiety itself is a reaction to a situation of threat. 'Threat,' however, is not always an objective phenomenon; it often depends on and results from subjective perceptions that can barely be eliminated through factual knowledge. Hence, living under occupation accumulates such threatening subjective perceptions in a given society into a dense atmosphere of pressure and tension. The complexity that follows from the accumulation of multiple subject positions under occupation must be addressed, not only in the moment of experiencing it, but also while looking back at it in the attempt to reintegrate the extraordinary that became 'ordinary'—however unreal it might again seem now, being viewed from the present. 'Culture,' so to speak, activates certain registers for coping with such a situation of distress. Constructing a tradition of hostility with the invader can be one reaction; by contrast, the attempt to draw on ideas of neighborhood, kinfolk, cultural exchange, and similarity in order to reorient oneself amidst the experience of constant menace can be another. Then, after a war, articulating and ascribing guilt are yet another important formula for negotiating the affective impact that war and occupation have had on subjects and societies (Kitchen 2011; Kellenbach and Buschmeier 2022).

We propose to understand the literature of occupation as a model for investigating such 'affected realities' of occupation. Studies on the connection between emotions and literature (for an overview, see von Koppenfels and Zumbusch 2016) have demonstrated that this is not only a matter of content but also of form. The literature of occupation does not simply reflect history, as spelled out above. Rather, it often employs complex narrative techniques, such as symbolic meanings, unreliable narrators, or temporal shifts to convey the multifaceted realities of living under occupation. Although not necessarily representational, the *récit* (Genette) communicates the emotional and social impact of this reality. It emerges as an influence of the experience of occupation, and it influences the readers with it. Of course, this is not exclusive to the literature of occupation, but, by using this mode, many texts that we discuss in this book connect European readers with a collective experience shared in their family histories. This might explain why we still see so many novels about the various 20th-century occupations in our very present. Contemporary occupation literature is an "affectively engaged mode[] of representing the past" (Landsberg 2015, 2). Alison Landsberg coined the term "prosthetic memories" for "personally felt public memories that result from the experience of a mediated representation of the past" (2015, 3) through which people did not actually live. Even if, for her, the term is directed toward forms of memory in popular movies, historical reenactments, and the like, her definition can be applied here too. Occupation literature, especially in Category c introduced above (cf. p. 31), partakes in prosthetic memory as a "new form of popular public cultural memory," as the reader

> does not simply apprehend a historical narrative but takes on a more personal, deeply felt memory of a past event through which he or she did not live. The resulting prosthetic memory has the ability to shape that person's subjectivity and politics. (Landsberg 2004, 2)

For Landsberg, what above have been described as postmodernist aesthetic techniques, are ways of "calling of attention to mediating devices," given they "have the effect of provoking the awareness that one is thinking" (Landsberg 2016, 6). These forms constitute a new relationship between affect and cognition with respect to the past, and their impact differs from mere emphatic identification, as they leave the consumer in a cognitive subject position. Affective modes of historical representations do not conflate past and present in some undifferentiated stream of events and feelings. On the contrary, they encourage the recipient to reconsider their relationship with an un-experienced past in the light of an aesthetic experience in the present. Landsberg argues that for the "history of mass trauma" (Landsberg 2015, 9), which military occupation obviously was and is, prosthetic memories can serve as a way to create a more holistic account of the past than any objectified historiography.

The term 'popular realism' has a strong negative connotation in literary criticism and emphasizes marketability over artistic merit. Therefore, it may not be entirely suitable for describing the literature of occupation, which has—as readers will see in this book—various forms and functions. We thus propose, instead, the term 'affective realism' to capture the main characteristic of this genre, and to acknowledge its working to establish prosthetic memories. Affective realism is realistic in its attempt to represent historical worlds as accurately as possible on the level of story (*histoire*), sometimes using familiar schemes and language on the level of discourse (*discours*). Most importantly, though, on both of these levels, affective realism is realistic in bridging the spatial and temporal gap between events and readers by showing affective modes of experiencing occupation. German author Olga Grjasnowa recently noted, on the relationship between literature and history, that their distinction is not a question of truth versus fiction; it is "a question of genre" (Grjasnowa 2022, 6).

Conclusively, this book posits that literary representations of occupation provide not necessarily a superior, but rather a *distinct* and *complementary* viewpoint to factual sources. Occupation literature enriches our comprehension of the historical complexities of military occupation, placing us in a more emotionally resonant relationship with a past that we may not have experienced firsthand, yet to which we remain intrinsically connected.

Structure of the Book

This book is divided into four parts, each of which will carry a brief introduction by Jeanne Glesener. Part one, "Literature and the World: Occupation as a European Experience," opens the volume with two chapters in which the theoretical framework and the hypotheses of the volume are elaborated. Chapters 1 and 2 start with considerations about the literature of occupation as a genre, arguing that literature is unique in its potential for depicting the historical realities of occupation. Writing that takes shape under or that focuses on occupation necessarily must find a specific way to incorporate the real into the fictional world. This part of the book discusses those ways and means. It examines the relationship between history and literature with respect to, most especially, the multifaceted ethical dilemmas that military occupations produced in everyday situations throughout Europe, both in their moment and in their wake. Each of these two chapters offers its own unique perspective. Chapter 1 is written by distinguished Belgian Dutch-language novelist and playwright Jeroen Olyslaegers, and he reflects on the production of an occupation novel. Chapter 2 presents three distinct case studies from different European regions and time periods to pinpoint occupation as a trans-European experience. Neither chapter asks how historiography can be understood as akin to narrative literature; on the contrary, both chapters illuminate how fictional literature aligns with (non-fictional) historical realities.

The five chapters in the second part, "Cultural Spaces of Occupation," testify to the varying geocultural transformations of occupied spaces, and how occupied and occupying writers used literary processes of intertextuality and interpretation to confer new meaning to them. Part 2 starts out with Chapters 3 and 4 analyzing how intertextual framing was used in order to cast the enterprise of occupation in all but mythic terms, such as in the topoi of occupying soldiers as Homeric heroes in instances where occupation was styled as tourism in travelogues, or where authors drew upon the Greek classics to illustrate the destruction of entire cultural landscapes and their populations. The following three chapters—Chapters 5, 6, and 7—while highlighting the social transformations that spaces underwent, as witnessed *specifically* in exiled and conscripted writers' ego-documents, novels, and poems, show how such transformations are also linked to the construction of conflicting images of self and other, and how these dynamic images form in response to the symbolic, material, and geographic domination of cities—their scapes, their spaces, and their resemantization and appropriation by the occupying forces.

Part three, "Writing Under/Against Occupation: Strategies of Resistance and Propaganda," takes a closer look at occupied territories as an intercultural contact zone and the devices used to implement cultural policy and propagandist discourses. While Chapter 8 highlights the role of occupiers who (in the highlighted cases) aimed at shaping the attitudes of the US-American public for propagandist purposes, Chapter 9 demonstrates how literary competitions were organized and promoted as a way of encouraging the occupied population to produce literature that aligned with the imposed ideology. This was another strategy to implement cultural policies that served the interests of the occupiers. The following two chapters, 10 and 11, focus on the book sector in times of war and, more specifically, on how the translation and circulation of texts, as well as the intercultural collaboration *on* texts, were promoted for the domination and re-education of the occupied population. Part 3 concludes that, in times of occupation, books and their authors functioned as cross-cultural brokers that shaped post-war European identity constructions. Both the materiality of the books and the agency of the authors contributed to this process of cultural exchange and influence.

Part four, "Remembering Occupation," concentrates on the enduring presence of occupation as a literary topic and on the memory discourses that it sparks in post-war cultural contexts, including but not limited to the realm of literature. Chapters 12 and 13 analyze how different occupations (Germans, Western Allies, and Soviets) experienced by the same territory (Germany, Latvia, and Estonia) are remembered differently and how this divergence in remembrance is conditioned by cultural, political, and historical or revisionist discourses. Chapter 14 closes this section with an investigation of the literary shaping of Soviet military rule in East Germany after 1945—an occupation that must not be named as such. Thus, it discusses the consequences of tabooing post-war occupation regimes in the charged atmosphere of the Cold War. Furthermore, part 4 discusses whether Soviet occupation can be considered and described as a mechanism pertaining to the colonial power matrix that determined the fates of small European nations under Soviet rule.

Notes

1. This is not to say that the experience of occupation is exclusive to Europe. The experience of colonial subjugation has shaped the memories of generations of the colonized who suffered from it.

2. Conservative intellectual Pascal Bruckner (2010) recently presented a similar argument, extending it to the whole 'West' and its colonial history.

3. The case of Ukraine is a very complicated one. Attempts to establish an independent state after World War I were hampered by the Second Polish Republic, the founding of the Soviet Ukraine, and occupations by Romania, as well as through territorial cessions to Czechoslovakia. In World War II, the Germans occupied the Ukrainian territory as part of the southern theater of the German–Soviet War, before the Red Army was able to defeat them and reestablish the Soviet Ukraine.

4. The most vivid and visible result of this change in perspective is probably the international and interdisciplinary "Occupation Studies Research Network," hosted by the Convenors Camilo Erlichman and Christopher Knowles at Maastricht University. Online: https://fasos-research.nl/occupationstudies/research-project/, accessed March 15, 2024.

5. This can now be researched through (translated) sources from societies under German occupation that an international network of scholars has recently started to publish. Online: http://www.societies-under-german-occupation.com/, accessed March 15, 2024.

6. In fact, it would be a very interesting and promising project to investigate similarities and differences in the literary representation of colonial and occupation settings. We stick to the terminological distinction between both, since the term 'occupation,' in its European semantic, merely refers to conflicts between nation states, which are, mostly, not the case when it comes to colonial aggressions. See our deliberations below.

7. It is true, however, that some types of violence, especially those involving sexual abuse, persisted and even escalated during occupations (see, for an example, Buschmeier's section on Mihuleac's *America de peste pogrom* in this volume).

8. As I cannot read Norwegian and no English translation has been published yet, I am referring to the German edition (Teige 2023). All translations are mine.

9. Demmin was the scene of one of the largest mass suicides after the war: in the region of 1,000 citizens killed themselves when the Soviet troops invaded and started to rape girls and women of all ages en masse.

10. A prevalent method in the occupation literature of the third category in our classification is to introduce some sort of historical diegetic framing. In Olyslaegers' *Wil* (2016/2019), the story is narrated by the great-grandfather to his great-grandchild. Christiane Kohl (2002) employs the narrative device of a journalistic investigation to convey historical accuracy for her novel about the German occupation in Tuscany

in 1944. Similarly, Katja Kettu (2011/2016) uses the fiction of discovered diaries and testimonies from eyewitnesses to simulate historical authenticity for her Finnish novel about the romance of a German *Wehrmacht* officer and a Finnish midwife.

11. For another example of such a temporal span, see Schumacher's chapter on Uwe Johnson's *Anniversaries* in this volume, Kalnačs' chapter on Latvian author Anšlavs Eglītis and Estonian author Jaan Kross, and Mamatsashvili's chapter on Georgian authors George Kipiani and Indo Inasari. For an example outside this book, Sofi Oksanen, in her novel *When the Doves Disappeared* (*Kun kyyhkyset katosivat*, 2012/2016), also tells about the turmoil of a forbidden love story in the transition of occupations from Soviet to German and back in Estonia.

12. For instance, the use of military force by a state to protect its citizens abroad or to prevent the proliferation of weapons of mass destruction (WMDs) has been justified as a form of self-defense rather than of occupation. The US-led coalition that invaded Iraq in 2003 claimed that this intervention was a necessary act of self-defense against the imminent danger of WMDs that the Iraqi regime ostensibly possessed. However, the legality and legitimacy of this preemptive war and its subsequent occupation were widely challenged by many states and legal experts, especially after it was revealed that the evidence for WMDs had been fabricated or manipulated. Some argued that the invasion constituted an act of aggression and a violation of international law, while others maintained that it fell within the scope of the right to self-defense. Using a similar line of argument, Vladimir Putin—in his speech shortly before the invasion of Ukraine in February 2022—claimed that he was defending the rights of those who suffered from the supposed oppression and violence of the Kiev regime. He argued that the Russian army would aim to "denazify" Ukrainian territories and prevent the "genocide" of Russians. The case of Ukraine also illustrates the challenges of enforcing international law in situations of military occupation, especially when a state disregards the principles and guidelines established by the Hague Conventions and other legal instruments. Since 2014, Russia has attempted to impose its own laws on Crimea and parts of eastern Ukraine, which are mostly unoccupied by Ukrainian forces but belong to an independent and functioning state. Russia asserted its sovereignty over parts of Crimea and Donbass, ignoring Article 43 of the 1907 *Hague Convention on Land Warfare*, which prohibits occupying powers from changing the legal status of occupied territories.

13. If we continue to use the term in a way that is limited to conflicts between sovereign states, then there is a risk of carrying the semantics of agents in the colonial enterprise into our analytic vocabulary.

14. This is a problematic issue in Stirk's differentiation between conquest and occupation (cf. Stirk 2016, 10–38), as it suggests that Europeans (and Americans) rather conquested land than occupied politically well-organized communities.

15. In his comment to Jeremy E. Taylor's blog entry "The Changing Face of 'Occupation Studies'": https://fasos-research.nl/occupationstudies/the-changing-face-of-occupation-studies/#comment-7 (from November 7, 2021).

16. For our purposes, we can set aside debates in international law as to whether it is required "that the foreign army has *actually* substituted its own authority for that of the ousted government" or "whether it is sufficient that the foreign army has only potential control, i.e., that it is actually controlling the area and therefore '*in a position*' to substitute its own authority for that of the former government" (Benvenisti 2009).

17. Momčilović's chapter discusses works of exactly this kind, though. They are written under occupation, and with respect to the very special circumstances that this situation meant for authors and publishers. This is to say: they are not simply written in a time of occupation, but rather the occupation was, so to speak, the precondition for their creation.

18. Which is made very clear by Eli Wiesel, probably the most important figure to put forward the idea of a testimonial memory culture since the 1970s (cf. Wiesel 1977, 9).

References

Anderson, Benedict. 2006. *Imagined Communities*. London: Verso.

Andersen, Tea Sindbæk, and Barbara Törnquist-Plewa, eds. 2017. *The Twentieth Century in European Memory: Transcultural Mediation and Reception*. Leiden: Brill.

Annus, Epp. 2012. "The Problem of Soviet Colonialism in the Baltics." *Journal of Baltic Studies* 43, no. 1 (March): 21–45.

Atack, Margaret, and Christopher Lloyd, eds. 2012. *Framing Narratives of the Second World War and Occupation in France, 1939–2009: New Readings*. Manchester: Manchester University Press.

Bähr, Johannes, and Ralf Banken, eds. 2005. *Das Europa des „Dritten Reichs": Recht, Wirtschaft, Besatzung*. Frankfurt am Main: Klostermann.

Baillargeon, David, and Jeremy E. Taylor. 2022. "Introduction: Spatial Histories of Foreign Occupation and Colonialism." In *Spatial Histories of Occupation: Colonialism, Conquest, and Foreign Control in Asia*, edited by David Baillargeon and Jeremy E. Taylor, 1–22. London: Bloomsbury Academic.

Bartusevičius, Vincas, Joachim Tauber, Wolfram Wette, and Ralph Giordano, eds. 2003. *Holocaust in Litauen: Krieg, Judenmorde und Kollaboration im Jahre 1941*. Köln: Böhlau.

Baßler, Moritz. 2022. *Populärer Realismus: Vom International Style gegenwärtigen Erzählens*. Munich: C.H. Beck.

Benvenisti, Eyal. 2008. "The Origins of the Concept of Belligerent Occupation." *Law and History Review* 26: 621–48.

———. 2009. "Occupation, Belligerent." *Max Planck Encyclopedias of International Law*. Accessed March 17, 2023, https://opil.ouplaw.com/display/10.1093/law:epil/9780199231690/law-9780199231690-e359.

Benz, Wolfgang, Johannes Houwink ten Cate and Gerhard Otto, eds. 1996-2001. *Nationalsozialistische Besatzungspolitik in Europa 1939–1945*. 10 Bde. Berlin: Metropol

Benz, Wolfgang, Gerhard Otto, and Anna Weismann, eds. 1998. *Kultur—Propaganda—Öffentlichkeit: Intentionen Deutscher Besatzungspolitik und Reaktionen auf die Okkupation*. Berlin: Metropol.

Biess, Frank. 2010. "Introduction: Histories of the Aftermath." In *Histories of the Aftermath: The Legacies of the Second World War in Europe*, edited by Frank Biess and Robert G. Moeller, 1–10. New York: Berghahn Books.

Biess, Frank, and Robert G. Moeller, eds. 2010. *Histories of the Aftermath: The Legacies of the Second World War in Europe*. New York, Oxford: Berghahn Books.

Bode, Christopher. 1988. *Ästhetik der Ambiguität: Zur Funktion und Bedeutung von Mehrdeutigkeit in der Literatur der Moderne*. Tübingen: Niemeyer.

Bogdal, Klaus-Michael. 2015. "Signaturen der Feindschaft: Literatur macht mobil." In *Literatura i vojna: Situacija 1914–1918 godov: XII s"ezd Rossijskogo sojuza germanistov Moskva 27–29 nojabrja 2014 goda*, edited by Natalija A. Bakši and N. S. Babenko, 41–57. Moscow: Jazyki slavjanskoj kul'tury.

Bruckner, Pascal. 2010. *The Tyranny of Guilt: An Essay on Western Masochism*. With the assistance of S. Rendall. Princeton: Princeton University Press.

Cantier, Jacques. 2019. *Lire sous l'Occupation: Livres, lecteurs, lectures, 1939–1944*. Collection "Seconde Guerre mondiale." Paris: CNRS éditions.

Conan, Éric, and Henry Rousso. 1994. *Vichy, Un Passé Qui Ne Passe Pas: Pour une histoire du XXe siècle*. Paris: Fayard.

Cooke, Miriam. 1996. *Women and the War Story*. Berkeley: University of California Press.

Cuomo, Chris. 1996. "War is Not Just an Event: Reflections on the Significance of Everyday Violence." *Hypathia* 11, no. 4: 30–45.

De Groot, Jerome. 2010. *The Historical Novel*. London: Routledge.

Dieckmann, Christoph. 2011. *Deutsche Besatzungspolitik in Litauen 1941–1944*. Göttingen: Wallstein.

———, Tatjana Tönsmeyer, and Babette Quinkert, eds. 2003. *Kooperation und Verbrechen: Formen der "Kollaboration" im östlichen Europa 1939–1945*. Göttingen: Wallstein.

Długoborski, Waclaw. 1996. "Kollektive Reaktionen auf die deutsche Invasion und die Errichtung der NS-Besatzungsherrschaft." In *Anpassung, Kollaboration, Widerstand: Kollektive Reaktionen auf die Okkupation*, edited by Wolfgang Benz, 11–24. Berlin: Metropol.

Enloe, Cynthia. 1983. *Does Khaki Become You? The Militarization of Women's Lives*. Boston: South End Press.

Erlichman, Camilo, and Christopher Knowles, eds. 2018. *Transforming Occupation in the Western Zones of Germany: Politics, Everyday Life and Social Interactions, 1945–1955*. London: Bloomsbury Academic.

Erlichman, Camilo, and Félix Streicher. 2022. "The Age of Metamorphosis: An Introduction." Occupation Studies Research. Accessed June 17, 2023, *Network*. https://fasos-research.nl/occupationstudies/the-age-of-metamorphosis-an-introduction/.

Erll, Astrid. 2011. *Memory in Culture*. Translated by Sara B. Young. Basingstoke: Palgrave Macmillan.

Feldmanis, Inesis. 2005. "Nacistu Okupacijas Politika Latvija (1941–1945): Petniecibas Problemas, Iespejamie Risinajumi Un Varianti." *Latvijas vesture* 1: 81–92.

Fortunati, Vita, and Elena Lamberti. 2008. "Cultural Memory: A European Perspective." In *Cultural Memory Studies: An International and Interdisciplinary Handbook*, edited by Astrid Erll and Ansgar Nünning, 127–40. Berlin: De Gruyter.

Fortunati, Vita, and Elena Lamberti, eds. 2009. *Memories and Representations of War: The Case of World War I and World War II*. Amsterdam: Brill.

Fühner, Harald. 2007. "Ein Volk Im Widerstand? Ein Volk Von Kollaborateuren?" *NiederlandeNet*. Accessed June 16, 2023, https://www.uni-muenster.de/NiederlandeNet/nl-wissen/geschichte/besatzung/widerstand.html.

Glynn, Ruth. 2015. "Engendering Occupation: The Body as Warzone in Liliana Cavani's *La pelle*." *Romance Notes* 55 no.3: 345–55.

Grjasnova, Olga. 2022. "Eine Frage der Gattung." *Historische Urteilskraft* 4: 6–9.

Gross, Aeyal. 2017. *The Writing on the Wall: Rethinking the International Law of Occupation*. Cambridge: Cambridge University Press.

Habermas, Jürgen. 2001. "Why Europe Needs a Constitution." *New Left Review* 11: 5–26.

Hague Conventions of 1907. Annex to the Convention: Regulations Respecting the Laws and Customs of War on Land—Section III: Military Authority over the Territory of the Hostile State. International Humanitarian Law Databases. Accessed March 15, 2024, https://ihl-databases.icrc.org/applic/ihl/ihl.nsf/ART/195-200052?OpenDocument.

Hobsbawm, Eric J. 1995. *The Age of Extremes: A History of the World, 1914–1991*. New York: Pantheon Books.

Hutcheon, Linda. 1988. *A Poetics of Postmodernism*. London: Routledge.

Kellenbach, Katharina von, and Matthias Buschmeier, eds. 2022. *Guilt: A Force of Cultural Transformation*. New York: Oxford University Press.

Kettu, Katja. (2011) 2016. *The Midwife*. Translated by David Hackston. Seattle: Amazon Crossing; Berlin: De Gruyter.

Kitchen, Ruth. 2011. "Another Side to the Story: Confessions of Guilt in Occupation Narratives." *French Cultural Studies* 22, no. 3: 207–17.

Kohl, Christiane. 2002. *Villa Paradiso: Als der Krieg in die Toskana kam*. Munich: Goldmann.

Koppenfels, Martin von, and Cornelia Zumbusch, eds. 2016. *Handbuch Literatur & Emotionen*. Berlin: De Gruyter.

Lagrou, Pierre. 2019. "States." In *Europe's Postwar Periods 1989, 1945, 1918*, edited by Martin Conway, Pieter Lagrou, and Henry Rousso, 103–20. London: Bloomsbury Academic.

Landsberg, Alison. 2004. *Prosthetic Memory: The Transformation of American Remembrance in the Age of Mass Culture*. New York: Columbia University Press.

———. 2015. *Engaging the Past: Mass Culture and the Production of Historical Knowledge*. New York: Columbia University Press.

Lebow, Richard Ned, Wulf Kansteiner, and Claudio Fogu. 2006. *The Politics of Memory in Postwar Europe*. New York: Duke University Press.

Lloyd, Christopher. 2003. *Collaboration and Resistance in Occupied France: Representing Treason and Sacrifice*. Basingstoke: Palgrave Macmillan.

Molasky, Michael S. 1999. *The American Occupation of Japan and Okinawa: Literature and Memory*. London: Routledge.

Morris-Suzuki, Tessa. 2005. *The Past Within Us: Media, Memory, History*. London: Verso.

Ninno, Fabio de. 2023. "The First Allied Occupation in Western Europe? Some Considerations of the Italian Experience as a 'Hybrid Case' (1943–1945)." Occupation Studies Research Network. Accessed June 13, 2023, https://fasos-research.nl/occupationstudies/the-first-allied-occupation-in-western-europe-some-considerations-of-the-italian-experience-as-a-hybrid-case-1943-1945/.

O'Keeffe, William J. 2013. *A Literary Occupation: Responses of German Writers in Service in Occupied Europe*. Amsterdam: Rodopi.

Oksanen, Sofi. [2012] 2016. *When the Doves Disappeared*. Translated by Lola Rogers. New York: Penguin Random House.

Olyslaegers, Jeroen. [2016] 2019. *WILL*. Translated by David Colmer. London: Pushkin Press.

Pratt, Mary Louise. 1991. "Arts of the Contact Zone." *Profession* 91: 33–40. Accessed March 15, 2024, http://www.jstor.org/stable/25595469.

———. 1992. *Imperial Eyes: Travel Writing and Transculturation*. London: Routledge.

Röger, Maren. 2015. *Kriegsbeziehungen: Intimität, Gewalt und Prostitution im besetzten Polen 1939 bis 1945*. Frankfurt am Main: S. Fischer.

Romijn, Peter. 2022. "Patriotic Duty or Gestapo Methods? Dutch Resisters and the Re-Occupation of Indonesia." Occupation Studies Research Network. Accessed June 13, 2023, https://fasos-research.nl/occupationstudies/patriotic-duty-or-gestapo-methods-dutch-resisters-and-the-re-occupation-of-indonesia/.

Rothberg, Michael. 2019. *The Implicated Subject: Beyond Victims and Perpetrators*. Stanford: Stanford University Press.

Rousso, Henry. [1987] 1991. *The Vichy Syndrome: History and Memory in France since 1944*. Translated by A. Goldhammer. Cambridge, MA: Harvard University Press.

Sapiro, Gisèle. 1999. *La guerre des écrivains: 1940–1953*. Paris: Fayard.

Stargardt, Nicholas. 2006. *Witnesses of War: Children's Lives under the Nazis*. London: Pimlico.

Stirk, Peter M. R. 2009. *The Politics of Military Occupation*. Edinburgh: Edinburgh University Press.

———. 2016. *A History of Military Occupation from 1792 to 1914*. Edinburgh: Edinburgh University Press.

Snyder, Timothy. 2010. *Bloodlands: Europe between Hitler and Stalin*. London: Bodley Head.

Teige, Trude. 2015. *Mormor danset i regnet*. Oslo: H. Aschehoug & Co.

Tönsmeyer, Tatjana. 2014. "Raumordnung, Raumerschließung und Besatzungsalltag im Zweiten Weltkrieg: Plädoyer für eine erweiterte Besatzungsgeschichte." *Zeitschrift für Ostmitteleuropa-Forschung* 63: 23–38.

———. 2015. "Besatzungsgesellschaften: Begriffliche und konzeptionelle Überlegungen zur Erfahrungsgeschichte des Alltags unter deutscher Besatzung im Zweiten Weltkrieg." Accessed June 16, 2023, http://docupedia.de/zg/toensmeyer_besatzungsgesellschaften_v1_de_2015.

Velmet, Aro. 2011. "Occupied Identities: National Narratives in Baltic Museums of Occupations." *Journal of Baltic Studies* 42, no. 2: 189–211. https://doi.org/10.1080/01629778.2011.569065.

Wiesel, Eli. 1977. "The Holocaust as Literary Imagination." In *Dimensions of the Holocaust: Lectures at Northwestern University*, 5–19. Evanston, IL: Northwestern University Press.

Wodianka, Stephanie. 2017. "The Emergence and Domestication of Chaos in the Contact Zone: 'The Rusty Giant from Rostock' or the 'Koloss von Züros.'" In *Chaos in the Contact Zone: Unpredictability, Improvisation and the Struggle for Control in Cultural Encounters*, edited by Stephanie Wodianka and Christoph Behrens, 7–18. Bielefeld: transcript Verlag.

LITERATURE AND THE WORLD: OCCUPATION AS A EUROPEAN EXPERIENCE

Introduction to Part 1

JEANNE E. GLESENER

Part one introduces considerations about the literature of occupation as a genre, all the while arguing that literature is unique in its ability to depict the historical realities of occupation. Writing that takes shape under or that focuses on occupation necessarily must find a specific way to incorporate the real into the fictional world. The following chapters discuss the ways and means of this incorporation and examine the relationship between history and literature with respect to the multiple and multifaceted ethical dilemmas that have been provoked by military occupations in everyday situations throughout Europe.

Opening the book is an essay by the renowned Dutch-language Belgian novelist and playwright **Jeroen Olyslaegers**. "Scars" provides us with a privileged insight into the crafting of his novel *Wil* (2016; *WILL*, English translation, 2019), set in the context of the German occupation of Antwerp. Both the strength and originality of *Wil* lie in its unerring ability to illustrate life under occupation by pointing out the transformation of the lived geographical, social, moral, and cultural spaces that occupation entails, and the new functions with which the cityscape (parks, buildings, streets, cafés, hotels, etc.) are invested.

Olyslaegers' essay details the very personal journey he undertook through the maze of family myths, post-war narratives of Flemish nationalists, and historical research on Antwerp during the occupation. Here, he concedes, much as we argue in the Introduction, that even the most meticulous historical research on occupation is incapable of conveying the full emotional impact that the lived experience entails. Taking as his guiding principle the geocultural space of the city itself and approaching it as a palimpsest not only of (hi)stories but of memories as well, and probing the scars left on the urban and moral fabric, he describes how the city impressed itself upon him both as a character and a witness. Olyslaegers explains how adopting the concept of psycho-geographical space as a critical lens became an efficient aesthetic tool to render vividly the affective reality of life in an occupied society. The essay also serves as a stark reminder of the extent to which occupation and the post-war discourses it generated are still very present in European urban, political, and mental landscapes.

The hypothesis that the experience of occupation serves as common ground for our European mentality from the 20th century until today is at the center of **Matthias Buschmeier**'s chapter. The legacies of occupations haunt European communities more than war does, so he contends, since they confront all affected societies with very complex ethical considerations that permeate the social fabric far beyond the imperatives of the battlefield, corroding the identities of both the occupier and the occupied in ways that persist long after occupation has ended. The chapter theorizes on the periodization of the literature of occupation, as well as on occupation's impact on text production. It also expounds on the significance of *when* a text was written: whether penned under the experience of occupation, shortly thereafter but still under the impression of it, or as memorial or revisionist literature in the present that accesses it through imagination or historical research. These specific temporal contexts of creation, says Buschmeier, have a bearing on the rendering and discursive framing of occupation. The chapter therefore takes a systematic look into the relationship between historical and fictional representations of the phenomenon.

It argues that literature—even though it does not, strictly speaking, qualify as a historical source—does give access to the affective realities of moral dilemma under occupation all the same. Furthermore, literature intervenes not just in the memory and identity politics of nation states, but also of the European community at large. Buschmeier illustrates these positions by his contextualized reading of three novels, focusing on different occupation regimes and set in different time periods: namely, *Le silence de la mer* (1941; *Silence of the Sea*, 1944) by Vercors, *De donkere kamer van Damokles* (1958; *The Darkroom of Damocles*, 1962) by Willem Frederik Hermans, and *America de peste pogrom* (2014; *Oxenberg & Bernstein*, German translation, 2018) by Cătălin Mihuleac. The juxtaposition of the texts allows Buschmeier to elaborate on the aesthetic, structural, and topical specificities of the genre of occupation literature by taking a closer look at the techniques of affective realism. It also lends itself to questions regarding how collective narratives of occupation sometimes attempt to hold fast to a comfortable oppositional dichotomy between resistance and collaboration—a dichotomy that, despite its persistence in the novels' respective national publication contexts, begins to break down in light of how novels such as these reveal instead the uncanny, morally ambiguous but existentially vital contact zone that opens up between these dichotomous positions.

CHAPTER I

SCARS. Writing on Occupation

The Reality Effect of Narrative and Psychogeographical Space, or The Case of *Wil*

JEROEN OLYSLAEGERS

Situationist Guy Debord first introduced the concept of psychogeography in his essay "Introduction to a Critique of Urban Geography," which he published in *Les lèvres nues*, no. 6, in 1955. In his opening paragraph of that essay, he defines it like this:

> Psychogeography could set for itself the study of the precise laws and specific effects of the geographical environment, consciously organized or not, on the emotions and behavior of individuals. The adjective psycho-geographical, retaining a rather pleasing vagueness, can thus be applied to the findings arrived at by this type of investigation, to their influence on human feelings, and even more generally to any situation or conduct that seems to reflect the same spirit of discovery.[1]

But it was the British fiction writer Iain Sinclair who linked this term with history in an urban landscape, more particularly in his book *White Chappell, Scarlet Tracings* (1987), wherein he looks at how the horrendous murders of Jack the Ripper have left marks on White Chappell, the neighborhood where the unfortunate victims were killed. In more recent years, Sinclair has taken some distance from his particular take on psychogeography, declaring that it has lost its usefulness during an interview with *The Guardian* published on April 24, 2004:

> For me, [psychogeography is] a way of psychoanalyzing the psychosis of the place in which I happen to live. I'm just exploiting it because I think it's a canny way to write about London. Now it's become the name of a column by Will Self, in which he seems to walk the South Downs with a pipe, which has got absolutely nothing to do with psychogeography. There's this awful sense that you've created a monster.

As a fiction writer, I sympathize with a writer who is fed up with the monsters he has created and that subsequently haunt other writers. Nevertheless, the way history has left its deep marks on a city has been a great source of inspiration ever since I started writing my novel *Wil* (originally published by Dutch publisher De Bezige Bij in 2016; *WILL*, English translation by David Colmer, published by Pushkin Press in 2020). In a certain sense, the 'psychogeographical' ghosts of the past are bound to appear when one decides to write a novel on the collaboration of the Antwerp police force during World War II, and when one actually lives in the old neighborhood where, in 1942, thousands of Jews were rounded up with the cooperation of that same police force (backed by the mayor) and ended up in Auschwitz.

In fact, the very first impulse to write a novel on this particular subject came after a psychogeographical jolt I experienced during a public talk conducted by historian Herman van Goethem. This must have been at the end of September 2013, and Professor van Goethem had invited me to discuss a police report that he found in the Antwerp archives. Together with writer Tom Lanoye and several interested students, we spent an entire day discussing his findings. The police report had described a razzia, or round-up, in which the policeman who wrote the report implicated himself as a participant who followed orders. We discussed the moral implications of this report, which was, of course, never presented to the attorney general, the mayor of Antwerp, or the German occupational forces. Did this policeman want to make a statement or not? Was there a significant subtext in his reporting? Although these questions were very interesting and our discussion very engaging, I was in a state of shock: the policeman had described a roundup in the Kruikstraat, where a Jewish person died by suicide in front of the policemen and where the rest of the family was found poisoned at the kitchen table. That particular house was just opposite the house where I lived. Suddenly it became impossible to unsee what my imagination delivered to me: two policemen ringing a doorbell across the street during a night of violent chaos in August 1942.

When I returned home after that stimulating day, the psychogeographical drama did not end just yet. I was in my writing room on the first floor when my mother called. While I was announcing that I planned to write a book on what happened in my street more than seventy years ago and listened to her reaction, I looked to the right at the Van den Nestlei, the street where a synagogue is situated and one of the main areas of the roundup during the night of August 15, 1942. My mother's voice stirred up a vague memory, and I asked her whether one of our family members lived on that street during the war. She confirmed that one of her aunts worked for a Jewish household in one of the fancy apartments. I told her what I learned about the razzias that August. After a small hesitation, my mother replied that my great-aunt kept on living there, not as a maid, but apparently as the lover of an *SS* officer.

Memories are buried in cities. What happened in the past sometimes emerges in the present, but the very nature of reality is that landscapes and cities may be scarred, but seldom indefinitely. The act of forgetting and getting on with your life is what has marked the post-war situation in Antwerp and in so many other cities in the world after the ordeals, the loss, and the personal tragedies. Both the horror and the nuances were allowed to be swallowed up by everyday life in the years that followed. The act of forgetting had quickly become a way of dealing with the ghosts. That lack of remembrance may shock contemporary society as an impossible, even immoral, lack of respect, but its signification goes beyond any morality imposed by us on the past. It is impossible to pay total respect to the past, although the so-called *Stolpersteine* of German artist Gunter Demnig do exactly that: they mark a house or a street corner where Jewish people who lived or worked were arrested and taken away to death camps. This happened on this exact spot, these stones tell us; this is real, these victims have names. In that way, they function as psychogeographical trigger warnings.

But before entering the psychogeographical space, I first had to make sure how the narrative space of a war novel could be defined. Indeed, the role of the police force in Antwerp during the occupation had never been source material for a novel before, and I felt a certain sense of responsibility I had never experienced during the writing of my other novels. Without the work of historians like Herman van Goethem, Lieven Saerens, and many others, my research would have been exhausting and would probably even have led to the abandonment of this writing project. There is reassurance to be found in a rigorous historical assessment of the past, with exact names and dates, locations and analysis, of what turned out to be an entire series of violent operations the likes of which the city of Antwerp had never experienced before in its nevertheless often-bloody history. But the full emotional impact cannot always be found in these brilliant historical studies. My task as a novelist was clear. I had to create a main character and narrator with whom the readers could identify and who could offer nothing less than a journey back in time to the darkest pages of Antwerp's history. Identification based on empathy is not only one of the most-used narrative devices; it brings us also back to the strange moral question people ask themselves when they are confronted with everyday life in World War II (or a narrative simulation of it). *What would I have done?* That is the basic question everyone asks, as if those horrors of the past can lead to a moral parlor game in which one can play the roles either way: a hero, a criminal, or a neutral bystander. It is significant that the memory of World War I does not raise these moral parlor game questions. In a certain sense, World War II will never be over, because of its moral ambiguity that keeps haunting one generation after the next—although one must admit that literature, movies, and television series each play their part, and not all of them focus on the moral questions involved but rather indulge in story lines that can be described as exploitative. The status of fiction, both on paper and on the screen, is never innocent though, no matter how responsible the artistic creators consider themselves to be.

In Flemish literature, fiction concerning World War II has focused for a long time on ideological collaboration and on the role of Flemish nationalism during that particular period. The so-called repression—the judicial condemnation of collaboration that manifested itself after the war in two waves, one immediately after the liberation and one after the first camp survivors returned—was bookmarked from the very beginning as the most significant historical fact of that period by the nationalists themselves. In fact, they recontextualized this as a revenge of the Belgian state against what the Flemish nationalists considered legitimate claims for more independence. In a way, this was one of the most successful narrative raids on the public consciousness after the war. To put it more bluntly: the use of repression turned out to be a highly efficient invasion of the narrative space. During these early post-war years, in fact all the way up to the eighties, the suffering of the Jews was therefore seldom mentioned, in lieu of the memory of the suffering of the collaborators, onto which nationalists projected the pitiless nature of the Belgian state. Several fiction writers, such as Hugo Claus and Louis Paul Boon, have attempted to nuance this raid on public memory by publishing novels in which the roots of this ideological collaboration were shown and exemplified. Nevertheless, the memory of World War II seemed cursed by this impossible claim of supreme victimhood of, and promoted by, Flemish nationalism.

Television journalist Maurice De Wilde broke this spell with his investigative series that started in 1982 with *De Nieuwe Orde* ("The New Order"), in which he showed how the pre-war years are crucial to understanding the ideological collaboration, illustrating that the collaboration was not accidental but, on certain levels, premeditated, the grounds for it prepared by growing radicalization. De Wilde often had to do the work of a historian, as not many academic articles had been published back then. His work caused a sensation in Flanders. This new narrative attacked some of the hypocrisies and deliberate vagueness that were still held as historical truths.

The invasion of narrative space by nationalist victimhood and the subsequent clash with the reality check of the historical television documentaries made by Maurice De Wilde was something I witnessed myself. I saw my maternal grandfather getting angrier and angrier while remaining glued to the screen. His take on collaboration in general, and his personal experience of the war years, became the narrative that dominated my pre-adult life. The few times he mentioned the fate of the Jews were drenched in pre-war antisemitism that can be summed up by the word 'profiteering.' For me, the conversations at the kitchen table functioned as a time capsule of the year 1947, the year my grandfather was released from prison after being sentenced as a collaborator. To a certain extent, I was fed up with the war, as I overindulged on the narrative of Flemish nationalism and of my grandfather in particular. What happened to the Jewish people during those years seemed unreachable and locked off by taboos. Even Maurice De Wilde was more concerned with the ideological collaboration and less with how bureaucracy made the genocide of Jews in Belgium possible. To his credit, not much of the latter was known back then, since it required years of archival work. This changed in the 1990s, when so many reliable, well-researched books and other texts were published that offered parts of the historical truth in detailed analyses.

The writing of my novel *Wil* was, in a way, a narrative exorcism of the stories that my grandfather had told me, but I realized this only at the last stage of the writing process. I always felt welcome in the house of fiction my grandfather had built, but questions about locked doors in that same house were never appreciated. He always made clear that my moral judgment was not based on experience and was therefore superficial and unrespectful at best. In a way, this is both true and untrue. A moral judgment many decades after the facts ignores the not-knowing that defines what writer Roberto Calasso calls "the unnamable present" (2019) wherein decisions are constantly made without knowing what the results might be. The lack of precognition does shed a light on the psychology of collaboration, as it does on anything else. All of us are permanently locked in the present, and often decisions that later turn out to be undefendable or unwarranted actions are part of the everyday experience. I also learned from an early age that condemning my grandfather did not help to understand his past. But his radical separation of his past actions from any moral judgment—at least by people like me, who had not experienced the war period—haunted me.

Narrative and moral space dramatically shape the past. In fact, at the end of his life, well past his nineties, my grandfather came under the spell of another narrative that was offered to him by the television series *Band of Brothers*, a 2001 American war drama miniseries based on historian Stephen E. Ambrose's 1992 non-fiction book of the same name. At the end of his life, my grandfather, through identification and empathy, finally saw the other side of the story by watching a band of American soldiers from D-Day until V-Day and sadly confessed that he had chosen the "wrong side." This is a case of tragic irony after solidifying his own position for decades, based purely on his personal experience and to be shared only on the condition that his listeners accepted it as historical truth.

From the very beginning, I was convinced that only street names were important in my novel. Antwerp itself is never mentioned. My narrative space was based on the research many historians had done, and the exact street names where violence happened truly were important. 'Antwerp' itself got in the way of telling a universal story peppered with localities. City life became a character of its own, seen through the eyes of a young cop in a particular city district that both combined the old Jewish neighborhood and the entertainment area around the Central Station. Back then, ordinary policemen made long walks and experienced life on a basic street level, where the bureaucratic decisions that were made in offices became real. Before the war, uniformed cops held the monopoly of authority in the streets; during the war years, this authority clashed with uniformed Germans, or even uniformed collaborators, who all claimed dominance of the public space. On a social level, city districts defined a lot more than in the present day. A cop normally stayed within the district where he grew up, which means that everybody knew him, and he knew many secrets no outsider could ever find out. My narrative space started to develop by studying all these factors. In a certain sense, I now realize that the idea of moral ambiguity, one of the main themes of my novel, developed as I was studying the geography of that city district and combining street names with historical facts. My main character, Wilfried Wils, is a young cop who has friends both in antisemitic circles and the milieu of the resistance. He is caught up between the two and has no clear idea what to do next: follow orders or not, intervene in a potentially dangerous situation or not. All these situations occur on a street level, going from the so-called pogrom on Easter Monday 1941 after the screening of an antisemitic movie and the organized protest against Jews in which he (albeit unwillingly) participates as a civilian, up to the roundup at the Van den Nestlei in August 1942, where he, in uniform, tries to obey orders during a horrible night of violence. There is no moral center in this narrative, although Wilfried Wils looks back on all this as an old man. Neither is there any ideology that would or would not motivate my main character. He just tries to survive, and the street names of those years still haunt him as an older man.

Meanwhile, the research I had done during the writing of the book evidently started to change the way I looked at Antwerp and its city life. It was the first time I realized that psychogeography can become very real, and the violence that happened in a particular street so many years ago started to mingle with my everyday experience of that same particular environment. After a while, it became impossible to look at Antwerp without looking through the prism of what happened during World War II. This was no longer a fictional memory house built by my grandfather, with vague references—but a city that was alive with historical facts on every street corner.

When *Wil* was published at the end of the summer of 2016, I expected an ideological controversy surrounding the narrative space that I had opened. But two things happened that totally surprised me. First, the book became an overnight success and was praised by readers with very different political backgrounds. It was immediately accepted that the role of the police and the mayor during that period had been highly problematic. That had not always been the case in the past. Second, the psychogeographic aspects of the novel were embraced in such a way that readers looked the streets up, and some organizations invited me to give guided walking tours. It was the first time in my career as a writer that I noticed how important historic reality has become in modern fiction. The fact that I described scenes that had really happened, mixed with invented characters and fictionalized situations, probably became part of the success of the novel. All of that could be revisited live by walking the same streets that I had described, and there is a dangerously thin line between respect for the past and a form of sensationalism. But at the same time, a genuine shock of the real went through the community of my own neighborhood, where most of what I described had happened. Together with a local school, a neighborhood network started to organize yearly remembrance walks in honor of the Jewish victims of the last roundup that happened on August 28, 1942. Together with historian Herman van Goethem, I was invited to read out loud several passages of my novel on the exact same streets and street corners that featured in my book. This was a true remembrance ritual that had not been guided by the city council or by any other official institutions; this was a so-called 'bottom-up' Remembrance Day, organized by local people who, after the psychogeographical shock that all this happened in their very neighborhood, wanted to keep the memory alive. At the time of the publication of *Wil*, there was almost no remembrance culture in Antwerp, apart from the small memory services the Jewish community organized among themselves. During the last couple of years, this has changed significantly. An advisory committee was set up, and many of its recommendations have been accepted and implemented for the future.

When historian Herman van Goethem published his book *1942* in 2019, he also concentrated on street names in his historical survey of that crucial year of the roundups in Antwerp. Things have come full circle between the historian and the novelist. In a way, I would like to think that we have influenced each other and that fate has brought both our works together, that fiction and historiography have made an impact on the psychogeographical reality of Antwerp by simply making the scars visible.

To conclude, I must return to the original police report that Van Goethem had introduced to me, and therefore, in a way, return to the crime scene, with all the street names and house numbers that you might expect in such a text. I confess that I have not read that report since that occasion when we spent the entire day discussing it. The policeman who offered it to his commanding officer is long dead. We will never know why he actually wrote a document that implicated himself as a participant who followed orders. Regardless, the report never got lost. Filed somewhere, it was waiting for a patient historian like Herman van Goethem, who spent ten years in the city archives, trying to clarify the mechanisms of bureaucratic collaboration in the city of Antwerp. Without all this research, the report would never have been found, and the writing therein lost. It described a reality that this policeman had experienced and, at the same time, opened up a future narrative space that engaged me as a writer—a space wherein the memory was still fresh and no scars were formed yet.

Notes

1. As a literary author, Jeroen was freed from some of the constraints of academic writing.

References

Calasso, Roberto. 2019. *The Unnamable Present*. Translated by Richard Dixon. New York: Farrar Strauss & Giroux [originally published in 2017 as *L'innominabile attuale*. Milan: Adelphi].

Debord, Guy. 1955. "Introduction to a Critique of Urban Geography." Translated by Ken Knabb. In *Critical Geographies: A Collection of Readings*, edited by Harald Bauder and Salvatore Engel-Di Mauro, 23–27. Kelowna, BC: Praxis (e)Press [originally published in *Les lèvres nues*, no. 6]. Accessed March 16, 2024, https://atrium.lib.uoguelph.ca/xmlui/handle/10214/1798.

Goethem, Herman van. 2019. *1942: het jaar van de stilte*. Antwerp: Pelckmans (Polis).

Home Box Office [HBO]. 2010. *Band of Brothers*. Produced by Mary Richards. Burbank, CA: Warner Home Video. DVD. Aired 2001, on HBO.

Olyslaegers, Jeroen. 2020. *WILL*. Translated by David Colmer. London: Pushkin Press [originally published in 2016 as *WIL*. Amsterdam: De Bezige Bij].

Sinclair, Iain. 1987. *White Chappell, Scarlet Tracings*. Uppingham: Goldmark.

———. 2004. "On the Road." Interview by Stuart Jeffries. *The Guardian*, April 24, 2004.

Wilde, Maurice de. 1982/1983. *De Nieuwe Orde*. BRT. Accessed March 16, 2024, https://www.youtube.com/watch?v=pschauvzxWw.

CHAPTER 2

Affective Realism

The Literature of Occupation through Regions and Ages – Vercors' *Le Silence de la mer* (1942), Willem Frederik Hermans' *De donkere kamer van Damokles* (1958), and Cătălin Mihuleac's *America de peste pogrom* (2014)

MATTHIAS BUSCHMEIER

Historical research has long adopted a nation-state paradigm to examine the occupation in World War II (as I discuss in this volume's Introduction). Traditionally, the collaboration–resistance dichotomy has dominated this perspective. This research design stems from, and to a certain degree continues to reflect, the fact that many new or restored states after 1945 relied on their occupation experiences to construct narratives of moral nation-state identity. After 1945, the 'purification' of national communities by way of punishing (a few) collaborators, along with the glorification of resistance movements, became a common postwar response and the core of many national rebirths throughout Europe. However, the nation-state paradigm has been criticized for overlooking the experiences of individuals and groups who did not fit neatly into the collaboration–resistance dichotomy, such as those who were coerced or forced into collaboration or those who engaged in acts of both collaboration and resistance. A more nuanced approach that considers the complexity of individual experiences and motivations is needed to fully understand the occupations during World War II.

The process of *Épuration* in France, for instance, was a necessary condition for creating myths of victimhood that aimed to absolve the new society from the (shared) stain of German-collaboration guilt that could not be easily erased. The moral superiority of the (individual) victim was projected onto the national collective. As Éric Conan and Henry Rousso have shown for France (Conan and Rousso 1994), this resulted in a historical representation and a memory politics that obscured the involvement of the French administration and police authorities in the persecution of the Jews and the resistance, in favor of imagining a unified national body. The nation was thus able to conceive of itself as a victimized collective that had overcome its victim status even during the war itself, as de Gaulle had already declared in his liberation speech at the Hôtel de Ville in Paris on August 25, 1944.[1] Literature played a significant role in constructing such a purified national self-image. For example, Louis-Ferdinand Céline's *D'un chateau l'autre* (1957) (*Castle to Castle*), which recounts his experience of witnessing the exiled Vichy government and many collaborators at Sigmaringen Castle, has a basic narrative structure that symbolically depicts a healing process not only for the ill author (who was deeply embroiled in the collaboration, and subsequently faced severe contention for this in post-war France), but for the whole nation. In Céline's representation, the collaborating France is portrayed with an undercurrent of guilt, cleverly concealed as benign, by depicting the Vichy regime as a mere farcical operetta:

> Representing Sigmaringen as an operetta not only meant devaluing the importance of the French collaborators' flight to Germany; in the immediate post-war years it meant doing so with the specific intent of partially or wholly exonerating the collaborators who had found temporary refuge in Germany at the end of the war. (Watts 1990, 31)

This story, as we have long known, is not peculiar to France, but shaped and continues to shape national memory discourses in many European countries: the Baltic States, Croatia, Luxembourg, the Netherlands, Norway, Romania, Slovenia, and Ukraine,[2] to name but a few, all had to make great sacrifices under German occupation and yet, equally, had strong fascist and/or Germanophile movements of their own on which the German occupiers could draw in order to organize and carry out the Shoah and which, after the war, posed a moral problem to national narratives of renewal and founding.

Ultimately, the experiences of occupiers and those occupied are necessarily far more intertwined and complex than the collaboration–resistance dichotomy has acknowledged. Occupation opens a "contact zone" (Pratt 1991) that also forces exchange and permanent communication, transforming the military front into a selectively permeable membrane of contact. On the one hand, occupiers rely on a local population's cooperation for their limited military resources, so that they do not have to deploy too many forces for order in the occupied areas. On the other hand, historian Tatjana Tönsmeyer (2015) argues that the occupied face a constant threat of violence and a struggle to survive under scarcity and food shortages, which compel them to enter into an asymmetrical relationship with the occupiers. The role of the occupied in this relationship should not only be viewed as one of passive suffering, but also as a space of active behavior aimed at survival. Doris Bergen also claims that "no option of non-involvement" (Bergen 2013, 23) exists for life under occupation. That said, acting under existential threats may involve ethical compromises. If the moral superiority of the occupied is seen as being inextricably woven with their powerlessness and passivity, then the revised notion of *agency* under occupation will inevitably entail guilt, which was either denied or attributed to specific individuals after the war, based on the cultural-political narratives of the liberated countries, and that sometimes led to individuals being cast out of their literal or national families. Naturally, occupation societies are characterized by a high degree of complexity, and this complexity gives rise to diverse moral perspectives (see the volume's Introduction). I argue that this multiplicity of moral positions could no longer be sustained after the war, as it challenged dominant narratives of national identity and collective memory.

This chapter examines three novels that depict how, amidst military occupations, individuals who grasp for agency both desire and struggle to be seen as people, rather than as enemies or (in most cases depicted here) as 'the occupied.' The novels represent different scenarios of occupation during World War II, in diverse geographical and temporal contexts.[3] They correspond to the periodization proposed in the Introduction of this volume. The first one, *Le Silence de la mer* (*The Silence of the Sea*) by Vercors, was written and published in 1941 and 1942, respectively, under the German occupation of France. It has been considered one of the most influential occupation novels ever since. The second, *De donkere kamer van Damokles* (*The Darkroom of Damocles*) by Willem Frederik Hermans, was published in 1958, more than a decade after the Nazi occupation of the Netherlands. Hermans had personally experienced the occupiers' oppression, after he refused to sign a loyalty declaration as a student. In his novel, by portraying an imaginary resistance fighter who is executed as collaborator, he not only ironically subverts the epic narrative of Holland's resistance against oppression but also mocks Allied post-war justice. Lastly, the third novel, *America de peste pogrom* ("America over the pogrom") by Romanian author Cătălin Mihuleac, was published in 2014 and represents a contemporary perspective on the very complex history of Romania's alliance with Nazi Germany, and its devastating consequences for the Jewish community. This latter novel is an example of the 'new' literature of occupation—that is, literature authored by individuals who never lived under the occupation but who still reflect on the fundamental impacts of the World War II occupations for their communities.

These three novels, as a literary intervention and despite their seemingly incomparable differences, share a common goal: to challenge collective narratives of occupation that rely on a simplistic binary opposition between resistance and collaboration. The ways in which they illustrate the trauma of the occupation experience continue to shape European memory to this day. I argue that these novels offer nuanced and complex representations of occupation that challenge dominant national discourses and invite critical reflection on this crucial period of European history.

Le Silence de la mer–Vercors (1942)

Le Silence de la mer (*The Silence of the Sea*), written by Jean Bruller under the pseudonym Vercors and published in 1942 as the first volume of the *Résistance* publisher *Les Éditions de Minuit* (Wickenberg 1996; Simonin 1994), is a famous example of occupation literature. This novel even appeared on *Le Monde*'s list of the 100 most important books of the 20th century. It is striking that the very same text was considered *the* Resistance novel,[4] due to its publishing history, and its realistic portrayal of France's collaborative subjugation. Ilja Ehrenbourg, for instance, declared in 1944 that it seemed only a collaborator could have written the book. Furthermore, Arthur Koestler in the immediate post-war period accused Vercors' French protagonist of being an inauthentic construct. "In spite of his versatile intelligence [he] has apparently never read a speech of Hitler's, nor seen a newspaper in the ten years between the Reichstag fire and the attack on Poland" (Koestler 1946, 20), Koestler sarcastically commented in *The Yogi and the Commissar* in 1943.

The founder of *Les Éditions de Minuit*, Pierre de Lescures, intended to offer a third path between militant communist resistance and general resignation. He called this third way a "Résistance pacifique" (Simonin 1994, 95). The publisher wanted to offer a proud image of France as a civilized nation that was upholding its cultural traditions even under the German occupation, and *Le Silence de la mer* has widely been read as the literary implementation of this propaganda agenda.

At this point, I am neither interested in the fascinating publishing history nor the autobiographical traces that Vercors, in various interviews, laid out himself about the German protagonist Werner von Ebrennac and the narrator's silent niece (see also the biography on Bruller/'Vercors' by Konstantinović 1969). In contrast, I read the novel with respect to the idea of occupation as an ambivalent zone of contact, in which obvious antagonism collapses little by little. In the style of the term "psychogeographical drama" that Jeroen Olyslaegers uses in his chapter of this volume (with reference to the city of Antwerp), *Le Silence de la mer* is the story of a psycho*spatial* drama between occupied and occupier.

This short novel (maybe "novella" is a more appropriate genre term here) displays the symbolic meaning of occupation in its literal sense. That is, as the occupation of space—an invasion of the alien power into the intimate realm of the private. Open violence in Vercors' book is absent; the German *Wehrmacht* officer who is billeted in the house of the narrator, an older man living with his niece, is portrayed as a cultivated, polite, and attractive man who admires French culture, speaks excellent French, and openly disapproves of the brutality of German warfare, as well as of the cowardice of French collaborator Marshall Pétain. Above all this, the German officer is an artist, a studied music composer by profession. The similarity of this character to Ernst Jünger has been remarked upon frequently over the years. The figure of the educated, elegant, and civilized German *Wehrmacht* officer—the narrative of the 'exceptional Nazi'—can be frequently found in the literature of occupation (such as, for instance, in the unfinished novel series *Suite française* by Ukrainian-born Jewish-French author Irène Némirovsky, who was murdered at Auschwitz), and it would be interesting to discuss in more depth the function of this motive (cf. John 1986). In Vercors' case, the portrayal of an 'exceptional Nazi' certainly serves as a projection for the fear the inhabitants face, which shows in the uncle's exclamation of relief, "Thank the Lord" (Vercors 2022, 73, subsequently cited as '*SM*'), regarding Ebrennac's civil respectability. To picture the enemy as a 'cultural friend' opens the curtain for the complex dynamic in this intimate chamber play.[5] For Vercors, it obviously was important to portray the occupier not as the 'ugly other' but as a cultural kinsman.

From the beginning, the closeness of the living quarters forces the occupied to stomach the physical and rhetorical presence of the occupier. Soon, Ebrennac's visits in the smoking room or the kitchen become an every-evening routine, the 'new normal' in the occupied house, and over the course of the story, Ebrennac seeks to transform from an intruder into a roommate. This transformation becomes visible when he strips off his military garb;[6] joining the uncle and the niece for his usual evening monologue, he dresses on one particular night in elegant civilian clothes (cf. *SM*, 75). Against his endless chatter on the deep connections between German and French culture, and on the nations' common duty to lead Europe, the niece's silence appears as an act of resistance—and Ebrennac notices it as such: "We have got to conquer this silence. We have got to conquer the silence of all France" (*SM*, 80).

Although she does not break her silence until the very end of the book, the closeness and intimacy of living together have an impact on the niece that she cannot escape, as her physical reactions prove:

> Silently, and with a grave insistence which still carried the hint of a smile, he was looking at my niece, at her closed, obstinate, delicate profile. My niece felt it, and I saw her blush slightly, and a little frown form gradually between her eyebrows. Her fingers plucked the needle perhaps rather too quickly and tartly, at the risk of breaking the thread.[7] (*SM*, 80)

In fact, the uncle observes these small and almost hidden gestures *repeatedly*. He recognizes her 'inner drama' (cf. *SM*, 90), torn between attraction and disgust for the occupier. The niece's blushing is a significant moment in this intimate play, and it is followed by a dramatic turning point: after a visit to Paris, Ebrennac suddenly shows up to the house in uniform again. From the look of things, he has transformed back into the occupier. But now the uncle observes in him something that unmasks his soldierly attitude as a lie. Again, the hand (as with the niece's sewing) is what signals this change:

> I learnt that day that, to anyone who knows how to observe them, the hands can betray emotions as clearly as the face [...]. And the fingers of that hand were stretching and bending, were squeezing and clutching, were abandoning themselves to the most violent mimicry, while his face and his whole body remained controlled and motionless.[8] (*SM*, 91)

In essence, the small, physical reactions of the occupier and the occupied come to resemble each other more and more, as the opposing parties begin to come closer not in words but rather in their emotional responses. The tension in the room, ever palpable, is now visible. The change that these characters undergo in subtlety and silence finally reveals itself most fully in the moment when Ebrennac confesses that he was wrong in his description of a German–French cultural unity—confesses that the Germans intend nothing else but to destroy the French culture. Ebrennac has decided to take the violence declared and enacted by his fellow German occupiers and turn it instead upon himself. He leaves to the Eastern Front to die, and in this last scene before leaving to Russia, the niece speaks her only word, bidding the departing officer his *adieu*.

Vercors condenses the occupation into an intimate theater. Its complexity does not show in the political and social positions or speeches of the figures but instead in the intricacies of body language and wordless intimacies. Ebrennac's loaded speeches about German–French spiritual unity contrast with the nuanced, balanced style of the text itself. Vercors' language resists the ideology-laced rhetoric of *both* the Germans and the violent resistance movement in France. And, as Laura Frost pointed out, it also resists "telling another story of Germany's 'rape' of France" (Frost 2019, 87); by contrast, *Le Silence de la mer* turns such standard rhetoric in anti-German propaganda of the villainous, occupying *boche*, with the implication of sexual violence as established since World War I (Frost 2019, 89–90), upside down. Ebrennac intends consensual "marriage" with France, not its "rape." Common metaphors for occupation as prostitution, penetration, and sexual abuse (Molasky 1999, 120–63) are transformed into a silent-because-forbidden romance story.

It is crucial that this romance of seduction manifests only on the subliminal level of the text, and not on the surface of linguistic utterance. The observing position of the uncle as narrator does not allow us to gain an inside perspective, neither of the niece nor of Ebrennac. Furthermore, the uncle's perspective reveals the complex triangle of relations and feelings. The suspense of silence becomes increasingly unbearable, until finally the niece cannot maintain it. One can only imagine how far the occupied would have allowed the occupier to advance into their intimate life beyond spatial configurations.

This complexity and ambiguity toward the occupier were what caused critics to accuse that the novel was born from a place of complicity with the enemy. In history, it was the change from persuasion to constraint in the German occupation policy that brought the truth of the parties' social positions back into focus; in the novella, it is the officer's return to combat at the Eastern Front—a move inspired by his own guilt at the German military's true intentions—that serves the same, thereby repealing all the ambiguities that the occupation had initially posed. Ebrennac's departure to the Eastern Front—"Off to Hell" (*SM*, 96), as he says—adumbrates not only his personal fate but a change in the character of the whole occupational regime. In fact, by the time of the text's publication in 1942, the situation in France had already changed: with the help of the French bureaucracy and police units, the Germans started to deport Jews to the death camps in the East, while hundreds of thousands of French men were forced to join the *Relève* (later called the *Service du travail obligatoire*). In response to these changing tides, from 1943, the *Résistance* turned increasingly violent, and the Germans answered this violence with brutal retaliations (Meyer 2000). However, *Le Silence de la mer* portrays a period when some educated German occupiers, such as Jünger or Hartlaub (on Hartlaub, see Siess' chapter in this volume), regarded the occupation as an opportunity for cultural exchange (see also Meyer and Klarsfeld 1999). Moreover, many French did not perceive that subset of Germans as uncivilized barbarians either. The novella's aesthetic poise reflects this moment after the armistice in 1940—and before the resurgence of violent occupation policies—through the tension of the unspoken. It effectively captures the complexities of the French–German relationship during the occupation, highlighting the nuances of collaboration and resistance. This is to say, the occupied house and its inhabitants function as a synecdoche for France's relationship with Nazi Germany.

Some critics have read the silence in the novella as a symbolic expression of nonviolent resistance against occupation, and, indeed, that is true to some degree. They view silence as a powerful strategy of the weak and oppressed against the strong and dominant. However, I contend that the novella mainly reveals the ineffectiveness of such silent resistance in confronting the oppressor; even within the story, silence does not expel the occupier. Namely, the house is not reclaimed by force, but rather the German occupier departs voluntarily; it is Ebrennac's disillusion with his German comrades—not the niece's refusal to speak to him—that drives him to leave the house, leave France, and face death at the Eastern Front. For the French in this novella, there is no liberation, whether through resistance or otherwise.

Such a narrative contradicted the post-war image of France as a victorious nation. *Le Silence de la mer*, thus, is a subversive text. After the war, Vercors' novel was easier to dismiss as historically inaccurate: after all, in history (unlike in the text), the occupier was not driven away by silence but by overwhelming military intervention. And the complex 'affective realities' of the subtle emotional relationship between the occupied and the occupier in the *narration* were then obscured by the Gaullistic *narrative* of a self-liberating nation—a nation that denounced any emotional attachment or even attraction to the former oppressor as a form of collaboration. The *Épuration* acted to erase the perception of an implicated community, replacing it with the vision of a nation liberated from "implicated subjects" (see Introduction and Rothberg 2019).

De donkere kamer van Damokles – Willem Frederik Hermans (1958)

The German occupation in the Netherlands made Willem Frederik Hermans a writer—a sentence with a double meaning. Hermans started writing as a literary author during the war, after having had to give up his studies in Geography due to his refusal to pledge his loyalty to the German occupiers. Moreover, his novel on the occupation, *De donkere kamer van Damokles* (*The Darkroom of Damocles*), published in 1958, made him a notorious *agent provocateur* in the Netherlands. The novel features the protagonist Henri Osewoudt, a cocky resistance fighter and ugly wannabe-hero who has been rejected for obligatory military service on account of his not being tall enough. The book describes him as a "diminutive freak, a toad reared upright" (Hermans 2020, 20, subsequently quoted as '*DD*') and as a man whose sole interest is the pursuit of sex—first with his first cousin Ria (*DD*, 20–1). (It is worth noting that Osewoudt resembles Günter Grass' Oskar Mazerath in *Die Blechtrommel* (*The Tin Drum*) [1959] in this respect of his outlook and sexual behavior.) Henri's interest in joining the resistance emerges within the plot as a way to escape his sense of his own insignificance.

Hermans chose a widespread genre in the tradition of the World War II resistance novel. It is a spy novel with "miraculous escapes, spectacular acts of sabotage and derring-do, heroic sacrifices, betrayals of double agents, torture sessions, liquidation of traitors and so on" (Lloyd 2003, 158). In contrast to the simplistic aesthetic standards of this tradition, however, Hermans turns his novel into a distorting mirror that leaves the reader without much orientation. The novel is strictly internally focalized, and thus readers are restricted to the limited perspective of its unreliable protagonist. Therefore, we—not unlike much of the research done on this topic (see Smulders 1983)—cannot even be sure about the ontological status of Dorbeck, the mysterious *doppelgänger* of Osewoudt and supposedly an important member of the resistance movement. Does he really exist, or is it all made up in Osewoudt's wish-fulfillment fantasy? What is more, Osewoudt has no driving ideology; he is neither a patriot, nor a communist, nor a supporter of the *Nationaal Socialistische Beweging* (NSB) like his neighbor Turlings, who slobbers over the Germans and their mission of a united Europe under German leadership.

Regardless of how one answers the question of whether Dorbeck exists, if Osewoudt is intended (as Oskar Mazerath) to be a representative figure, and if readers are brought into the same position toward the events as the protagonist himself, then the novel also depicts the resistance movement as a chimera. In turn, the reader must conclude that if the Netherlands' resistance movement was indeed a chimera, then the conviction that gave ground to the Netherlands' post-war identity politics—of having been a country in resistance against the Nazi occupiers—reveals itself as an act of collective self-delusion. This approach is in line with Hermans' mission (in his writing outside this novel) to accuse self-declared members of the resistance, such as the Jewish scholar Friedrich Weinreb, to be mere impostors: a still-ongoing debate in the Netherlands.

Furthermore, in this novel, occupation itself is not represented as a state of exception. On the contrary, the Dutch Home Guard defenders, which Osewoudt joined after being rejected by the military, look like the occupiers of 25 years earlier: Osewoudt wears German spiked helmets from World War I, and his old rifle is not shut once:

> He went to the back room and took his uniform from the cupboard. The uniform was dark green, like a forestry man's. A German helmet went with it, army surplus from the Great War. […] All Osewoudt was allowed to do was stand guard with an old rifle, on the sidelines as usual. In the blazing sunshine, to the accompaniment of birdsong, he was obliged to visualise the monstrous guns for himself. No one had any intention of attacking the post office.[9] (*DD*, 26–27)

It is right after this passage that the notorious Dorbeck, who introduces himself as a member of the resistance movement, enters the scene. For everyone but Osewoudt, however, who considers himself a resistance fighter after meeting Dorbeck, life goes on just as normal: "Soon the blue tram was running to its normal schedule again. Everything returned to normal, only things were somewhat busier for a while" (*DD*, 30). Shortly later: "The sun shone. It was a fine day. There were people walking about, including some unarmed German soldiers. It was almost as if nothing had changed, as if things would stay the same forever" (*DD*, 35). And even after Osewoudt assassinates a man on command without knowing anything about his political background, the protagonist is able to live on, as "if the war simply faded from his existence" (*DD*, 51).

It would be inaccurate to claim that the novel ethically justifies the actions of the resistance movement; for a significant portion of the text, German soldiers are not depicted as threatening in any way, and yet, nevertheless, Osewoudt continues to kill on command. For instance, while his participation in the assassination of Lagendaal, a Dutch collaborator with the Gestapo, might be seen as a legitimate target of military resistance, Osewoudt's actions become more questionable when he strangles a female Dutch National Youth Storm leader on his way to Lagendaal's house. The Youth leader, a blonde woman with "beddable, smashing legs, too!" (*DD*, 144), as Henri remarks instantly to his female comrade, had simply been on her way to collect Lagendaal's child for a trip, unknowing of the assassination plot. Osewoudt finds her attractive and is even drawn to her dead body. His female accomplice, simply called 'the girl,' bluntly comments: "I bet you'd have raped her if I hadn't been around. You should have seen your face!" (*DD*, 155). Once inside the home, Osewoudt also snaps the neck of Lagendaal's wife without hesitation or remorse (see *DD*, 159) before shooting Lagendaal and kidnapping their five-year-old son.

Despite his questionable conduct, though, the occupation provides Henri with a sense of identity that he lacks in his ordinary life. He views the occupation as an opportunity rather than a threat. In fact, he is afraid that the end of the war will return him to his mundane existence as a tobacconist:

> Because if the Germans were beaten, what would a girl like Marianne still see in him: an uneducated, unattractive tobacconist, a man who didn't even need to shave and who, in a liberated Holland, would have lost every chance of being either hero or martyr?[10] (*DD*, 210)

Instead, at the war's end, Osewoudt—as his *doppelgänger* Dorbeck—finds himself charged by the Allies for collaboration with the Germans, and for murder, because in this novel the line between being a hero of the resistance and being a traitor to the Dutch nation is blurry. Indeed, before the war even ends, when a German Gestapo officer named Ebernuss (a name actually phonetically very close to Ebrennac) spends weeks interrogating Osewoudt, he recognizes that he and his prisoner—the former a Nazi and the latter a self-fancied resistance fighter—would be very alike after the war (cf. *DD*, 254–55).

The novel's representation of the resistance is provocative, but even more challenging is the depiction of the Allied investigation of Osewoudt's case. The same facts that the novel initially presents through his perspective are now used against him by the Allied investigators. Moreover, Osewoudt feels that the Nazi

Ebernuss was more accurate in his accusations than the Allied officers. Osewoudt begins as an imaginary hero of the resistance, but he meets his end by being declared a collaborator—and shot down. Ironically, he becomes a victim because of the fact that he was *not* passive, but rather had actively striven for agency amidst the occupation. The occupation thus transformed Osewoudt into Dorbeck, the latter of whom the reader cannot be sure ever existed. However, the occupation also devours its own offspring and condemns to death anyone who takes part in it—regardless of their allegiance.

In this regard, Hermans' novel highlights the complex and unpredictable nature of life under occupation, wherein individuals may be forced to make difficult moral decisions in order to survive.[11] It also underscores the destructive impact that occupation can have on individuals, regardless of their actions or intentions, and suggests that the line between victim and perpetrator can become blurred amidst such an ambiguous milieu, in a self-reinforcing cycle of violence.

The truth of the narrative remains ambiguous for Hermans' readers, who were both eyewitnesses and active participants in the real historical events. Along the course of the fifteen years since the war's end (before the book's publication), they encountered conflicting accounts of the past and the present alike; just as in Osewoudt's case, the former Nazi occupiers and the present-day Allied prosecutors drew different conclusions from the very same evidence, and the subjectivity of individual perspectives revealed two distinct 'realities' of the occupation. What appears to be factual dissolves into illusion, and what is exposed as deception could also be authentic—as Osewoudt at one point articulates in his interior monologue:

> Who can you trust? Perhaps the doctor is in league with Ebernuss, maybe the Germans are even now busy matching the telephone number I gave the doctor with the address, maybe Marianne will be arrested in the next half-hour. [...] Who can be trusted? Everyone's deceiving everyone else.[12] (*DD*, 191)

In essence, occupation, as it is displayed by Hermans, is a state of vagueness not just in which moral and juridical norms can become blurry, but also in which these same norms turn upside down at short notice.

De donkere kamer van Damokles challenged, and continues to challenge, any simplistic or monolithic interpretation of the Dutch experience under occupation. It also raised a provocative question about the country's identity politics after the war, which, like France, had constructed the image of itself as a nation that resisted and opposed its occupier in an unequivocal way. Instead of humoring this national self-concept, the novel exposes the complexities and ambiguities of the Dutch situation[13] both during and after the war by employing, as its device, a chatoyant protagonist who, though he seems to have chosen the right side during the occupation, at the same time is represented as an inbreeding, sexually abusive, growth-challenged murderer (note his slight physical stature as a metaphor for his stunted personal development), whose deeds are substantially more motivated by self-image concerns than by any true political ideology. Such a figure—much like Oskar in *The Tin Drum*, which was published only a year later—fits perfectly the genre of the modern picaresque novel. Unlike Oskar, however, Osewoudt fails to understand until the end that he is not the rogue hero he believes he is, but rather is fooled by the complex world of intrigue around him.

Ultimately, by giving his book the appearance of a spy novel, Hermans leaned into the immediate post-war popularity of this genre of occupation literature—but his masterful trick was really to hide an existential novel within it. *De donkere kamer van Damokles* depicts the occupation period not as a time of heroic adventures but as a bizarre grotesque. To Hermans, this account of history is a closer approximation to reality than any moral realism or ideological truth that he suspected within any sort of existentialism as the 1950s' literary *mode à la jour*.[14]

America de peste pogrom–Cătălin Mihuleac (2014)

How different things look when we pull ourselves away from Central and Western Europe to the East, and from the perspective of occupied non-Jews to Jewish life and suffering in the context of occupation. In his 2014 novel *America de peste pogrom*, which has not been translated into English yet, Romanian author Cătălin Mihuleac tells a transgenerational story of two Jewish families, the Oxenbergs and the Bernsteins, from the city of Iași, the capital of historic Moldavia. Before exploring this novel itself, it is pertinent first to provide some important historical context regarding the treatment of Romania's Jews. For this analysis, I will provide a more detailed historical context, as this particular history may be still less well-known to Western audiences.

Until 1944, Romania was a German ally and had invited German troops into its territory to prepare the invasion of the Soviet Union from the south. However, when Romania declared war in 1944, the Germans, now Romania's enemy, already occupied parts of the country. Thus, the case of Romania is a combination of the fourth and fifth categories of occupational regimes that we have presented in this volume's Introduction. It would be a harsh trivialization, though, to call it a "pacific occupation" (Benvenisti 2009); the country's initial alliance with Germany enabled Romania's regime to carry out the murder of hundreds of thousands of Jews. As such, it is important to note that using the term "occupation" for Romania (as well as for other cases in Category 5 where local antisemitism was lethal and rampant) is a double-edged sword, since the German occupation was also referenced as an argument for deflecting any guilt about the so-called "Romanian Holocaust"; Romanians found it handy to blame the whole affair purely on the German occupiers (Benz 2022, 89; Shafir 2012). In fact, in Mihuleac's novel, the narrator itself refers to the (real-life) Communist Romanian historians Aurel Kareţki and Maria Covaci, who even served in German *SS* units that allegedly prepared the Iaşi pogroms (see Mihuleac 2018, 226, quoted as '*ApP*').[15] In Iaşi, a series of anti-Jewish pogroms were initiated by the Romanian government under General Ion Antonescu. In these events, almost 15,000 people were killed from June 29 to July 6, 1941, just days after Romania had joined World War II on the German side. The narrator, however, insists that "the *copyright* for the pogrom lies with the Romanian Authorities" (*ApP*, 226, emphasis in the original).

Since November 1940, Romania had already been an official ally of Nazi Germany (cf. Benz 2022, 87). In preparation for their joint invasion into the Soviet Union, and in order for Germany to secure Romanian and subsequently (after also invading Ukraine) Ukrainian oil fields, German troops from the 11th Army, along with *SS* units and the military intelligence service of the *Wehrmacht*, were redeployed close to the "new" Soviet–Romanian border. Iaşi was the headquarters of the 198th infantry division of the *Wehrmacht* 30th Army Corps. In addition to a long-standing tradition of antisemitic attitudes and policies that were intensified by the Antonescu Regime—which came to power with the help of Hitler's Germany in the late-summer of 1940—the Romanians hoped to regain the Bessarabian territory, which had been occupied by the Soviets as a result of the "Hitler–Stalin Pact," also called the "German–Soviet Friendship and Border Contract" from September 1939. Moreover, Romania had suffered various territorial losses to Hungary and Bulgaria (Ioanid 1993, 119) as a consequence of the "Second Vienna Award" in 1940.[16] The territorial integrity of the multiethnic nation was at risk, and the aggressive policies against Jews and other ethnic minorities can be seen as an attempt to enforce a Romanian identity that was, at the time, built on the racist idea of blood.

In the Romanian press, the image of the Jew as intruder was widespread (Ioanid 1993, 121) and juxtaposed with the occupying power of Soviet Bolshevism. The Iaşi pogrom itself was mostly executed by "the Iaşi police, backed by the Bessarabia police and gendarmerie units. Other participants were army soldiers, young people armed by SSI agents, and mobs who robbed and killed, knowing they would not have to account for their actions" (International Commission on the Holocaust in Romania 2004, 19). All this happened with the knowledge, approval, and assistance of the *Wehrmacht*'s intelligence service, the *Abwehr*, under the command of Major Hermann von Stransky. This widespread participation was also a result of bandied rumors about "Judeo-Bolsheviks" who had supposedly allied with the Soviets to enable an invasion of Moldavia. In fact, however, the pogrom, as well as the start of deportations of Jews from Moldavia to Romanian camps, must be placed in direct context with the start of Operation Barbarossa (Nazi Germany's invasion of the Soviet Union), whose southern flank the Germans launched from Romania and directed toward the industrial centers of Ukraine. It is also evident that the pogrom was deeply connected to the Soviet occupation in Bessarabia; the Romanian Government feared losing more territory and wanted to regain Bessarabia. Meanwhile, the German side believed that the population's disaffection in Soviet-occupied territory would reduce the need for German troops to invade it (cf. Blau 1955, 14), which was no small consideration, since the Soviets outnumbered the German military forces in the region. Even more important to the *Wehrmacht* was that no Jewish or Communist partisan movement could become a threat at the rear—especially when Hitler decided that the 11th Army's tasks in Romania were mainly to secure communication lines for replenishment and to tie down the region's Soviet forces so that they could not be redirected toward the advance of the German army group's north wing (cf. Blau 1955, 35). For all these reasons, in addition to ideological ones, the purge of any possible "Jewish-Bolshevik" resistance was warmly welcomed by the German military forces around Iași. Thus, the pogroms in Romania cannot be isolated from the German military occupation[17]—nor, to be clear, are they merely a function of it. The Iași pogrom itself, as well as the case of Romania, displays the interconnectedness of changing occupational regimes in its most terrible way.

Although Romanian responsibility for the pogrom was officially accepted by the Government of Ion Iliescu in 2004, Mihuleac, a non-Jewish Romanian, faced scathing criticism and was threatened with murder for *America de peste pogrom* by patriotic groups and press, which mirrors a trend in Romanian memory culture to conceal, or at least to reinterpret, Romania's role as an ally of Nazi Germany. Such critique builds on the post-war argumentation by Antonescu, who strictly denied the historical reality of any large-scale collaboration between the Romanian people and the Germans, at least beyond the incontrovertible abundance of Romanian *SS* recruits (Pălimariu 2019, 152). Despite the criticism that he faced after his book's publication, Mihuleac had in fact dug into archival documents to immerse himself in the authentic historical background of his story.[18]

The novel intertwines the biography of Suzy, a Romanian woman who occasionally works as a tour guide in Iași, with Dora Bernstein, an American tourist with Romanian roots. She guides Dora and Dora's son Ben around the city for the pogrom's 60th anniversary. Later, Suzy marries Ben, moves to Washington, D.C., and as part of the new family, begins looking into the family history with the help of a historian named Sever, who researches the history of the pogrom from various archives.[19] It turns out that Suzy's mother-in-law, Dora Bernstein, is in fact Golda Oxenberg, the only member of her family to survive both the pogrom and its aftermath; Dora's/Golda's father and brother had survived the pogrom but died on one of the overcrowded deportation trains. The novel's extradiegetic frame suggests that Suzy herself gave the results of this historical research to the author, Mihuleac, who then transformed it into a novel. Thus, two very popular means within the literature of remembrance are brought together: the genre of the transgenerational family novel, and accompanying strategies of authentication: the preceding dedication—actually a paratext—is signed by the author himself but also by the fictional Suzy.

This novel's fictional setting, in fact, brings to mind the scandal of German author Wolfgang Koeppen. In 1948, Jewish survivor Jakob Littner had asked the young Koeppen to edit his autobiographical work to meet the stylistic demands for publishing. In 1992, however, Koeppen and his publisher Suhrkamp (re-)released the text with only minor changes, this time presented as a novel of Koeppen's own artistry, reducing Littner's authorship now to an oral report transmitted through the former publisher's *notes* to Koeppen (as Koeppen wrote in the new preface to *Jacob Littners Aufzeichungen aus einem Erdloch*). Koeppen, a member of the *Tätervolk*, simply appropriated the victim's voice for himself (Klüger 2020). By contrast, Mihuleac, as a non-Jewish Romanian, avoids such fraud and resulting criticism (cf. Fischer 2022, 162–73) by restaging a similar scenario *within* the fictional frame of the novel. By this narrative means, Mihuleac's novel can legitimately feature as a literary second-hand testimony (Pălimariu 2019, 160) of the affective realities of the pogrom.

Mihuleac draws attention to many antisemitic stereotypes by using these same stereotypes to describe certain characters: Golda's younger brother Lev is operating his own credit bank at the age of 13, some of the Jewish characters have crooked noses, and many of the Jewish characters consider themselves intellectuals and/or are members of the economic, cultural, and educated elite of Iași who look down on Romanian peasants and working-class people.[20]

Moreover, the novel itself is characterized by a brutal and highly sexualized language. To describe the growing antisemitic tendencies that culminated in the pogrom, Mihuleac frequently applies the rhetoric of penetration—a common metaphor for occupation. At the beginning of Part 3, for instance, in which the events of June 29, 1941 are described, the girl Golda, who was taught German and admires German culture just as her mother Roza does, witnesses the brutal gang rape of her mother by Romanian police officers, neighbors, and a German *Wehrmacht* officer. In this scene, Roza first comes into contact with this German officer in connection with an occasion on which her husband Jacques, a

gynecologist by profession,[21] and her son get arrested; she hopes that, by appealing to him—"how handsome he looks in his elegant uniform" (*ApP*, 211)—he
will show leniency with her family, since she believes that, even as a soldier, he
represents the refined German culture she admires. She even presents to him a
reference letter regarding her translation of Romanian prose fiction into German, as evidence of her love of German culture, believing in the "cultural alliance between both countries … comparable to the brotherhood between the victorious German army and the Romanian…" (*ApP*, 172, ellipses in the original),
as she said to her husband some days before. In contrast, though, to Ebrennac in
Vercors' *Le Silence de la mer*—and instead like the German officers with whom
Ebrennac spoke in Paris—the officer that Roza approaches only ridicules her assumptions about German culture.

At this point in the scene, the focalization now switches to Roza's perspective.
To save her husband's and son's lives, she decides to sacrifice her body to the German officer—a common manifestation of coercion or force during the war that has
frequently been dismissed throughout history as 'horizontal collaboration.' In civil
life, the German officer had been rejected by a woman he loved, but occupation
opens up a realm of new sexual opportunities for him—albeit not by romantic
relations with the enemy (*à la* the hint of romance in Vercors' novel) but rather by
exploitative means: in free, indirect speech, we hear the officer thinking, "War is a
wonderful thing. Thanks to the war, he will have enough women. Without count-
ing, without mercy" (*ApP*, 218). In spite of his disgusting behavior, Roza tries to
please him sexually: "meekly, she undresses him, admires the perfect proportions
of a hero of antiquity" (*ApP*, 218), hoping that, by trying to create a good experience for the officer, she might help to ensure her loved ones' safety. Nevertheless,
her act of submission takes a cruelly unexpected turn when it becomes a gang rape.

The humiliated female body, here, becomes a demystified allegory of occupation and distortion, and accordingly Mihuleac presents multiple perspectives on
this bodily occupation. For the German soldier, this is an event to document,
just like a tourist or travel photographer might—and in fact, this is how German
soldiers liked to imagine themselves during the occupations (see Meid's chapter
in this volume, and see our book cover that stems from a travel guide for German
soldiers in occupied Belgium). The images that the Germans captured in the
novel, however, reveal the occupation for what it truly was, especially for Jews:
an experience of brutal, dehumanizing violence:

> The German delightfully contemplates this [rape] and asks himself whether the
> light would be sufficient for taking a photograph. Then he suggests that he and
> his Romanian officer-comrade should penetrate the dirty Jewish madame simul-
> taneously, and namely into the neighboring orifices, just as the Romanian and

> German brothers-in-arms invade hostile Russia, shoulder to shoulder. The Romanian officer joyfully agrees upon the suggestion: "Soldiers, I command you: cross the Pruth!" (*ApP*, 219)

One could argue that a detailed depiction of gang rape (and I spare the reader an even more disgusting photography scene [cf. *ApP*, 289]) is a mere example of war-porn writing. However, right after this quoted passage, the narrative perspective shifts back to Roza's bodily sensations and her feelings of helplessness and humiliation, and thus to a very different reality; even the style of the writing itself changes, to the fragile sound of sentence fragments.

Amidst all of this, beyond the victim's and the perpetrators' realities, we encounter another reality with which we, as readers, are juxtaposed: that of the witness. Young Golda, observing the horrific act in shock, still believes that a German must be able to save her mother. Golda escapes the scene and hurries toward the city's bursar to reach the German chief commander (at the time, Major General Otto Röttig). On her way, she runs into the turmoil of the pogrom, where Romanians strip any valuable clothes off the murdered Jews. Eventually Golda slips and falls onto a pile of naked corpses. An old woman approaches to kill her, and in her despair, Golda cries out—in German, because she still believes in the nobility of Germans and their culture—"Mein Vater! Mein Vater, Hilfe!" (*ApP*, 238). Ironically, it is indeed a German officer, a father, who saves her life. "Leave her alone, both! *Off you go*! The rigorous command from the mouth of a German officer brings some fresh air" (*ApP*, 239). He asks Golda to tell him something nice in German, and she remembers a poem that she once wrote on vacation with her parents in Warnemünde, in Northern Germany, reciting it to him with a trembling voice. Golda's use of poetic language successfully enables her to connect, emotionally, with the occupier. Moved, the officer asks her to write this poem down for his daughter at home—with a valuable fountain pen, given to him by a Jew in the latter's own desperate and futile attempt to bribe the German to save his life.

I argue that these two scenes—the gang rape and the child's recitation of the poem—condense the contradictory realities of occupation in a striking way. The changing focalizations and the pluralization of narrative subjectivities enable the novel to grant access to the emotional dilemmas that arise in situations of violent excess, in which cultural assumptions about the occupier are unmasked as mere self-deception, or are invoked—sometimes in tragically misguided futility—as a life-saving strategy. Here, one person's rescue manifests through the writing instrument of another whose life has already been taken.

To conclude, I shall turn once more to the relationship between historiography and literature, since this relationship is consistently reflected across the novel: Suzy receives most of her knowledge about the pogrom from her historian friend Sever. But neither was the subjective reality of Roza's brutal gang rape to be recorded in the historical sources, nor did the fates of innumerable, horribly abused women make it into the country's official history books. Thus, only the literary account is capable of bringing this occupational reality back before our eyes and searing it into our memories. For Mihuleac, it is the failure of Romanian national historiography that urged him to write this novel, and this very labor made him an enemy in the eyes of the 'patriotic.'

The novel does not intend to present an alternative reality. Instead, it aims to help the reader access a dimension of reality that lies beyond the scope of any historiography that understands the history of occupation rather flatly as a mere history of "heroic fights for the freedom of the fatherland" (*ApP*, 298). Indeed, contemporary historiography has largely moved beyond overt identity politics. However, the novel introduces a distinct form of memory: an *ekphrasis* of the *aisthesis* of occupation, or more simply, what Alison Landsberg (2004) termed "prosthetic memory" (see the Introduction for further discussion). This approach forges an affective link with the past for those who did not experience it directly, and for those whose recollections have been obscured or entirely eclipsed by the nation's official historical narratives. To penetrate these barriers, Mihuleac opts for a violent exposure of the reader to this history, marked by its vehement language and stark portrayals of sexual violence.

Conclusion

This chapter analyzed three novels that depict diverse experiences of living under occupation. The novels differ in their aesthetic approaches, historical backgrounds, and the spatial and temporal aspects of these elements.

However, despite their differences, each of these novels exposes a menu of ethical complexities and moral dilemmas that occupation entails. The stories told therein are not just about armies and politics but about ordinary people caught in extraordinary circumstances. They reveal the ways in which individuals struggled—and nonetheless often failed—to maintain their lives and dignity in the face of violence and oppression. Just as importantly, they also challenge any simplistic imagining of the occupation, and they resist the narratives of national identities that rely on clear antagonism to justify the nation's moral legitimacy.

For example, in *Le Silence de la mer*, the antagonism (if one can even use such a word to define the main characters' dynamic) is anything but overt; the French hosts and their German lodger Ebrennac are trapped in a silent standoff, wherein each party secretly yearns for a genuine connection, yet is prevented from achieving this by the social and political barriers of the occupation. The niece is especially torn between her attraction to Ebrennac and her loyalty to her country and uncle. She cannot reconcile her feelings with the harsh reality of being occupied, and spatially as well as emotionally invaded by an enemy force.

The chapter also examined how the authors employ various literary techniques to convey the complexity and ambiguity of human relationships during the time of occupation, and how these relationships challenge the dominant narratives of nationalism, heroism, and victimhood. For example, Osewoudt in Herman's *De donkere kamer van Damokles* fantasizes about being a heroic resistance fighter, but his actions are driven by insecurity and delusion more than by personal morals or political convictions. Given motives such as his, Osewoudt's (and Herman's) version of the Netherlands' occupation history is distorted and unreliable. Ironically, in his view, it was the Gestapo officer who understood him better in his version of history than the victorious Allies; although he has fought against the Germans, the Allies ultimately do not consider him one of their own.

While Osewoudt aims to be recognized for his antagonism toward the Germans, enacting his resistance overtly, the main characters of *America de peste pogrom*, Golda and Roza, attempt to 'resist' simply by aiming to survive, therefore taking actions that appear (on the surface) more like cooperation and appeasement. These characters, who both identify with German culture, hope for the occupiers to see them as (cultural) allies rather than as enemies, and that this understanding can save their loved ones and their lives. However, their cultural affinity to Germany blinds them to the reality of the limitless brutality that the occupation has unleashed. For example, Roza tries to impress the German officer with her intelligence and taste, hoping that he will see her as more than a Jewish woman to be exploited. She also wants to find some humanity in him, and to be seen as a lover who cares for him as an individual—not just as a convenient object for his pleasure. This scene shows the psychological coping mechanisms that many women under occupation had to adopt in order to survive. The mother's and daughter's dreams of a civilized and cultured German presence in the Romanian–Russian borderland are shattered by violent sexual assault and deadly deportations.

Golda, too, wants someone to recognize the part of her that loves German language and poetry. She is not just a child witnessing the horrors of a pogrom; she is a child who recites a poem to a German officer amidst a pogrom, and he spares her (and a rabbi's) life temporarily—not because he recognizes her humanity, but because the poem triggers some nostalgic memory of his own childhood and daughter. In this scene, even though Golda escapes the horrors of occupation with her life (ultimately all the way to the United States), the rift between occupier and occupied is not bridged but rather is re-inscribed in a bitter way: Golda writes down the poem with a golden fountain pen that a desperate Jew gave to another German sergeant in exchange for his life—unsuccessfully.

All of these novels display the potential—or sometimes even just the hope—for empathy and compassion in the face of violence and oppression. They also reveal the moral complexities and the struggle for dignity and recognition that are faced by those who live under occupation. These literary works do not rely on a strict mimetic approach to represent the reality of occupation. Rather, with each employing a distinctive style and perspective to convey an affective dimension of occupation that often escapes the historical record, these novels complicate and challenge the dominant narratives and expectations of how life under occupation should be seen and remembered. In this way, they exemplify the kind of 'affective realism' that we proposed (see the Introduction to the volume on this terminology) as a key feature of the literature of military occupation.

Ultimately, the psychogeography depicted by these and any other novels of their genre transcends the end of the war and the immediate post-war period. Their affective realism strives to portray historical worlds faithfully on the story level, sometimes using familiar schemes and language on the discourse level, and sometimes even by explicitly irritating such schemes and use of language. More importantly, though, novels such as these aim to *bridge* the spatial and temporal gap between events and readers by revealing the affective modes of experiencing occupation on the levels of both story and discourse. This literary genre also relates to our present situation: in a paradoxical way, the literature of occupation links different times and places by emotionally invoking a 'past' experience that is still embedded in our communities' present. Although each occupation novel might address a specific national context, a comparative perspective reveals the lasting impact that the military occupation of World War II has had not just on our 'national' minds—but on our European ones.

Notes

1. "Paris ! Paris outragé ! Paris brisé ! Paris martyrisé ! Mais Paris libéré ! Libéré par lui-même, libéré par son peuple avec le concours des armées de la France, avec l'appui et le concours de la France tout entière, de la France qui se bat, de la seule France, de la vraie France, de la France éternelle." https://www.ina.fr/ina-eclaire-actu/25-aout-1944-paris-outrage-paris-brise-mais-paris-libere (August 24, 2022).
2. A crucial step in this analysis is to employ the typology of occupations that was established in the introductory chapter of this book. This typology allows for a systematic and rigorous comparison of different forms of occupation and their implications for social inequality. By using this framework, we can avoid oversimplifying or generalizing the complex and diverse realities of occupation structures and dynamics.

3. All authors discussed in this chapter are male authors. For a female perspective on occupied France, see my forthcoming chapter: "Die Gegenwart des Opfers. Besatzungsliteratur als weibliche Gegengeschichte: Irène Némirovskys *Suite française* (1942/2004)." In *Position und Stimme des Opfers,* edited by Saskia Fischer, Matthias N. Lorenz, and Deborah Fallis. Berlin: Verbrecher Verlag, 2024.

4. As the subtitle of the bilingual edition by Brown and Stokes reads, cf. Vercors 2022. In fact Bruller/Vercors came back to the topic in his novels *Les Armes de la nuit* (1946) and *La Puissance du jour* (1951). On the development of his literary treatment of the French resistance movement see Kidd 1999.

5. A very similar strategy is also used in *America de peste pogrom*, which will be discussed later in this chapter. At this point, I am only giving one quote: "You can be assured that by such cultivated soldiers who ravish your soul with such heavenly musical chords, no evil can be inflicted" (Mihuleac 2018, 211). Since I do not read Romanian, and no English translation is available, I am referring to the German translation. All translations from the German version are mine.

6. Laura Frost (2019, 80–82) dismisses this important fact. Ebrennac does not attract the niece due to his handsome military look in uniform but rather as a civilian; see *SM*, 75.

7. "Il regardait ma nièce, le pur profile têtu et fermé, en silence et avec une insistance grave, où flottaient encore pourtant les restes d'un sourire. Ma nièce le sentait. Je la voyais légèrement rougir, un pli peu à peu s'inscrire entre ses sourcils. Ses doigts tiraient un peu trop vivement, trop sèchement sur l'aiguille, au risqué de rompre le fil" (*SM*, 50).

8. "J'appris ce jour-là qu'une main peut, pour qui sait l'observer, refléter les émotions aussi bien qu'un visage […]. Et les doigts de cette main-là se tendaient et se pliaient, se pressaient et s'accrochaient, se livraient à la plus intense mimique tandis que le visage et tout le corps demeuraient immobiles et compassés" (*SM*, 61–62).

9. "Hij ging nnar de achterkammer en nam zijn uniform uit de kast. Het uniform was donkergroen als het uniform van een boswachter. Er hoorde een Duitse helm bij, opgekocht uit oude voorraden na de oorlog van '14–18'. […] Osewoudt mocht niets anders doen dan op wacht staan met een oud geweer. In de stralende zon, onder het gezang van vogels, moest hij zelf de monsterlijke kanonnen verzinnen zoals altijd. Niemand was van plan het postkantoor aan te vallen" (Hermans 1994, 20–21).

10. "Want als de Duitsers verslagen zouden zijn, wat zou een meisje als Marianne dan nog voor hem kunnen voelen: een onontwikkedlde sigarenwinkelier, met ook nog een ontoonbaar uiterlijk, een man die niet eens een baard had en in een bevrijd vaderland zelfs niet meer de gelegenheid zou hebben een martellaar of een held te zijn?" (Hermans 1994, 171–72).

11. This applies more to Oswoudt's Jewish girlfriend, Marianne, than to Oswoudt himself. Nobody forces Oswoudt to do what he does. Moreover, most of the time he was more concerned about his assumed post-war glory than about the moral character of his

deeds. As a Jew, Marianne takes all the risk when she comes back from her safe harbor in England to join the Dutch resistance.

12. "Wie is te vertrouwen en wie niet? Misschien is de doctor alleen maar een handlanger van Ebernuss, misschien zijn de Duitsers nu bezig uit te zoeken op welk adres het telefoonnummer thuishoort dat ik de dokter heb obgegeven, misschien wordt Marianne over een half uur gearresteerd. […] Wie is nog te vertrouwen? Iedereen bedriegt iedereen" (Hermans 1994, 155).

13. In the Belgian context, Hugo Claus with his seminal 1983 work *Het verdriet van België* (*The Sorrow of Belgium*) served a role remarkably similar to this.

14. See van Rooden (2012) with regard to Hermans' novel *Ik heb altijd gelijk* (1951), and Mukherjee (2007) with regard to *The Darkroom of Damocles*.

15. Later it says: "The true guilty of the pogrom became allies of the Soviet Union after August 23, 1944. […] Many were decorated by Stalin" (*ApP*, 256).

16. The novel (cf. *ApP*, 144) mentions that this loss of territories was attributed to "Judeo-Bolshevism" by Antonescu, although forced upon Romania by Hitler and Mussolini.

17. Which becomes evident when realizing that, already in 1940, the so-called "Marcks Plan," by Brigadier General Erich Marcks, envisaged the attack on the Soviet Union also from Romania and the region of Iași. See Blau (1955, 5).

18. I am drawing on interview statements that the author provided to one of my students, Nina Brennecke, for her master's thesis.

19. This is a narrative means found quite frequently in the 'new' literature of occupation in order to integrate historical knowledge into the story. See also the discussion of Trude Teige's *Marmor danset i regnet* in the Introduction of this volume.

20. This point merits further discussion. How can Mihuleac justify the repetition of antisemitic stereotypes in his novel, which aims to confront Romanians with their complicity in the Shoah? One tentative answer to this challenging question is that Mihuleac may want to imply that even if all the antisemitic stereotypes were true, they would not warrant a pogrom and a subsequent genocide.

21. For the importance of this motif and for Romanian research literature and critique, see Pălimariu (2019).

References

Benvenisti, Eyal. 2009. "Occupation, Belligerent." Oxford Public International-al Law. Accessed March 17, 2023, https://opil.ouplaw.com/display/10.1093/law:epil/9780199231690/law-9780199231690-e359.

Benz, Wolfgang. 2022. "Verbündete, Satelliten, Freunde des Deutschen Reiches." In *Deutsche Herrschaft: Nationalsozialistische Besatzung in Europa und die Folgen*, edited by Wolfgang Benz, 77–100. Freiburg: Herder.

Bergen, Doris. 2013. "What Do Studies of Women, Gender, and Sexuality Contribute to Understanding the Holocaust." In *Different Horrors, Same Hell: Gender and the Holocaust*, edited by Myrna Goldenberg and Amy H. Shapiro, 16–37. The Stephen S. Weinstein series in post-Holocaust studies. Seattle: University of Washington Press.

Blau, George E. 1955. *The German Campaign in Russia: Planning and Operations (1940–1942)*. German Report Series No. 20–261a. Washington: Department of the Army Pamphlet.

Céline, Louis-Ferdinand. 1957. *D'un chateau l'autre*. Paris: Gallimard.

Conan, Éric, and Henry Rousso. 1994. *Vichy, un passé qui ne passe pas: Pour une histoire du XXe siècle*. Paris: Fayard.

Fischer, Saskia. 2022. "Just Another 'Legend of the Forgiving Jew'? The Art of Coping with Wrongdoing and How Literature Can Assist." In *Guilt, Forgiveness, and Moral Repair*, edited by Maria-Sibylla Lotter and Saskia Fischer, 153–77. Cham: Springer International Publishing.

Frost, Laura. 2019. *Sex Drives: Fantasies of Fascism in Literary Modernism*. Ithaca, NY: Cornell University Press.

Hermans, Willem Frederik. [1958] 1994. *De donkere kamer van Damokles*. Amsterdam: Oorschot.

———. 2020. *The Darkroom of Damocles*. Translated from the Dutch by Ina Rilke. London: Pushkin Press.

International Commission on the Holocaust in Romania. 2004. *Final Report. Presented to Romanian President Ion Iliescu*. Bucharest. Accessed March 16, 2024, https://www.ushmm.org/m/pdfs/20080226-romania-commission-holocaust-history.pdf.

Ioanid, Radu. 1993. "The Holocaust in Romania: The Iasi Pogrom of June 1941." *Contemporary European History* 2, no. 2: 119–48. https://doi.org/10.1017/S0960777300000394.

John, S. Beynon. 1986. "The Ambiguous Invader: Images of the German in Some French Fiction about the Occupation of 1940–44." *Journal of European Studies* 16, no. 3: 187–200.

Kidd, William. 1999. "Vercors. – Writing The Unspeakable: From *Le Silence de mer* (1942) To *La Puissance du jour* (1951)." In *European Memories of the Second World War*, edited by Helmut Peitsch, Charles Burdett, and Claire Gorrara, 46–54. New York: Berghahn Books. https://doi.org/10.1515/9781782389637.

Klüger, Ruth. 2020. "Der Dichter als Dieb? Der Fall Littner-Koeppen." In *Gelesene Wirklichkeit: Fakten und Fiktionen in der Literatur*, 2nd ed., 135–42. Göttingen: Wallstein Verlag GmbH.

Koestler, Arthur. 1946. *The Yogi and the Commissar*. New York: Macmillan.

Konstantinović, Radivoje D. 1969. *Vercors, écrivain et dessinateur*. Bibliothèque française et romane 17. Paris: Klincksieck.

Landsberg, Alison. 2004. *Prosthetic Memory: The Transformation of American Remembrance in the Age of Mass Culture*. New York: Columbia University Press.

Lloyd, Christopher. 2003. *Collaboration and Resistance in Occupied France: Representing Treason and Sacrifice*. Basingstoke: Palgrave Macmillan.

Meyer, Ahlrich. 2000. *Die deutsche Besatzung in Frankreich 1940–1944: Widerstandsbekämpfung und Judenverfolgung*. Darmstadt: Wiss. Buchges.

Meyer, Ahlrich, and Serge Klarsfeld, eds. 1999. *Der Blick des Besatzers: Propagandaphotographie der Wehrmacht aus Marseille 1942–1944*. Bremen: Temmen.

Mihuleac, Cătălin. 2014. *America de peste pogrom*. Iași: Editura POLIROM.

———. 2018. *Oxenberg & Bernstein*. Übersetzt aus dem Rumänischen von Ernst Wichner. Wien: Paul Zsolnay Verlag.

Molasky, Michael S. 1999. *The American Occupation of Japan and Okinawa: Literature and Memory*. Routledge Studies in Asia's transformations 1. London: Routledge.

Mukherjee, Neel. 2007. "A Dutch Classic to Rival Camus." *The Daily Telegraph*, September 13, 2007. Accessed March 16, 2024, https://www.telegraph.co.uk/culture/books/fictionreviews/3667861/A-Dutch-classic-to-rival-Camus.html.

Pălimariu, Ana-Maria. 2019. "Überreife Hebammenkunst: Zeugenschaft, auch für die Zeugen in Oxenberg & Bernstein von Catalin Mihuleac." In *Narrative des Peripheren in posthabsburgischen Literaturen des zentral(ost)europäischen Raums*, edited by Ana-Maria Pălimariu and Wolfgang Müller-Funk, 151–68. Jassyer Beiträge zur Germanistik 12. Konstanz: Hartung-Gorre.

Pratt, Mary Louise. 1991. "Arts of the Contact Zone." *Profession* 91: 33–40. Accessed March 15, 2024, http://www.jstor.org/stable/25595469.

Rooden, Aukje van. 2012. "Het gelijk van de schrijver: Willem Frederik Hermans' fictieve discussie met Jean-Paul Sartre." *Nederlande Letterkunde* 17, 159–77. Accessed March 16, 2024, https://www.dbnl.org/tekst/_ned021201201_01/_ned021201201_01_0011.php.

Rothberg, Michael. 2019. *The Implicated Subject: Beyond Victims and Perpetrators*. Stanford: Stanford University Press.

Shafir, Michael. 2012. "Denying the Shoah in Post-Communist Eastern Europe." In *Holocaust Denial. The Politics of Perfidy*, edited by Robert S. Wystrich, 27–66. Berlin: De Gruyter.

Simonin, Anne. 1994. *Les editions de minuit 1942–1955: Le devoir d'insoumission*. Paris: IMEC Editions.

Smulders, Wilbert. 1983. "De literaire misleiding in 'De donkere Kamer van Damokles.'" PhD diss., Rijksuniversiteit te Utrecht.

Tönsmeyer, Tatjana. 2015. "Besatzungsgesellschaften: Begriffliche und konzeptionelle Überlegungen zur Erfahrungsgeschichte des Alltags unter deutscher Besatzung im Zweiten Weltkrieg." Docupedia-Zeitgeschichte, 18.12.2015. Accessed March 16, 2024, http://docupedia.de/zg/toensmeyer_besatzungsgesellschaften_v1_de_2015. http://dx.doi.org/10.14765/zzf.dok.2.663.v1.

Vercors. 2022. *Le Silence de la mer/The Silence of the Sea: A Novel of French Resistance during World War II by "Vercors,"* edited by James W. Brown and Lawrence D. Stokes. Translated from the French by Cyrill Connolly. London: Bloomsbury Academic.

Watts, Philip. 1990. "The Ghosts of Sigmaringen." *Studies in 20th Century Literature* 23, no. 1: 27–41.

Wickenberg, Ernst-Peter. 1996. "Verlegen unter deutscher Besatzung: Anne Simonins Quellenstudien zum französischen Widerstandsverlag *Les Éditions de Minuit.*" *Internationales Archiv für Sozialgeschichte der deutschen Literatur* 21, no. 2: 176–85.

CULTURAL SPACES OF OCCUPATION

Introduction to Part 2

JEANNE E. GLESENER

This part testifies to the varying geocultural transformations of occupied spaces and how literary processes of intertextuality and interpretation were historically used by both occupied and occupying writers to confer new meaning to them.

The opening chapter investigates one of the most popular German texts about Greece: Erhart Kästner's travelogue, *Ölberge, Weinberge* (1953) ("Mountains of Olives, Vineyards"). Its popularity is remarkable, given that it is the revised and sanitized version of a veritable bestseller from the Third Reich, namely *Griechenland. Ein Buch aus dem Kriege* (1942) ("Greece: A Book from the War"). The 1942 travelogue, bypassing the murderous reality of the occupation, is an extraordinary document in that it participated in promoting tourist ventures to Greece as a holiday—a harrowing example of trying to introduce a semblance of normalcy to a situation that was everything but. **Christopher Meid**'s comparison of the two versions of Kästner's book focuses on the poetics of mythologizing the occupier's experience and how that very gesture was motivated differently during and after the war. As Meid's careful reading shows, the occupied territory of Greece is refigured into a legitimate cultural space by reactivating the topoi of German cultural history and rekindling the idea of a kinship between Greeks and Germans. The *Wehrmacht*'s uncouth soldiers are modeled on Homer's bold Achaeans, only braver and more heroic, thereby also stressing the racial superiority of the conquering Germans. Furthermore, after the war, the affective reality of the destruction that was wreaked upon Greece by occupation and civil war does not impact Kästner's poetic stance when, as Meid underlines, he again falls back on mythology (the Oedipus myth, in this case) to explain away the suffering and the crimes committed.

Following from Meid's emphasis on the aesthetic strategies of mythologization that have been employed to avoid engaging the occupier's moral responsibility, the next chapter shows how an antique text from the European classical tradition was used, not to glorify, but to expose the wantonness of the *Wehrmacht* during its occupation of Italy. Comparing Xenophon's *Anabasis* (380–360 BCE) to Jewish-German philologist, poet, and Word War I veteran Rudolf Borchardt's *Anabasis* (1944)—a report on his exiled family's forced return from Italy to the German Reich—**Jan Andres** examines how Borchardt channels the experience of occupation through intertextual reference to this ancient source. He shows how the pre-text of the classical European tradition was used as a narrative strategy that gave Borchardt an approach to reflect both on Italy's situation under *Wehrmacht* occupation and on his own predicament. Adopting Xenophon's semibiographical posture and the stylized wavering between fact and fiction for his own memoir, Borchardt not only manages to convey the emotional strain of his situation as a Jewish-German exiled writer under constant threat of deportation, but also to express his dismay at the *Wehrmacht*'s wanton and willfully destructive behavior toward the occupied territory. Andres' contextualized reading of the *Anabasis* makes plain that the devastation Borchardt laments is not only that of the cultural and social landscapes of occupied territories, but also the fact that these very acts of wanton destruction equally signal the rupture with the Prussian military tradition by which Borchardt lived.

Much like the genre of memoir can, ego-documents such as private diaries and letters can deploy narrative strategies capable of blurring the fine line between fact and fiction. When written under the strain of occupation, they can become a coping mechanism for distancing oneself from the pervasive, inhuman horrors witnessed or, on the contrary, an outlet to give room to how that very reality affects the writer emotionally. Analyzing the ego-documents of Felix Hartlaub, a young German historian assigned to the Historical Archive Commission in Paris as part of the occupying forces, and of Tami Oelfken, persecuted by the National Socialist regime for her socialist and pacifist views and thereafter thwarted in trying to publish her books in the French occupation zone, **Stefanie Siess** contrasts works produced under two different occupying regimes to investigate how artistic expression is shaped respectively by the role of the author *and* by the character of the occupying regime itself. Looking at these writers' semi-documentary works through the conceptual lens of how they represent the 'other,' Siess also discusses the relevance of these texts and other such ego-documents as cultural representations of a specific moment in time: sources that provide indispensable insights into the lived experience of everyday life and that map the conflicting mentalities under occupation.

Mapping—as a concept and a literary device—is also what foregrounds **Atinati Mamatsashvili**'s approach to the representation of occupied cities in her own chapter. Bringing together disparate novels that portray life under occupation or during liberation in Tbilisi, Paris, and Luxembourg allows Mamatsashvili, in a stringent comparative perspective, to isolate the recurring spatial patterns used by Georgian emigré writers Indo Inasari and George Kipiani and by German exiled writer Maria Gleit to convey the occupation experience. Inasari and Kipiani focus, respectively, on Paris in the aftermath of the liberation and on Tbilisi, a city occupied by the Bolsheviks; Gleit describes life in Luxembourg during Germany's four-year occupation of the country. The chapter asks how mental space (perceived and represented) and social space (constructed and produced) interact in a fictional text that portrays an urban space—a space that is, at once, 'produced' by the new oppressive regime and yet represented by the narrative processes that manage to subvert the regime in turn. Resorting to spatial dichotomies—legal–illegal and clandestine–legitimate—allows Mamatsashvili to map the reinterpretations (be they forced or existential) of all kinds of geocultural and psychosocial spaces, such as city and landscape, home and hospitality, legitimacy and invisibility, all occurring in the aftermath of ideologies imposed by brute force.

The final chapter in this part brings together earlier explorations on cultural spaces of occupation by emphasizing how mythology, classical literature, and (specifically, in this case) religious master narratives act as ideological lenses to foster discourses of supremacy and legitimation by drawing on the tenets of European cultural history. Reading Luxembourgish writer Pierre Gregoire's trilogy *Europäische Suite* (1951–1952) ("European Suite"), which depicts two regimes of occupation against his war experience in Nazi-occupied Luxembourg and in concentration camps, and that expounds on the theme of spiritual and secular martyrdom that underlies his work, **Daniela Lieb** showcases how Gregoire casts a literary alter ego to construct a historical continuity from the Nazi occupation of Luxembourg to the presence of the Red Army in the Soviet occupation zone. Lieb explains how Gregoire's use of Roman Catholic discourse figures leads him to conceptualize the construct of an anti-European 'East,' stylized as comprising the barbarian and culturally inferior *homo sovieticus* against whom the 'West' was able to define itself as the one and only 'real' Europe.

CHAPTER 3

Military Occupation as Tourism?

Griechenland. Ein Buch aus dem Kriege (1942) and
Ölberge, Weinberge (1953) by Erhart Kästner

CHRISTOPHER MEID

Philhellenism, Travel, and Politics

The idea of a special relationship between the Greeks of antiquity and the Germans of modern times has been influential since the late 18th century (cf. Fuhrmann 1995; Landfester 1996). To the rest of Europe, this extreme form of philhellenism seemed alien; British literary scholar Eliza M. Butler even described it as the "tyranny of Greece over Germany" (cf. Butler 1958). Butler's study was first published in 1935, at a time when the National Socialist rulers were adapting the traditional philhellenic ideals to their ideology. National Socialism's yearning to align itself with ancient Greece found its most effective expression in the Olympic Games of 1936, whose accompanying program—particularly, the Olympic torch relay invented for the occasion—propagated the idea of cultural translation (cf. Large 2007).

The National Socialists initially also sought good relations with the modern Greek state and its authoritarian ruler, General Ioannis Metaxas (cf. Zacharioudakis 2002), and at the same time tried to strengthen Germany's influence within Greece (cf. Koutsoukou 2010). An illustrative example of this strategy is the anthology *Unsterbliches Hellas* (1938) ("Immortal Hellas"), which was edited by the Greek diplomat Charilaos Kriekoukis and Karl Bömer, an official in the NSDAP's Foreign Policy Office. It highlighted the ties between the two states. Moreover, the volume's contributors consistently strove to highlight the ostensible parallels both between the Germanic tribes and the ancient Greeks, and between modern Greece and the National Socialist German Reich (cf. Kriekoukis and Bömer 1938).

This affinity for all things Greek, however, was to change drastically in 1941, when Italy invaded Greece (cf. Fleischer 1986). After the Greeks were attacked and pushed Mussolini's troops back as far as Albania, the German army intervened, and the ensuing years of Germany's tyranny over Greece are among the darkest in Greek history. From April 1941 to late summer 1943, Greece was under German, Italian, and Bulgarian occupation; thereafter, it was exclusively under German rule. Even if the German occupiers had initially assured the Greek people of their appreciation (cf. Hitler 1942, 29), the situation in occupied Greece presented a completely different picture. Greece, which relied on food imports, was now cut off from foreign food supplies. Moreover, although "the occupation itself proceeded with little violence, the soldiers took food and requisitioned what they liked" (Mazower 1993, 23). According to the Red Cross, "about 250,000 people had died directly or indirectly as a result of the famine between 1941 and 1943," and 100,000 of those died in the famine's very first winter (cf. Mazower 1993, 41). Meanwhile, because the birth rate (as birth rates are apt to do in wartime) declined "over the same period, the Red Cross reckoned that the total population of Greece was at least 300,000 less by the end of the war than it would otherwise have been, as a result of food scarcity" and the simultaneous decline in births (Mazower 1993, 41).

At the same time, underground movements, such as the communist ELAS (*Ellinikos Laikos Apeleftherotikos Stratos*, or Greek People's Liberation Army) and the bourgeois EDES (*Ethnikos Dimokratikos Ellinikos Syndesmos*, or National Republican Greek League) waged a successful partisan war against the occupiers (cf. Tsoutsoumpis 2016): in the winter of 1943 into 1944, partisans controlled almost four-fifths of the country. However, the German and Italian occupiers reacted with great brutality. Shootings of civilians were documented as early as August 1941. Sometimes, entire villages fell victim to the so-called expiation measures (cf. Mazower 1993), such that, by the end of June 1944, 1,339 villages had been completely or partially destroyed and about 30,000 people had died as a result of the German and Italian reprisals (cf. Rondholz 1997, 161f.). Added to all this violence, from March 1943 onwards, the Jewish population was deported; out of about 70,000 Greek Jews, approximately 58,000 were murdered in the Shoah (cf. Mazower 1993, 235–261).

Yet somehow—all this horror notwithstanding—many German soldiers saw their stay on the shores of the Mediterranean as something like a holiday. Accordingly, Greece was a popular place of service for members of the *Wehrmacht* (cf. Mazower 1993, 201). Moreover, the occupation policy was also aimed at suggesting a semblance of normalcy in many areas of life, especially in the realm of culture, for the occupying German personnel. For instance, soon after the fighting ceased, the German Archaeological Institute resumed its excavations in Greece (cf. Hiller von Gaertringen 1995). Furthermore, the *Wehrmacht* leadership explicitly promoted tourism among the occupying troops and supported them logistically; the local command in Athens even organized city tours and visits to archaeological sites (Hiller von Gaertringen 1994, 129f.). Lectures, concerts, and author readings for German troops were held in Athens as well. By organizing such events, the *Wehrmacht* tried to demonstrate how cultured the occupiers were. Moreover, they maintained the illusion that a 'normal' life was possible in times of war and terror.

Besides popular academic treatises and travel guides for the occupiers, among the propaganda were publications by soldiers (cf. Anonymus 1941; Generalkommando 1944), a number of whom painted the occupation as a holiday. Their texts, some of which betray literary aspirations, were aimed at the reading public of the Third Reich and at fellow soldiers alike.

It is important to recognize that "forms of forced mobility" (Brenner 1997, 143),[1] which also include participation in war, cannot be described as travel per se, since forced mobility is, by definition, involuntary (Brenner 1997). It might initially seem strange, thus, to speak of these texts as 'travel literature.' However, because the participants in a war often experience a perspective shift (cf. Brenner 1997, 144), the occupiers' texts often follow the conventions of the travelogue genre all the same—even though their attitude of leisure changes nothing about the fundamental dubiousness of their literary (or, for that matter, military) ventures.

The book *Wir marschieren gegen Griechenland* (1942) ("We Are Marching Against Greece"), by the officer G. J. Graf, is a striking example of how war experience and tourist perception blend. In his book, Graf describes some German soldiers as they enjoy themselves on the Thermaic Gulf. He observes, in particular, "a blond soldier" who is having coffee on a terrace: "He smiles and takes a leisurely drag on a cigarette. As he does so, he watches the busy traffic on the street while a boy is cleaning his boots" (Graf 1942, 104).[2] Here, in essence, the soldier is described as a tourist recovering from the exertions of conquest. In line with this attitude of tourism, Graf complains that he cannot visit any more of the country's sights because the campaign is already over:

> Our regiment will not march further south, although we would all have liked to see the city of Larissa, the monastic republic on Mount Athos, the city of Athens with the Acropolis and the many artistic monuments from the history of ancient Hellas, the port of Piraeus, Thermopylae, the ancient site of the Olympic Games, and much more. (Graf 1942, 113f.)[3]

Graf's attitude finds its parallels in the numerous photographs taken by German soldiers in occupied Greece:

> [The] miscellaneous photographic material portrays an image of Thessaloniki as a city that is a 'tourist destination,' a place where, at least for the soldiers pictured, everyday life was not affected by the atrocities of war and the Nazi crimes against humanity. (Katsaridou and Motsianos 2022, 6)

While Graf's text is a revealing period document that can, at best, claim historical interest, Erhart Kästner's travelogues are a different matter; Kästner's travel writing was the beginning of an impressive literary career, with a special role played by his book *Griechenland. Ein Buch aus dem Kriege* (1942) ("Greece: A Book from the War"). This book is particularly interesting because, in it, he combines the description of his travels in Greece with reflections on larger historical processes. In doing so, Kästner links basic assumptions of Nazi racial doctrine with philhellenic topoi in order to stylize the German occupiers of Greece as legitimate successors to the ancient heroes. The ideologically purified second version of this book, which appeared in 1953 under the title *Ölberge, Weinberge* ("Mountains of Olives, Vineyards"), also engages in comprehensive interpretations of history—the difference being that now Kästner reflects on an all-encompassing historical fate that would also be responsible for the horrors of the occupation.

Escapism as Propaganda: *Griechenland. Ein Buch aus dem Kriege* (1942/43)

In 1941, Erhart Kästner, a librarian who had completed his doctorate in 1927 with a thesis on Goethe, was transferred to Greece as a non-commissioned officer. Private letters leave no doubt that Kästner was averse to National Socialism, which was fed by an ultimately anti-democratic elitism (cf. Hiller von Gaertringen 1994, 41–47). At the same time, he obviously had no qualms about putting himself at the service of the regime if he could benefit from it. The transfer to Greece is a good example of this: Kästner was sent there because he had pretended (cf. Hiller von Gaertringen 1994, 61–128) to be able to speak modern Greek in order to get stationed there, as he had always wanted to visit it.

In Greece, Kästner wanted to see as much of the country as possible. Thus, together with his friend, the painter Helmut Kaulbach, he developed a plan to write an illustrated book that, as Kästner and Kaulbach stated in their proposal to their superiors from January 1942 ("Plan für ein Griechenlandbuch"), would give "officers and enlisted men who spend longer periods of time in Greece during the war a small book of memories and an introduction to the monuments and beauties of the country" (Hiller von Gaertringen 1994, 96). Army authorities approved. This meant that Kästner and Kaulbach could travel throughout the occupied country, the army providing them with a means of transport.

They completed the manuscript in the summer of 1942, and the book first appeared in a non-public edition for members of the *Wehrmacht* that autumn. When the book was published, Kaulbach was no longer alive: he had died of a war injury on October 10, 1942 in Russia, where he had been transferred (cf. Nauhaus 2003, 97).

In the summer of 1943, then, several thousand copies of a second edition were printed for the general book market (Hiller von Gaertringen 1994, 107). This latter fact clearly indicates that their travelogue met all political expectations: in a time of extreme paper shortage, only texts compatible with the political ideology were printed at all (cf. Barbian 2010, 275). Given that the demand both within and outside the *Wehrmacht* was great, the planned follow-up projects (this time without Kaulbach's collaboration)—a book on Crete and one on the Greek islands—could expect a similarly good response. The book on Crete, however, did not appear until 1946. A collection of travel essays on the Greek islands was published posthumously in 1975.

Regardless of the specific reason for its creation, the completed *Griechenland* shows that its author certainly pursued high artistic ambitions. With his attempt to write an artistically ambitious travelogue about Greece, Kästner had consciously aimed to place himself within an illustrious tradition of German-language literature. As Hugo von Hofmannsthal had noted in an aphorism from 1919, Greece served as a destination of almost religious significance, especially for German authors who considered Greece a spiritual home: "[We,] even more than the other nations, treat antiquity as a magic mirror from which we hope to receive our own figure in a foreign, purified appearance" (Hofmannsthal 2015, 34). In a later essay, Hofmannsthal stresses that of "all the journeys we undertake, the journey to Greece is the most spiritual" (Hofmannsthal 2022, 112). It becomes "a spiritual pilgrimage" (Hofmannsthal 2022, 112) that is dedicated to an idealized past. Hofmannsthal thus articulates a tension between Greece's fame as a historical destination on the one hand and its sensually experienced present on the other: modern travelers, he exclaims, "had forgotten that this landscape could exhale a scent other than that of memories" (Hofmannsthal 2022, 112). This tension between the expectations of travelers, who have an idealized image of Greece and especially of antiquity, and their (often disappointing) experience of the country they visit is constitutive of modern German travel literature about Greece as well (cf. Meid 2012).

Kästner was very familiar with these traditions. For example, the most important and most widely read travelogue about Greece is by Gerhart Hauptmann, for whom Kästner worked as a private secretary during 1936 and 1937. In his *Griechischer Frühling* (1908) ("Greek Spring"), Hauptmann describes how he approaches Greece's lost (i.e., ancient) culture through compelling experiences in nature (cf. Meid 2012, 34–81), repeatedly emphasizing in his writing the similarities between Greece and Germany. When Kästner, in a letter to his former employer from September 1942, describes his own book as a "little belated follow-up to the Greek Spring" (Nauhaus 2003, 381), he is certainly partially right.

However, Kästner goes far beyond his role model in ideological terms. His *Griechenland* also belongs decidedly to Nazi literature, with which it shares thematic and stylistic similarities. For one, it should be noted that the travelogue was one of the most popular genres of the Third Reich (cf. Brenner 1997; Graf 1995). Capitalizing on readers' interest in travel literature, numerous texts on Greece in the 1930s and 1940s were written with a decidedly geopolitical orientation: for example, Carl T. Wiskott's *Griechenland im Auto erlebt* (1936) ("Greece Experienced by Car"), Heinrich Hauser's *Süd-Ost-Europa ist erwacht. Im Auto durch acht Balkanländer* (1938) ("South-Eastern Europe Has Awakened: by Car through Eight Balkan Countries"), and Lutz Koch's *Reise durch den Balkan. 20 000 Kilometer Autofahrt durch Ungarn, Rumänien, Bulgarien, die Türkei, Griechenland, Albanien und Jugoslawien* (1941) ("Journey through the Balkans: 20,000 Kilometers of Car Travel through Hungary, Romania, Bulgaria, Turkey, Greece, Albania, and Yugoslavia"). Works such as these combine what are, at first glance, two contradictory tendencies: an idealization of Greek antiquity and landscapes, paired with a focus on the modern means of transport that German travelers used—the automobile. In other words, the cult of technology is combined with the worship of antiquity. Finally, most contemporary travelogues about Greece emphasize the idea of cultural translation, mostly in the context of the 1936 Olympic Games (cf. Meid 2012, 270–79). Kästner's text marries all of these characteristics—the cult of technology, the cult of antiquity, and the cult of nature—and surpasses its predecessors in its own ostentatiously stylistic ambition.

Obviously, Kästner embraced philhellenic traditions and adapted them to the demands of propaganda literature: central points of his book justify the German occupation of Greece in reference to philhellenic traditions, while, at the same time, the devastating reality of the war is conspicuous for its absence in numerous passages. Instead, Kästner's travelogue centers on the notion of Greece as a timeless place of nature and myth: the numerous prose miniatures paint idyllic landscapes flooded by light, which, in turn, facilitate the traveler's personal development and epiphanies. Kaulbach's accompanying drawings, which depict beautiful landscapes and ruins, reinforce this tendency toward romanticization—and away from Greece's wartime reality.

Of course, Kästner's idyllic passages should not obscure the fact that the historical narrative he systematically unfolds is essentially racist. His book deals rather obsessively with the relationship between ancient Greeks and modern Germans, framing the entire work with an opening chapter that describes the journey to Greece and a concluding chapter that describes the flight back home to Germany. In this last chapter, "Flight over Greece" (*Flug über Griechenland*),

Kästner describes the Greek landscape from a bird's-eye perspective and envisions the historical and mythological events that took place there. For him, the similarity between Germany and Greece is immediately evident: "The German lives half in Hellas anyway, as long as he is in Germany; but when he comes to Greece, he is surrounded everywhere by the German" (Kästner 1943, 268). This statement—which hardly goes beyond the positions articulated in Gerhart Hauptmann's *Griechischer Frühling*—stresses the idea that there is indeed a special affinity between ancient Greeks and modern Germans, who therefore feel at home in Greece. For Kästner, Greece was "north in the south" (Kästner 1943, 269), the home of an originally Nordic people:

> The two holiest sites of the Greeks, Delphi and Mount Olympus, seem the most Nordic. Delphi: a high alpine valley. Mount Olympus: a northern mountain. It is as if distant memories were echoing here, memories of a people who had been displaced to the south, who had become happy in the south, but who nevertheless did not lose a yearning for the north in the depths of their hearts. (Kästner 1943, 269)[4]

Here, granted, Kästner does not refer to Nazi ideas in particular. Rather, he is echoing a line of tradition that was commonplace in German cultural history long before the Nazis. That is, Kästner's commitment to this idea of a kinship between Greeks and Germans (a predominant supposition from even before his own time) might be dismissed as a simple artifact of the eccentricity of one intellectual tradition (that of Germany) seeking a role model in another (that of Greece)—were it not for the aggressive consequences of this idea, which were particularly disastrous for the Greeks of Kästner's era.

Indeed, in the 19th and 20th centuries, the question about the origins of the modern Greeks was much discussed. Of particular importance is the Byzantinist Fallmerayer, who, in 1830, in his *Geschichte der Halbinsel Morea während des Mittelalters* ("History of the Morea Peninsula during the Middle Ages") had declared that the "race of the Hellenes [was] extinct in Europe" (Fallmerayer 1830, I). Instead, in Fallmerayer's view, the modern inhabitants of Greece were of Slavic descent—a quite-controversial thesis that was taken up again, and radicalized, in the so-called race studies of the 20th century in whose German textbooks the ancient Greeks are described as a Nordic Aryan people, biologically related to the Germans of the present. The influential Nazi ideologist Alfred Rosenberg, in his version of this theory, stated that Greeks and Romans had then 'degenerated' in antiquity as a result of interracial mixing (cf. Rosenberg 1934, 35), an idea shared by the Freiburg racial scientist Hans F. K. Günther (cf. Günther 1929). Werner Kulz summarized these positions as follows: "The Greek people [...] are, to us, precisely because we know them so well from antiquity, the clearest example of a complete racial transformation" (Kulz 1937, 19). Kulz reinforces this assertion for the present day when, referring to Slavic migrations during the Middle Ages, he states that there was no continuity whatsoever between ancient and modern Greeks, even if the latter saw it differently:

> But even if, for example, in a hostel for the strangers visiting the ruins of the palace of Mycenae, an 'Agamemnon' cleans the shoes, 'Eumaeos' tends the pigs, and 'Socrates' washes the plates—the Hellenic people has died for all time. (Kulz 1937, 57)

These biologistic assumptions are the basis of Kästner's image of history. Just as Alfred Rosenberg did in his notorious *Der Mythus des 20. Jahrhunderts* (1930) ("The Myth of the 20th Century"), Kästner narrates cultural history in relation to race. According to this view on ancient history, the Greeks of antiquity came as conquerors from the north; soon, they 'degenerated' because they reproduced with the 'inferior' local population. A further decline occurred during the Migration Period, when Slavic tribes invaded Greece. Kästner claims that "the Greeks were [...] strangers in this land, wanderers who came, blossomed, and died after giving the world the most exquisite gift" (Kästner 1943, 162). In other words, for Kästner, it is clear that the modern inhabitants of the country have little in common with the ancient Greeks. As he sees it, the German occupiers now take their place, and they do so legitimately. At about the time that Kästner's book was written, Hitler had remarked: "When we are asked about our ancestors, we always have to refer to the Greeks" (cited in Picker 1963, 159).

The importance of this historical context for Kästner's text is shown by the fact that he discusses this context at length in his framing chapters. For instance, in the opening chapter of his travelogue *Fahrt nach Griechenland* ("Journey to Greece"), Kästner describes an early morning train journey to Athens. His train stops for some time next to another train that is carrying German soldiers and weapons:

> They were [German] men who had come from Crete and were now heading for a new destination and a new battle. Our train slowly pushed its way along the neighboring line of wagons. On the open, flat railway wagons, the guns, the motor cars, and the wheels stood firmly moored. They were powdered with dust and spoke more clearly of the hardships they had endured than the men did. On top and between [their guns] sat, stood, and lay equanimously the heroes of the battle, magnificent figures. They all wore only shorts, some also pith helmets, and squinted through their sunglasses into the bright morning. Their bodies were burnt copper-brown by the Greek sun, their hair white-blond.

> There they were, Homer's "blond Achaeans," the heroes of the *Iliad*. Like them,
> they came from the north; like them, they were tall, bright, young, a race radiant in
> the splendor of its limbs. They were all there, the young Antenor, the massive Ajax,
> the lithe Diomedes, even the radiant, blond-haired Achilles.[5] (Kästner 1943, 9)

For the narrator, there can be no doubt that the Homeric heroes are present in the occupying soldiers. In accordance with racist interpretations of Homer, which highlight in particular his portrayal of blond heroes (cf. Sieglin 1935), Kästner emphasizes that the German soldiers embody the same heroic type as the figures of the Greek epics. There is one important difference, though: modern warfare requires greater heroism than the battle of Troy:

How different then should they [the Homeric heroes] have looked from these here [the German soldiers], who serenely bore their heroism and, quietly and comradely, as if it had been nothing, spoke of the battles on Crete, which were probably much more heroic, much bolder, and much more bitter than all the battles for Troy. Who on earth would ever have had more right to compare himself with [the Homeric heroes] than these [German soldiers]—who did not think of it? They came from the hardest of victories, and drove toward new and unknown deeds. There was not one of them who had not left his comrade, his friend, down there. Around each of them hovered the wingbeat of fate. Homeric air was blowing (Kästner 1943, 9f.).[6] Kästner's attempts to surpass Homer culminate in a nude bathing scene with clear homoerotic overtones:

> Suddenly, a completely classical picture emerged. Sparkling in the light of this
> morning and in the splendor of their young nakedness, this crowd of conquerors
> cavorted along the foreign sea, and it seemed as if an immortal race that had been
> thought lost had naturally returned and taken possession of this shore, or as if
> they had always been there and the mountain of the gods had never looked down
> on anyone but them. (Kästner 1943, 10)[7]

Strangely enough, some scholars have used this passage as an opportunity to place Kästner in the vicinity of the so-called inner emigration (cf. Schnell 1976, 96). Nothing could be more wrong: it is precisely the aestheticization of the occupying forces that serves to celebrate a racist historical narrative. By describing the soldiers as bathers, Kästner makes the violent conquest seem like a beach holiday. This also corresponds to the standard propaganda in which photos of *Wehrmacht* members enjoying a bath in the sea were widely circulated. Graf's *Wir marschieren gegen Griechenland* also contains such a photo (cf. Graf 1942, 104).

If we look at how Kästner describes and evaluates the Greeks of the present, his descriptions here, too, confirm the impression that his travelogue is a deeply racist text. For example, Greek children playing with a blonde girl of Danish descent appear as "little lemurs and monkey faces" (Kästner 1943, 84). For Kästner, the modern Greeks are only a footnote in history—but at least they should be treated gently:

> Even the Romans, less reverent in cultural matters than we are obliged to be, left Athens undestroyed. They did so with a justification that should be remembered today in an hour of discontent against modern Greece. For they resolved to "exercise leniency against the living for the sake of the dead." (Kästner 1943, 46f.)

Kästner, who was not an ardent National Socialist, is nonetheless the prototype of a literary opportunist; he used the opportunities offered by the occupation of Greece to pursue his tourist inclinations on the one hand, and to launch his literary career on the other. It is hardly surprising that he took part in the occupiers' cultural program by giving a series of lectures advertised as *Dichter im Waffenrock* ("Poet in Regimentals") (Hiller von Gaertringen 1994, 119). Those who are familiar with Germany's timid manner of coming to terms with the past in the 1950s will find it equally unsurprising that, only ten years after the war, Kästner could be celebrated as the propagator of a Christian-humanist image of Greece.

History, Myth, and Fate: *Ölberge, Weinberge* (1953)

Strangely enough, Kästner's *Griechenland* marked the beginning of a successful literary preoccupation with Greece. Immediately after the war, while he was a British POW, he began revising his texts about Greece. In 1946, he published *Crete* after ensuring that it contained no incriminating passages. When *Ölberge, Weinberge. Ein Griechenlandbuch* ("Olive Mountains and Vineyards: A Book on Greece")—the heavily revised version of *Griechenland* appeared in 1953, the response was overwhelmingly positive. Kästner's view of Greece has since influenced younger generations' approach to the country at least as much as Hauptmann's *Griechischer Frühling* influenced readers from Kästner's own generation. The new version also contained drawings by the late Kaulbach; however, Kästner had reduced their number from 100 to 48 and, in particular, omitted the pictures that showed people and buildings, instead including largely harmonious depictions of nature (cf. Nauhaus 2003, 106).

The basic Christian orientation of Kästner's travelogue is already evident in its title, which refers to the biblical Mount of Olives near Jerusalem (cf. Hiller von Gaertringen 1994, 239). Compared to his 1942 version, Kästner has made a complete turnaround; whereas, at that time, the blood myth in the wake of Alfred

Rosenberg formed the backdrop of Kästner's ideological considerations, Kästner is concerned by 1953 with determining the relationship between Christianity and antiquity in a harmonious way (cf. Hiller von Gaertringen 1994, 343–402). His aim is to synthesize both spheres under decidedly Christian auspices: "Thus we are baptized Hellenes" (Kästner 1953, 49). The book plays out across two times: on the one hand, it contains many of Kästner's descriptions from the 1942 book and from other texts he had written during the war, while on the other, it describes experiences from the first post-war trip that he made to Greece as well, in 1952. This contrast enables the author to view his own role from a distance. However, it is precisely this clarity of perspective that gives rise to a number of problems—for example, when Kästner declares in retrospect, "If I had learned at that time that I had been granted a full four years in this country, I think I would have been bursting with joy" (Kästner 1953, 13f.), his glee at the fact that the war enabled him to travel as a tourist betraying the fact that he blatantly ignores his own involvement in the occupation. His elitist criticism of tourism also seems problematic (not least of all for its hypocrisy), when he points out that, during the war, he was able to visit the ancient monuments undisturbed, which were now overrun by tourists:

> At that time we did not even need to steer clear of Mycenae, Epidauros, and Delphoi, where in peacetime it is difficult to escape the foreigners' motor coaches. They were deserted, as the wilderness of the Greek mountains and coasts always is anyway. (Kästner 1953, 23)

Ölberge, Weinberge does contain large parts from the older book, such as the bathing scene quoted above. In the new version, though, Kästner no longer refers to the conquerors as Homeric heroes, but rather leaves it at the heroic aestheticization of the naked soldiers, who are now portrayed as ignorant objects of fate:

> Spring '41. I will always remember a picture from the morning of the journey to Athens. […] There were paratroopers from Crete and an anti-aircraft battery; on the flat railway wagons stood moored the guns, powdered over with dust, on and between them stood and sat the fighters, shorts, sunglasses and pith helmets. Their bodies had been burnt to a copper color in the few days, their hair white-blond. […] In young nakedness, the foreign crowd cavorted at the foot of Mount Olympus, and Homeric air blew unexpectedly. With the ignorant, the landscape painted itself a picture of memory.[8] (Kästner 1953, 14f.)

More than just making artistic changes to the work, it should be noted that Kästner also goes so far as to describe the conditions under which his earlier book had been written, and he openly addresses Germany's war crimes. Thus, the new version of his text comments on and reflects the conditions of its creation. At the same time, he presents these historical contexts in such a way that they become part of his metaphysical interpretation of history (which is rather typical of the 1950s). In this sense, *Ölberge, Weinberge* can also be understood as an attempt to come to terms with guilt—though not the individual guilt of the writer, who, in retrospect, portrays himself as an outsider and opponent of the regime, thereby completely ignoring his influential role as a propagandist for the Nazi occupation. Rather, Kästner now tries to understand the historical events from a philosophical point of view, on the macro level. In doing so, he clearly addresses the horrors of war and takes them as a starting point for broader reflections on history. For example, Kästner explicitly describes the consequences that the hunger winter of 1941–1942 had for the Greek civilian population:

> I reached the edge of a grave that was as long and as wide as a classroom. On both sides, ramparts piled up. The tracks of a cart led up from the side.
> Apparently, dead bodies had been driven in during the day and immediately placed in the pit from the cart, without coffins, as is the case in war and in times of plague. This time, in the winter of '41–'42, it was hunger; in Piraeus alone, fifty starved to death every day; sometimes only forty, then again sixty. In Athens it was worse: if you walked through the streets early in the day, you could see twelve or fifteen starving people on the tarmac from the castle to Omonoia Square; just above the grates of the underground railway, where a little warmth rose, there were usually four or five.[9] (Kästner 1953, 68f.)

At first glance, Kästner has added a documentary dimension to his travelogue. However, he does not mention the *causes* of this famine. Instead, he places his observations in a religiously tinged, historical–philosophical scheme: with recourse to traditional stereotypes about the south, he explains the misery in Greece as the expression of a necessity inherent to world history. Here, as elsewhere, he uses ancient mythology as a means of explanation. By referring to commonly known stories, he diverts attention from questions of guilt and responsibility. Thus, the Oedipus myth serves him as an interpretive device to make misery comprehensible:

> Ten thousand grandchildren of Oedipus, ten thousand [people with] swollen feet; except now, [they have] oedema no longer from punctured heels [like Oedipus did] but from hunger. Such outbreaks of misery, such heaves of suffering, belong to the image of the south. Here, they always exist as a possibility. The exemplary suffering of beggars, cripples, and blind people on the streets means that suffering is always present, whereas it is hidden in our country.[10] (Kästner 1953, 71)

Through this mythological reference, the author equates the suffering of innocent people caused by political and military action with the suffering of Oedipus, who has involuntarily committed terrible crimes. What could have been the starting point for a reflection on human-made suffering is suddenly declared an example of a special southern disposition. In Kästner's perspective, the famine does not occur because of German or Italian occupation; rather, it is a symptom of the south, which makes the region attractive for travelers because it gives them lessons on the course of world history: "This universality, this powerlessness of suffering (which is contagious) is one of the reasons why one travels to countries like this Hellas" (Kästner 1953, 71).[11] Traveling to Greece means, for the tourist from Central Europe, testing one's limits; in southern countries, according to Kästner, the traveler can observe the dissolution of permanent structures, and even the dissolution of history itself:

> Today, one travels in order to find out what it is like when the peoples have completely slipped into the void of history. For that is what it is, that they no longer have any history there; they are only aftermaths, only stories. Where orderly power, with its pillars, arches, tensions, floors has collapsed, there is only leveling, rubble. Only abandonment. Only mass, and faith.[12] (Kästner 1953, 71f.)

In Kästner's view, this decay is the necessary first stage on the way to a faith that can only develop real strength in times of need. Misery is, thus, the precondition of a religious mood; as such, it serves a useful function.

In these passages of *Ölberge, Weinberge*, Kästner looks back on the occupation period from a 1950s perspective. However, he also describes far more concrete and immediately affecting encounters with the past. In the chapter "Village Feast" (*Dorffest*), Kästner first recalls the Oedipus myth when describing a hike through the valley of Chaironea. Soon afterwards, he informs the reader about a crime that took place nearby in the 20th century:

> Walking like this, I was able to avoid the village of Distomo, which, eight years ago, during the war, was the scene of a monstrous slaughter. The *papas* [priest] of the village, willingly or not, had sent two lorries full of soldiers into the partisan ambush near Steiri, which was followed by a systematic revenge—senseless murder of women, children, and peasants—such as a country still remembers after a hundred years.[13] (Kästner 1953, 231)

Kästner leaves no doubt whatsoever about the criminal nature of the act of revenge committed by the *Waffen-SS*, which massacred almost all the inhabitants of the village of Distomo in a so-called reprisal action in June 1944 (cf. Mazower 1993, 212–14; Králová 2016, 57–59). The traveler from Germany not only feels horror but also deep shame, and wants to avoid the traces of the past. However, by an almost fantastic coincidence, on this very day, the village festival is taking place in Distomo. Survivors of the massacre who are working in a field near the road urge Kästner (who is not recognized as German) to take part in the celebration. Only at the last moment does he manage to resist the "strange request to hold a drinking session in the village square of the place of blood" (Kästner 1953, 232). Nevertheless, in the neighboring village of Steiri, he ends up obliged to take part in a celebratory drinking session anyway, where the cheerful surroundings and general exuberance lead Kästner to "offer an ovation to life, to the survival that consumes the horrors of history" (Kästner 1953, 233). Here, as in the literature of the turn of the century, life appears as a mythically exalted force against which individual experiences of misery must recede. And although Kästner mentions the "horrors of history," the question of guilt and responsibility fades into the background. In Steiri, Kästner presents a cathartic experience that was not least caused by destiny: "But it seemed destined to me to celebrate in this depressing area" (Kästner 1953, 233).

Kästner's rather courageous confrontation with German war crimes, thus, takes place in an almost mythical setting. He is more concerned with banishing the horror, which is absorbed into a religious horizon, than with a rational reappraisal of the past. This attitude creates an ambivalent impression: on the one hand, Kästner names German crimes very clearly, while on the other, he implicitly excuses them by referring to a vague 'fate' (cf. Hiller von Gaertringen 1994, 339). Because of this, this text of occupation literature becomes a text of self-exculpation.

Such tendencies are symptomatic of how German guilt was dealt with in the literature of the 1950s (cf. Meid 2015); by explaining all suffering metaphysically, Kästner tends to blur the lines between perpetrators and victims. Considering the genesis of his travelogue, his second version can also be read as a literary reappraisal of the occupation of Greece, which, in any case, still manages primarily to satisfy the needs of the perpetrator community.

*

An analysis of Kästner's Greece books cannot give a realistic impression of Germany's occupation of Greece. However, these books are an interesting source for historians because they show how Kästner smoothly adapted his image of both ancient and modern Greece to the changing ideological demands of the Nazi and post-Nazi periods alike, and was, therefore, surprisingly able to build a literary career on his activity as a propaganda author, without any difficulty.

When William J. O'Keeffe says of Kästner and other authors of his generation that their "literary output [...] sought, with some success, to attest to civilised values despite the contradiction in its authors' situations" (O'Keeffe 2013, 223), he completely fails to recognize the propagandistic effect of these works, which aestheticized and mythologized German rule. Kästner was certainly a "political and literary opportunist" (Strohmeyer 2006, 110) whose literary glorification of the brutal occupation regime led to his being referred to as the "Arno Breker of the pen" (Fleischer 1988, 35), in other words, the literary equivalent of the most famous sculptor of the Third Reich.

Notes

1. All translations from non-English sources are my own.
2. „Mit Vergnügen beobachte ich einen blonden Soldaten, der in einem Korbsessel vor einem Kaffee an einem schön gedeckten Tischchen Platz genommen hat. Vor ihm steht eine Tasse Kaffee, er zieht schmunzelnd und behaglich an einer Zigarette. Dabei schaut er dem regen Verkehr auf der Straße zu, während ein Junge ihm die Stiefel putzt."
3. „Unser Regiment wird nicht weiter nach Süden marschieren, obwohl wir alle die Stadt Larissa, die Mönchsrepublik auf dem Berge Athos, die Stadt Athen mit der Akropolis und den vielen Kunstdenkmälern aus der Geschichte des alten Hellas, den Hafen Piräus, die Thermopylen, die antike Stätte der olympischen Spiele und vieles andere gerne gesehen hätten."
4. „Die beiden heiligsten Stätten der Griechen, Delphi und der Olymp, muten am nördlichsten an. Delphi: ein Hochalpental. Der Olymp: ein Nordberg. Es ist, als ob dabei ferne Erinnerungen nachklängen, Erinnerungen eines in den Süden verschlagenen, im Süden glücklich gewordenen Volkes, das dennoch im tiefen Grunde seines Herzens ein Heimweh nach Norden nicht verlor." (269)
5. „Es waren Männer von Kreta, die von dort kamen und nun einem neuen Ziel und einem neuen Kampf entgegengingen. Unser Zug schob sich langsam an der nachbarlichen Wagenreihe entlang. Auf den offenen flachen Eisenbahnwagen standen fest vertäut die Geschütze, die Kraftwagen und die Räder, von Staub überpudert und deutlicher von den überstandenen Strapazen redend als die Männer. Darauf und dazwischen saßen, standen und lagen gleichmütig die Helden des Kampfes, prachtvolle Gestalten. Sie trugen alle nur die kurze Hose, manche den Tropenhelm, und blinzelten durch ihre Sonnenbrillen in den hellen Morgen. Ihre Körper waren von der griechischen Sonne kupferbraun gebrannt, ihre Haare weißblond. | Da waren sie, die ‚blonden Achaier' Homers, die Helden der Ilias. Wie jene stammten sie aus dem Norden, wie jene waren sie groß, hell, jung, ein Geschlecht, strahlend in der Pracht seiner Glieder.

Alle waren sie da, der junge Antenor, der massige Ajax, der geschmeidige Diomedes, selbst der strahlende, blondlockige Achill." (9)

6. „Wie anders denn sollten jene ausgesehen haben als diese hier, die gelassen ihr Heldentum trugen und ruhig und kameradschaftlich, als wäre es weiter nichts gewesen, von den Kämpfen auf Kreta erzählten, die wohl viel heldenhafter, viel kühner und viel bitterer waren als alle Kämpfe um Troja. Wer auf Erden hätte jemals mehr Recht gehabt, sich mit jenen zu vergleichen als die hier—die nicht daran dachten? Sie kamen vom schwersten Siege, und neuen, unbekannten Taten fuhren sie entgegen. Keiner von ihnen, der nicht den Kameraden, den Freund da drunten gelassen hätte. Um jeden von ihnen schwebte der Flügelschlag des Schicksals. Es wehte homerische Luft." (9f.)

7. „Unversehens ergab sich ein völlig klassisches Bild. Sprühend im Licht dieses Morgens und im Glanz ihrer jungen Nacktheit tummelte sich die Schar dieser Eroberer am fremden Meer, und es schien so, als sei ein verloren geglaubtes, unsterbliches Geschlecht wiedergekehrt und habe mit Selbstverständlichkeit Besitz genommen von diesem Ufer, oder als seien sie immer dagewesen und der Götterberg habe nie auf andere niedergeblickt als auf sie." (10)

8. „Frühjahr 41. Von der Fahrt nach Athen wird mir ein Morgenbild immer in Erinnerung sein. [...] Es waren Fallschirmspringer von Kreta und eine Flakbatterie; auf den flachen Eisenbahnwagen standen vertäut die Geschütze, überpudert von Staub, darauf und dazwischen standen und saßen die Kämpfer, kurze Hose, Sonnenbrille und Tropenhelm. Ihre Körper waren in den wenigen Tagen kupfern gebrannt, ihre Haare weißblond. [...] In junger Nacktheit tummelte sich am Fuß des Olympos die landfremde Schar und unversehens wehte homerische Luft. Mit Ahnungslosen malte die Landschaft sich ein Erinnerungsbild." (14f.)

9. „Ich gelangte an den Rand eines Grabs, das so lang und so breit wie ein Schulzimmer war. Beiderseits häuften sich Wälle. Von der Seite führten die Gleise eines Karrens heran. | Offenbar hatte man tagsüber Tote herzugefahren und sie vom Karren sofort in die Grube gelegt, ohne Särge, wie es im Krieg und in Pestzeiten ist. Diesmal, im Winter 41 auf 42, war es der Hunger; allein im Piräus verhungerten Tag für Tag fünfzig; manchmal fielen nur vierzig an, dann wieder sechzig. In Athen war es schlimmer; wer am frühen Tag durch die Straßen ging, konnte vom Schloß bis zum Eintrachtsplatz auf dem Asphalt zwölf oder fünfzehn Verhungerte sehen; allein über den Rosten der Untergrundbahn, wo ein bißchen Wärme aufstieg, lagen gewöhnlich vier, fünf." (68f.)

10. „Zehntausend Ödipusenkel, zehntausend Schwellfüße; jetzt aber Ödeme nicht mehr von durchstochenen Fersen, sondern Hungerödeme. Solche Ausbrüche des Elends, solche Wuchten des Leidens gehören zum Bilde des Südens. Hier sind sie immer als Möglichkeit da. Das exemplarische Leiden der Bettler, Krüppel und Blinden auf den Straßen bewirkt, daß Leiden immer anwesend ist, während man bei uns dergleichen versteckt." (71)

11. „Dies Allgemeine, diese Ohnmacht des Leidens (sie ist ansteckend) ist einer der Gründe, weshalb man Länder wie dieses Hellas bereist." (71)

12. „Jetzt reist man, um zu erfahren: wie das ist, wenn die Völker noch vollends ins Geschichtslose glitten. Denn das ist es doch, daß sie dort keine Geschichte mehr haben; es sind bloß noch Nachwehen, bloß noch Geschichten. Wo geordnete Macht mit ihren Säulen, Wölbungen, Spannungen, Stockwerken niederbrach, ist bloß noch Eingeebnetes, Schutt. Bloß noch Preisgabe. Bloß noch Masse und Glauben." (71f.)

13. „Wenn ich so ging, konnte ich das Dorf Distomo meiden, das vor acht Jahren, im Krieg, der Schauplatz eines ungeheuerlichen Blutbades war: der Pappas des Dorfes, mit oder ohne Willen, hatte zwei Lastwagen voller Soldaten in den Hinterhalt der Partisanen bei Steiri geschickt, darauf folgte eine planvolle Rache, sinnloses Morden an Frauen, Kindern und Bauern, wie es ein Land noch nach hundert Jahren im Gedächtnis behält." (231)

References

Anonymus. 1941. *Ein kleiner Spaziergang durch Saloniki: Andenken vom Einmarsch der deutschen Truppen in Saloniki—9. April 1941.* Saloniki: Italienische Buchdruckerei A. Akuaroni, Ermusstrasse 19.

Barbian, Jan-Pieter. 2010. *Literaturpolitik im NS-Staat: Von der "Gleichschaltung" bis zum Ruin.* Frankfurt am Main: Fischer Taschenbuch.

Brenner, Peter J. 1997. "Schwierige Reisen: Wandlungen des Reiseberichts in Deutschland 1918–1945." In *Reisekultur in Deutschland: Von der Weimarer Republik zum'Dritten Reich,'* edited by Peter J. Brenner, 127–76. Tübingen: Niemeyer.

Butler, E. M. 1958. *The Tyranny of Greece over Germany: A Study of the Influence Exercised by Greek Art and Poetry over the great German Writers of the Eighteenth, Nineteenth, and Twentieth Centuries.* Boston: Beacon Press.

Fallmerayer, Johann Jakob. 1830. *Geschichte der Halbinsel Morea während des Mittelalters: Ein historischer Versuch.* Stuttgart and Tübingen: Cotta.

Fleischer, Hagen. 1986. *Im Kreuzschatten der Mächte: Griechenland 1941–1944 (Okkupation—Resistance—Kollaboration).* Frankfurt am Main: Lang.

———. 1988. "Siegfried in Hellas: Das nationalsozialistische Griechenlandbild und die Behandlung der griechischen Zivilbevölkerung seitens der deutschen Besatzungsbehörden, 1941–1944." In *Griechenland—Entfernungen in die Wirklichkeit: Ein Lesebuch,* edited by Armin Kerker, 26–48. Hamburg: Argument.

Fuhrmann, Manfred. 1995. *Europas fremd gewordene Fundamente: Aktuelles zu Themen aus der Antike.* Zurich: Artemis & Winkler.

Generalkommando, ed. 1944. *Der Peloponnes: Landschaft—Geschichte—Kunststätten. Von Soldaten für Soldaten.* Athens: Christu.

Graf, G. J. 1942. *Wir marschieren gegen Griechenland: Erlebnisse eines Infanterie-Geschütz-zuges vor und während des Einsatzes in Griechenland. Geschildert von dem Mitkämpfer Dr. G. J. Graf. Oberleutnant in einem Infanterie-Regiment.* Mit Bildern. Saarlautern: Hausen.

Graf, Johannes. 1995. *"Die notwendige Reise:" Reisen und Reiseliteratur junger Autoren während des Nationalsozialismus.* Stuttgart: M & P.

Günther, Hans F. K. 1929. *Rassengeschichte des hellenischen und des römischen Volkes.* München: Lehmann.

Hauptmann, Gerhart. 1996. *Griechischer Frühling: Reisetagebuch Griechenland—Türkei.* Edited by Peter Sprengel. Berlin: Propyläen.

Hauser, Heinrich. 1938. *Süd-Ost-Europa ist erwacht: Im Auto durch acht Balkanländer.* Berlin: Rowohlt.

Hiller von Gaertringen, Julia Freifrau. 1994.*"Meine Liebe zu Griechenland stammt aus dem Krieg": Studien zum literarischen Werk Erhart Kästners.* Wiesbaden: Harrassowitz.

———. 1995. "Deutsche archäologische Unternehmungen im besetzten Griechenland 1941–1944." *Mitteilungen des Deutschen Archäologischen Instituts*, Abteilung Athen 110: 461–90.

Hitler, Adolf. 1942. *Der großdeutsche Freiheitskampf.* Vol. 3: *Reden Adolf Hitlers vom 16. März 1941 bis 15. März 1942.* Munich: Zentralverlag der NSDAP.

Hofmannsthal, Hugo von. 2015. "Buch der Freunde." In *Sämtliche Werke: Kritische Ausgabe,* edited by Rudolf Hirsch. Vol. 37: *Aphoristisches, Autobiographisches, frühe Romanpläne,* edited by Ellen Ritter, 9–62. Frankfurt am Main: S. Fischer.

———. 2022. "Einleitung zu 'Griechenland' von Hanns Holdt." In *Sämtliche Werke: Kritische Ausgabe,* edited by Rudolf Hirsch. Vol. 35: *Reden und Aufsätze,* no. 4, edited by Jutta Rißman, Ellen Ritter, Mathias Mayer, and Katja Kaluga, 112–21. Frankfurt am Main: S. Fischer.

Kästner, Erhart. 1943. *Griechenland: Ein Buch aus dem Kriege.* Zeichnungen: Helmut Kaulbach; Berlin: Gebrüder Mann.

———. 1953. *Ölberge, Weinberge: Ein Griechenlandbuch.* Mit Federzeichnungen von Helmut Kaulbach. Wiesbaden: Insel.

Katsaridou, Iro, and Ioannis Motsianos. 2022. "Escaping the War Horror: 'Tourist' Photographs of Thessaloniki under the German Occupation (1941–1944)." Accessed March 16, 2024, https://visual-history.de/2022/06/07/katsaridou-motsianos-escaping-the-war-horror/. https://doi.org/10.14765/zzf.dok-2394.

Koch, Lutz. 1941. *Reise durch den Balkan: 20 000 Kilometer Autofahrt durch Ungarn, Rumänien, Bulgarien, die Türkei, Griechenland, Albanien und Jugoslawien.* Mit 118 Aufnahmen des Verfassers. Berlin: Deutsche Verlagsgesellschaft.

Koutsoukou, Phädra. 2010. "Die NS-Kulturpolitik gegenüber Griechenland in der Vorkriegszeit: Olympia 1936, Förderprogramme Geisteswissenschaften, Abwerbung griechischer Künstler." In *Hellas verstehen: Deutsch-griechischer Kulturtransfer im 20.*

Jahrhundert, edited by Chryssoula Kambas and Marilisa Mitsou, 139–55. Cologne: Böhlau.

Králová, Kateřina. 2016. *Das Vermächtnis der Besatzung: Deutsch-griechische Beziehungen seit 1940*. Cologne: Böhlau.

Kriekoukis, Charilaos, and Karl Bömer, eds. 1938. *Unsterbliches Hellas*. Berlin: Andermann.

Kulz, Werner. 1937. "Kurze Rassengeschichte des griechischen Volkes." In *Europas Geschichte als Rassenschicksal: Vom Wesen und Wirken der Rassen im europäischen Schicksalsraum*, edited by Rolf L. Fahrenkrog, 17–57. Leipzig: Hesse & Becker.

Landfester, Manfred. 1996. "Griechen und Deutsche: Der Mythos einer 'Wahlverwandtschaft.'" In *Studien zur Entwicklung des kollektiven Bewußtseins in der Neuzeit*, edited by Helmut Berding. Vol. 3: Mythos und Nation, 198–219. Frankfurt am Main: Suhrkamp.

Large, David Clay. 2007. *Nazi Games: The Olympics of 1936*. New York: Norton.

Mazower, Mark. 1993. *Inside Hitler's Greece: The Experience of Occupation, 1941–44*. New Haven: Yale University Press.

———. 1995. "Militärische Gewalt und nationalsozialistische Werte: *Die Wehrmacht* in *Griechenland 1941 bis 1944*." In *Vernichtungskrieg: Verbrechen der Wehrmacht 1941–1944*, edited by Hannes Heer and Klaus Naumann, 157–90. Hamburg: Hamburger Edition.

Meid, Christopher. 2012. *Griechenland-Imaginationen: Reiseberichte im 20. Jahrhundert von Gerhart Hauptmann bis Wolfgang Koeppen*. Berlin: De Gruyter.

———. 2015. "Schuld und Entlastung: Reiseberichte von Erhart Kästner, Walter Jens und Rolf Bongs." *treibhaus. Jahrbuch für die Literatur der fünfziger Jahre* 11: 218–41.

Nauhaus, Julia M. 2003. *Erhart Kästners Phantasiekabinett: Variationen über Kunst und Künstler*. Freiburg im Breisgau: Rombach.

O'Keeffe, William J. 2013. *A Literary Occupation: Responses of German Writers in Service in Occupied Europe*. Amsterdam: Rodopi.

Picker, Henry. 1963. *Hitlers Tischgespräche im Führerhauptquartier 1941–1942*. Edited by Percy Ernst Schramm. Stuttgart: Seewald.

Rondholz, Eberhard. 1997. "'Schärfste Maßnahmen gegen die Banden sind notwendig…: ' Partisanenbekämpfung und Kriegsverbrechen in Griechenland. Aspekte der deutschen Okkupationspolitik 1941–1944." In *Repression und Kriegsverbrechen: Die Bekämpfung von Widerstands- und Partisanenbewegungen gegen die deutsche Besatzung in West- und Südeuropa*, edited by Ahlrich Meyer, 130–70. Berlin: Verlag der Buchläden Schwarze Risse, Berlin/Rote Straße.

Rosenberg, Alfred. 1934. *Der Mythus des 20. Jahrhunderts: Eine Wertung der seelisch-geistigen Gestaltenkämpfe unserer Zeit*. Munich: Hoheneichen.

Schnell, Ralf. 1976. *Literarische Innere Emigration 1933–1945*. Stuttgart: Metzler.

Sieglin, Wilhelm. 1935. *Die blonden Haare der indogermanischen Völker des Altertums: Eine Sammlung der antiken Zeugnisse als Beitrag zur Indogermanenfrage*. Munich: Lehmann.

Strohmeyer, Arn. 2006. *Dichter im Waffenrock: Erhart Kästner in Griechenland und auf Kreta 1941–1945*. Mähringen: Balistier.

Tsoutsoumpis, Spyros. 2016. *A History of the Greek Resistance in the Second World War: The People's Armies*. Manchester: Manchester University Press.

Wiskott, Carl T. 1936. *Griechenland im Auto erlebt: Mit dreiundachtzig Bildern von Dr. Paul Wolff & Tritschler*. Munich: F. Bruckmann.

Zacharioudakis, Emmanouil. 2002. *Die deutsch-griechischen Beziehungen 1933–1941: Interessengegensätze an der Peripherie Europas*. Husum: Matthiesen.

CHAPTER 4

Banished from an Occupied Exile

Rudolf Borchardt's *Anabasis* Fragment (1944)

JAN ANDRES

When Rudolf Borchardt was forced to flee Italy by the German military in 1944, large parts of the country were still occupied by the German *Wehrmacht*, which itself was under mounting pressure from Allied forces. Though its title, *Anabasis*, invokes a classical model, Borchardt's seemingly autobiographical and fragmentary account of his escape—set against the backdrop of occupation and invasion—is of a kind that was possible only in the 20th century, with its extremes of war and violence. Borchardt's text is therefore an altogether different *Anabasis* from that suggested by its title's intertextual reference.

Xenophon's *Anabasis*, for centuries a set text in the teaching of ancient Greek, has historically enjoyed a remarkable reception in German literature. In *Meergruß* ("Sea-Greeting"), the poem that opens the second cycle of *Die Nordsee* (1826) (*The North Sea*) Heinrich Heine quotes what is perhaps the best-known passage in Xenophon's text, the cry of the returning Greeks as they finally come within sight of the sea:

Thalatta! Thalatta!	Thalassa! Thalassa! [The sea! The sea!]
Sei mir gegrüßt, du ewiges Meer!	Greeting to you, you eternal sea!
Sei mir gegrüßt zehntausendmal,	Greeting to you ten thousand times
Aus jauchzendem Herzen,	From the glorying heart,
Wie einst dich begrüßten	As once greeted you
Zehntausend Griechenherzen,	Ten thousand Greek hearts,
Unglückbekämpfende, heimatverlangende,	Misfortune-fighting, homeward-longing,
Weltberühmte Griechenherzen.	World-renowned Greek hearts.
(Heine 2014, 141)	(Watkins 1944, 141)

The cry itself is a direct quotation, with Heine clearly referring to the celebrated *March of the Ten Thousand*, by which name Xenophon's *Anabasis* is also known.

Even before Heine, Christoph Martin Wieland discussed the work in his epistolary novel *Aristipp* (1800–2), a book famous in its day, now largely forgotten:

> Xenophon's *Anabasis*—which, since its principal subject is *retreat*, might no less aptly be called *Katabasis*—was already familiar to me when I received your letter from Rhodes. *I* too read it with pleasure, and though I daresay certain qualifications may be in order as regards the high value which you accord this work, I must nonetheless confess that it would be no easy matter to tell a story so wonderful in itself as the march and retreat of the ten thousand Greeks with less ostentation and greater sincerity of tone. (Wieland 1984, 195)

The story of a march and a retreat: further intertextual references to the *Anabasis* may be found in European literature—in Arno Schmidt, for instance, but also in James Joyce, as Wolfgang Will has pointed out in his recent monograph (Will 2022, 13–15). Will also mentions the text that stands at the center of the present study and that, though its title explicitly refers to Xenophon, is perhaps the least known within the chain of reception alluded to here.

I shall begin by calling to mind the ancient 'pre-text' before examining how a German writer in exile could find in it an approach to representing his own experience of occupation. Rudolf Borchardt's *Anabasis*, written in 1944, leaves no doubt that its description of conditions in and around Lucca, then under German occupation, draws on Xenophon's account—which, we may safely assume, Borchardt would have known well as a former classical scholar. Although we cannot be certain as to whether he composed this memoir with an edition of Xenophon in hand, his family's recollections observe that he often referred to the text and carried a copy with him.[1]

The Pre-Text: Xenophon's *Anabasis*

Xenophon's *Anabasis* was composed sometime between 380 and 360 BC. Its author was a Greek aristocrat who had studied under Socrates and who, at about age thirty, joined an army of Greek mercenaries in the pay of the Persian Prince Cyrus in 401 BC. The *Anabasis* tells of this campaign, which Cyrus fought to replace his brother Artaxerxes on the throne. In this dynastic conflict, the struggle of a satrap against a king, Xenophon acted as something of an 'embedded journalist'[2] (Will 2022, 22). Some three or four decades later, he set down his recollections, which have become known as the *Anabasis*—meaning 'ascent' or 'climbing up.' However, the famous subtitle *The March of the Ten Thousand* was not used by Xenophon himself, and the army is more likely to have numbered 13,000 men.[3] This memoir, autobiographical in structure but with considerable literary stylization, comprises seven books and may be considered a classical antecedent of the genre of autofiction so popular today. Beyond being a seminal text for an entire genre, it is also used in teaching ancient Greek to this day. Xenophon's memoir tells not only of the army's march up the country—its *anabasis*—but also of its descent or *katabasis* and its *parabasis*, its march along the coast toward the Bosporus and ultimately homewards. The campaign lasted two years and covered several thousand kilometers.[4]

In the first book,[5] Xenophon describes Cyrus's preparations for the campaign, the recruitment of the army of mercenaries, and the first encounter between the enemy brothers at the Battle of Cunaxa, probably near Babylon. Cyrus, who led from the front, is killed and commemorated by Xenophon in a lengthy eulogy, a panegyric on the late king's character. This might well mark the end of the campaign and thus of the narrative. Instead, the second book describes the election of a new leader, Clearchus, under whom the army begins its homeward progress. It is at this point that the katabasis may be said properly to begin; only the first book describes an anabasis in a strict sense (Flower 2012, 5). In this second book, the returning army is watched and followed on its journey by Tissaphernes, a Persian satrap, who takes advantage of dissension among the Greeks and invites some twenty-five Greek generals and captains to his camp, where Tissaphernes then has them arrested and murdered. This leaves the Greeks once more—quite literally—decapitated and leaderless. It is only in the third book that the anonymous, extradiegetic narrator introduces the author: "There was a man in the army named Xenophon, an Athenian"[6] (Xenophon 1921, vol. I, 419). This Xenophon is thus introduced as a character with a backstory.

One night, Xenophon has a dream that prompts him to address the disoriented troops, rousing them to elect new generals and to elevate him, a civilian, to the rank of officer. Pressed by the Persians, the Greeks head first for the Tigris and then for Kurdistan and the Armenian highlands. This march through central Anatolia, the subject of the fourth book, is full of losses and privations for Xenophon's army, as well as repeated skirmishes with the local population. It ends in Trapezus (Trebizond), a Greek city on the Black Sea, where the Greeks celebrate their apparent deliverance with games and sacrifices.

Yet along the course of the next several books, the problems of discipline and provisioning that earlier beset the expedition reappear, and the army marches on, pillaging along its way. The command of the Ten Thousand suffers a rift between Xenophon and another captain, causing the army briefly to break down into ethnic factions. Xenophon, however, in a display of his political acumen and rhetorical ingenuity, succeeds in reuniting it.

The seventh and last book tells of the Greeks in Byzantium, the sacking of which Xenophon is able to avert. Unrest among the survivors—by this point, probably no more than five to six thousand hoplites (Flower 2012, 5)—over the topic of an outstanding debt for duties performed for the Thracian king Seuthes, forces Xenophon to make two long speeches in his defense. Xenophon (the author) here depicts Xenophon (the officer) as a person of rhetorical gifts and moral integrity (Xenophon 1921, vol. II, 327ff.). In the end, the surviving mercenaries are hired by Sparta, once more to do battle with Persians. Xenophon leads his men back to the region from whence they came and where the struggle with the Persians continues. Their journey has thus reached its end.

Only the first book is, therefore, properly called an anabasis, and whether the title of the larger work is even Xenophon's own title for it remains controversial (Flower 2012, 5). In any case, the larger *Anabasis* depicts the Greek army, the Persian forces, and the country where the events unfold as part of a self-portrait. Yet this self-portrait of Xenophon as a captain in the Greek army is drawn, as it were, in the third person. To be more precise, the *Anabasis* is a homodiegetic narrative with zero focalization, but in which the author shares a name with his character.

The Post-Text: Borchardt's Topical Reappropriation (1944)

It is this literary and historical relation of events, written in the early 4th century BC, to which Borchardt's title alludes. The point he makes by using this title in 1944, after he and his family were forced to leave Italy, is at least threefold. First, he offers an eyewitness account of occupation and a military campaign. Second, in so doing, Borchardt, like his model Xenophon, records his observations of the landscape and people amid the shifting tides of occupation. The result, third, is a mixture of seemingly factual autobiography and fictional literature—in other words, a kind of autofiction in which author and speaker appears to be identical, but should be kept apart analytically.[7] Beyond that, however, the reference is fairly loose. Unlike that of Xenophon, Borchardt's text follows no obvious structure, nor does it reach a conclusion, remaining a fragment. Moreover, the 'I' that narrates events is clearly both author and character; Borchardt's narrative is homodiegetic albeit (again unlike Xenophon's) with largely internal focalization. Nevertheless, the title as paratext serves to maintain a strong link between the two works.

The argument to be developed here is that, if we take the term initially to denote only a return home in wartime, Borchardt's anabasis may be said to be twofold. The first, negative anabasis is that of the *Wehrmacht*, which is on the retreat from the American and British armies and is plundering its way up the Italian peninsula. Second, there is the largely positive anabasis of the Borchardt family, headed by Rudolf, the paterfamilias. Though it is forced and leads back to the dangerous German Reich, this anabasis—like Xenophon's—ends surprisingly well in the face of constant perils, with the family's liberation.

Under the Third Reich, Borchardt, who was of Jewish descent and had lived more or less permanently in (initially self-imposed) Italian exile since 1903, was banned from publishing and hence *de facto* from exercising his profession in Germany.[8] Yet he was also a German veteran of World War I, having volunteered in August 1914 and served first as a private; then as a non-commissioned officer; and finally, from 1917, in the general staff. When the war broke out, to do anything else but serve seemed out of the question. Borchardt was undoubtedly a patriot and, like his admired friend Hugo von Hofmannsthal, a conservative who prioritized such values as tradition and education, particularly the idea of literary tradition as a unifying force (Hofmannsthal's *Schrifttum*), and the need—as Borchardt put it—for a 'creative restoration' (*schöpferische Restauration*). Such attitudes are often placed under the heading 'conservative revolution,' another term popularized by Hofmannsthal. Culturally and politically, Borchardt certainly was a man of the right, a nationalist and a conservative, and was drawn—if only for a time—to such seemingly-great men as Mussolini. Yet National Socialism repelled him, and by no means only because its racial laws classified him as a Jew. Borchardt was never comfortable with his Jewishness, nor did he practice any other faith. That he should have chosen to remain in Italy in the 1930s and 1940s is therefore due not only to his affection for the country, his passion[9] for flowers and landscaping, or his admiration for the architecture. For a German Jew and his family, Italy was also a place of refuge, of an exile motivated first by cultural longing and then by political necessity. The political dimension of his exile in Italy came to the fore after 1933, even though Italy itself began to introduce antisemitic legislation in the late 1930s and discrimination intensified.

By early 1943, Borchardt's Italian refuge was beginning to look dangerously shaky –all the more so when, in September of that year, Mussolini was deposed and Italy signed an armistice with the Allies, leading to a German military occupation. The family had to leave the Villa Bernardini outside of Lucca, its home for twelve years.[10] Finding an affordable substitute was no easy matter, and the Borchardts finally took lodgings in the Villa Pallavicino in Forte dei Marmi, though they never felt comfortable there. In his letters, Borchardt claims no longer to have worked there, indeed, to have been unable to do so, which may perhaps be something of an exaggeration.[11] To obtain the necessary residence permit, Borchardt lied about his ancestry, changing his mother's Jewish-sounding name and claiming to be 'Aryan.'[12] He was well aware of the danger he faced under German occupation.

In spring and early summer 1944, the Allies, having first landed in Sicily the previous year, were closing in on Florence. The Borchardts again had to move, back to the vicinity of Lucca, where, in early May, they found a warm reception from Estella Castoldi at the Villa Poggio al Debbio.[13] In mid-August, a German medical officer in the rank of captain was billeted in the villa, and another German captain took lodgings next door. It was the latter, named Dörner, who on August 29[14] ordered the family to join the occupation troops on their northward retreat. If this was not an outright arrest, it was at any rate an order that brooked no refusal, and an ill-prepared attempt at escape that evening failed. The family was ultimately taken by the *Wehrmacht* to Innsbruck, which Rudolf Borchardt at least perceived as the first stage of their deportation. Yet in Innsbruck, for reasons that have yet to be explained, the family was released; to their own surprise, the Borchardts were simply let go. Only a few weeks after this forced return to the *Reich*, on January 10, 1945, Rudolf Borchardt died in Tyrol, leaving the manuscript of *Anabasis* unfinished. It seems to have been the last text on which he worked and, as such, represents his fragmentary legacy.

At the center of this autobiographical fragment is the Borchardts' stay at the Castoldi family's Villa Poggio al Debbio. The events play out against the backdrop of the US Fifth Army's advance against the 16th *SS Panzergrenadier Division* "Reichsführer-SS" and thus against the so-called "Gothic Line" of German defenses across northern Italy. Borchardt, in the role of Xenophon, describes the situation as the German occupation comes under pressure from the Allied advance. The *Wehrmacht*, in his view, had abandoned the Prussian military tradition and was terrorizing Italy and its people with acts of arbitrary cruelty. Worse still was the SS, which had never participated in the Prussian tradition in the first place. It is telling that it was the SS that arrested the family in the pouring rain after the botched escape attempt on August 31.[15] Borchardt felt that the aforementioned medical officer, who was attached to the *Sicherheitsdienst* (SD) and is referred to in the text as "Dr. Schneider," had personally spied on and betrayed him.

Perceiving German military rule as a form of anarchy or arbitrary rule, Borchardt notes that "Hitler's troops [were] the unrestricted masters of this defenseless country where there was no longer any Italian authority to ensure the authority and protection of the law" (Borchardt 2003, 30; the book will henceforth be cited in the text as "*RBA*"). His *Anabasis* is one of a number of autobiographical texts distinguished by its specific mixture of fact and fiction.[16] Borchardt is a narcissist with a propensity to speak highly of himself and his achievements.[17] But he is also a writer and above all an orator who, throughout his life, addressed the political situation of his day. In any case, this is a document whose veracity and value as a source ought to be subjected to critical scrutiny; in the interests of caution, one would do well initially to treat the text as at least semi-fictional. This is apparent in certain passages and aspects of the text; for instance, in the way his hostess Estella Castoldi becomes "Mrs. N." An even more striking instance is Borchardt's conversation, toward the end of *Anabasis*, with the captain, which appears in the form of a stage dialogue (and is typographically rendered as such) while also suggesting that it is a transcript taken verbatim or at least reproduced from memory. Although the text remains a fragment, its author clearly wished it to be seen as an autobiographical account that was truthful and, above all, politically percipient.

Borchardt's Account of the German Occupation in the Post-Text

> It was around Christmas 1942 that the first shock of reality rent the veil behind which we still believed our old world to be sheltered. Our Italian base, so broad and happy, vanished beneath our feet, and Saltocchio was lost. (*RBA* 17)

This sentence opens Borchardt's account, combining the military image of a "base" that was "lost" with the perhaps-surprising notion that, in the midst of a world war that by then had incontrovertibly become a war of destruction, there was still a safe "old world" to be shattered. A political analysis of events is not far behind, however, delivered as the Borchardts move house:

> I shall list all my errors and mistaken calculations here; they will give order to the picture. The result was settled, and no matter how many bloody decimal places one wanted to take it to rather than rounding it off behind the point had no more bearing on the result. The African disaster [i.e., the surrender of the German Africa Corps in May 1943] and the unopposable landing in Sicily [i.e., Operation Husky, July 9–10, 1943] gave, as I know, the Italian generals the cue to make their move, a move urged and awaited by all of Italy. The Russian disaster [i.e., the encirclement of the Sixth Army at Stalingrad in winter 1942–43], which had consumed Hitler's great army, meant that there, too, the desperate race for the better time was lost forever, and won by the other side. Our generals, too, moved closer together in order to draw, in line with our conscientious military tradition, the conclusions and to look out for the character who would have been Prussian enough once more to act as Yorck had done. (*RBA* 19)

Faced with a twofold military disaster, in the south as well as the east, Borchardt waited for the German generals to act as their Italian counterparts had done by deposing Mussolini. The reference is to the Convention of Tauroggen, an armistice between Prussia and Russia signed on December 30, 1812 by Prussian Field Marshal Johann David Ludwig Count Yorck von Wartenburg without his king's consent, ultimately turning Prussia against Napoleonic France. Borchardt was probably looking to establish a parallel with Stauffenberg's attempted assassination, for he would have been aware that the *Wehrmacht* was not able to sue for peace while Hitler remained in charge.

A second, concealed allusion may also be at play here: Peter Graf Yorck, one of Stauffenberg's co-conspirators, was a descendant of Yorck of Tauroggen. Since he relates the events of that month, Borchardt would have written these words no earlier than August 1944—that is, after the failed attempt on Hitler's life. However, Borchardt claimed already to have been certain of the German defeat by 1943. As far he was concerned, the war was decided, and the last officers with any sense of responsibility were looking for a way out, which put them at odds with Hitler. Borchardt thus claims to have at least anticipated resistance to Hitler from within the military by 1943.

Borchardt, who had hoped to "wait out" the final defeat in Forte dei Marmi, nonetheless found himself on a "slanted track upon which we sank" (*RBA* 20). Although his refuge is situated amid "hills lacking any hinterland of military interest" (*RBA* 21), there is a steady trickle of evacuations and "forced guests" with local homeowners. For their part, the Borchardts, as already mentioned, took lodgings with the Castoldi family in Michele de Moriani near Lucca. Although the welcoming Estella Castoldi may objectively be said to have been the savior of the homeless family, tensions soon erupt between her and Borchardt, whose portrait of his landlady verges on slander. She is called simply "N." (as mentioned above), described as supposedly half-English and yet loathing England, while also as being ashamed of Italy (*RBA* 22). As early as 1940, Borchardt claims, he had explained to her

> that all was lost and that the run of victories from country to country [i.e., the *Wehrmacht's* so-called *Blitzkrieg*] was merely a terrible stay of divine vengeance, and that the war would end with Germany's downfall and with her dropping out of European history for two hundred years. (*RBA* 22)

Again, Borchardt assumes the mantle of the political analyst and prophet who had foretold the end barely a year into the war. "N.," however, has had the temerity to deprecate the "wise and Christian countryfolk" (*RBA* 23)—the Tuscan locals—as "half foreign, half-witted, and lacking instinct." She therefore understood neither the Italian people nor, of course, the wider political situation (*RBA* 23). Yet in Borchardt's view, these very locals were more finely attuned to political currents than the lady of the house, to whom the country remained foreign: "Every day laborer had an unerring sense of the lasting political yield of the victorious harvests reaped lightning-fast by military technology" (*RBA* 23). It is consistent with Borchardt's exalted view of Italy that he should, as early as 1940, attribute such military perspicacity even to simple and, politically, most-likely-uninformed agricultural laborers—and, of course, to himself. "N.," by contrast, is declared a stranger in Italy, a foreign body.

The depiction of his hostess that follows inverts the classical model. Where Xenophon had laid Cyrus to rest with a panegyric, Borchardt resorts to character assassination, heavily deploying national and gender stereotypes to disparage his allegedly overbearing landlady:

> On her own family's side and from shared schooldays, Mrs. N. had been familiar with the royal house, and specifically with its fiercest female representatives. [...] Like others of her kind, she took her prefabricated notions and prejudices, the stereotyped parroting of half-understood dogmas, to constitute her character, making her the terror of reasonable and agreeable conversation. Even allowing for the disharmonies of her ambiguous origins, she was a most pitiable person, though she elicited no sympathy. (*RBA* 26)

The hostess is accused of stereotypical thinking—framed in a stereotypical view of an intercultural background.

Mrs. N. was now "reduced to making her closest circle miserable with her chastisements and her fanaticism"; the "measure of her blinkeredness and self-righteousness" made her recognizable as having a particular "type of female tyranny and lunatic obsession with order" (*RBA* 27). Her character and intellect placed her in stark opposition to that "wisest, most civil, and most flexible of peoples," that is, the Italians, upon whom "she tries to inflict herself as the Jehovah of all deserved punishments and narrowly apportioned mercies" (*RBA* 27). Portraying this unfortunate woman as a divine punishment on Italy is, of course, ludicrous, but Borchardt is far from finished: in her fanaticism, N. had "dreamed in Fascism the ideal bridge between her English and her Italian halfness"—"an idiotic dream" (*RBA* 27). For in spite of Fascism—"a vulgar crew"—Italy had remained itself, "with more light and less shadow than most of her sister peoples" (*RBA* 28).

Borchardt gives no indication here of his own former fascination with Mussolini. Instead, he sets himself, the Italomaniac, up in opposition to N., who had, in his estimation, never known, loved, or understood Italy. From National Socialism, she had adopted such "picture-book terms" as "discipline, fanaticism, stoutness of heart, heroism of mind, hardness, greatness." In them, her immeasurable vanity had found their "idol"—for which "she had of course to make a rule of shutting off her ears and eyes against reality" (*RBA* 28). On the one hand, a woman who had lost touch with reality over her addiction to cookie-cutter ideas; on the other, a male author whose gaze is acute and even prophetic: in its gendered assumptions, too, this image of Estella Castoldi is pure cliché. Looking back, Borchardt's wife, Marie Luise (known, in her personal life, by the affectionate nickname "Marel"), found his perception of Castoldi to have been a "delusion" (Schuster 2003, 372).

Borchardt's own analysis of the war and world politics is set off in sharp relief from that which he attributes to his landlady. He distinguishes between a positive vision of an authentic Germany and its perversion by National Socialism:

> But this horrible confusion between German Germany and Nazi Germany, between true German character and substance and the demons that took possession of both, this dazzling fallacy from which Hitler continued to derive all his credit, indeed ever more so, […] did, however, provide the angry woman with sophistic arguments. After all, old Germany really had been betrayed by Italy in 1914. The Peace of Versailles had indeed been a crazed and reckless assault on that real and true Germany, and nobody who accepted it without being firmly resolved in due course to break its yoke was worthy of being called a German. (*RBA* 29)

The narrator here assumes the voice of a chauvinistic Great War veteran who objects to the Treaty of Versailles as a supposed humiliation imposed on Germany. This position was widespread among conservative soldiers, and one on which they thoroughly agreed with the Nazis. This view of the Versailles settlement all too often fed into a general rejection of the Weimar Republic, which was seen as tarnished from birth with treason and a defeat that was not acknowledged as such. Instead, it was widely held that the German army had been 'stabbed in the back,' and this myth bred hostility within the republic.

Borchardt soon moves on to his first description of the German forces occupying Italy:

> Hitler's troops, beaten across the Tiber and pushed against the mountains, the unrestricted masters of this defenseless country where there was no longer any Italian authority to ensure the authority and protection of the law, treated their supposed allies—which they still were, though the legal foundation was a fiction—in the capacity of conquerors. There might be isolated instances of a wiser officer carrying the day and treating the Italians with gentleness and understanding, but even such instances lacked any deeper understanding of the national character, to the understanding of which the older Germany in particular had devoted a century of scrupulous and affectionate labor. The Italians—who, wherever they went, were jostled, constrained, shoved hither and thither by prohibitions, threats, orders barked in ill-chosen words rendered cruder still in translation—stepped smoothly aside, smiled, chattered in broken German and obeyed, and with shrugs

and brave faces yielded to the demands that the beaten and ill-provisioned army made of them, at first on pretexts, then point-blank [...]. (*RBA* 31)

The occupying forces come as conquerors with no awareness of what they have conquered, and above all with no respect for the country's language, culture, or history—in short, everything that in Borchardt's mind makes up Italy and made it the destination for art-loving Europeans taking the Grand Tour in the 18th and 19th centuries. At least the locals often proved wily enough to outwit the coarse Germans.

The German retreat from Pisa, which American forces entered on July 26, spells the "horrific crushing of this city I loved above all others" (*RBA* 55). A few days later, the scene of the battle is Florence, where the destruction includes blowing up the bridge across the River Arno. It is "only with inward horror" that Borchardt can hear German officers "speaking my language [...] amid such a catastrophe of our culture" (*RBA* 55). The feeling resembled that of "gazing across the courtroom into the inscrutable face of a brother lost in time and eternity" (*RBA* 55). But although the occupation and the crimes committed under it signified a cultural rupture and a watershed in German–Italian relations, Borchardt's use of the term "our culture" indicates his continued belief in the idea that the cultures shared some common foundations. The German officers, however, appear as 'lost brothers,' irrecoverably separated from Borchardt, the war veteran, who finds himself bristling at the sound of the German language—in which, all the same, he continues to write.

Of himself and his family, Borchardt claims that they had

> done what was in our power to mediate between the army and the local population, to settle conflicts, and especially to make easier the unpleasant trade of the German soldiers and corporals, whose ignorance of the language and the pressure to carry out repulsive orders put them in an invidious position, especially when they were decent lads. This army, hungry and morally adrift, its very fabric rotted and riven by defeat, now quite literally lived off the land. Virtually the entire country around Lucca, the plains as well as the hills, had by army decree been declared a "requisition zone," that is to say, lawless. (*RBA* 34–35)

What is evident from this passage is that Borchardt assigns responsibility for the crimes committed under the occupation to the officers rather than to the men. His view of the *Waffen-SS* is even more negative. There is a slight connection here to the events related by Xenophon, particularly the fifth book, which tells of a starving army and its depredations. In Borchardt's view, the *Wehrmacht* in 1944 was acting not primarily out of greed or malice (both of which he finds in the *SS*) but from sheer necessity, without the restraint imposed by Prussian education and principles. Material scarcity has a corrosive effect on military discipline and morals:

> I wish to add that, in view of my political and intellectual principles, of my educa-tion and my life's experience, I could only look on in horror and had indeed been compelled to close my eyes to the fact that my own compatriots were covering this defenseless and, to me, sacred country in their tyrants' lost war […]. I shall never forget the effect upon me of the first appearance of the clay-yellow, sack-like uniforms of the National Socialist tropical army in Viareggio, in the pearly light of that transfigured Tyrrhenian shore, and the voices, gestures, profiles, physiog-nomies, accents—not much in themselves, but unbearable in this atmosphere—of this group of strangers which had ceased to adapt or assimilate as every nation had learned to do in Italy […], the memory of whose image is accursed for their entire nation and served gradually nearly to extinguish, in the Italian imagina-tion, the German humanity of the nineteenth and twentieth centuries, of which I and my life's work formed part. (*RBA* 41–42)

The uniforms of the Africa Corps stand in an almost allegorical dichotomy with the cultivated landscape of Italy and its sparkling sea, a holy land analogous to Palestine itself. With the occupation, an awareness of German humanity is ex-punged from Italy's cultural memory. The loss is mutual.

Borchardt, while maintaining his fundamental sympathy for the ordinary sol-dier, is nonetheless dismayed at the destruction wreaked by the *Wehrmacht* and the troops' behavior. Yet, remarkably, even at this point he still speaks of the war primarily as a desecration of culture. There is no mention yet of war crimes against the civilian population:

> But that this war, lost long ago in each of its theaters and in the entirety of its conception […], should have rolled its rapacious sword and its crushing hooves over the museum of the occidental centuries only to visit destruction upon it and to rush into its own destruction nearly broke my heart and at first made it nearly impossible for me to see in the unfortunate German compatriot the brother who, though he appeared here in a get-up repellent to me and painted all over with swastikas, had nonetheless remained the old faithful, simple, and honest man […]. (*RBA* 43)

There is nothing disparaging about Borchardt's reference to Italy as a museum. He admired tradition, and its landscape, shaped by historical forces, was the very thing that fascinated him most about Italy. Borchardt's "Villa" essay is only one expression of this admiration, albeit a particularly notable one. The destruction of Italy does nothing to arrest the destruction of Germany, and that is why Borchardt keeps the ordinary soldier at a distance—who, in any case, has ceased to be a compatriot in the Prussian sense by wearing the swastika.

These general assessments of the *Wehrmacht's* conduct and of the political situation, the diagnosis of a failure to accept that the war is irrecoverably lost, are followed by comments on why the *Wehrmacht* (and, worse, the *SS*) behaved in such a violent and culturally ignorant manner. The Nazi influence, Borchardt concludes, had broken the continuity of the Prussian military tradition, to which he sees himself as belonging, and opened the door to depravity. Borchardt draws a sharp distinction between the Prussian military until the end of World War I and its successor under Nazi rule, particularly at the officer level. He thus departs from the stereotype of the educated, cultured, and refined officer that often appears in the literature of occupation. Borchardt finds the reason for the egregious policies of the occupation regime in the loss of a military tradition that had held up certain values and attitudes. It had

> taken on the force of terrible evidence that Hitler's army, cobbled together in a few years from mediocre cadres, once it had played and squandered its surprise trumps, had nothing more to bring to the table than the traditional but primitive military achievements […] of German bravery, moved recklessly across bloody chessboards, that those old senior staff officers who had thrown their lot in with Hitler counted among their number not one true general, and that the fast promotion attendant upon fake revolution had not been enough to produce one, and that instead the already seemingly innumerable marshals by the Party's grace compared even to Napoleon's better marshals […] only slightly more favorably than did Europe's grim oppressor himself to the great Napoleon. (*RBA* 45–46)

Hitler is no Napoleon, let alone a military commander of comparable stature—Borchardt may be alluding to Hitler's lowly beginnings as an obscure corporal in the Great War. As for his field marshals—such as von Kluge, von Brauchitsch, von Witzleben, or Keitel, who were promoted after the German victory over Norway—Borchardt finds them incapable of fighting a war that is, in any respect, 'decent'. The Nazis lacked stature; their logic was that of the Party, not the military:

> Their claims to be continuing the traditional German officer, even of the First World War, whose peculiar and time-honored spirit and substance would have been as incomprehensible to them as would have found his attitude, his character, and, in the higher ranks, his proverbial education in military academies and staff

> positions inaccessible, were to be met only with silence, and only by averting one's
> eyes from the outward appearance of young persons, some of them barely past
> boyhood, in uniforms garishly adorned with tin medals, stars, crosses, ribbons,
> and images of horror, which permitted comparison with the serious cloth of the
> Prussian officers and his badges of honor, precious only by virtue of their scarcity,
> less still than they had done in the Great War [...]. (*RBA* 46–47)

The war is depicted as an act of vandalism and desecration resulting from a lack of cultural and military education. In Borchardt's view, the Nazis have replaced professionalism and integrity with tinsel, with outward trappings and an inflation of honors given away lightly.

Recalling Ernst Jünger and the esteem in which he held his Iron Cross and the *Pour le Mérite* that he received toward the end of World War I—as recalled particularly in *In Stahlgewittern* (1920) (*Storm of Steel*)—another source of Borchardt's thinking can be identified in the form of a (soldierly) new nationalism, or a so-called '*ästhetischer Fundamentalismus.*'[18] The rupture of Prussian traditions appears here, first, as a problem of education; even in its secondary aspect as a military problem, it is attributed to a lack of education. Borchardt, true to his self-image as a scholarly, classically educated writer, is thus able to pity the German officer whom he is practically forced to overlook, while at the same being forced to live with the pain that Italy's misery has caused, and continues to cause, him:

> To me, the German officer who appeared as the bearer and representative of this
> shameful and futile, murderous and suicidal policy, as the oppressor of treacher-
> ous Italy was [...] at best a pitiable figure [...], from whose cause and share of guilt
> my true and essential patriotism I was henceforth separated, by having pledged
> myself to the German name and the German past. (*RBA* 50)

As was earlier the case for Hitler himself, the term used here to describe the role of the German officer corps as "oppressor" is "*Zwingherr,*" suggesting a premodern, indeed medieval form of violent and arbitrary rule. Patriotism properly so called, in Borchardt's view, is what separates the German as a type—with Borchardt as its representative—from the modern German army. The *Wehrmacht* had broken the continuity of the Prussian tradition and, doomed to fail, did so with ignorant ferocity.

Borchardt's condemnation of the *SS*, to which he assigns the principal responsibility for the war crimes perpetrated under the occupation, is far harsher. Granted, recent historians have found such a clear distinction between the *Wehrmacht* and the (*Waffen-*)*SS* to be largely untenable, since both forces were not only fighting the same campaign but also carried out joint operations. It is in discussing the *SS*, however, that Borchardt first mentions Italian civilian casualties:

> When the last purely-military commandant in Lucca gave way to the SS, absolute plunder began, and with it the systematic destruction of this glorious cultural landscape [...], the shocking manhunt from which even our closest friends in their venerable villas were not exempt, or were not exempt until we summoned up all means of defense, [and] the cold-blooded murder of harmless refugees from endangered areas, who were seized in the mountain forests as alleged *francs-tireurs* and whose bodies were dumped at intervals on the country roads. (*RBA* 36–7)

Plunder, arbitrary murder, and manhunts under the pretext of fighting partisans—it was the *SS* that was out to kill Italian civilians. What is remarkable here is the emphasis Borchardt places on the fact that his friends in the fine villas of which he was so fond had also suffered under, and to some extent fended off, the *SS*. This may serve to highlight his part as an ally and indeed savior of the population, though it is far from clear to what means he, a Jewish-German exile, would even have had recourse.

What he certainly realized, both as a passionate gardener and a cultural historian, was that the occupiers were depriving the occupied of their means of support in the long term by destroying the country's agricultural infrastructure:

> When the wheat harvest, which had been rich for the first time in years, could not be ground because each day the SS laid waste to one of the great and glorious mills that were the pride of this modern agricultural landscape [...], when marauding soldiers, plucking the best white grapes, threatened to leave nothing for this country [already] robbed of all wine, when the coarseness of their drivers caused trucks to be hidden, not under infertile leafy boughs, but under olive branches as thick as an arm and heavy with fruit [...], when this beaten and condemned army of a beaten and doomed country [...] battered and razed [the area] as a future battlefield, Mrs. N.'s general political paroxysm became appreciably reduced to trembling for her own existence on her own ground. (*RBA* 37–38)

Olives and wine, the symbols of this region and its economic foundation, are, for different, reasons destroyed by the army of a doomed empire, making the act seem even more senseless. While the wanton destruction threatens the livelihood of the local population, Borchardt turns this concern against Mrs. N. (Estella Castoldi), accusing her of selfish concern for her property.

A prototypical instance of Borchardt's condemnation of the *SS* as the driving force of an immoral and destructive occupation can be found in his physiognomic sketch of Dr. Schneider, an *SS* man by whom he feels watched and betrayed: "A boyish lanky person in whose pale, always somewhat-uptilted face the features were half-womanish, half-shifty" (*RBA* 60). Having begun with gendered stereotypes, the description moves on to geographical and cultural ones:

> (I)n his features there were German and Slavic elements, which, though originally refined in character, could combine to form an irritating mask, then again to dissolve and bring to light something childish—reminiscent perhaps of a spoiled girl—and something truly childlike that was not displeasing. (*RBA* 61)

Slavic and effeminate features are the terms in which Borchardt chooses to discredit a member of the *SS*:

> His wispy hair, kept too long, strikingly was already going gray around a face still maturing into manhood as though, within him, nature was making a symbolic example, as in certain pathological cases of plant life, of developmental capacities freezing even in the earliest stages of formation [*Bildung*]. (*RBA* 61)

To make matters worse, the imputation of lacking masculine maturity and *Bildung*—a lack that Borchardt had already identified in the *Wehrmacht* and its officers—is supplemented by animal imagery: there was "something of a minor beast of prey, weasels, polecats, little predators" about Schneider (*RBA* 61). In sum, then Schneider is dismissed as a small animal, a creature of instinct—a predator of sorts, but no lion. From today's perspective, such stereotypes must, of course, seem problematic—not least because, by describing a human being as a "little predator," Borchardt veers close to a political metaphor deployed by the Nazis themselves. In any case, Borchardt leaves no doubt that he regards the *SS* as an even more corrupt bunch than the *Wehrmacht*, which by its actions had disqualified itself from fulfilling the role, both military and moral, of a German army.

While Borchardt's political analyses and his views of the military situation and the occupation leave little to be desired in terms of clarity—though just how early he came to these realizations is open to question—the consequences he draws for his own conduct seem limited. He defines his own position as a passive one, ultimately invoking the autonomy of art:

> The poet who knows that it is his vocation to regard and to respect the hair-thin line between yes and no, between the most intense passion of the symbolic attitude and the first tentative interventions in the causality of action—on this, the whole nature of poetry depends, and Dante and Goethe thought nothing of

getting on the wrong side of both parts in order to remain faithful to their own sovereignty—the poet has thus already acted by denying himself. (*RBA* 53)

This is the confession of a non-political man who believes that it behooves him, as an artist, to be passive and who, nonetheless, by virtue of his education, has a clear and incorruptible view of the course of history. Borchardt is either unable or unwilling to resolve this blatant contradiction. He is merely the observer of occupation. War and occupation seem also to elude poetic representation in the narrower sense, being instead assigned to the realm of personal experience and, hence, autofiction. This may explain the reference to Goethe, who, after all, took a similar approach in his *Belagerung von Maynz* (1822) (*Siege of Mainz*) and *Campagne in Frankreich 1792* (1822) (*Campaign in France 1792*).

Concluding Remarks on the German Occupation of Italy in the Anabasis

In conclusion, there are four points I would like to make concerning Rudolf Borchardt's perception of the German occupation of Italy:

First, to Borchardt's mind, occupation policy is always both military and cultural policy. He makes no separation between these realms because any military intervention in the Italian landscape means an intervention in tradition and culture, and because every act of destruction means the rupture of a tradition.

Second, the German troops are accused of disrespecting the Italian people and the Italian cultural tradition, and of doing so out of ignorance of the country, the language, and its traditions. In Borchardt's view, the crimes of the occupation are the result not least of a lack of education, being possible only through *Unbildung*.

Third, Borchardt distinguishes between the two principal branches of the German occupation army. The *Wehrmacht* has already completely lost the Prussian military tradition among both its officers and its men, though he generally takes a milder view of the latter. His worst opprobrium, however, is reserved for the SS, which he blames for the bulk of the crimes and the wanton destruction. Dr. Schneider, whose type and physiognomy are described in terms that make him a grotesque allegory of the SS, stands as a representative of the whole, even though he is a medical officer rather than a front-line soldier.

Fourth, although Borchardt takes pride in his own military training and experience, he does not cast himself in the role of a potential resistance fighter. He continues to conceive of himself primarily as a poet and, in this specific instance, a cultured observer seeking to leave to posterity a testimony that is also a self-portrait. The decisive factor in his perception of historical events is his self-image as a connoisseur and admirer of Italy, which conditions his view of the occupation. Ultimately, the relation to Xenophon remains rather superficial, apparently motivated in large part by the ancient author's description of a campaign ending in a perilous return home. Borchardt's narrative style is quite different from Xenophon's, and the narrator himself in Borchardt's *Anabasis* is given a far more prominent voice. All told, Borchardt's is the far more strongly autobiographical text—though it is stylized and tends to make too much of its author's political perspicacity.

Translated by Joe Paul Kroll

Notes

1. Borchardt scholarship has so far not discussed the *Anabasis* in much detail, though a seminal and richly documented edition is now available: Borchardt 2003 (see p. 9 for Borchardt's reading of Xenophon). The *Anabasis* and the context of its writing are discussed in Sprengel 2015, 413–24.
2. Will 2022, 22.
3. The information is taken from Will 2022 and another highly informative monograph: Flower 2012.
4. Xenophon 1921.
5. The summary is based on the primary text and on the concise accounts and reconstructions provided by Flower 2012 and Will 2022.
6. Xenophon 1921, vol. I, 419.
7. On this, see Wagner-Egelhaaf 2013. A concise reconstruction of the genesis of the term can be found in Zipfel 2009.
8. Cornelius Borchardt, "Erinnerungen an 1944/45," in: Borchardt 2003, 207; see also Sprengel 2015, 353ff.
9. *The Passionate Gardener* was the title of a book on which Borchardt worked in the 1930s, published posthumously: Borchardt 2020.
10. On the sequence of events, see Sprengel 2015, 413-24; in much detail, Schuster 2003 and Borchardt 2003, 253–372, 261.
11. Schuster 2003, 281, with reference to Borchardt's correspondence with Rudolf Alexander Schröder.
12. Sprengel 2015, 414.
13. Schuster 2003, 285.
14. Schuster 2003, 292; Sprengel 2015, 416–17.
15. Schuster 2003, 294, with reference to an account by Marie Luise Borchardt.

16. Prominent examples being the *Rudolf Borchardts Leben von ihm selbst erzählt. Mit einem Nachwort von Gustav Seibt*, Frankfurt a.M.: Suhrkamp (2002), or the monstrous, pornographic novel among Borchardt's unpublished works: *Weltpuff Berlin*. Reinbek: Rowohlt (2018).

17. On the accusation of narcissism, see Kauffmann 2003, espc. 4–21.

18. See Stefan Breuer's numerous works on the subject, e.g., *Die radikale Rechte in Deutschland 1871–1945* (2010), particularly the chapters on "new nationalism." See also Breuer 1995, 148–68. Borchardt is called "Der Gegenkönig."

References

Borchardt, Cornelius. 2003. "Erinnerungen an 1944/45 (1999)." In Borchardt, Rudolf, *Anabasis: Aufzeichnungen, Dokumente, Erinnerungen 1943–1945*, edited by Cornelius Borchardt/Rudolf Borchardt Archiv, 207–52. Schriften der Rudolf Borchardt-Gesellschaft. Munich: Rudolf-Borchardt-Gesellschaft.

Borchardt, Rudolf. 2020. *Der leidenschaftliche Gärtner*. Berlin: Matthes & Seitz.

Breuer, Stefan. 1995. *Ästhetischer Fundamentalismus: Stefan George und der deutsche Antimodernismus*. Darmstadt: Wissenschaftliche Buchgesellschaft.

———. 2010. *Die radikale Rechte in Deutschland 1871–1945: Eine politische Ideengeschichte*. Stuttgart: Reclam.

Flower, Michael A. 2012. *Xenophons's Anabasis, or The Expedition of Cyrus*. New York: Oxford University Press.

Heine, Heinrich. 2014. *Sämtliche Gedichte: Kommentierte Ausgabe*, edited by Bernd Kortländer. Stuttgart: Reclam.

Kauffmann, Kai. 2003. *Rudolf Borchardt und der "Untergang der deutschen Nation.": Selbstinszenierung und Geschichtskonstruktion im essayistischen Werk*. Tübingen: Niemeyer.

Schuster, Gerhard. 2003. "Chronik der Ereignisse 1943–1945." In Borchardt, Rudolf, *Anabasis: Aufzeichnungen, Dokumente, Erinnerungen 1943–1945*, edited by Cornelius Borchardt/Rudolf Borchardt Archiv, 253–372. Schriften der Rudolf Borchardt-Gesellschaft. Munich: Rudolf-Borchardt-Gesellschaft.

Sprengel, Peter. 2015. *Rudolf Borchardt: Der Herr der Worte. Eine Biographie*. Munich: C.H. Beck.

Wagner-Egelhaaf, Martina, ed. 2013. *Auto(r)fiktion: Literarische Verfahren der Selbstkonstruktion*. Bielefeld: Aisthesis.

Watkins, Vernon. 1944. "Poems from Heine's 'Die Nordsee.'" *Life and Letters To-Day* 42: 141–47.

Wieland, Christoph Martin. 1984. *Aristipp und einige seiner Zeitgenossen*. In *Sämmtliche Werke [Reprint]*. 16 vols, edited by Jan Philipp Reemtsma/Hamburger Stiftung zur

Förderung von Wissenschaft und Kultur. Vol. 11. Nördlingen: Greno Verlagsgesells-
    chaft.
Will, Wolfgang. 2022. *Der Zug der Zehntausend: Die unglaubliche Geschichte eines antiken
    Söldnerheeres*. Munich: C.H. Beck.
Xenophon. 1921. *Anabasis*. 2 Vols. Translated by Carleton L. Brownson. Revised by John
    Dillery. Loeb Classical Library 90. London: Harvard University Press.
Zipfel, Frank. 2009. *Autofiktion: Zwischen den Grenzen von Faktualität, Fiktionalität und
    Literarität?* In *Grenzen der Literatur: Begriff und Phänomen des Literarischen*, edited by
    Simone Winko et al., 284–314. Berlin: De Gruyter.

CHAPTER 5

German Writers as Occupiers and Occupied

Franco-German Representations in the Works of Felix Hartlaub (1940–1941) and Tami Oelfken (1945–1955)

STEFANIE SIESS

In 1940, Felix Hartlaub was a young historian and a talented artist, assigned to the Historical Archive Commission in occupied Paris as part of the German occupying forces. He processed his experiences by working on literary sketches written in the style of a diary. They contained precise, vigilant observations of everyday life in occupied Paris, the impoverishment of the city, and its inhabitants. Throughout this work, Hartlaubs's attitude toward his role as an occupier remained thoroughly contradictory. An inner distance becomes clear in his prose, which, however, remained free of any political consequence in his actions (Weichelt 2020, 217).

Tami Oelfken, by contrast, was a 57-year-old woman at the end of World War II. Formerly persecuted by the National Socialist regime for her socialist and pacifist views, she tried to publish her books in the French occupation zone. She also chose the genre of diary entries or an epistolary style for her literary treatment of the end of the war and the early post-war period. Her work reveals a strong discrepancy between (on the one side) the possibilities and opportunities available to former victims of Nazi persecution and to women in the postwar period, and (on the other) their self-proclaimed right to participate in the creation of a new democratic state (Habermann 1988, 31).

In this chapter, I analyze and contrast the works of these two authors, which were produced under the circumstances of two very different occupational regimes. These are mainly Felix Hartlaub's *Kriegsaufzeichnungen aus Paris* (2011, first published 1950) ("War Notes from Paris") and Tami Oelfken's *Fahrt durch das Chaos. Ein Logbuch aus Zeiten des Kriegs* (1946) ("Journey through Chaos. A Logbook from Times of War"), as well as unpublished diary notes and correspondence.[1] Special consideration is paid to questions of genre, especially to the relationship between literature and ego-documents. How is artistic expression shaped by the role of the author, as well as by the character of the occupational regime itself? Social representations as images-in-flux of self and other are examined, first through the lens of a German occupier in France, then of a German writer occupied *by* the French. How are these images influenced by the experiences of war and occupation? Which transfers, similarities, and differences can be identified when analyzing the works and experiences of these two authors?

Methodologically, the research works with the French concept of *représentations sociales* (social representations), originally a concept from social psychology (cf. Durkheim 1898; Moscovici 1961). It later found its way into historical sciences as part of the *Nouvelle Histoire* movement (New History). From the structuralist *histoire des mentalités* (history of mentalities) by the first generation of the Annales school in Paris, establishing a social history in the early 20th century, said movement developed in France in the 1970s and proclaimed a new cultural history (cf. Le Goff, Chartier, and Revel 1978). The sub-discipline of *histoire de representations* (history of representations), while still asking questions about collective and social mentalities, is more skeptical about the possibility of attributing mentalities to entire social classes or categories. Representations are no longer seen as simple mental reflections of sociopolitical reality, nor as a superstructure in the Marxist sense, but rather as spheres of action in which historical actors encounter, perceive, and represent one another. There is no longer a clear line separating sociopolitical reality from its symbolic and cultural representation. In his programmatic text of 1989, Roger Chartier calls such historiography *histoire culturelle du social*, a new cultural history of the social (Chartier 1989, 1511).

The concept therefore goes beyond that of images of the self and other. Representations are used as an approach to writing cultural history, as they are the essential medium that reveals collective patterns. As such, they are a useful category of analysis for studying societies under war or occupation. The French word *représentation* can have three different meanings in German: *Vorstellung* (idea or imagination), that is, the mental aspect, which includes cultural and national stereotypes, as well as influences from previous times of war and occupation; *Wahrnehmung*, the perception of self and other during the actual encounter of occupier and occupied; and finally *Darstellung*, the symbolic expression in text and image. In the study of Felix Hartlaub's and Tami Oelfken's texts, these three aspects can be applied to elaborate Franco–German representations under occupation.

Both authors produced literary works as well as ego-documents, such as letters and private diaries not intended (or, at least, not initially intended) for publication. Yet especially in the case of artists, drawing a clear distinction between separate genres of texts can sometimes be difficult. As such, for the question of genre and of literary expression during occupational experiences, a definition of the term 'ego-document' is necessary, as well as a reflection on literary texts, or more generally on art, as sources in the historical sciences.

Recent historical research, following the suggestions of the Dutch historian Rudolf Dekker from the 1970s, understands ego-documents as sources that provide information about a person's view of himself or herself, primarily and initially autobiographical texts (Dekker 2002, 7). Dekker's fellow Dutchman Jacob Presser described "egodocuments" in 1958 as texts in which "the author tells us something about his personal life and feelings," or, to put it even more generally, in which "an ego intentionally or unintentionally reveals or conceals itself" (Presser 1969, 286). Access via ego-documents offers a very personal and subjective approach to history. In the 'unveiling' of the self, the other—the unknown—also becomes clear. Such documents are therefore not only suitable for biographical studies, but also offer great opportunities for insights into the history of everyday life and mentalities.

'Ego-documents,' as a concept or a category of analysis, can be understood in both a broader and a more limited way (cf. Schulze 1996). Classically, the term refers to autobiographical writings, diaries, and letters, but its definition can also include drawings or photographs. Even in court or hospital records, an ego can show and hide itself, as Presser put it, especially when autobiographical writings are not available, which is often the case with, for example, works on everyday working-class life. In this broader sense, an ego-document need not be self-produced.

In more limiting definitions, certain elements can be set as exclusionary factors, such as the unity of 'ego' and author, or the intention to publish. This last element would distinguish literary texts written for publication from texts written to cope with everyday life or with intimacies and emotions intended to remain private. Writing as a social practice can have different functions and intentions, it can be a political, artistic, or intimate act, or all of the above. To approach this, an interdisciplinary discussion between historical and literary studies can be helpful (cf. Depkat and Pyta 2021). Philipp Lejeune's idea of an 'autobiographical pact,' in which the author of an autobiography or of other ego-documents makes a pact—a contract—with his readers in which he promises to tell his life, and nothing but his life, in all its details, offers a further separation between ego-documents and literature as fiction. The claim to truthfulness is meant to set the autobiographical genre apart from literary texts (Lejeune 1975, 8).

In the case of both Hartlaub and Oelfken, the difficulty of the distinction between ego-documents and literature, ego-documents and fiction, arises; they cannot always be clearly distinguished from each other, especially in the case of fragmentary notes. Instead, the different types of texts complement each other and only give a conclusive picture when viewed together.

A German Writer as Occupier in France: Felix Hartlaub (1940–1941)

The writer and historian Felix Hartlaub (born 1913) disappeared without a trace from Berlin in the final days of World War II in 1945, at just 31 years old. Only in 1955 was he officially declared dead. He left behind a small oeuvre of literary and private writings: fragments and observations from the midst of a catastrophe that, with their evocative power and precision, would make a permanent place for him in post-war German letters (cf. Hartlaub 2022). As a historian with a doctorate in military history, he was posted to Paris in 1940 to conduct archival research in the occupied foreign ministry at the Quai d'Orsay. As a result, he was part of the occupation forces, but with a civilian mission. He stayed until September 1941, when he was redeployed to Romania as a soldier (Marose 2005, 13).

During his time in Paris, Hartlaub recorded his impressions of the city in notebooks that document with unparalleled immediacy the daily realities of the occupation. Although written in the style of a diary and therefore remaining fragmentary, his "War Notes" (*Kriegsaufzeichungen aus Paris*) can be attributed to his larger body of literary work. A narrative figure emerges, a nameless literary "He" takes on the role of the distanced describer and reflects on the task and attitude of his colleagues, as well as of the Parisian population. Without embellishing, Hartlaub describes the impoverishment of Paris, the atmosphere of repression and depression, and the proud attitude of the French population. He sketches scenes of great urgency and symbolic power that bring out the will to inhumanity that he encounters, as well as the progressive process of the individual's desensitization in a society dominated by inhuman ideals. At the center of his literary critique are his colleagues, most of whom willingly follow National Socialist ideology and act without any scruples, despite their education or religion.

In his writings, Hartlaub chooses the perspective of the *flâneur*, the lonely melancholic who conquers the city through wanderings (O'Keeffe 2013, 42). In the process, a desperate, almost Kafkaesque atmosphere is created.[2] The narrative figure, like his author, wears civilian clothes, is tormented by embarrassment and shame, and would prefer to be invisible. Hartlaub himself calls his notes "*Tagebuchoid*" (i.e., diary-like) (Hartlaub 2002, 470). Despite this resemblance, however, Hartlaub consistently writes about himself in the third person, creating a *doppelgänger* to maintain his personal distance. As such, there is no clear unity of 'ego' and author, and many entries are left undated. Other typical formal elements that can characterize diary entries as well, such as a personal address, are also not given. The short texts are captioned with references to places in the city where he makes his observations ("Place Pigalle," "Quai," "Place des Vosges"), describe the narrator's activity ("Evening stroll," "Coming back from

Fontainebleu"), or pointedly summarize an experience ("International crisis at the knocking-shop," "Propaganda"). They show the directness and the documentary character of a diary, but a personal distance is maintained. Observations are rarely directly evaluated or emotionally tied back to the author.

While traditional definitions of 'diary' put introspection or emotional effusion at the center, Katherine Roseau considers the diary as a 'place' for identity construction (Roseau 2020, 1124). She argues that understanding of the self arises from interactions with others, and therefore extrospective texts must not be excluded from the diary genre. If we follow this definition, the 'War Notes' can be considered an ego-document. Nevertheless, Hartlaub shows and expresses clear literary and artistic ambitions that go beyond that genre. In a draft letter to the legal philosopher Gustav Radbruch, a friend of his father's whom he met in Heidelberg before the war, he describes his literary ambition to approach the "invisible," the "decisive," by musing:

> The best thing I can do is simply tell [...] what is visibly evident on an everyday basis in the urban area through which my daily paths pass; perhaps this is the closest I can get to the invisible, which is of course the decisive thing. (Hartlaub 2002, 467, my translation)[3]

His literary style corresponds to the demands of the *Kahlschlagliteratur* of the post-war period. The language is characterized by brevity, stripped of ideology and emotion (cf. Böll 1979). Abbreviations are prominent, underlining the texts' documentary and fragmentary character. Another ambition of Hartlaub's writing is documentation for posterity; his training as a historian is evident. He notes at the end of 1941: "The profound justification of writing history becomes clear to me only during these times [...]. It is necessary to write down a lot, because anything other than private personal sources will hardly be available and valid later on" (Hartlaub 2002, 412).[4] He thus anticipated the scientific approach of the current chapter: the engagement with 'private personal sources,' with ego-documents, to gain knowledge about mentalities and representations during a time of war and occupation (Marose 2005, 20).

In his letters from Paris to family and friends, not intended to be published and thus more clearly assignable to the category of ego-documents, Felix Hartlaub himself emerges more as an individual. As in his 'War Notes,' he takes on the role of the distanced describer, but he also describes the state of his inner self. The desire to publish his notebooks after the war becomes clear, but also how closely the sketches were based on his personal observations (Krauss 1958, 11).

Son of a bourgeois family, Hartlaub was first introduced to France during a school exchange[5] and while traveling with his father in the early 1930s; he understood and spoke French. These previous sojourns in France and his Francophile background influenced the ideas and images (*Vorstellungen*) that he formed and held about himself and the French. In Paris in 1941, he never for a moment lost the awareness that now he was there as a member of an occupying army. His low rank sharpened his sense of injustice and shame in the face of the oppressed population. For years, he saw the relationship between the Germans and the French discredited. He assumed that he and his colleagues, Germans in general, would never be able to come back to Paris or France "in peace and as individuals" after this war and occupation.[6] Yet with the curiosity of an inquisitive contemporary historian, he had welcomed his transfer to enemy territory: "One must see the annihilation of Europe from close up," he writes (Grünbein 2011, 154).[7]

Hartlaub's attitude toward National Socialism and occupation remained contradictory. On the one hand, he maintained a correspondence with the German communist resistance, namely by way of letters he exchanged with his close friends, Klaus, Irene, and Erna Gysi, whom he had met during his studies in Berlin.[8] On the other hand, he was in Paris as part of the occupation forces and later even became very close to the National Socialist leadership in the restricted area of the Führer's headquarters.[9] In his writings, self-critical, clear-sighted reflections of his willingness to conform alternate with desperate attempts to keep concessions to a barbaric regime as low as possible by retreating into isolation. In contrast to his Jewish friends, such as the Gysis or Rudolph Kieve, all of whom were forced to emigrate for some time, Felix Hartlaub was not in a life-threatening situation and avoided a radical change in his own circumstances. In a letter to Kieve from 1933, he talks about the possibility of emigration to the USA—a prospect he rejected because, as a writer, he felt bound to the German language: "Living, yes, but what to do and have? The only thing I have, or perhaps will one day be able to have: *la lingua tedesca* and what can be done with it" (Hartlaub 2002, 22).[10] Hartlaub was certainly no stranger to the things that were happening around him; the "rapid wear and tear of human sensibility" that he observed during National Socialist rule and occupation burdened him immensely—and yet he remained trapped in opportunism and the desire to be invisible (Weichelt 2020, 163).

This dichotomy shows in his notes from Paris. Hartlaub documents surprising, precious moments of beauty that are usually immediately displaced by the oppressive reality of the occupation—like on the Seine, where he mingles with the silent population under the protection of his civilian clothes:

> A cold east wind along the banks of the Seine, early morning. Dust mixed with fluffy, golden-brown plane-tree seeds, which catch on the fresh horse droppings. [...] One of the women takes measures against the sand blown up by the biting wind. All in black, a loose, threadbare coat, woollen shawl, and mittens. [...] Her

eyelids suddenly stiffen, the eyes narrow, a flash from the side: an elegant little French four-seater limousine rolls up, with yellow wheels, pleasingly curved bonnet and back end. Inside, bolt upright, despite the danger of hitting their heads, somewhat too close together, sit three German uniforms, field-gray, black, and silver [...]. For a second, their gaze shifts to the corner of their eyes, a quick probe to the left, then fixed straight ahead again. (Hartlaub 2022, 55–56)[11]

The beauty of the city, the poverty of the population, the cold of winter, the omnipresent threat of the occupiers, the latter's luxurious lifestyle, all come to light through this 'Impression,' as the title suggests. An atmosphere of violation and stagnation becomes clear. Representations in the sense of perceptions of self and other during the actual encounter of occupier and occupied (*Wahrnehmung*) become very apparent in those texts.

In the ministry building on Quai d'Orsay, plundered and destroyed by the Germans after the invasion, Hartlaub experiences, as he writes, "Pompeian effects":

The dust is already a quarter of an inch thick. The result is like Pompei: all the calendars say 14/6/40 [the day of the German invasion]. Newspapers consumed by the sun [...]. In the bare, tube-like room belonging to the *huissier* [usher], who was just finishing the mail [...], there is a kettle, a tin of sardines. Top hats, little ladies' umbrellas lie strewn across the tables, a powder puff. (Hartlaub 2022, 127–28)[12]

While the population must fish along the Seine in hopes of getting lunch that day, the occupiers live in luxury. With barely concealed disgust, Hartlaub describes visages resembling those in Otto Dix's paintings, pale, sinister faces with chubby necks and crew cuts. A *Landser* (low-ranking German soldier) drags antiques through the streets under both arms, gossips about Parisian brothels, and parties in the cafés of Rue Montmartre, surrounded by French girls who sell themselves out of poverty (Pflohmann 2011). Hartlaub notes the greed and the will to exploit that characterize the mentality of the occupiers, but also of their families and friends back home in Germany, who wrote letters to get their hands on luxury products from France. He describes the extent of the looting—mail-order looting included—and the misery of the population:

Incidentally, you cannot imagine what our *Habebalds* and *Eilebeuter* [derogatory terms for greedy Germans], especially the latter, even if they are only present through the letters they write, have done here. Without that, the relationship with the population would be better, satisfactory as it may be. Large parts of the city have been completely emptied. You can easily recognize the *Allemand* [German] by the cardboard box under his arm. (Hartlaub 2002, 448–50)[13]

Yet here, too, his role remained ambivalent, also profiting from the lifestyle as an occupier and from the decline in prices. He acquired a cheap catalogue of French classics from the antiquarian bookshops in Paris, and he was aware that he could only afford it under the circumstances of occupation.[14]

In the following, he addresses the atmosphere of the city, the attitude of the population, and the Parisian women who particularly attract him, but whom he does not approach because of his status as an occupier, as well as on account of his shyness:

> The city—there is little to write about. Of course, it also has its charm, a very hidden, very sad charm. [...] The discipline of the population, the wise attitude through all classes, is quite unique. [...] [T]he inimitable chic cannot be killed. [...] The women, predictably, impress me mightily. [...] But the Parisian woman is an 'absolute epitome,' certainly the highest occidental product. (Hartlaub 2002, 448–50)[15]

He expresses compassion and admiration for the occupied population but feels outcast by it; his initial notion that he might receive preferential treatment or even not be recognized as a German (due to his language skills and his unclear status as a civilian) did not prove true. The Parisians were even more suspicious, because they did not recognize him as an occupier at first:

> My idea of being considered a native here was naïve. Your walk and your look betray you immediately, all the callowness and sadness you carry. If you're indeed overlooked one moment, the next there is a doubly palpable flinch. In a way, I would have a much easier time here in uniform; everything is clear from the first moment. Like this, in civilian clothes, I sometimes run the risk of being seen as a 'spy.' My embarrassment, which makes me completely stiff and has also completely deprived me of French, totally cuts me out everywhere, as if with rusty scissors. (Hartlaub 2002, 450)[16]

Hartlaub failed to find a desirable role for himself with his colleagues or among the 'cold' Parisians; he only found an "in-between and fragmented identity" (Roseau 2020, 1135). In the encounter, during a time of occupation—a time of crisis—he takes an uncomfortable look at social representations as images of self and other, of German occupiers and of occupied Parisians. The only way he can come to terms with the contradictions between and within his own role and identity is through artistic expression (*Darstellung*), through distanced description, through withdrawal—but also through compassion. While William O'Keeffe's evaluation that the literary output of German authors in service in occupied Europe attested to "civilized values despite the contradiction in its authors' situation" might not fully apply to Erhart Kästner (see Meid, this volume; O'Keeffe 2013, 223), it does apply to Felix Hartlaub.

A German Writer Occupied by the French: Tami Oelfken (1945–1955)

Tami Oelfken (1888–1957) grew up as Marie Wilhelmine Oelfken in the Blumenthal district of Bremen. The daughter of a middle-class family, she worked as a teacher and reform pedagogue before and during World War I. She described herself as a socialist and pacifist and joined the *Spartakusbund*, a Marxist revolutionary movement, as well as the KPD (the German communist party), which she quit again in 1924. After the war, she resigned from the state school service and founded her own reform school in Berlin in 1928, which she was able to defend against the Nazis until 1934, when she was banned from her profession as a teacher. A continuation of her school in exile in Paris and London failed.[17]

After her return to Berlin in 1939, unable to teach in Germany, Oelfken concentrated more on her writing. In 1942, she was served with a second professional ban: a lifetime writing ban. As writing had become her only way of supporting herself, she now had to depend on friends for food, shelter, and her supply of paper. The paper was especially important because she had been keeping a detailed diary, a so-called logbook of life in war-time Germany since 1939 (later published under the title "Journey Through Chaos: A Logbook from Times of War").[18] In 1944, she moved to Überlingen on Lake Constance to be close to friends. This region had become a gathering place for German intellectuals in internal emigration, partly because of its proximity to neutral Switzerland (cf. Bosch 2007). Oelfken continued her logbook there until 1945, followed by a private, unpublished diary, which she kept until 1956.

She was already an older woman when the war was over, twenty-six years older than Felix Hartlaub. Her world views (*Vorstellungen*) were shaped by her socialization during the *Kaiserreich* and her political and professional experiences during the Weimar era. Oelfken was a self-confident woman whose loud personality and lifestyle caused offense in various contexts. She remained unmarried all her life, which was not unusual for a teacher; moreover, her parents already considered her "unmarriageable" as early as childhood because of a birth defect involving her hips, which was clearly visible, and that limited her physically

(Fiedler 1995, 42). Outwardly, her status as a single woman was largely accepted, but from her private diary it becomes clear that she felt romantic love exclusively for women and had lived in same-sex relationships. This unpublished diary is the only place where she discusses this part of her life: "I have very rarely dreamed of a male lover in my life."[19] Oelfken finds her own term for women whose sexual orientation diverges from heteronormativity: the "Tuggas." She uses the word as a term of endearment for her former love, with whom she is still friends, but also as a collective term, for possible future partners, who were difficult to find under such historical and political circumstances that required secrecy: "The Tuggas are thin on the ground."[20]

Nazi policies generally turned a blind eye to women's homosexual intimacy, but only if it did not disturb 'normality' (cf. Eschebach 2012; Plötz 2005).[21] That said, even during National Socialism, it was possible for Oelfken to live in relationships with women, but only completely in private, in hiding. As commonly observed for women during National Socialist times and in the early Federal Republic of Germany, she often changed residences and lived as a subtenant, alone, or with a (to the public) "platonic" girlfriend.

Although her lifestyle was probably known to the *Gestapo*, she was persecuted mainly for her political views and her books, which led to her professional bans. In the logbook, she describes the persecution she faced in 1939 in Berlin, but also the advantage in this case of being "just a woman":

> I received a notice from the Gestapo to appear for questioning 'in my own affairs' at Alexanderplatz. [...] This is not the first time that I have been put under the microscope. This time I am only worried because my record of sins in National Socialist Germany is more than overdrawn. The anxious question over two sleepless nights is, what have they found out about all the forbidden acts? [...] My black leather diary is in the hands of a friend from Peru, with whom it is well kept in the extraterritorial desk drawer. So they couldn't have found that either. [...] So what the heck might they have been 'snooping in my affairs'? I don't know. I rely on the protection of my white-hot rage and the fact that I'm 'just a woman after all.' (Oelfken 1946, 128–30)[22]

She mentions her 'black leather diary,' which she was hiding and which became the source for her later-published 'logbook.' Like Hartlaub, Oelfken chose the genre of diary entries and an epistolary style for her literary treatment of war and occupation (*Darstellung*). Her 'logbook' served as a private self-consolation but was also written with the intention of publication after the war. It is not a chronicle of events, but rather a mixture of diary-like notes and fictitious letters to her close circle of friends. Her records are as emotional as they are expressive about everyday life under dictatorship. Oelfken reflects on her self-image as a persecuted person, as well as on German mentalities under National Socialism (*Wahrnehmung*). Full of hope for a new beginning after the war and a sense of responsibility, the notes express a strong wish to be actively involved as an artist and educator in building a new democratic Europe:

> If there shouldn't even be room for us—for us who have never lost our sense of justice and human dignity since 1933 and who, as you quite brightly recognize, are the ones who receive art and give art—who should there be room for? (Oelfken 1946, 407)[23]

The book is an impressive document of inner emigration and the resistance of a person persecuted by the Nazis; 'inner emigration' not in the sense of looking the other way, but describing how, without being in exile or in organized resistance, one could retain intellectual independence and help other persecutees in Nazi Germany, even if this involved a high risk (cf. Bosch 2003).

It concludes with the description of Oelfken's experience of the end of the war in Überlingen, where she welcomed the French occupation soldiers as liberators. The Allies became bearers of hope:

> O my French brothers! The war is over! Is over at last! Your day of victory is our day of freedom! Have our thanks! We have bought our freedom with our defeat, with your victory. It is dearly paid for. It is the most precious thing on Earth. We will guard our freedom like our most precious treasure. (Oelfken 1946, 418)[24]

Unlike Hartlaub's "War Notes," the "logbook" does not remain in extrospection. While Hartlaub describes his surroundings and does not give a direct insight into his own emotions and thoughts, his personal opinions only becoming fully clear in his letters, Oelfken's logbook gives both: extro- *and* introspection. This difference can also be applied to their lives and actions. Oelfken did not withdraw, not as a person and not as a writer. She wanted to be visible and was eager to participate in politics and society, despite the risks she faced in being so outspoken. Where Hartlaub's adherence to civilized values comes without any real risk (as he remains, despite his private disapproval, part of the regime), Oelfken *is* taking such risks.

After the war, besides working on and trying to publish her literary projects, Oelfken wrote letters to her friends and to business partners. Her correspondence from 1945 to 1955 with her friend and publisher Werner Wulff documents the desperate attempt of a politically marginalized woman to publish her books in post-war Germany. Wulff, who was also persecuted during the war and active in the resistance, was one of the first publishers in southern Germany to receive licenses from the French military government to publish books after the war. In 1946, his publishing house in Überlingen (Wulff Verlag) published Oelfkens' logbook. The letters between Oelfken and Wulff serve to maintain their business relationship; contracts are concluded, and details of publications are discussed. But the special relationship between the two is also addressed, a relationship characterized by friendship and solidarity, as well as by occasional disagreements. Their correspondence shows an oppressive monotony, waiting for licenses and paper allocation, and existential problems of a material and professional nature. Copies of articles and conversations with other personalities from the cultural sphere are attached in their correspondence (Oelfken 1988, 31).

Moreover, some of the letters describe Oelfken's and Wulff's cooperation with the French occupation authorities, including Alfred Döblin (see Sandra Schell's chapter in this volume), who worked as a literary inspector (*Literaturinspektor*) in Baden-Baden at this time. His duties included pre-censorship and publication approval of books in the French zone of occupation. He also approved Oelfken's manuscripts:

> Furthermore, Volkmar writes me that in the whole Russian zone, not one publisher has yet received a proper license [...]. So, we are better off in the French zone. (Oelfken 1988, 46)[25]
>
> I therefore firmly expect that the approval for the 'Sonnenuhr' will also arrive in the next few days, especially since you have already received confirmation from Mr. A. Döblin how much he appreciates this work. (Oelfken 1988, 50)[26]

In the immediate post-war period, the conditions and opportunities for Oelfken's literary work and publishing seemed to develop in a positive direction. But her hopes for rehabilitation and for success after liberation were not to be fulfilled. Since 1945, she had been applying for reparations as a victim of National Socialism. The proceedings dragged on for years and ended with an unsatisfactory settlement in 1955 (Hansen-Schaberg 1997, 139). Moreover, Oelfken was soon ostracized in the cultural establishment of the Adenauer state and became one of the largely ignored writers of the post-war period: in 1951, Oelfken had contributed to an anthology that advocated for collaboration with GDR authors and spoke of a future reunification of Germany. It was edited by publisher Willi Weisman in Munich, and famous authors such as Alfred Döblin and Anna Seghers were also featured, but Oelfken specifically was severely criticized for her contribution, most notably in an article in the newspaper *Die Zeit*, written by Paul Hühnerfeld, who claimed that she had "dangerously pacifist ideas" (Habermann 1988, 9). Subsequently, some West German publishers shunned her.

Publishing houses were certainly affected by the Allies' denazification and re-education measures, but they mostly only changed their programming, not so much their owners or staff (Habermann 1988, 11). As such, personal continuities and networks from pre-war times were very evident in the cultural scene, and the zeitgeist was characterized by strong anti-communist sentiment. Joseph Caspar Witsch, co-founder of the well-known publishing house Kiepenheuer & Witsch, no longer dared to publish Oelfken's books, despite an existing contract (cf. Dietz and Lokatis 2011, 244–47). Nor did *Die Zeit* publish Oelfken's response to their article, in which she defended herself but did not give in. The text reveals a strong political self-image and a vision of a democratic, reunified Germany in the future:

> Solidarity of the intellectuals, freedom, and reason in a free country, are conditions of life for me. [...] As long as I have my own heart and mind, I prefer to rely on that heart and mind. I am not a person of the masses. [...] Don't you have enough imagination to even fathom a democratic Germany in the future? [...] I gladly and unequivocally declare to you here that I am an active pacifist in the land of freedom, which you certainly cannot imagine. I am no longer in any party, and I vote secretly. I am a socialist. I hate the fact that, in a free Germany, people still can't get out of the habit of snooping around in the private sphere of every citizen. (Oelfken 1988, 65–66)[27]

Her reply to Witsch's rejection letter, likewise, expresses personal disappointment, but also disappointment about the manner in which democracy was developing in Germany. Oelfken makes a comparison with France to show that democracy must be able to endure differences of opinion:

> Dear Dr. Witsch,
> My attitude and my political opinion were well-known to you during our negotiations, which ran for almost two years. [...] The two pages I contributed from the 'logbook' to the *West-Ostgespräch* [the aforementioned anthology] in Munich were written in '41. For any reader who is also of good will, it is clear from the text that it is equally unsuitable for communist as well as for capitalist propaganda. [...] Unlike you and Mr. Paul Hühnerfeld, I hope and believe that Western and Eastern Germany will one day be Germany again. It seems to me that you do not hope that, because if you did, you would have to think today that, in the near future, we will have a general German parliament again, as is the custom in a democratic country. So, you would have to know that in such a parliament, as is the case in France, a communist can sit next to you whom you cannot beat to death. [...] What you personally experienced in the Soviet Zone is just as irrelevant for the German future as what I experienced in the Third Reich. It is the lack of democratic consciousness that messes with the brains of many people. [...] You promised

> me the first payment by the first of April, which you revoked on April 20. […] Your
> refusal today and its explanation are an open boycott. (Oelfken 1988, 99–101)[28]

After this dispute and the destruction of her reputation, Oeflken no longer found much publicity and became increasingly impoverished. The French occupation initially brought professional opportunities, but soon enough it became apparent that German mentalities were very slow to change. Democracy had to be learned. As an avowed socialist, as well as a disabled older queer woman seeking publicity, Tami Oelfken embodied several marginalized intersections. She remained a controversial figure and did not find her place, even in the new democratic Germany. Still, that did not stop her from expressing herself. "You shall not be silent…" ("Du sollst nicht schweigen…") is the title of the final chapter of an unpublished book from the last years of her life (Habermann 1988, 7).

Conclusion

In my analysis, I have offered insight into the works and correspondence of two authors who worked in very different contexts of war and occupation, both describing, in their own way, the decline of human values that comes with such times, especially during and after National Socialist rule. These authors chose similar types of texts for their literary activity: diary-like notes, written in notebooks, some of which were initially intended as private diaries and only later intended for publication; or, alternatively, an epistolary style. In times of war and occupation, experiences and thoughts must be recorded immediately, as documentation for the future. Writing as a practice also fulfills a function of constructing and deconstructing images of self and other. In both cases 'the others' are other Germans, as well as the French, appearing (at turns) both as occupied and as occupiers. The social representations that are described move along the spectrum between friend and enemy, agency and passivity, collaboration and resistance, repression and liberation.

Felix Hartlaub did not have to fear persecution or censorship because of his affiliation with the occupying forces; he was in a privileged position, despite his inner distance and criticism of the actions and demeanor of his colleagues. He withdrew as far as possible, trying not to attract attention, even in his prose. For the occupied Parisians, however, there were only very few freedoms left under occupation, and they had no option of withdrawing from it. The effects of the repressive National Socialist regime become clear in Hartlaub's atmospheric descriptions.

Tami Oelfken, on the other hand, was persecuted during the war herself. The French occupation brought her more freedom: she no longer had to live in exile or fear for her life, and she was no longer affected by regime-imposed professional bans. The professional and personal disappointments she experienced in the post-war period were due less to conditions of occupation than to only slowly changing German mentalities, for whom democracy remained alien for a long time and anti-communism provided a new—and old—enemy image against which to rally.

Notes

1. Felix Hartlaub's literary fragments were published for the first time in an incomplete and edited form by his sister Geno Hartlaub in 1950; a complete edition of his work did not appear until Ewenz 2002. His notes from Paris were separately published in 2011 under the title *Kriegsaufzeichungen aus Paris*. In 2022, the first English translation was published under the title *Clouds Over Paris. The Wartime Notebooks of Felix Hartlaub*. Tami Oelfken's diary from 1939 to 1945 was published in 1946 under the title *Fahrt durch das Chaos. Ein Logbuch aus Zeiten des Kriegs*. Her correspondence with publisher Werner Wulff and other personalities from the cultural sphere of the post-war period was published in 1988 under the title *Noch ist es Zeit. Briefe nach Bremen 1945 bis 1955*. Copies of her unpublished diary from 1949–1956 can be found in the Felder Archives in Bregenz, *Vorlass Manfred Bosch*, N61/1, N61/2.
2. Franz Kafka being Hartlaub's literary idol; see Marose 2005, 53.
3. All translations from non-English sources are my own. Hartlaub 2002, vol. 1, 467: "Am besten erzähle ich […] einfach was sich alltäglich in dem Stadtgebiet, durch das meine täglichen Wege führen, sichtbar zeigt; vielleicht kommt man gerade damit dem Unsichtbaren, das natürlich das Entscheidende ist, am nächsten." Draft letter to Gustav Radbruch, March 1, 1941.
4. Cf. Marose 2005, 20: "Die tiefe Berechtigung der Geschichtsschreibung wird mir erst in diesen Läufen klar […] Man müßte viel aufschreiben, denn andere als private persönliche Quellen werden später kaum vorhanden sein und gelten." Letter from Romania to the parents, October 1941.
5. In 1930, Hartlaub spent half a year in Strasbourg with the family of the sociologist Maurice Halbwachs, famous for his concepts of collective memory. During his assignment in Paris, they met again, but Hartlaub describes the encounter as distant and unpleasant; Hartlaub now was perceived as the occupier. Meanwhile, the Halbwachs family stood on the other side of history, Jewish on the maternal side and socialist on the paternal side. The two Halbwachs sons joined the Resistance during the occupation. They nevertheless welcomed their former exchange student in their home and had a polite conversation about the politically neutral subject of literature. Cf. Hartlaub 2002, vol. 1, 454–55, letter to the parents, December 28, 1940.

6. Hartlaub 2002, vol. 1, 447: "Wir sind uns alle darüber klar, dass wir hier im Frieden und als Einzelne nie mehr hinkönnen." Letter to the parents, December 5, 1940.

7. Hartlaub 2002, vol. 1, 412: "Man muß die Vernichtung Europas aus der Nähe sehen." Letter to the parents, June 20, 1940.

8. Klaus Gysi, his mother Erna, and his wife Irene were active in the communist resistance. In 1935, Klaus was expelled from the Friedrich Wilhelm University in Berlin because of his Jewish roots. He then went to Cambridge and Paris, where he was temporarily interned. In 1940, he returned to Germany with his wife at the decision of the German Communist Party and lived illegally in Berlin until the end of the war. After the war, he joined the Socialist Unity Party of Germany (SED) and became head of the Aufbau publishing house in the German Democratic Republic (GDR). Klaus and Irene Gysi are the parents of *Die Linke* politician Gregor Gysi; see Hartewig 2004.

9. From May 1942 to March 1945, he was stationed at the so-called 'War Diary' department of the High Command of the *Wehrmacht*, again as a historian. During that time, he continued his notebooks, now under the title "Notes from the Führer's Headquarters" (*Aufzeichnungen auf dem Führerhauptquartier*) (Hartlaub 2002, 147–240).

10. Hartlaub 2002, vol. 1, 22: "Leben schon, aber was tun und haben? Das einzige, was ich habe bzw. vielleicht einmal werde haben können: *la lingua tedesca* und was sich damit anstellen läßt." Letter to Rudolph Kieve, October or November 1933.

11. Hartlaub 2002, vol. 1, 66, "Impression": "Kalter Ostwind den Seinekai entlang, früher Vormittag. Staub, vermischt mit flaumigem goldbraunem Platanensamen, der am frischen Pferdemist hängenbleibt. [...] Eine der Frauen, die gegen den sandhaltigen scharfen Wind angeht. In schwarz, loser verschlissener Mantel, wollenes Schultertuch, wollene Fausthandschuhe [...] Ein plötzliches Erhärten der Lider, die Pupille verengt sich, ein Glanz von der Seite her: Eine elegante kleine frz. viersitzige Limousine kommt gerollt, mit gelben Rädern, gefällig abgerundetem Kühler, Heck. Drin sitzen steil aufgerichtet, trotz der Gefahr, an die Decke zu stossen, etwas eng nebeneinander, drei d[eutsche] Uniformen, feldgrau, schwarz und silber [...] Die Blicke sind eine Sekunde lang im Augenwinkel, ein Sondenstich nach links, dann wieder starr geradeaus."

12. Hartlaub 2002, vol. 1, 119: "Staub liegt schon einen halben Finger dick. Pompejanische Effekte: Die Kalender zeigen alle den 14.6.40. Die von der Sonne ausgezehrten Zeitungen (...) In dem schlauchartigen, kahlen Zimmer des Huissiers [Amtsdiener], der gerade die Post fertig machte (...) steht noch der Teekocher, die Sardinenbüchse. Zylinder, kurze Damenschirme liegen über den Tischen, eine Puderquaste."

13. Hartlaub 2002, vol. 1, 448–50: "Im Übrigen könnt ihr euch nicht vorstellen, was unsere Habebalds und Eilebeuter, vor Allem Letztere, wenn sie auch nur brieflich anwesend sind, hier angerichtet haben. Ohne das wäre das Verhältnis zur Bevölkerung besser, so befriedigend es auch sein mag. Grosse Teile der Stadt sind völlig leergekauft. Am Karton unterm Arm erkennst du mühelos den Allemand." Letter no. 87 to Gustav Friedrich and Erika Hartlaub, December 9, 1940.

14. Hartlaub 2002, vol. 1, 465: "Die Bücher sind relativ schandbar billig. [...] Nie im Leben werde ich die gewisse Liquidität besitzen, die mir hier jetzt eignet. Die Gelegenheit, einen einigermassen vollständigen und einheitlichen Bibliotheksrayon zu schaffen, ist einmalig." Letter to the parents, February 24, 1941.

15. Hartlaub 2002, vol. 1, 448–50: "Die Stadt—es lässt sich wenig schreiben. Sie hat natürlich auch so ihren Reiz, einen sehr verborgenen, sehr traurigen. [...] Die Disziplin der Bevölkerung, die weise Haltung durch alle Schichten hindurch, ist ganz einzigartig. [...] der unnachahmliche Schick ist nicht tot zu kriegen. [...] Die Frauen beeindrucken mich, wie vorauszusehen, mächtig. [...] Aber die Pariserin ist eben ein 'schlechthinniger Inbegriff', sicher das abendländische Höchstprodukt." Letter no. 87 to Gustav Friedrich and Erika Hartlaub, December 9, 1940.

16. Hartlaub 2002, vol. 1, 450: "Naiv war meine Vorstellung hier als Einheimischer angesehen zu werden. Gang und Blick verraten einen sofort, all die Unausgegorenheit und Traurigkeit, die man mit sich herumschleppt. Wird man tatsächlich einen Augenblick lang übersehen, so gibt es im nächsten ein doppelt fühlbares Zurückzucken. In gewisser Weise hätte ich es hier in Uniform viel leichter; da ist alles vom ersten Moment an klar. So, in Zivil, laufe ich manchmal Gefahr, als „spion" angesehen zu werden. Meine Verlegenheit, die mich völlig steif macht und mir auch das Französische völlig verschlagen hat, schneidet mich vollends wie mit einer rostigen Schere überall." Letter to the parents, December 9, 1940.

17. Biographic references on the website of the *Bremer Frauenmuseum*: https://bremer-frauenmuseum.de/2017/03/23/oelfken-maria-wilhelmine-gen-tami/, accessed November 29, 2022.

18. German title: *Fahrt durch das Chaos. Ein Logbuch aus Zeiten des Kriegs.*

19. Unpublished diary: Felder Archives, Bregenz, Vorlass Manfred Bosch, N61/1, N61/2, March 9, 1952.

20. Unpublished diary: Felder Archives, Bregenz, Vorlass Manfred Bosch, N61/1, N61/2, November 20, 1950.

21. Since its introduction in 1872, Paragraph 175 threatened same-sex desire in Germany. This also applied to non-heterosexual women, even if they were less affected. Even during the Nazi era, when a separate department existed to prosecute homosexuals, women were not charged under § 175. Female homosexuality, however, was classified as 'asocial' behavior in terms of Nazi ideology. The persecution of non-heterosexual women was thus carried out along 'racial' factors, or social and political criteria. In the Federal Republic of the 1950s and 1960s, the still existing § 175 acted as a threat. Homoerotic desire was still under suspicion (cf. Patzel-Mattern, Katja, Schmidt, Mirijam: Lesbian* Life Worlds in the German Southwest (ca. 1920s–1970s)—Subproject II: The Boundaries of the Private: Legal and Private Frameworks, https://www.uni-heidelberg.de/fakultaeten/philosophie/zegk/histsem/mitglieder/patzel-mattern/lesbischelebensweltensuedwesten.html, accessed December 20, 2022).

22. Oelfken 1946, 128–30: "Von der Gestapo erhielt ich die Aufforderung, zu einer Verneh-mung ,in eigenen Angelegenheiten' am Alexanderplatz zu erscheinen. […] Es ist nicht das erste Mal, dass ich unter die Lupe genommen werde. Ich bin diesmal nur deshalb beunruhigt, weil mein Sündenkonto im nationalsozialistischen Deutschland mehr als überzogen ist. Die bange Frage in zwei schlaflosen Nächten ist, was haben sie von den vielen verbotenen Handlungen herausgekriegt? […] Mein schwarzes Ledertagebuch ist in Händen eines Freundes aus Peru, bei dem es in der exterritorialen Schreibtisch-schublade gut aufbewahrt ist. Das können sie also auch nicht gefunden haben. Also was zum Teufel mögen sie ,in meinen Angelegenheiten' herumgeschnüffelt haben? Ich weiß es nicht. Ich verlasse mich auf den Schutz meiner weißen Wut und darauf, dass ich ,doch nur eine Frau bin.'"

23. Oelfken 1946, 407: "Wenn nicht einmal für uns Platz sein sollte—für uns, die wir seit 1933 nie das Gefühl für Gerechtigkeit und Menschenwürde verloren haben und die wir, wie Sie ganz hell erkennen, diejenigen sind, die Kunst empfangen und Kunst ge-ben—für wen sollte dann noch Raum sein?"

24. Oelfken 1946, 418: "O ihr meine französischen Brüder! Der Krieg ist zu Ende! Ist end-lich zu Ende! Euer Tag des Sieges ist unser Tag der Freiheit! Habt Dank! Wir haben mit unserer Niederlage, mit eurem Sieg, unsere Freiheit erkauft. Sie ist teuer bezahlt. Sie ist das kostbarste Gut der Erde. Wir wollen die Freiheit hüten wie unseren höchsten Schatz."

25. Oelfken 1988, 46: "Außerdem schreibt mir Volkmar, daß in der ganzen russischen Zone noch nicht ein Verlag eine richtige Lizenz erhalten hat […]. Also sind wir in der französischen Zone noch am besten dran." Wulff to Oelfken, January 30, 1946.

26. Oelfken 1988, 50: "Ich rechne daher fest, daß die Genehmigung für die ,Sonnenuhr' auch in den nächsten Tagen eintrifft, zumal Sie von Herrn A. Döblin bereits bestätigt bekommen haben, wie sehr er diese Arbeiten schätzt." Wulff to Oelfken, April 5, 1946.

27. Oelfken 1988, 65–66: "Solidarität der Geistigen, Freiheit und Vernunft in einem freien Land, sind für mich Lebensbedingungen. […] So lange ich ein eigenes Herz und einen eigenen Verstand habe, ziehe ich es vor, mich auf dieses Herz und diesen Verstand zu verlassen. Ich bin kein Mensch der Masse. […] Haben Sie nicht genug Phantasie, um sich ein zukünftiges, demokratisches Deutschland auch nur vorzustellen? […] Ich erk-läre Ihnen hier gern und eindeutig, daß ich im Lande der Freiheit aktive Pazifistin bin, worunter Sie sich gewiß nichts vorstellen können. Ich bin in keiner Partei mehr und wähle geheim. Ich bin Sozialistin. Ich hasse es, daß man sich im freien Deutschland immer noch nicht abgewöhnen kann, in der privaten Sphäre jedes Bürgers herum zu schnüffeln." Unpublished response to Hühnerfeld's article in *Die Zeit*.

28. Oelfken 1988, 99–101: "Sehr geehrter Herr Dr. Witsch, meine Haltung und meine politische Meinung waren Ihnen im Verlauf der Verhandlungen, die fast zwei Jahre liefen, bekannt. […] Die beiden Seiten, die ich aus dem Logbuch dem West-Ost-gespräch in München beisteuerte, wurden im Jahre 41 geschrieben. Für jeden Leser,

der auch nur guten Willens ist, geht aus dem Text eindeutig hervor, daß er gleichermaßen für die Kommunisten und die Kapitalisten ungeeignet zur Propaganda ist. [...] Zum Unterschied zu Ihnen und Herrn Paul Hühnerfeld hoffe und glaube ich, daß West und Ostdeutschland eines Tages wieder Deutschland sind. [...] Es scheint mir, Sie hoffen das nicht; denn wenn Sie es hoffen würden, dann müssten Sie schon heute daran denken müssen, daß wir in naher Zukunft ein allgemeines deutsches Parlament wieder haben, wie es in einem demokratischen Land Sitte ist. Sie müßten also wissen, daß in einem solchen Parlament, wie es in Frankreich der Fall ist, neben Ihnen ein Kommunist sitzen kann, den Sie nicht totschlagen können. Was Sie persönlich in der Ostzone erlebt haben, spielt dabei genau so wenig eine Rolle, wie es für die deutsche Zukunft unwichtig ist, was ich im Dritten Reich erlebt habe. Es ist der Mangel demokratischen Bewußtseins, der bei vielen Menschen die Gehirne in Unordnung bringt. [...] Sie stellten mir die erste Zahlung zum ersten April in Aussicht, die Sie am 20. April widerriefen. [...] Ihre heutige Absage und deren Begründung ist ein offener Boykott." Letter from Oelfken to Dr. Witsch, May 15, 1951.

References

Böll, Heinrich. 1979. "Bekenntnis zur Trümmerliteratur." In *Heinrich Böll: Werke. Essayistische Schriften und Reden 1: 1952–1963*, edited by Bernd Balzer, 31–34. Cologne: Kiepenheuer & Witsch.

Bosch, Manfred. 2003. "Nachwort." In *Oelfken Tami: Fahrt durch das Chaos*, edited by Manfred Bosch, 347–77. Lengwil: Libelle.

———. 2007. *Bohème am Bodensee: Literarisches Leben am See von 1900 bis 1950*. Lengwil: Libelle.

Chartier, Roger. 1989. "Le monde comme representation." *Annales. Économies, Sociétés, Civilisations*. 44, no 6: 1505–20.

Dekker, Rudolf, ed. 2002. *Egodocuments and History: Autobiographical Writing in its Social Context since the Middle Ages*. Rotterdam: Hilversum Verloren.

Depkat, Volker, and Wolfram Pyta. 2021. *Tagebücher zwischen Text und Quelle: Geschichtswissenschaft und Literaturwissenschaft im Gespräch*. Berlin: Duncker & Humblot.

Dietz, Nicole, and Siegfried Lokatis. 2011. "Tobbys Wunsch? Tami Oelfken zwischen den Fronten bei Kiepenheuers." In *100 Jahre Kiepenheuer-Verlage*, edited by Siegfried Lokatis and Ingrid Sommer, 244–47. Berlin: Ch. Links.

Durkheim, Émile. 1898. "Représentations individuelles et représentations collectives." *Revue de Métaphysique et de Morale* 6: 273–302.

Eschebach, Insa, ed. 2012. *Homophobie und Devianz: Weibliche und männliche Homosexualität im Nationalsozialismus*. Berlin: Metropol.

Ewenz, Gabriele Lieselotte. 2002. "Einführung in Leben und Werk." In Hartlaub, Felix, *In den eigenen Umriss gebannt: Kriegsaufzeichnungen, literarische Fragmente und Briefe aus den Jahren 1939 bis 1945*, edited by Gabriele Lieselotte Ewenz, 7–41. Frankfurt a.M.: Suhrkamp.

Fiedler, Ulf. 1995. "Vom roten Plüsch zur Räterepublik: Das abenteuerliche Leben der Tami Oelfken." In *Dichter an Strom und Deich*, edited by Ulf Fiedler, 41–49. Bremen: Hauschild.

Grünbein, Durs. 2011. "Der Verschollene." In Hartlaub, Felix, *Kriegsaufzeichungen aus Paris*, 147–63. Berlin: Suhrkamp.

Habermann, Ursel. 1988. "Zur Einführung." In *Noch ist es Zeit: Briefe nach Bremen 1945 bis 1955*, 7–34, Frankfurt a.M.: tende

Hansen-Schaberg, Inge. 1997. "Tami Oelfken (1888–1957)." In *"etwas erzählen.": Die lebensgeschichtliche Dimension in der Pädagogik*, edited by Inge Hansen-Schaberg, 132–41. Hohengehren: Schneider.

Hartewig, Karin. 2004. "A German Jewish Communist of the Second Generation: The Changing Personae of Klaus Gysi." In *Dark Times, Dire Decisions: Jews and Communism*, edited by Jonathan Fraenkel and Dan Diner, 255–74. New York: Oxford University Press.

Hartlaub, Felix. [1950] 2002. *In den eigenen Umriss gebannt: Kriegsaufzeichnungen, literarische Fragmente und Briefe aus den Jahren 1939 bis 1945*, edited by Gabriele Lieselotte Ewenz. 2 vols. Frankfurt a.M.: Suhrkamp.

———. 2011. *Kriegsaufzeichnungen aus Paris*. Berlin: Suhrkamp.

———. 2022. *Clouds over Paris: The Wartime Notebooks of Felix Hartlaub*. Translated by Simon Beattie. London: Pushkin Press.

Krauss, Erna. 1958. "Der Mensch." In *Felix Hartlaub in seinen Briefen*, edited by Geno Hartlaub and Erna Krauss, 11–17, Tübingen: Wunderlich.

Le Goff, Jacques, Roger Chartier, and Jacques Revel, eds. 1978. *La nouvelle histoire: Les encyclopédies du savoir moderne*. Paris: Retz.

Lejeune, Phillippe. 1975. *Le Pacte autobiographique*. Paris: Édition du Seuil.

Marose, Monika. 2005. *Unter der Tarnkappe—Felix Hartlaub*. Berlin: Transit.

Moscovici, Serge. 1961. *La Psychanalyse, son image et son public*. Paris: Presses universitaires de France.

Oelfken Tami. 1946. *Fahrt durch das Chaos: Ein Logbuch aus Zeiten des Kriegs*. Überlingen: Wulff.

———. 1988. *Noch ist es Zeit…: Briefe nach Bremen 1945 bis 1955*. Edited by Ursel Habermann. Frankfurt a.M.: tende.

O'Keeffe, William J. 2013. *A Literary Occupation: Responses of German Writers in Service in Occupied Europe*. Amsterdam: Rodopi.

Pflohmann, Oliver. 2011. "Ein Skizzenbuch gegen den braunen Spuk." Deutschlandfunk. August 10, 2011. Accessed March 17, 2024, https://www.deutschlandfunk.de/ein-skizzenbuch-gegen-den-braunen-spuk-100.html.

Plötz, Kirsten. 2005. *Als fehle die bessere Hälfte: 'Alleinstehende' Frauen in der frühen BRD 1949–1969*. Königstein: Helmer.

Presser, Jacob. 1969. *Uit het werk van dr J. Presser*. Amsterdam: Polak & Van Gennep.

Roseau, Katherine. 2020. "A Diary without the 'I': Embodiment and Self-construction in Felix Hartlaub's Extrospective Second World War Paris Writings." *Textual Practice* 34, no. 7: 1123–39.

Schulze, Winfried, ed. 1996. *Ego-Dokumente: Annäherung an den Menschen in der Geschichte*. Berlin: Akademie.

Tami Oelfken's unpublished diary 1949–1956, Felder Archives Bregenz, Vorlass Manfred Bosch, N61/1, N61/2.

Weichelt, Matthias. 2020. *Der verschwundene Zeuge: Das kurze Leben des Felix Hartlaub*. Berlin: Suhrkamp.

CHAPTER 6

Literary Representations of Occupied Cities

Tbilisi, Paris, and Luxembourg[1]

ATINATI MAMATSASHVILI

This chapter examines the literary representation of three occupied cities—Tbilisi, Paris, and Luxembourg—in works composed in the 1930s and 1940s by Georgian and German writers in exile, principally in France and Luxembourg. Among the Georgian writers who fled the country after the occupation of Georgia by the Bolsheviks in 1921, there are some who stress the two regimes of occupation: that by Nazi Germany of France (where many exiled Georgian writers settled) and that by Soviet Russia of Georgia. In this sense, it is interesting to consider the texts of two different Georgian authors, George Kipiani (1908–1986) and Indo Inasari (1895–1952), the former focusing on Paris in the aftermath of its liberation from the Nazis, and the latter on Tbilisi under occupation by the Bolsheviks. Overlapping in part with these other two occupations, Luxembourg also remained in the grip of the Nazis for four years, with Germany intending to make it part of the Reich. Maria Gleit (1909–1981) was a German writer and journalist, "author of antifascist novels and children's books" (Heimberg 2002, 41), who left Germany with her husband as soon as Hitler came to power and settled in Luxembourg in 1938. She moved to the USA a year later. In her novel *Katrina: A Story of Luxembourg*, published in English in 1945 and dedicated to her Luxembourgish friends, she focuses on the resistance network in that city.

In each of the three cases we are considering here, the writer, forced into exile, looks at a city (which may be in his own country) that is occupied by an oppressor (who may be his own compatriots). This chapter's main objective of exploring the *external* view of these cities in the grip of murderous ideologies is to examine how mental space (perceived and represented) and social space (constructed and produced) interfere (Lefebvre 1991) in fictional texts that stage an urban space as produced by the new oppressive regime and, simultaneously, as represented by the narrative process that manages to turn the space upside down. To reflect on this proposed viewpoint, we will proceed by focusing on both the private and public spaces created and arranged by the occupier—spaces that involve, from the outset, the inclusive–exclusive duality, in which the notion of being included is as strong and separate as that of having been expelled. In such cases, neutrality seems almost impossible: either you are part of the community, or you are not. Anyone who chooses to (or who *must*) be part of that community must stay within the ranks, participate in all sorts of inaugurations, and form part of the newly created (social) space, simply by virtue of constituting it: in other words, one must either participate in its creation or else be rejected, persecuted, forced to withdraw from the legal space, and go underground (i.e., become invisible) in order to survive. This condition applies equally to the dislocated and deracinated exile who flees the country: because he refuses to be part of the community, he has no choice but to leave it if he, too, wishes to survive.

Hence, the notion of 'social space' will allow us, on the one hand, to account for the experience of isolation within a society (regardless of the unique context of the individual's isolation/exile) and, on the other, to think about the forms of resistance that may nevertheless arise among the isolated—for social space is not a fixed space, but rather one that is perennially under construction. Thus, the mental space (i.e., designated and desired space) is constantly confronted with the existing social space. It is in this way that the social space itself, by inspiring various measures (including the creation of resistance networks and movements, hiding places, etc.) plays an inadvertent role in generating other (illegal) spaces: hidden spaces.

While literary texts, by way of their textual organization, offer the possibility of rendering—notably—not a dichotomy of excluded/included spaces but instead the co-existence of legitimate and illegitimate spaces, we will also call upon a pictorial example that lends an additional dimension of analysis: notably, a painting of an attic, executed in the midst of the occupation by the Dutch-Belgian painter Jan Cox (1919–1980). This latter, non-literary creative work will allow us to examine—through its staging of a closed space from which the other ('open,' legally sanctioned) space is absent—the terrifying dimension of the claustration and imprisonment in occupied societies, to which man, doomed to destruction, is henceforth condemned to live.

Why Bring These Settings Together? (Tbilisi–Luxembourg; Paris–Luxembourg; Paris–Tbilisi)

It might seem unusual to combine these disparate literary works, or even these cities. However, the reasoning is quite simple: with each work offering an external perspective on its respective setting, examining these three works in tandem allows us to find commonalities in the construction and experience of disparate spaces, introducing two, or even three,[2] distinct regimes of occupation: that of Georgia by Soviet Russia, that of France by Nazi Germany, and that of Luxembourg by Nazi Germany.

While the Tbilisi case introduces a political regime and historical context that differ on several points from the Nazi occupations (namely, Georgia endured the Soviet regime), we can nevertheless find an important commonality between Tbilisi and Luxembourg's respective occupations: both places were annexed. Specifically, Luxembourg was annexed by Nazi Germany in 1942, which was not the case for France, and Georgia was annexed in 1921 by Soviet Russia and remained part of the Soviet Union for more than seventy years.

Another similarity can be drawn between Paris and Luxembourg through each writer's view of the respective city: namely, each of these writers takes an *external* view, being *foreign* to the city in which he or she finds him- or herself in exile. The Georgian writer George Kipiani is in exile in Paris, having fled the Soviet regime, and it is Kipiani's portrayal of Nazi-occupied Paris that I will consider here. In turn, Maria Gleit is a German writer who fled Nazi Germany with her Jewish husband, and her novel, written in exile, portrays her view of the occupied city of Luxembourg, where she had lived in the late 1930s; even though she was no longer in Luxembourg at the time of its occupation, she wanted to paint a portrait of the city where she had lived and of its inhabitants. Finally, a Georgian writer who finds himself in exile in France makes the link between Tbilisi and Paris—and, more broadly, between Georgia and France. When George Kipiani writes his text that joins the two cities, his exile 'home' (Paris) has been liberated from its occupier by the Soviets, while his original home (Tbilisi) is still occupied by the forces of Stalin—the 'great' winner of World War II. Like Kipiani, Indo Inasari was also in Paris when he wrote the novel that I analyze here. However, Inasari's host city does not appear at any point: it is on Tbilisi and Georgia in general—under the sway of Soviet ideology—that his text, composed in Paris in the 1930s, is focused. Thus, all three authors are emigrant writers, and it is particularly from this perspective—the condition of the emigrant: the one who does not speak entirely from the place where she or he is, nor entirely from the place where he is no longer (Schütz 1944)—that I shall develop the reasoning on cities occupied under extreme historical conditions.

The 'external' perspective of the emigrant writer is understood in a sociological sense: in his essay "The Stranger: An Essay in Social Psychology," speaking of the "typical situation" (Schütz 1944, 499) of a stranger who finds himself in a new social group, Alfred Schütz immediately links the exilic condition to cartography, in the sense that handling a map is an action inextricably linked to the identification of oneself (and one's location) *on* this map, and to the orientation that presupposes himself standing at the center of the surrounding world. For, as Schütz notes, in order to be able to use the map correctly, one "has first of all to know his standpoint in two respects: its location on the ground and its representation on the map" (Schütz 1944, 504). This means, on a sociological level, that in order to engage with a cultural model, a group member must be able to identify himself as an internal member of the group in question, and that this identification is possible only if he has a clearly "definite status" (and is "aware" of it) within the group to which he belongs (Schütz 1944, 504). Identifying in this way permits him a particular orientation (i.e., he may orient himself *from* the center), whereas the stranger lacks this 'internal' member status. Therefore, since the stranger finds everything unfamiliar, he is unable to "consider himself as the centre of his [new] social environment" (Schütz 1944, 504), and a (spatial) "dislocation" (Schütz 1944, 504) occurs. It is from this dual 'external' location (that is, in relation to the group to which he arrives *and simultaneously* the group to which he no longer belongs) that I will first consider the functioning of the "illegitimate country"[3] (Inasari 1936, 130)—the sole 'legal' space in which those who are marginalized are no longer admitted.[4] Second, I will consider the place of those who have lost their homes, are escaped prisoners, or are rebels and resistance fighters—all of whom constitute the clandestine space, the only space to which they are now entitled. Finally, I will illuminate the manner in which fiction manages to make this clandestine, illegal space *visible*, through the lens of the émigré.

Tbilisi: The City that Expels versus the Village that Shelters

"She did not consider the city as a protector of men"[5] (Inasari 1936, 7)—this is the conception that governs the anti-Soviet novel "The Shadow of a Truth" (ჩრდილი ერთი სინამდვილის), composed by Georgian writer Indo Inasari[6] in 1934 and published in Paris in 1936 in Georgian. Inasari was exiled in Paris in 1929 after, like many of his contemporaries, fleeing the Soviet regime. The chief commonality among the literature by Georgian emigrants in the 1930s is that the authors' experience of exile often links them to the figure of the stranger, the outcast, who lives on society's margins. Even if the author is very grateful to the host country (which, for most Georgian authors, was France), it is rather with the figure of the *clochard* that Georgian writers and poets identify themselves. One of the reasons for this is undoubtedly literary exclusion: these writers often publish in Georgian and lack close links with French intellectuals and writers, unlike their predecessor generation, the Georgian Symbolists, some of whom had traveled and lived in France before World War I and developed close contacts with their French and Belgian artist contemporaries. The exclusion of Georgia's exiled writers, by contrast—along with the nostalgia they felt for the

Soviet-invaded homeland they left behind—obviously determined the themes and orientation of their emigration literature.

Set during the Soviet period, when Georgia was occupied by the Red Army, Inasari's "The Shadow of a Truth" focuses on three characters, including resistance fighters and collaborators. The first, Tbatana, is a young student in Tbilisi whose rented room in the city is 'legally' stolen from her by a Soviet citizen, thus rendering Tbatana homeless. The second, Otaridi, is a character sent to the Gulag, but who manages to escape and leads a peasant revolt for the liberation of Georgia from Soviet rule. The third, Goubadi, is a young Soviet-indoctrinated functionary who kills his own parents at the end of the book out of ideological conviction. The images of the camps incorporated in this novel often overlap with those evoked by Varlam Shalamov (Shalamov 2018) almost three decades later in his *Kolyma Stories*.[7]

The author's personal experiences, in fact, formed the basis for the novel's plot. After the occupation of Georgia by the Red Army in 1921, he was arrested by the Bolsheviks and imprisoned for a year in Metekhi prison in Tbilisi; as a member of the National Guard, he was considered a 'dangerous person.' After his release, he became a member of the Union of Proletarian Writers, and in 1924, he was admitted to study in the Philosophy program of the State University of Tbilisi. Together with other philosophy students, Inasari founded a group named Adamianossani, the term derived from the Georgian word '*adamiani*' meaning 'man' or 'human.' Inasari himself developed the group's concept. He finished his studies in 1929, but he was counted for some time among the 'undesirable and dangerous persons for the state' on account of his literary and political activities, while Adamianossani was conceived as an anti-Soviet organization.

In autumn of that year, these pressures finally forced Indo Inasari to leave the country with his wife. Upon his arrival in Paris, he founded the newspaper *Adamianossani*, which changed its name in 1937 to *Mouzaradi*. It was during his period of exile in Paris that his novels "The Shadow of a Truth" (ჩრდილი ერთი სინამდვილის, in Georgian), "National Equity and the Sterile Flower" (*L'équité nationale et la fleur stérile*, in French), and the "Beggar of the Soul" (სულის მათხოვარი, in Georgian, with some extracts translated into French) were written. He returned to Georgia after World War II in 1947 and was deported with his family in 1951. One year later, he disappeared without a trace. According to sources, he was killed during torture by the Cheka.

The edition of "The Shadow of a Truth" that I have at my disposal comes from the archives of Guram Sharadze, a Georgian historian and philologist who brought Georgian archives from Paris to Tbilisi in the 1990s. This particular copy of the book features a hand-written dedication by Inasari to David Marjanishvili: "In memory of our encounter in exile": "პატივცემულ დავით

მარჯანიშვილს ხსოვნად ლიტოლვილებაში შეხვედრის. ავტორი"). It bears the signature "The author." It can be assumed that the David Marjanishvili to whom Inasari dedicated this copy was the Georgian émigré by that name who acted as a correspondent and member of the editorial staff for the weekly newspaper *Saqartvelo*[8] (published in Berlin from 1942 to 1945), a newspaper founded by the Georgian Legion of Vermarcht, which consisted of 30,300 Georgian émigrés devoted to fighting against the Soviet Union to liberate Georgia from the Bolshevik Occupation. Marjanishvili was also a founding member of the patriotic organization *Kartlosi*, which published the Paris edition of the same newspaper.

From the start, Inasari's novel portrays the city as a space hostile to man—an external space to which man moves, or from which he distances himself, because his *real* house, his true home, is in the village. The city is a place that attacks rather than protects. When we talk about 'space' here, it is in the sociological sense of the term, which includes not just the place itself but also the goods connected to it, as well as the relational and geographical networks contained therein; for example, the apartment, the yard, the university, the police station, the street, and even the neighbors and friends—all portrayed as dimensions or 'places' of mobility and movement within the novel. This geo-social-spatial network is mainly established through the displacements, expulsions, and relationships that the protagonists (mainly Tbatana) create. It is interesting that the main character, Tbatana, a young woman, and the two other protagonists—Goubadi and Otaridi, who are men—are all originally from the village but move to the city. Tbatana and Otaridi move there to pursue their education, and Goubadi moves there to advance his career as a Communist official. Yet this rural-to-urban migration proves pivotal and ultimately detrimental for all three: (a) Tbatana loses her home, her mother, and her brother, and she becomes a homeless beggar; (b) Otaridi is sent to the Gulag, although he survives and goes on to lead insurgents against Communist ideology; and (c) Goubadi, indoctrinated by Soviet ideology, kills his own parents out of political conviction, after which he loses his mind.

As for the geographical arrangement of the story, the text's narrative and schematic development focus on four different places: the Gulag, the city, the village, and—linking the latter two—the forest. That is, while the city stands as a place that breeds evil and attacks man, the village presents itself as a place of shelter, and the forest represents the path that unites the one with the other; though the forest encompasses danger (in this way, parallel to the city), it also affords access to return to a place of safety (the village). The Gulag remains a place apart from all the rest: it is the place of death and torture.[9]

The antagonism between the one that aggresses and the one that shelters (i.e., the city versus the village) becomes more apparent when Tbatana's mother Bia decides to follow her daughter to Tbilisi in order to find out about her son (Tbatana's brother), who has been arrested by the Soviet authorities and imprisoned in the city, and of whom she has no news. All the more important, however, is that this is the occasion on which Bia *discovers* the city: while Tbatana had moved there already to pursue her studies, Bia had never left the village before. Alas, when they arrive at Tbatana's home at night, tired after a long journey, it is a stranger who opens her door and says that the apartment now belongs to him. This is the dialogue that plays out between the astonished Tbatana and the stranger:

> "What do you want?" [Stranger]
> "This is my home." [Tbatana]
> "What?!"
> "This is my home," Tbatana continued to assert, more confidently.
> "Citizen, you have surely not fallen from the moon, this is a Soviet country," [the stranger] said calmly and wanted to go back to his apartment as if nothing had happened…
> "This is my home, it's mine… get out…" [Tbatana] pushed the door. Bia watched with amazement the fight between her daughter and the madman. She had imagined Tbilisi differently. (Inasari 1936, 76)

The stranger's insistence upon his right to take what (he knows) belongs to another is based on "the right that every citizen has in the Soviet state" (Inasari 1936, 76): "every flat that is free is yours… Go ahead and look for your own place and please don't bother me again, otherwise [...]," he trails off with the suggestion of an unspoken threat (Inasari 1936, 76).

Tbatana and Bia's trip to the city becomes a tragedy: the old woman, who "imagined Tbilisi differently," is left without a roof over her head. Tbatana, driven out into the street with her mother, doggedly tries to get her home back. Her journey through the city is quite impressive: she goes to the police station, to her university, and to her friends (whom she ultimately cannot find)—all to no effect. At the same time, her old mother, who has remained in the apartment's courtyard (note that the mother stays put, as opposed to her daughter's night-time movements from place to place), is ultimately not allowed to stay there either. This depiction of how easily the city threatens homelessness is coupled with the outraged hostility that the place exhibits: while the daughter desperately seeks a solution, her tired mother in the courtyard is jeered on all sides by the former neighbors, who see the two women as *intruders* in the building and want to chase Bia *out of the yard, too.* One particularly compelling detail about the neighbors' antagonism toward Bia is the fact that such behavior completely contradicts Georgian customs, which value excessive hospitality.[10] In other words, through this interaction, we see that the city has become a place devoid of old values—having lost what was inherent to Georgia's very character. It is the city that takes the son away from the mother (Bia's son being imprisoned in Tbilisi), and it is the city that deprives the mother and daughter of their rightful home. Left with no domicile, they become homeless.

All this said, what is even more interesting about "The Shadow of a Truth" is the fact it renders indissoluble the link that exists between spaces and (Soviet) ideology: it is in the city that one's personal peace is ruined, and he may find himself inadvertently on the wrong side of the law. In the city, homes become occupied by the Soviets, innocents are imprisoned and tortured by the Cheka, families are broken up, and morals have degenerated—for example, the neighborhood's behavior toward the old woman is a clear indication of this. In the end, the city is the place where the Soviet regime has taken root, and, as such, the Soviet regime now rules the *urban space*: the old woman is chased out of the courtyard (i.e., a semi-public, open space), the daughter is expelled from her home, and the search for help through the city comes to nothing; no one offers aid. It is these events in the city that reveal to us that the Soviet regime (in other words, the Soviet ideology) has succeeded in creating a new man, the Soviet man, *homo sovieticus*, who differs entirely from the 'old' man—the Georgian man.

This fundamental shift in ideology is simultaneously reflected not just in the spatial modeling but also in the links that people have with one another, the places they inhabit, and where they are moving.

One Sixth of the Globe is Communism

What is curious about the spatial distribution of this novel is that not only does space become a metaphor for ideology (i.e., the city *is* communism), but, in fact, the metaphor also works the other way around: communism (and therefore ideology itself) becomes a metaphor for geographical space. In one poignant exchange, some peasants who have staged a revolt declare, "We will all die, but we will not adopt communism"—to which Goubadi, the avowed communist, retorts: "Are you going against communism? Against a sixth of the globe?" (Inasari 1936, 145)

This is how the communist protagonist greets the revolting peasants—including his own father. The ideology is expressed in terms of a *metaphor* that is spatial, and it thus takes on a different tangibility. How, especially in such small numbers, to resist such a *large spatial* entity: one-sixth of the globe?

Spatial metaphors play a considerable role in the text. For example, the city is presented elsewhere in the book as "one big *hotel*" [my emphasis]. In this case, rather than the aggrandizing invocation of "globe," the use of the word "hotel" serves to minimize or to consolidate, in a sense:

> You know yourselves that all these houses stand separately, but otherwise in their essence "the whole city represents one big hotel," and in this hotel it is the master's business to decide to whom he will distribute this or that room… […] and the master of this "city hotel," you know, is the government. (Inasari 1936, 129)

This is the response that the police commissar gives to Tbatana when she asks for help in recovering the apartment that a Communist stole from her. In other words, according to the new ideology, the visual arrangement of the urban spatial division is illusory: even if the houses are built separately from each other, they are, in reality, one and the same building, without any private walls and in which everything is collective—hence the metaphor of the hotel (a collective space that is owned and operated by a party other than its occupants) in substitution for the house (a space that is truly private and often privately owned). In Soviet-occupied Georgia, the 'home' no longer exists; it is up to the *maître d'hôtel* to *allocate* a room to his *temporary* residents.

In this sense, it is not only the city's spatial arrangement that is radically changed by Soviet ideology (the city reduced to a single building, i.e., the hotel), but also the city's very *essence*, in that the notion of a private home is now defunct. The words "It's mine," "It belongs to me," must be banished from the vocabulary. Everything must become *common*: the wife, the children, the dwelling place, life itself, because "this is communism" (Inasari 1936, 141). It is an "illegitimate country" (Inasari 1936, 130) in which the protagonists now must live, while the term 'country' acts as a mere metaphor—its pre-occupation meaning rendered defunct—and incorporates the habitable spaces that the 'undesirable' protagonists no longer have any right to occupy, except under marginalized or illegal conditions (if they were left homeless, escaped from the Gulag, etc.).

Honest words no longer hold any power here, overshadowed by the lies of those who hold high positions in the new system: "In the illegitimate country, the word of someone who occupies such a great position would be taken as the truth, and who will believe me, the wretch that I am?" (Inasari 1936, 130), thinks Tbatana, reflecting on Goubadi and his position in society. The novel even contains a chapter titled "The Man and the Communist" (Chapter XXX), which contrasts the man with the man-communist. The latter is portrayed as lacking all human characteristics.

The final scene of the novel moves to the village, where a gathering of villagers has come to listen to a prophet who is none other than Tbatana's mutual love interest, the protagonist Otaridi, who was imprisoned, tortured, and then sent to the Gulag by the Cheka. He managed to escape and return to the village, which had become a place of resistance. He preaches there the absolute necessity of personal freedom and political independence:

> Why have you taken from man what was his own? You want to give us what is common and you tell us that Communism, the Communist system, its state organization is better, and that is why you are torturing us today? […] [T]he best system is the one that can be changed… An organization, of a system, that is open to change based on the will of men, is the only kind that can offer an ideal form of happy, serene existence… And when can the system be changed according to one's desires?
>
> When men have the right to do so, when they are free.
>
> That is why the pre-determined form of existence that is not based on freedom represents violence, violence… (Inasari 1936, 212–14)

The village is represented as a pillar of resistance and, simultaneously, as a shelter: if all evils are possible in the city, it is to the village that the protagonists return in order to escape from the Soviet system. In escaping, they have triumphed over the regime, however minimal this triumph may be.

Yet it is also to the village that Goubadi returns, the indoctrinated protagonist who kills his own parents over the Soviet ideology that has poisoned his mind. This murder has been a step too far in Goubadi's rabid pursuit of his beliefs, a final straw atop a pile of atrocities he has committed for the cause; finding the burden of this final act too heavy, he takes to wandering the forest, where the villagers find him in a state of madness—asking every passerby whether he has seen his mother… whom Goubadi has personally killed. His ultimately homicidal loyalty to Soviet ideology brings to mind a quote by Victor Klemperer: "Words can be like tiny doses of arsenic: they are swallowed unnoticed, appear to have no effect, and then after a little time the toxic reaction sets in after all" (Klemperer 2000, 15). Although Klemperer was speaking of Nazism and Nazi rhetoric, his words are perfectly applicable to the spaces where other totalitarian regimes take hold, and even though Nazism certainly differs on several levels from Soviet ideology, the two still retain a certain similarity, especially for the fact that both regimes treated the project of engendering the new man as the very center of the process of indoctrination. Indeed, this transformation of a person into an *ideologized* person also haunts us from Nazi times—visibly: in the pages of George Grosz's expressionistic lithograph, "They Couldn't Resist" from his *Interregnum* portfolio (Grosz 1936/1976), everyone marches "in rows" (as Ödön von Horvath would have formulated[11]), the gesture of the Nazi salute uniting everyone in harmony.

Underground Men: *Katrina*

In her novel *Katrina: A Story of Luxembourg* (1945), which Maria Gleit dedicates to her stay in Luxembourg and the struggle of the Luxembourgers against their occupiers, two worlds coexist: on the one side, the underground world, and on the other, the new world created and governed by the Nazis, their collaborators, and those who keep silent. The underground world into which Gleit invites us is that of the city of Luxembourg, with its secret passages that allow the organization of a resistance network. From there, through the people involved, this network extends to the villages and forests, where those who have faced danger (e.g., resistance fighters, rebels, escapees from prisons and camps) were able to find hidden shelter and assistance. The novel depicts the struggle of Luxembourgers (particularly those in the underground) against Nazism, with the story playing out from 1942 to 1944. Its larger plot revolves around the rescue of a Luxembourgish child at risk of being taken to Germany to be raised as a Nazi; the novel concludes with Luxembourg's liberation.

At the start of the book, fifteen-year-old protagonist, Katrina Specht, a Luxembourgish girl, joins the resistance and helps to organize a secret pilgrimage to the *Consolatrice des affligés* (Our Lady of Consolation) statue in Luxembourg City—an activity forbidden under the occupation. This pilgrimage dates from the 17th century, and while Our Lady of Consolation was originally considered the protector of Luxembourg City, the devotional act took on an increasingly nationalistic dimension that grew stronger during World War II, when Europe's occupied peoples were subjected to the prohibition of pilgrimages and other religious practices (Hurlock 2022, 37). Although *Katrina* features a range of characters, including collaborators, traitors, and those who remain passive, the 'place' to which the book's resistance fighters and/or persecuted individuals are relegated is the *hidden* spaces: these characters are not to be seen, their faces only appearing in broad daylight very discreetly. Their lot is an underground life; to show their faces in the open would mean being stopped by soldiers in the streets, denounced by collaborators, and so forth.

In this novel, as in the case of Inasari's above, the antinomy between the city and the village appears from the start, where the city, full of Nazis, is portrayed as a place of 'danger'—a word the text repeatedly invokes. When Katrina wants to accept her Aunt Amalia's invitation to stay with her in Luxembourg City, Katrina's family wants to prevent her from doing so, particularly because of the 'danger' that she is liable to run into there:

> The city was full of soldiers, Germans, of course, and of guards in yellow uniforms, called the SA. Father said it was dangerous for a young girl to live in such

a city; Katrina had retorted that here, too, they had their 'Yellow'—a man called Herr Kuhn who had taken possession of the parsonage in the village. No one could be safe in times like these, she had said to Father. (Gleit 1945, 3)

Indeed, by the time the story begins, the "Grand Duchy of Luxembourg had been overrun and occupied by the Nazis" for two years; from start to finish, the novel contains variations on the refrain "[a]nd the whole city is full of Nazis" (Gleit 1945, 18). However, although Katrina's village, by contrast to the city, does not suffer particularly under the Nazis, the entire "country [was] in chains and [there were] endless edicts of the tyrant to be obeyed," which cause "misery" (Gleit 1945, 7). Nonetheless, these edicts and laws must be obeyed by anyone who hopes to live his or her life in relative 'peace'; in other words, those who desire peace need to conform.

The underground world is made up of resistance fighters, along with people who are imprisoned or sent to the camps—all of these people having been eliminated from the public space and thus rendered invisible. Alternatively, having escaped from prisons and camps, some of these individuals go into hiding and live 'invisibly' all the same. Such is the Wunderlich family: the husband has escaped from a concentration camp and is hidden in Katrina's village house by her father. Mr. Wunderlich had been involved in resistance activities, which consisted of publishing an underground newspaper—the activity for which he was interned in the camp. Mr. Wunderlich's wife Marianne, meanwhile, is in Luxembourg City and involved—like her husband—in the resistance. When Paul Joachim, a German civilian boy Katrina's age who lives in her village, finds Mr. Wunderlich's clothes, he thinks the man has escaped from the prison in Luxembourg City "where all the *unreliable* elements of your country" (Gleit 1945, 58, emphasis in the original) are held.

Complicating the Wunderlichs' situation still further is that they also have a baby, Sebastian, who is "in danger" (and will be saved later by Katrina). One might ask why Sebastian is in "*constant* danger" (my emphasis) throughout this novel. In fact, before the baby himself even appears, his precarious situation is already mentioned: we first learn of Sebastian when Rosamunde, a peasant woman from the village, asks Katrina to see Marianne Wunderlich and bring the baby to Rosamunde in the village, as he is in "danger." By the time Katrina sees the baby herself, he is six months old, and at this moment, while she looks at him in his mother's arms, Katrina compares him to Moses:

Sebastian seemed to her like Moses in his ark of bulrushes among the flags by the river's brink. Never had she seen anyone as *content* as he, and, perhaps, as *safe*. For what in all the world *could happen* to a baby like him? He was not more than six months old.[12] (Gleit 1945, 105, my emphasis)

It is not certain that the comparison with Moses would suggest that the child is Jewish, but this mention is not anodyne, and it could nevertheless suggest a certain similarity of condition with the Jews, who were also in "constant danger" at that time. Recall that Maria Gleit—the author herself—had fled Luxembourg with a Jewish companion, so the plight of the Jews was more than likely a theme of personal significance to her.

In any event, elsewhere, when Katrina sees little Sebastian a second time two years later, her mission is *still* to *rescue* him, but this time from the hands of Paul Joachim's mother, into whose hands Sebastian had eventually fallen due to a misunderstanding. By this point in the story, Frau Joachim has lost her Nazi son Paul; he has died because he will not betray refractories. Now she wishes to flee to Germany to raise Sebastian there and make a Nazi out of him.[13] Katrina's aim the second time she is tasked with the wellbeing of this child is, thus, to save him specifically from becoming a Nazi. However, even though the reasons for the first rescue remain unarticulated throughout the novel, a few details in relation to Sebastian could evoke a Jewish child in danger in occupied Luxembourg. First, *false papers* were needed for when he was to be handed over to Rosamunde, to save his life. Second, Sebastian's *blond, blue-eyed appearance* is portrayed as a matter of surprise. When Katrina sees him after two years—he is now two and a half—the book describes her reaction as follows:

Sebastian! She had not expected him to have the blond curls, the long, upturned lashes, the rosy cheeks. Breathless with delight and anxiety, she bent over him and touched his hands. [...] The child opened his eyes. Dark-blue eyes with an almost-black sheen. (Gleit 1945, 218)

Katrina's surprise, states the text, is due to the fact that she did not expect him to have blond curls or dark-blue eyes. This astonishment, together with the book's repeated references to the young child being *in danger* and the fact that Katrina had associated him in his infancy with the Bible story from the *Book of Exodus* about the *baby Moses* being left in a basket among the reeds by his mother so as to prevent him from being *killed* as a Hebrew boy, all indeed seem to suggest to the reader that the child could be Jewish, even if the text never makes an explicit claim to that end. Interestingly, while these vagaries—mere *suggestions* about the danger that even the youngest of Jews faced—are the novel's only hint of a reference to the experience of Luxembourg's Jews at all, this element introduces an additional dimension to the underground space by involving, even if not naming, the Jews alongside the undesirable (invisible) groups. For, the main focus of the fable remains—as stated above—life under the occupation, and especially the particular situation in which Luxembourg found itself, in relation to the rest of occupied Europe, as an annexed territory:

> And by the way, the Yellow had added before he left, the strike was at an end, Luxembourg was legally a part of Germany now, hundreds of unreliable elements who were opposed to this state of affairs were being deported to labor and extermination camps in Poland and East Prussia, other scores of people had been shot in the streets—but order was restored again throughout the Gau Moselland, trains were running, factories working, the stubbornness of the people was broken, once, said the Yellow, and for all… (Gleit 1945, 196)

The novel emphasizes how this annexation was executed, how Luxembourg was incorporated into the Reich: "legally." All opposition has been "broken," which is to imply that the "unreliable elements" have been evicted; they were deported to the labor or extermination camps, leaving only the obedient among the community. Luxembourgers as a nation no longer exist. They have become Germans. French has been banished: "'They have proclaimed the annexation of the Grand Duchy of Luxembourg today,' he explained. 'We are not Luxembourgers anymore; we are Germans, or so they say. We are part of the Great German Reich'" (Gleit, 1945, 150). And in this world, as Indo Inasari also emphasizes of Soviet-occupied Georgia, ideology takes the place of man, or rather thinks *in the place* of man:

> [T]hey announced that from now on all Luxembourgers were Germans, and that they should not only be extremely grateful for this good fortune, but also from now on must never again undertake to think any thoughts but those allowed to them by the Nazis. (Gleit, 1945, 174)

Annexation, however—becoming German—includes simultaneously thinking like a Nazi. Those who constitute the underground world are totally non-existent within the Nazi world, as if the former exist outside the grounds, outside the living space, of their previous communities. Hence, the word "vanished" comes up in reference to those who manage to escape the camps, the prisons, the Nazi space—such as "the priest [who] seemed to have *vanished* from the earth"[14] (Gleit, 1945, 176, emphasis in the original). The space of resistance is an unseizable space, a space that cannot exist as *geographical* space (after all, when one inhabits this space, one is "vanished from the earth")—but it is a space from which one can nevertheless lead a struggle. A space that is not visible but, all the same, definitely exists, such as the underground passages of Luxembourg City, or the cellars where the refractories called 'deserters' hide—a space that the village priest, also, secretly joins.

In this context, an interesting episode arises when the Nazi guards are searching for Raymond, a resistance fighter; as they check the city's districts, the houses' rooms are ransacked and "*change* their appearance" (Gleit, 1945, 132, my emphasis). Yet once the Nazi guards have left—having failed to find the man (who ultimately entered Mrs. Wunderlich's room to hide)—the city takes on an unusual appearance: "The houses seemed to move even closer to one another in their desire for protection. Only the house of Madame Wunderlich, apart as it stood, appeared, even in distress, too proud to signal defeat" (Gleit 1945, 134). The occupation of the city by the "new masters" (Gleit 1945, 132), as the book often calls them, seems to introduce metaphorically an urban reorganization through a fantastical element (i.e., buildings that move). Raymond's enigmatic 'disappearance' from Mrs. Wunderlich's house (where he entered and where the guards did not find him) is explained by the underground passages that allow for displacement and a hidden existence. "We have a secret passage here, Katrina... That's what he came to my house for, you see?" (Gleit 1945, 141). It is, in fact, this sort of "subterranean passage" (Gleit 1945, 141) that also allows the printing of underground newspapers to continue—an activity about whose utility the young Katrina feels rather skeptical.

In the subsequent section, we come back to a work of Georgian exile literature and see that the hidden spaces—which, in Gleit's case, allow the refractories to 'disappear,' enable the characters to save lives, and lead ultimately to a victory over the oppressor's regime—do not always facilitate an equally victorious final result.

George Kipiani: "From Reality to Reality: The Liberation of Paris—At the Heart of a Georgian Exile"

George Kipiani's book *Poetic Works: 1930–1965*, published in Paris in 1965, consists of poems written in Georgian between the 1930s and 1960s and is concluded by an essay titled "From Reality to Reality." This essay has the distinction of being the book's only work that is presented there in two languages; that is, the Georgian version of the essay was translated into French. There is a note at the bottom of the page that this translation was made by a certain M. L. Z., but it is also possible that Kipiani translated his work by himself and then had his translation reviewed by a translator; Kipiani had a habit of self-translating without attributing his translations to himself.[15]

This text at the very end of the book interests me the most. Composed in 1944, "From Reality to Reality" is followed by a subtitle: *La libération de Paris.*

Au cœur d'un exil géorgien ("The Liberation of Paris: At the Heart of a Georgian Exile"). The story transpires over the course of one day and focuses on the narrator-protagonist, a Georgian emigrant (most likely Kipiani himself), who, on the day of Paris's Liberation, goes out for a walk in the streets. The passersby he meets, the joy he sees all around him, provoke equivocal feelings: on the one hand, he shares the happiness of the locals' liberation—as a Georgian, he can empathize with the experience of one's country being occupied. On the other hand, the sight of the Soviet insignia, the Stalinist flag—Russia now having become Hitler's great conqueror—leaves the narrator feeling deeply distressed for the fate of Georgia, which is still under the sway of the bloody tyrant, Stalin.

While he walks through the streets of Paris at the very moment of its liberation, a passerby addresses him, remarking that the weather is pleasant, and the interaction inspires the following reflection in the narrator's mind:

> Yes, for the country where I live, the weather is indeed fine that day! France—until then bound hand and foot—has just broken its chains and thrown off the heavy slab that crushed its chest… France is celebrating Victory. [...] Alas, today, my kind-hearted host, you will not hear me—for I am in pain… (Kipiani 1965, 262)

This pain comes from the fact that he notices, in one of the city squares, the "strange flag dipped in blood. The flag of the traitor, the occupier, the unsatisfied despot"[16] (Kipiani 1965, 267)—the red flag bearing the hammer and sickle. It goes without saying that the flag Kipiani notices in the square is the Soviet flag. The fact that Paris is celebrating the victory of a tyrannical ally—the Soviet Union—provokes a feeling for the poet that contrasts with that of liberated France, because his native Georgia is still "under the Russian sway."

Let us briefly consider the textual differences between the two versions. Only the French version has a subtitle, which is absent from the Georgian one. Instead, the latter bears a dedication: "To Ketevan Dadiani's daughter" (ქუმღვნი ქეთევან დადიანის ასულს). So let us note at the outset that the Georgian *national* context is removed in the target language (French) and that therefore this latter version is more concise. Consider the following excerpt from the Georgian version (my translation); the lines that appear below in italics are missing from the French text and appear *only* in the Georgian one:

> This is a strange flat I live in.
> I don't like it. *It doesn't like me either. We can't stand each other.*
> My infinitely restless soul cannot rest. *I feel like running away, recounting something to someone, telling something to someone, maybe someone will understand me. Understand what? I don't know either.*[17]

I close the door behind me and go out into the street.
Paris is a vast and beautiful city, but for me, as much as this city is beautiful, it
is also rude; as much as it is smiling, it is also full of sorrow, where the laughter
of others—translates into tears for me. The happiness of others—is my misfortune
and so,
I tread with my emaciated feet, my mind in disarray
The sunburnt asphalt pavement.
A passerby greets me:
"Good morning! Nice weather, isn't it?"
Nature is astonishing: it has endowed each language
With particular expressions.
We both know that the weather is fine;
We both see clearly, and yet,
It seems essential to confirm it:
"Nice weather, isn't it?"[18] (Kipiani 1965, 261–62)

According to Christian Lagarde, changing language involves "rethinking oneself" (Lagarde 2013, 11). From this perspective, the question to be asked is precisely why the author chose to self-translate, and especially why he chose to translate only *this particular text* and not any others from the same book? Moreover, why did he not translate this text in its entirety? These choices indicate—quite blatantly—that Kipiani was "rethinking" his original (Georgian) thoughts and how they would be received by his French audience.

Although the passage above is just a small excerpt, it should be noted, first, that in the fuller text, the French version suppresses and reduces to a minimum the Georgian-national context. This becomes apparent not only through the discrepancy between the Georgian and French subtitles (the former version forgoing a subtitle entirely), but above all by the omission of proper nouns that carry very strong socio-historical connotations in reference to the trauma of Georgia's occupation by Russia. The transposition of these proper nouns into the French version would be entirely devoid of any understanding or meaning unless accompanied by an exegesis each time. This problem concerns proper nouns such as—for just a few examples—"Tabakhmela" and "Kodjori" (names of Georgian places) or names of months ("August," "February"); all of these terms would be immediately recognizable to a Georgian readership, as they evoke the Sovietization of Georgia and the country's bloody struggles against its Russian occupier, yet—without an explanation at the bottom of the page—would have no meaning for, or be confusing to, the French public.

Second, the French version is also almost entirely devoid of any of the Georgian version's criticism of the Soviet Union. In fact, instead of expressing itself in terms of "despot," "bloody," or "occupier" with regard to the figure of Stalin (as the Georgian version does), the self-translated French version is nearly silent, or at the very least anemic, on these themes. It replaces them with comparatively subtler expressions, such as "the iniquity of things" or "even the villains seem good to you"—simply indicating that victorious France, rid of fascism, fails to perceive the true face of its ally: Stalin. Thus, the (self-)translation almost entirely *conceals* the intensity of the author's feelings at the time of the liberation; the truth and the reality are suggested, but not expressly stated.

From then on, the quasi-mutism on historical events, the alienation (linguistic, cultural) of the writer-emigrant from the space in which he is inscribed at the moment of writing, shows his total solitude, as well as the inability—of literature—to make important truths of his heard. Kipiani's narrator-protagonist thus makes clear that liberation—the open emergence into and the reclaiming of the public space—does not necessarily mean leaving clandestinity behind.

Clandestinity, therefore, deserves further exploration, and it is this condition that I will now address—this time through a pictorial example that takes us back to the spatial claustration that man experiences in the face of unprecedented events.

What is the Place of the Exiled within Legitimate Space?

It is undoubtedly *Les clandestins du quai Van Dijck* (1942) ("The Clandestines of the Van Dijck Quay")[19], a painting by Belgian painter Jan Cox, that can best illustrate the spatial arrangement in which protagonists evoke this condition of the person enclosed in confined spaces—and, accordingly, absent from open, visible, and identifiable spaces.

Painted during the occupation of Belgium, this work shows three protagonists, each in a different posture and all in a confined space. Probably an attic, the space is entirely closed in on itself and off from the outside; it lacks even a single window (or, at least, no window is visible). For although the interplays of light and shadow on the floor might suggest a source of light, the perspective adopted does not reveal the presence of any opening through which this exterior light might emerge. Within the space, there is but a single piece of wooden furniture, seemingly a bed. A woman lies on it, eyes closed, in a position of despair. Another figure, probably a child or teenager, is sitting on the bed, resting their face in their hands as they gaze upwards, as if waiting for salvation—a posture that at once seems to blend expectation with despair. The third figure, at the far edge of the image, is essentially in the background, seated on a wooden staircase that leads nowhere and whose height reaches the ceiling. A candle illuminating his face shows a look of extreme fear; he seems completely terrified.

The sensation of this absolutely closed place (there is a door ajar revealing only darkness behind it) gives the impression of, on the one hand, a disaster having already happened and, on the other, an expectation—an expectation linked not to some kind of hope, but rather to a fear of being discovered. Thus the title of the painting, which centers on the condition of clandestine people.[20] Several visual elements indicate that this could be a family in hiding and not a group of resistance fighters, in an absolutely precarious position—no visible food, and not even any clear impression of clothing (the characters instead appear to be *draped* amorphously in cloth, rather than wearing any distinct styles). Their total despair and terror could reflect the condition of Jews, especially in 1942 when the first roundups were being organized in Belgium. Besides, if Cox had wanted to paint resistance fighters, he would probably not have depicted two adults with a child.

This image, which bears witness to the immediacy of the historical events—to the clandestine, *outlaw* condition—in which certain categories of people suddenly found themselves is a kind of anticipation of the painter's later works that depict the atrocities of World War II. "It took thirty years before I could visually express any of the horror and despair I have witnessed and suffered in the war" (Cox 1976, 9), Cox notes about the late paintings in which he illustrates the *Iliad*. This war experience makes him feel that there is no longer anything to be proud of as a human being (Cox 1976, 9). "I have lived all these years with the melancholy of disillusion and the nearly guilty feeling for my miraculous survival. I have seen innocent people beaten to death" (Cox 1976, 9).

Across Cox's works, there is a kind of claustration of a living body, of its imprisonment in a constricted space. This shrinking of (living) space, often staged in various ways—whether in the visual arts, in literature, or any other artistic medium—introduces complex questions regarding the effects that such claustration can produce. Throughout the arts, and especially in the literary texts we are dealing with here, the repercussions of historical events of oppression, injustice, and disenfranchisement are routinely approached from the perspective that man was evicted from a space he no was longer authorized to occupy. This gradual contraction of his universe finally forced him into total invisibility: he was driven out of space long before the gas chambers were put in place and the Gulag was created.

Analyzing images (whether photos, advertisements, films, etc.) in relation to space—given that every image inherently contains an "error" (i.e., an illusion) for the fact that it is, by nature, an incomplete representation—Henri Lefebvre notes that an image can in no way "expose" its error on a space, but, on the contrary, "the image is more likely to secret [that error]" (Lefebvre 1991, 96). The error or illusion is thus "reinforced" by the image, instead of being "revealed" (Lefebvre 1991, 96)—for the error lies in the way that an image "fragments" a space (Lefebvre 1991, 97). Indeed, an image itself is a "fragment of space" (Lefebvre 1991, 97).

"Cutting things up and rearranging them, *decoupage* and *montage*—these are the alpha and omega of the art of image-making" (Lefebvre 1991, 97). The optical and visual world (which includes the artist's eye, the drafter's pencil, or the photographer's lens) is an "integral and integrative," "active and passive," part of the illusion (Lefebvre 1991, 97). Nevertheless, an exception could occur, "the tenderness or cruelty" of the artist could "transgress" the "limits of the image" (Lefebvre 1991, 97) and another reality, another truth than that of exactness, may then emerge.

The same is undoubtedly true of the texts analyzed above, if we consider these texts as akin to those images that capture fragments of space. Do these works manage to transcend exactness and reveal another reality, through the fragments of space that their narratives create?

Let us take George Kipiani's Paris as an example: the 'artist's eye' places before the reader a space in which figures and their dynamics—passersby, a jubilant crowd, the relationships we observe between strangers who exchange smiles and platitudes (meaningless conversations, people simply eager to communicate after so much suffering)—contribute to an atmosphere of joy that animates the whole city. In addition, places that Kipiani lists are attached to a certain Parisian (and national) urban symbolism: the narrator passes the Tomb of the Unknown Soldier "buried under a heap of multicolored flowers," the "Champs-Élysées and the great resplendent cafés" (Kipiani 1965, 263). But this joyful reality is suddenly interrupted: he mentally transports himself to his homeland, seeing himself running to his childhood home where his mother should be waiting. In fact, Kipiani's narrator begins his story by closing the door behind him as he leaves his exile home ("I close the door behind me and go out into the street" [Kipiani 1965, 261]). In his daydream, he "runs" *toward* the house of his childhood—but there, his mother ('Deda')[21] lies dying on the bed. His pained reverie constitutes a large portion of this text, ending finally with a return to the 'real' space: once again, as earlier in his excursion, someone on the streets of Paris remarks on what a nice day it is.

The two spaces that interfere here, by means of—according to the Lefebvrean formula—artistic "tenderness or cruelty," manage to reveal another truth: one that is not visible from the perspective of anyone but the narrator, an émigré who keeps his *mutism* among the French passersby ("I can't utter a word or even a sound", Kipiani 1965, 262). He does not express himself. The fragment of a whole other space—the Soviet space, seen in the blood-red flag—is not even visualized linguistically (as the French version of the text is devoid of the words that the Georgian version invokes for the Soviet leader). But it is notably the story of his dream (the images of his dying mother, the visions of his devastated homeland) that implicitly introduces, in the French version, what the narrator does not outright articulate from the Georgian version concerning the historico-political context. Thus, this other space—the world in which the Soviet flag of the liberator can be seen as that of a bloodthirsty tyrant—is indeed present in the French version regardless (even though not directly articulated there), behind the façade of the jubilant crowd.

"Those who produced space," writes Lefebvre, "were not the same people as managed it, as used it to organize social production and reproduction" (Lefebvre 1991, 48). If we transpose this reasoning to the context on which this chapter focuses, those who actually produce space (at least in the fictional worlds explored here) are indeed those who do not manage it, but they *contribute to* shaping it: the escaped prisoners, the resistance fighters, dislocate the newly constituted and recently organized space—a "repressive" (Lefebvre 1991, 49) space—from which they were evicted. The underground space in *Katrina* breaks down the space that the new masters have imagined. For it is not enough to imagine and design, or even to produce—because spaces exist in *permanent* production, as Lefebvre points out. And we can observe the same process with Inasari: within the new Soviet space, in which women are chased and assaulted and men suffer for resisting the new ideology (i.e., they are sent to the camps and killed), a marginal space—one of resistance fighters—is nevertheless emerging and thus reshaping the existing, 'official' one.

Conclusion

Through the works examined here, a space emerges that is constructed on the margins of 'legal,' supposedly 'legitimate' space. This new marginal space is formed by those who have no right to be part of the legitimate space or, in other words, even simply to exist. But the type of space that emerges in these works here is also a *literary* space constructed by a 'foreign' gaze—by someone who is not really part of the geographical place about which he writes to begin with.

Indeed, he is not part of *any* geographical place anymore: his are the gaze and the perspective of the exile.

Not only does he find himself exiled *from* a place; he retains his exile condition wherever he lives. In this sense, he is not able to participate fully in the experience of the space where he lives. Take Kipiani in Paris, for example; even when the liberation occurs, due to how his exile experience *conditions* his sentiments, he is unable to embrace the liberation as uncomplicatedly as the Parisians do. Furthermore, unlike the Parisians', his voice remains neglected and unheard even when Nazism comes to an end, for the other violent regime is still present—not only in a separate geographical place far away (i.e., his native Georgia) but also right *there*, in the very space in which he finds himself exiled: Soviet insignia, which has now appeared in Paris, comes to haunt the streets in which he walks.

While Kipiani at least tries to articulate (partially) his words for the audience of his host country, some exile authors remain confined to absolute mutism. Here, we look to Inasari, who traces a narrative about Soviet atrocities, knowing from the outset that no one will hear him—except the exiled Georgian minority. Yet in Inasari's case, just the same as Kipiani's, we see how the marginal (i.e., literary) space is constituted backwards, from within the official, institutional one.

At the same time, exile writers show us that the spaces outside of the (institutional) legal space can actually *save* those who are marginalized. Recall how, in Gleit's novel, the marginal space is what allows the resistance to rescue a child from the grips of the Nazis. In this sense, Gleit's oeuvre (much like Jan Cox's painting) makes the illegal, technically 'nonexistent' space visible for the reader (spectator) and thus—by rendering it visible—attempts to restore 'reality'[22] to this 'invisible' space by integrating it back into the space from which it has been extirpated.

Notes

1. This work is linked to the project WRITERS, supported by NIAS—Netherlands Institute for Advanced Study in the Humanities and Social Sciences. All quotes from non-English resources are my translations.
2. In the sense that the Nazis' regimes in France and in Luxembourg differed.
3. Indo Inasari, a Georgian writer, refers to the Soviet space as an "illegitimate country." This designation refers, on the one hand, to the regime's hijacking of the entire legislative and social system and, on the other, to Russia's 'illegitimate' occupation of Georgia. This term could also be applied to the other regime—the Nazi regime.
4. Soviet, as well as Nazi ideology form the only 'legal' space to which one must conform; all those who do not conform or who oppose it are immediately marginalized or eliminated.
5. As no official English translation exists, the author of this chapter has translated all passages seen here from the Georgian texts.
6. Indo Inasari is the pseudonym of Nikoloz Inasaridze.
7. Varlam Shalamov's *Kolyma Stories* deal with his experience in the Kolyma camps, where he spent more than seventeen years after being arrested for anti-Soviet propaganda. The stories are unique in their genre and provide a harrowing account of the reality of the Gulag. See Shalamov 2018.
8. Georgian word for 'Georgia.'
9. Since this is a very broad and complex subject, it will not be developed here.
10. The work of the famous Georgian writer, poet, and playwright Vazha-Pshavela (1861–1915), *The Host and the Guest*, probably best describes this Georgian custom: even if the guest turns out to be the worst enemy of the village, and consequently of the host in

whose house he is staying, the latter will defend him with a weapon in his hand against the whole village that demands his punishment—because what prevails above all other concerns is his *condition* of being the *guest*.

11. See *A Child of Our Time* (1938).
12. I emphasize to highlight how much the text insists on the fact of his 'safety' on the one hand and the 'danger' he faces on the other.
13. "You see, he's very precious to me. He's my nephew [lies Frau Joachim not to admit that she stole the child], but I intend to raise him as if he were my own son. I lost my own son, you see. He turned traitor to our holy Nazi cause. But this little boy in the back room, he'll become a real Nazi. I'll see to that" (Gleit 1945, 217).
14. I emphasize.
15. See Sharadze 1991, 282, 301.
16. This sentence is present only in the Georgian version, as the French and Georgian versions differ from each other. I will return to this point later.
17. I have kept the triple use of 'someone' from the original. As for the concept of 'understanding' in connection with the condition of exile, of stranger, in George Kipiani's and in other Georgian emigrant authors' works, due to the breadth of the subject, I will not dwell on it in this chapter.
18. The original version (Italics indicate Georgian text that I translated into French):
    Il est étrange cet appartement que j'habite.
    Je ne l'aime pas. *Il ne m'aime pas non plus. Nous ne pouvons pas nous supporter.*
    Mon âme infiniment agitée n'y trouve pas de repos. *J'ai envie de fuir, raconter quelque chose à quelqu'un, conter quelque chose à quelqu'un, peut-être que quelqu'un me comprendra. Comprendra quoi ? Moi non plus, je n'en sais rien.*
    Je referme la porte derrière moi et sors dans la rue.
    Paris est une ville vaste et belle, mais pour moi autant cette ville est belle, autant elle est grossière; autant elle est souriante, autant pleine de chagrin, où le rire d'autrui—se traduit en larmes pour moi. Le bonheur d'autrui—est mon malheur et ainsi,
    L'esprit en déroute, je foule de mes pieds amaigris
    La chaussée asphaltée brûlante de soleil.
    Un passant me salue :
    "Bonjour ! Beau temps, n'est-ce pas ?…"
    La Nature est étonnante : elle a doté chaque langue
    D'expressions particulières.
    Tous deux nous savons qu'il fait beau;
    Tous deux nous voyons clair, et cependant,
    Il apparaît indispensable de le confirmer :
    "Beau temps, n'est-ce pas ?"
19. According to the editions, the title of the painting, whose current collection is unknown, can differ. In one of the variants, it is entitled *La dissimulation du quai Van*

Dyck. Other versions propose the following titles: *Les résistants du quai Van Dyck*, 1942 (Devillez 2003, 216); *Les clandestins du quai Van Dijck*, 1942 (Duvosquel and Deraeve 1992, 15). The imagine is in a private collection; a reproduction can be found online at: https://www.wikiart.org/en/jan-cox/the-hiding-1942 (accessed February, 21 2024.)

20. Jan Cox, who returned from Brussels after the Gestapo failed to appreciate his paintings—judging them to be 'degenerate'—settled in Antwerp on the Ernest Van Dyck Quay, where "his attic studio soon became a refuge for trapped friends and maquisards, both foreign and Belgian" (Corbet 1952, 11). It is also known that he painted these friends.

21. The Georgian word 'deda,' meaning 'mother,' is transcribed into French. This transposition of the word from one language onto the other further accentuates the exilic dimension and the intensity of the feeling.

22. If we take the word in the sense that Inasari uses it.

References

Corbet, Augus. 1952. *Jan Cox*. Antwerp: De Sikkel.

Cox, Jan. 1976. *L'Iliade d'Homère*. Exhibition 26 March—23 May 1976. Brussels: Musées Royaux des Beaux-Arts de Belgique.

Devillez, Virginie. 2003. *Le retour à l'ordre: Art et politique en Belgique*. Brussels: Éditions Labor.

Duvosquel, Jean-Marie, and Jacques Deraeve, eds. 1992. *La jeune peinture belge: 1945–1948*. Introduction by Ph. Roberts-Jones. Curated by Serge Goyens de Heusch. Brussels: Crédit Communal de Belgique.

Gleit, Maria. 1945. *Katrina: A Story of Luxembourg*. Illustrations by Nedda Walker. New York: Charles Scribner's Sons.

Grosz, George. [1936] 1976. *Interregnum*. Faksimiledruck der Ausgabe New York 1936. Mit einem farbigen Frontispiz und 64 Tafeln. Frankfurt a.M.: Propyläen.

Heimberg, Anke. 2002. "'Schreiben kann man überall. Das ist das Gute an meinem Beruf': Die Schriftstellerin Maria Gleit (1909–1981) im Exil." In *Gender—Exil—Schreiben*, edited by Julia Schöll, 41–68. Würzburg: Königshausen und Neumann.

Horvath, Ödön von. 1938. *A Child of our Time*. Translated by R. Wills Thomas. With a foreword by Franz Werfel and an appreciation by Stefan Zweig. London: Methuen.

Hurlock, Kathryn. 2022. "Peace, Politics, and Piety: Catholic Pilgrimage in Wartime Europe, 1939–1945." *War and Society* 41, no. 1: 36–52.

Inasari, Indo. 1936. ჩრდილი ერთი სინამდვილის. *L'Ombre d'une vérité* ["The Shadow of a Truth"]. Paris: J. Nikichine.

Kipiani, George. 1965. *Œuvres poétiques: 1930–1965*. Paris: l'auteur, 11, rue Villedo.

Klemperer, Victor. 2000. *LTI: The Language of the Third Reich*. London: N. J., Athlone Press.

Lagarde, Christian. 2013. "Avant-propos. L'autotraduction: *terra incognita* ?" In *L'Autotraduction aux frontières de la langue et de la culture*, edited by Christian Lagarde and Helena Tanqueiro. 9–22. Limoges: Lambert-Lucas.

Lefebvre, Henri. 1991. *The Production of the Space*. Translated by Donald Nicholson-Smith. Oxford: Blackwell.

Schütz, Alfred. 1944. "The Stranger: An Essay in Social Psychology." *American Journal of Sociology* 49, no 6 (May): 499–507.

Shalamov, Varlam. 2018. *Kolyma Stories*. New York: New York Review Books.

Sharadze, Guram. 1991. უცხოეთის ცის ქვეშ ["Under the Foreign Sky"]. Vol. 1. Tbilisi: Merani.

CHAPTER 7

Semantics of Occupation(s) in Pierre Grégoire's *Europäische Suite* Trilogy

Catholicism, Anticommunism, and the Idea of Luxembourgish Exceptionalism

DANIELA LIEB

The role of armed conflict in the formation of nations and nation-states has increasingly come within the purview of historical research (Langewiesche 2000, 26–31; 2019, 261–336), and such is also apparent in the case of Luxembourg. The Grand Duchy, which owes its statehood to the reorganization of Europe after the Coalition Wars against Napoleon (1792–1815), began to manifest a sense of its own identity during what became known as the Luxembourg Crisis (1867), when the country was at risk of being sold to France.[1] An important vehicle for the consolidation of a discrete national identity, however—perceived as distinct mainly by comparison to neighboring Germany—was the occupation of neutral and demilitarized Luxembourg by German troops during World War I (Pauly 2011, 82–86). Afterwards, the 1930s represented a precarious period in the realm of foreign policy when, on the one hand, the country was struggling to come to terms with the trauma of World War I while, on the other hand, fearing for its independence in the face of National Socialist expansionism. Finally, the cardinal experience of the second occupation of Luxembourg on May 10, 1940, and the country's de facto annexation by the Third Reich (Pauly 2011, 93–104), completed the nation-building process.

While the enforced conformity (*Gleichschaltung*) of all areas of political, social, and cultural life (Conter et al. 2020, 100–43) meant that only a small number of Luxembourgish authors continued to publish during the occupation (Conter et al. 2020, 334–423), the liberation by US troops on September 10, 1944—and especially the return of citizens from resettlement, prison, and concentration camps in 1945 (Pauly 2011, 102)—resulted in an extensive body of texts, most of them factual reports (Conter et al. 2020, 427–579). With additional groups of people (conscientious objectors, deserters, escape agents), along with the inclusion of the first and second post-war generations, this body of writing continues to grow even now.

By comparison, fictional output has been much scanter, although it is experiencing an extraordinary boom at the moment, especially in the form of novels.[2] Against this backdrop, Pierre Grégoire's trilogy *Europäische Suite* (1951–52) ("European Suite") is a remarkably rare exception, despite its being partly autobiographical, the author having spent almost five years in Nazi prisons and concentration camps. Its singular nature is no doubt due to the fact that Grégoire (1907–1991), unlike most other chroniclers of the war, was already a long-established writer at the time of the work's publication. Not only was he able to look back on many years of working as a journalist on the editorial staff of the *Luxemburger Wort* ("Luxembourg Times"), the Grand Duchy's most important daily newspaper, where he had been in charge of the culture desk since 1933; he also had several literary publications to his credit, including the collection of poems *Im Atemwarm der Ewigkeit* ("In the Warm Breath of Eternity"), with which he achieved his first big literary success in 1936, and the novel *Semlia. Die benedeite Kraft der Erde* (1939) ("Semlia. The Blessed Power of the Soil"). As early as 1945, immediately after his return from Mauthausen, Grégoire published his *Kleines Vorspiel zum KZ* ("Little Prelude to the Concentration Camp"). This was followed a year later by *Die Cäsur der Entscheidung: Gefängnisse und Konzentrationslager 1940–1945* ("The Caesura of Decision: Prisons and Concentration Camps 1940–1945"). With these personal accounts, the author made a substantial contribution to the codification of Luxembourg's experience of the war. Perceived as both a historical and an existential watershed, this experience also permeated Grégoire's tracts *Die Gnadenstunde des Abendlandes* ("The West's Hour of Grace"), published in 1950 under the pseudonym Gregor Stein and *Rot sind die Reiter der Apokalypse* (1950) ("Red are the Horsemen of the Apocalypse"), published under the pseudonym Erio. Both deal with the political architecture of post-war Europe from a distinctly Roman Catholic point of view.

The present chapter focuses on three complementary strands of discourse in *Europäische Suite.* First, it aims to show the means by which the trilogy draws a line of continuity from National Socialist dictatorship to communist dictatorship—political systems for which Grégoire suggests that the values of the Roman Catholic 'West' are the only possible corrective; the 'West,' in turn, only achieves full legitimacy when set against the contrasting backdrop of an 'East' that is at once morally inferior and in need of redemption. Second, this chapter examines the question of how, and with which ideological intentions, the trilogy systemically inscribes itself into contemporary Roman Catholic/conservative Luxembourgish literature. Finally, the chapter aims to outline how all the figures of thought in Grégoire's *Suite* are packaged and mobilized to serve the notion of a Luxembourg that is superior in terms both of ethics and civilization.

The analysis does not always follow the chronological order of the events described in the novel but rather is thematically organized. Such an approach is fitting, given the structure of the *Suite* itself, which presents a relatively poor plot that serves as a mere backdrop for ideological concerns.

Spain as the Road to Damascus

At 600 pages, *Europäische Suite* is the longest and ideologically densest work of fiction within Grégoire's wide-ranging 46-volume oeuvre. It is also the most complex regarding its temporal and spatial structure. The first two parts of the trilogy, titled *Der spanische Wirbel* ("The Spanish Vortex") and *Der deutsche Totentanz* ("The German Danse Macabre"), appeared as a single volume in 1951; the third part followed in 1952 under the title *Das russische Gespensterballett* ("The Russian Ghost Ballet"). The role of publisher fell to *Der Freundeskreis* ("The Circle of Friends"), a Roman Catholic book distributor founded in 1937 or 1938 (exact year unknown) with Grégoire's participation. To ensure wider distribution, *Der Freundeskreis* included the trilogy in its recently launched series of "obligatory books" (*Pflichtbücher*).[3]

Europäische Suite narrates the life and suffering of a young Luxembourger called Camille Hubert. In the first part, he abruptly leaves his home country after falling out with his relatives and initially travels to France. In Marseille, he meets a Spanish expatriate, alongside whom he volunteers in the Spanish Civil War, joining the Republican side. With the conflict in Spain (1936–39; for a history of events, cf. Collado 2006), Grégoire refers to an event that was the subject of extensive and controversial public discussion in Luxembourg, especially in the two daily newspapers, *Luxemburger Wort* and *Escher Tageblatt* ("Esch Daily News"), which competed both politically and ideologically. Moreover, the Spanish Civil War was, in many ways, interwoven with domestic Luxembourgish realities. In the opinion of left-wing circles in particular, the struggle in Spain was the prelude to a much greater, even global conflict—a view that also finds its way into the trilogy. Indeed, Camille addresses the events in Spain as "the world's opening battle for the highest gift of humanity" (Grégoire 1951, 73)[4] and infers a duty to support the democratically legitimized Republican order. The Civil War, in which Hitler's Germany (as well as Mussolini's Italy) intervened on the side of the insurgents from the summer of 1936 onwards (Collado 2006, 91–166), is often associated with Nazi expansionism and, following the occupation of the Rhineland in March 1936, with growing concern for the survival of Luxembourg's neutrality. "Spain's freedom is our freedom, for behind Franco and Mola stand Hitler and Mussolini. If Spain were to become a deployment zone for

Hitler's Germany, our fate would also be sealed," warned Victor Bodson, Socialist Deputy in Luxembourg's national legislature and Luxembourg's Vice-Consul to the Spanish Republic.[5]

At the same time, the conflict in Spain seemed an acute reflection of the problems at home: the political landscape in Luxembourg was divided into a right-wing conservative and a left-wing liberal camp. This polarization came to a head in June 1937, when the controversial "Muzzle Law" (*Maulkorbgesetz*) was narrowly rejected in a referendum (Wehenkel 2012). The law, ostensibly designed to ban the Communist Party, actually sought to prevent *any* political activity that was not along the lines of government policy. When the international community's increasing involvement in the Civil War finally spread to the Grand Duchy, 88 men who can be identified by name (Wehenkel 1985, 53–54; 1997, 119–21) joined the ranks of the International Brigades (Berg 2005). Most were miners and metalworkers from the heavily industrialized south of the country. However, in April 1937, at the height of the debates surrounding the "Muzzle Law," the Chamber of Deputies passed legislation criminalizing participation in the Spanish Civil War. This law was in keeping with the policy of non-interference initiated by London (Collado 2006, 144–66), and it applied to citizens of Luxembourg as well as foreign nationals who were resident in the Grand Duchy (except for the Spanish). This measure was of fundamental importance for the status of those who had fought in Spain, both upon their return to Luxembourg in 1938–39[6] and following the occupation of the country by German troops on May 10, 1940. By the end of 1940, and with the help of lists previously drawn up by the Luxembourg police, most of those who had returned from Spain had been arrested and deported to German prisons and concentration camps. Any Italian nationals among their number were extradited to fascist Italy (Wehenkel 1997, 93–106).

This, briefly, is the historical background against which Grégoire set the plot of *Europäische Suite*. As will become evident, the protagonist Camille Hubert's deployment to the Spanish front is the pivotal point in the trilogy in two respects: on the one hand, it serves as the trigger for the protagonist's conversion from an atheist to a religious worldview and, on the other hand, it is the reason for his persecution by the National Socialist occupation forces.

Grégoire was a staunch Roman Catholic and, as we shall see, he created his hero along autobiographical lines. It may initially seem surprising, then, that he has this same hero fight on the side of the Spanish Republic and (at least initially) act as a mouthpiece for anti-clerical positions.[7] However, the unfolding plot makes it clear that Grégoire is merely setting the scene for Camille's commitment to Roman Catholic values and, by doing so, the author is preparing to introduce the discourse figure of the unavoidably religious basis of all historical action. That includes, first, morally discrediting the Republican troops; during the voyage to Barcelona, Camille meets several future members of the International Brigades whose lack of discipline and whose deficient ethos (being mainly braggarts, drunkards, and womanizers) make Franco's victory seem inevitable. These shortfalls are principally concentrated in a character who is given the moniker of 'the Tilsiter,' who operates on behalf of the Soviet Union. With this figure, Grégoire not only creates the German Other—indispensable to forging Luxembourg's national identity since World War I—but also the radical Other of a non-, even an *anti*-European 'East': "For he is a German. No, he is already a 20th-century Muscovite. But we, my friends, are still the great Europeans, the last true Westerners" (Grégoire 1951, 59). This idea of an opposition between the communist 'East' (constantly expanding its politico-ideological sphere of influence) and the (necessarily Roman Catholic) 'West'—an opposition that it is impossible to overcome—goes on to occupy an increasingly prominent place in the second, and especially the third, part of the trilogy.

Figure 1: Devotional image of the *Christus cardiophorus*, 1906. Diocesan Archives of Luxembourg (DAL), Théophile Walin Bequest 172_0307.

Camille's conversion to Roman Catholic values is precipitated by his spectacular rescue, thanks to a statue of the Sacred Heart of Jesus, an iconographic representation of the Savior carrying his heart in his hands (an image most formally known as the *Christus cardiophorus*). In this pivotal scene, Camille and his fellow fighters are defending a village against Francoist troops, and they are holed up in its church when the Sacred Heart sculpture softens the impact of a falling roof beam and saves Camille from certain death. He is subsequently rescued by enemy soldiers and taken to a military hospital, where one of his feet is amputated.

Another decisive influence on Camille's future appears in the guise of Luxembourgish national Jeannie Jacobs, a fervent Roman Catholic and devotee of the Sacred Heart, whom he had scorned and reviled for her religiosity at the beginning of the book. Now, on his sickbed, he is nursed by a veiled young woman who turns out to be Jeannie. Her face is marked by three deep, cross-shaped scars, inflicted by a Republican soldier when she had tried to protect a Sacred Heart statue from desecration. Under the influence of Jeannie, with whom he falls in love, Camille progressively distances himself from his former atheism. At the end of *Der spanische Wirbel,* the pair, now engaged, return to Luxembourg together.

Biographical Aside 1: The Author as Fictional Character

By having his protagonist turn toward Roman Catholicism, Grégoire may conceivably be offering an analogy of his own transition from progressive to conservative literature. The author made his debut in the left-leaning journal *Junge Welt* ("Young World") in 1928. Yet just a year later, he turned to denominational publishing bodies and institutions; for example, the student magazine *Academia*, the neo-conservative *Jonghémecht* ("Young Homeland"), and the Sankt Paulus publishing house, which was run by the diocese of Luxembourg. During his later career as a journalist and writer, which spanned more than half a century, Grégoire would increasingly make his mark as an unwavering Roman Catholic intellectual.

It is interesting to observe how Grégoire constructs numerous parallels between his own life[8] and that of Camille Hubert, especially in *Der deutsche Totentanz.* On May 10, 1940, the day the Grand Duchy was occupied by the *Wehrmacht,* Grégoire wrote an article titled *Luxemburg von den Deutschen besetzt* ("Luxembourg Occupied by the Germans"). When this and other writings fell victim to the censorship that the occupier immediately imposed, the *Luxemburger Wort* editors decided not to recast the printing plates. Instead, as Grégoire explains in his account *Die Cäsur der Entscheidung,* they opted to excise the offending passages from the lead plates and print them blank. "Accordingly, the newspaper appeared on that 10th of May with four large, white oases in its twelve-page textual desert" (Grégoire 1946, 26). Only the title and the first sentence of his own article were visible. Then, between May 17 and 29, Grégoire published the column *Von Tag zu Tag* ("From Day to Day"), based on the *Mein Kriegstagebuch* ("War Diary") of Batty Esch, a fellow journalist who had been arrested by the *Gestapo* on May 11. In defiance of the censors, Grégoire repeatedly attempted:

> to show my compatriots, in veiled hints, the path they must take to safeguard our country's existence. I know I am playing a dangerous game, one that may not always succeed, since many contributions are simply deleted by the *Sonderführer*, but I venture to do so tirelessly, with increasing pleasure whenever I prevail. (Grégoire 1946, 34)

In early September of that year, inspired by the sight of a worker from the south of Luxembourg who was armed with a club and who was defiantly displaying a pin with the red national lion,[9] Grégoire wrote and distributed the poem *Lôsst Klöppele wuessen!* ("Let Clubs Grow!"). In it, he calls on his compatriots to stop felling oak trees and let them grow instead, for when the war is over, they will be needed for clubs to beat the Nazi collaborators and drive them out of the country.

Figure 2: Pins (*Spéngelen*, in Luxembourgish) with national symbols, 1939. Archives communales de Sanem. Photograph: Christof Weber.

On the sixth of that month, Grégoire was taken into custody, along with three fellow journalists, following a search of the *Wort*'s editorial office. He was held in Luxembourg's city prison and later transferred to Trier. After being briefly released, he was re-arrested on December 17 and was moved to Berlin. It was not until July 1941, the following year, that a so-called protective custody order (*Schutzhaftbefehl*) was issued against him. The charges included tendentious reporting and establishing a secret anti-German organization. On August 8, Grégoire was sent to Sachsenhausen concentration camp, where he remained until October 20, 1944, when he was transferred to Mauthausen. At Mauthausen, he and five other Luxembourgish inmates joined an international resistance group set up shortly before the camp was liberated. He set out on his return journey to Luxembourg on May 25, 1945.

These key biographical data form the narrative framework of the second volume of *Europäische Suite*. Back in Luxembourg, Camille Hubert volunteers for the French and Belgian air forces at the outbreak of World War II but is rejected because of his amputated foot. Anticipating Hitler's invasion of Luxembourg, he sets up a resistance network. However, he (like Grégoire) is arrested by the *Gestapo* and moved to Germany. With the help of a German dissident, he manages to escape and makes his way back to Luxembourg but (also like Grégoire) is once again arrested and deported to Germany. After a long ordeal in various prisons, he is interned (here, too, like Grégoire) in Sachsenhausen concentration camp.

As a former Spanish Civil War fighter, Camille is assigned to a punishment unit at Sachsenhausen, where he meets the Tilsiter again. Shortly before the war's end, the camp *Kommandant* decides to set up a camp brothel and sends for a randomly selected inmate from Ravensbrück women's concentration camp. She turns out to be none other than Jeannie Jacobs, who had been arrested because of her close links to Camille. However, before the brothel is set up, Jeannie and Camille manage to escape. Shortly afterwards, they encounter the first Red Army units. At this point, in parallel with the impending rupture of the anti-Hitler coalition, the novel begins to draw on Roman Catholic discourse figures and a Western ideology with religious overtones—to which the Soviet Union stands in irreconcilable opposition.

Europäische Suite as a Martyrs' Mirror of the Occupation

Toward the end of *Der deutsche Totentanz*, the notion of a 'West' based on Roman Catholicism increasingly takes shape. In Camille Hubert's judgment, however, the Western world has been exposed to destructive forces since the beginning of the modern era, a process that temporarily culminated in the tyranny of

National Socialism. The following installment, *Das russische Gespensterballett*, leaves no doubt that Bolshevism poses a much more acute threat, first establishing its hold on Europe by dispatching political commissars to the Spanish Civil War, and now continuing its expansion unimpeded in the Soviet occupation zone. The proposition of continuity between National Socialist and communist dictatorship is central to the trilogy; with it, Grégoire harks back to a mentifact he had previously developed in the tracts *Die Gnadenstunde des Abendlandes* and *Rot sind die Reiter der Apokalypse* in 1950.

Moreover, it appears that with the *Suite*, he fashioned a fictional framework for the figures of thought he had already outlined in his earlier texts. In these earlier texts, just as in the trilogy, author and *dramatis persona* merge to become one voice; Grégoire's fictional and expositional utterances coalesce into a single continuum of speech shared by all his writings. In light of this observation, not only is it virtually impossible to make an accurate distinction between novel and essay; it is also not very productive, as it blinds the reader to ideological continuities and convergences.

Die Gnadenstunde des Abendlandes, published before the trilogy, had been the result of Grégoire's critical examination of the European Movement's cultural conference, held in Lausanne at the end of 1949. It communicates his rejection of the secular direction taken on that occasion. The relatively slim volume already contains the essential outlines of his Western ideology: that as a result of the Reformation, the Enlightenment, and the bourgeois revolutions, Europe has lost its denominational unity and hence its politico-spiritual primacy, ultimately degenerating into a "Cape of Bad Hope on the continent of Asia" (Grégoire 1950a, 13). Only a comprehensive Christian—that is, Roman Catholic—renaissance is presumed capable of restoring the West's historical supremacy. In this context, Grégoire updated some of the proposals put forward in the 1930s by the *Luxemburger Wort*, especially by its main ideologue Batty Esch, in favor of transforming the Grand Duchy into an ecclesiastical corporative state. To these, Grégoire added the vision of a messianic-soteriological figure that would restore the lost *unitas catholica* and wrest Europe from the supposed Asian hegemony. The idea of an *ecclesia militans* led by the papacy, which would return Europe to the rank of a "continent above all continents" (Grégoire 1950a, 87), becomes ever more explicit.

In this context, the theme of spiritual and secular martyrdom is given special weight. According to Grégoire, the present, more than any other historical era, is especially suited to firm up Christian resistance and produce numerous martyrs, those "prudent masters and chosen spirits" who "give humanity back its belief in the meaning of existence" (Grégoire 1950a, 84). In keeping with this idea, *Rot sind die Reiter der Apokalypse* repeatedly refers to religious persecution in the communist countries of the Eastern Bloc, particularly the persecution of (mainly Roman Catholic) dissident clerics, such as Archbishop Alojzije Stepinac of Zagreb, Archbishop Ivan Sarič of Sarajevo, or Jozsef Mindszenty, Roman Catholic Primate of Hungary.[10] In accordance with this well-established trend in Grégoire's thinking, Camille Hubert and Jeannie Jacobs sacrifice themselves at the end of *Europäische Suite* to save the life of a child (the embodiment of 'defenseless' Europe in the face of the communist onslaught). By that act, they become 'blood witnesses' and reach the end of the path on which they first embarked in Spain.

In *Mein Buch der Tausend Sprüche* (1969) ("My Book of a Thousand Sayings"), Grégoire says of himself that even before he became interested in politics, ethics, metaphysics, and theology had long since "played their role [in him] and never finished" (Grégoire 1969, 253). With this cluster of themes, he turns his attention to an essential aspect of the history of the church and salvation, namely the concept of the Imitation of Christ. This notion, which originally referred to the way of life practiced by the disciples and the early church, underwent a fundamental transformation over the course of its historical and theological development. It changed from largely non-binding discipleship (*akolouthein*) to obligatory and regulated imitation of Jesus (*mimesis* or *imitatio*). From one era to the next, this, in turn, was variously interpreted as life testimony or blood witness (*martýrion*). In the 2nd century, the letters of Ignatius of Antioch and the description of the martyrdom of Polycarp of Smyrna introduce an interpretation of *imitatio*, in the sense of a genuine experience of Christ's sufferings (Milchner 2004, 7–48). Numerous passages from *Europäische Suite, Die Gnadenstunde des Abendlandes*, and *Rot sind die Reiter der Apokalypse* suggest that it is precisely this early Christian ideology of martyrdom—which incorporates pagan notions of a 'noble death,' as well as later mystical ideas—that underpins Grégoire's understanding of an ethically, politically, and culturally productive acceptance of the cross. To that effect, Camille repeatedly emphasizes the parallel between Christian antiquity and the year 1945, and then continues by recommending the Passion as the most suitable means of overcoming the European 'crisis':

> We are too apt to deny ourselves the redemptive power that arises from dolor as a balm of His sorrows, because we are too lukewarm and too sluggish to render the frightfulness of the Lord's crucifixion fruitful through sharing in His torture. But the most powerful creative force grows out of fires survived, and all destruction, even the most distant and the most terrible of the soul, can be healed by activating the Passion. That is the greatest contradiction and probably the most incomprehensible. But it alone can be capable of driving the well-meaning individual, who is beginning to live according to the intentions of the dying Redeemer, [...] through all torments, to spur them on to all actions, and in all situations of earthly

> futility to discover the solution to mundane problems in the Eternal above. […]
> No time has been more favorable than ours, which has strung suffering next to
> suffering and adversity next to sorrow, if we are to secure for humanity all the
> possible ways of fully grasping the meaning of the first Passion in its voluntary
> recreation, of burning out humanity's core in order to fill it with the driving force
> of a greater expectation. (Grégoire 1952, 185)

As a consequence, *Europäische Suite* not only ties in with concepts of *imitatio*
theology, but also with the religious building blocks of Luxembourg's national
identity: after World War I, and increasingly during the 1930s, the idea that the
country enjoyed a privileged relationship (especially applicable in times of crisis)
with God and the Virgin Mary came into ever sharper focus. Against this backdrop, the theological charge of World War II seems entirely unsurprising. This
took the form of, for instance, establishing a cult of the Comforter of the Reset-
tled[11] in Bohemian and Silesian camps, or symbolically aligning Grand Duchess
Charlotte with the Virgin Mary, as occurred in particular circles of the resistance
(Conter et al. 2020, 61–62). The liberation of Luxembourg and its later recognition as an equal partner within the post-war political order (for example, as a
founding member of the North Atlantic Treaty Organization NATO in 1949), or
within the framework of European integration, gave fresh impetus to the confident notion that the country enjoyed special status within the salvation event.
This is also clearly expressed in a passage from the final chapter of Grégoire's
Cäsur der Entscheidung:

> God needs Luxembourg so He can fulfil part of His great plan with her. And as
> much as we have recognised, in this most recent world war as in the previous one,
> that it would be more proper to remain quite modest and say, "Luxembourg needs
> God," we are no less aware—from experiencing those same wars—that He has
> preserved her twice most miraculously, for us and hence for Himself. (Grégoire
> 1946, 233)

Also revealing at this point is the fact that the occupation of Luxembourg (which
was in breach of international law), combined with the country's large number of
war victims in relation to its total population, and the extensive destruction following the Battle of the Bulge (December 1944–January 1945), rapidly brought
about a martyrological interpretation of the war experience (Conter et al. 2020,
517–20, 570–72). To this day, the multiple *Places des Martyres* (Martyrs' Squares)
and *Rues des Sacrifiés* (Roads of the Sacrificed) found throughout the Grand
Duchy continue to perpetuate this view in the public space. The *Musée National
de la Résistance* (National Museum of the Resistance) in Esch-sur-Alzette, which

Figure 3: *Musée National de la Résistance* in Esch-sur-Alzette (2008).
Photograph: Frank Schroeder.

has existed since 1956 and was, for decades, ideologically controlled by former resistance fighters, also has a normative effect in this respect. A sarcophagus containing human remains outside the main entrance, plus several urns filled with soil from various concentration camps in the foyer, unquestionably confer upon the institution the character of a reliquary of Luxembourg's resistance.[12] In terms of the history of ideas, the *Europäische Suite*'s discourse on martyrdom fits seamlessly into this context.

Grégoire's Barbarian 'East': On the Genealogy of a *locus terribilis*

In *Das russische Gespensterballett*, Camille Hubert and Jeannie Jacobs decide to return to Luxembourg. A breathless odyssey across the Soviet occupation zone begins, during which the protagonists are constantly exposed to the twofold risk of either being seized by Russian occupation troops or tracked down by the Tilsiter. The latter wants to eliminate Camille on behalf of the Union of Soviet Socialist Republics (USSR) because of the information he acquired during the Spanish Civil War (i.e., about the communist infiltration of the West). In a parallel plotline, Nikela Holper, a friend of Camille's who has returned from forced resettlement, engages the Luxembourgish officer René Travor to search for the missing pair. At times, Travor is assisted by Maria Dominique, former communist and confidante of the Tilsiter's, who is now a renegade. It is conceivable that Grégoire has woven elements of his own life into the narrative, specifically his return from Mauthausen concentration camp.

During their perilous trek, Jeannie and Camille repeatedly encounter Red Army troops, whose 'primitive nature,' 'stupidity,' and 'bestiality' are frequently highlighted. The contrast between the 'satanic' *homo sovieticus* and the values of the Roman Catholic 'West' becomes more and more distinct. The irrevocable dichotomy of 'East' and 'West' is entwined with the previously outlined martyr ethos, which recommends a productive, heroic death on the cross to the best and noblest of Europeans as the only means of redeeming the 'West.'

It has become a commonplace of cultural studies to recognize and examine how collective identities constitute themselves by excluding the ethnic, cultural, and linguistic Other. Given that field of reference, it is worth pursuing the question of how not only the *Suite* but also Grégoire's earlier works *Die Gnadenstunde des Abendlandes* and *Rot sind die Reiter der Apokalypse* conceptualize the construct of an anti-European 'East' against which the 'West' is able to define itself as the one and only 'real' Europe. Examining the term 'Eastern Europe' shows that it does not describe a fixed geographical area. As a 19th-century coinage and creation, it instead reflects the West's changed historical awareness following the remapping of Europe at the Congress of Vienna (1815). Before that date, Slavic peoples—above all, Russians and Poles—were assigned to the North, in accordance with ancient tradition. The East was reserved for the 'Orient' (not least the Holy Land). Locating Russia in the North allowed lines of continuity to be established with 'barbarian' peoples of late antiquity (e.g., the Goths) and their attacks on the Roman Empire. It also enabled association with attributes such as darkness, cold (up to and including 'General Winter'), and certain animals (the 'Russian bear'), as well as recourse to the Old Testament identification of the North as the seat of Satan and of evil. The construct of savagery and menace acquired an additional aspect when the weighty ideological baggage borne by the term 'Orient'—due to the confrontation between the European powers and the Ottoman Empire—was transferred to post-Petrine Russia. The discursive expansion and the new ambiguity of the 'East'—coupled with the concurrent terminological reduction of 'North' to the Scandinavian peninsula—led to the idea of Russia's otherness vis-à-vis the West being codified. The anti-Bolshevik furore of the inter-war period and the formation of blocs during the Cold War cemented the formula of the "rift between East and West" (Lemberg 1985[13]).

It was from this iconological cache that both *Europäische Suite* and the earlier tracts, *Die Gnadenstunde des Abendlandes* and *Rot sind die Reiter der Apokalypse*, derived the notion of a barbaric 'East,' with which "the finer measures of our West" (Grégoire 1952, 66) are contrasted. In the *Suite*, this construct begins with crimes of the Red Army, especially rapes and thefts of jewelry and watches, to which Camille Hubert is an eye- and earwitness when he crosses the Soviet occupation zone. The image thus evoked of the "violators of honor from the steppes" (Grégoire 1952, 9) is complemented by the concept of "idiots from the East," a concept Grégoire had already developed in *Rot sind die Reiter der Apokalypse* (Grégoire 1950b, 146); this occurs after the encounter with a soldier called Vasya Demidov (an aptonym composed of French *demi* and German *doof*, i.e., 'half-wit'), who is incapable of even winding a wristwatch. Moreover, it is striking that Grégoire has recourse to vocabulary borrowed from the fields of zoology, pathology, and racial hygiene—vocabulary previously deployed in the 1930s by the *Luxemburger Wort* as part of its approach to 'Bolsheviks,' including domestic left-wing forces. Accordingly, in *Rot sind die Reiter der Apokalypse*, here is talk of "hyenas of historical materialism" (Grégoire 1950b, 199), "parasitism" (Grégoire 1950b, 77), "plague germ," "bacillus of corruption," infected "cells," and contaminated "bloodstreams" (Grégoire 1950b, 94). He also invokes the original semantics of the term "barbarian" in the sense of onomatopoeic reduplication ('blah blah'). From this perspective, political and cultural otherness, especially communism and non-Catholicism, are seen as a deformation of 'nature,' particularly as a perversion of a 'healthy' Luxembourgish constitution. Even linguistic difference is easily rendered in biological terms: as *Rot sind die Reiter der Apokalypse* implies, Western European tongues cannot possibly pronounce Slavic languages. As such, Slavic names are supposedly not articulated, but "spat out" (Grégoire 1950b, 46); in order to pronounce them properly, the (Catholic) Westerner would need a 'sick,' 'denatured' tongue. The *Suite* concludes this 'diagnosis' with the hostile stereotype of the animalistic, cognitively and culturally inferior barbarian from the 'East,' who, since the Spanish Civil War, has been ushering in the "most nightmarish reign of all times, that of bestiality" (Grégoire 1952, 72) in Europe, driven by ignorance of Western values, blind hatred, and the will to destroy.

It is interesting to note that with the topos of the barbarian, Grégoire draws on traditional Slavophobic figures of thought that hark back to the German Empire (Schaller 2002). These were adopted by National Socialism, racially exacerbated, and turned into an essential ideological component of the struggle for *Lebensraum* in the East. At the same time, (exiled) German dissidents like Klaus Mann or Ernst Toller employ almost identical discursive strategies to delegitimize the Hitler regime by qualifying Nazis as savage, stupid, and uncultured barbarians (Wagner 2016). Grégoire himself makes abundant use of such rhetoric in his writing, for instance in the second volume of the *Suite*. Moreover, his portrayal of National Socialist and Soviet barbarity as equivalents prefigures the equation of fascist totalitarianism with its communist counterpart, the latter being widespread in the post-communist states of Eastern Europe, and the idea of a second, 'red Holocaust' that derives from it. This form of 'memory appropriation,' in which the crimes against European Jews during World War II are relegated to the background in favor of highlighting one's own suffering under communism, takes center stage in Jelena Subotić's monograph *Yellow Star, Red Star* (2019, 6–13, 17–44).

In Western historiography, extending the concept of the 'East' has resulted in the idea of a (semi-)Asian Russia, to which supposedly 'Oriental' characteristics, such as backwardness, despotism, cruelty, disorder, and irrationality, are attributed. Added to this are associations from the semantic field of hordes, swarms, multitudes, and sheer quantity not covered by the notion of 'North.' Both the *Suite* and its predecessor *Rot sind die Reiter der Apokalypse* follow this line of tradition, for instance by qualifying the Soviet Union as the epitome of a mass

Figure 4: Cover of *Rot sind die Reiter der Apokalypse* by an unnamed graphic artist.

society (Grégoire 1950b, 9) or by advancing the idea of Russian "hordes" invading the West (Grégoire 1952, 184). Along with a poetics of the flat landscape (the 'Russian steppes,' Grégoire 1950b, 238; 1952, 9, 113), these further reinforce the notion of Russia's alien nature in comparison to Europe.

In keeping with this discursive practice, *Rot sind die Reiter der Apokalypse* places Slavic ethnicity in a *locus horribilis* of deliberate geographical vagueness; for example, in the wasteland of the "Russian Empire" (Grégoire 1950b, 248) or the unfathomable "great red space" (Grégoire 1950b, 58). Such Orientalization strategies also lead to supposed continuities with Central Asian horse peoples; in this view, the Russians are "Mongol types" and, as such, followers of a "Tatar-barbarian doctrine of existence" (Grégoire 1950b, 88). Lenin, Stalin, and Molotov appear as successors to the Mongolian Khagans. According to the chapter *Im Osten nichts Neues* ("Nothing New on the Eastern Front") in *Rot sind die Reiter der Apokalypse*, the "red tide" inundating Europe—and the continent's imminent transformation into a Soviet fringe—is nothing other than a reenactment of the Mongol invasions of the Middle Ages. In this context, it is hardly surprising that Grégoire explicitly refers to *Ystoria Mongalorum*, written in the 1240s by Johannes de Plano Carpini, a Franciscan monk and explorer from Italy. Once Grégoire has delineated the continuity of the Mongol Empire and the Soviet Union, the eschatological interpretation of Mongol expansion allows him to declare Russia the domain of Cain, Lenin a half-demon, and Stalin the perfect embodiment of Satan. The title of the tract, and the matching cover design, only gain their full significance in light of such interconnections.

Nostos: A Genre Shared within Luxembourgish Literature?

In *Der deutsche Totentanz*, Camille Hubert, appalled by his compatriots' passivity in the face of foreign policy developments and by their careless assessment of the looming world war, founds a resistance group even before the German invasion. By having his protagonist return from Spain specifically at a time when Luxembourg is experiencing a serious crisis due to aggressive German expansionism, Grégoire presumably inscribes himself in a firmly established narrative that has been hitherto widely ignored by literary scholars.

As Pit Peporté, Sonja Kmec, Benoît Majerus, and Nicolas Margue demonstrate in their essential monograph *Inventing Luxembourg* (2010), Luxembourg's nation-building processes always operate both centrifugally and centripetally. The effect of this complementary counter-flow is also evident in developments during the 1930s, which were precarious in terms of foreign policy. The concept of legitimate Luxembourgish statehood,[14] as directed toward Germany, always goes hand in hand with the idea, aimed at the domestic sphere, of seamless national cohesion beyond all economic, social, or ideological particularities. After 1935 at the latest, literature, especially where it is conservative–denominational in kind, was substantially involved in the project of the symbolic integration of all Luxembourgers into a (supposedly) homogeneous community. What is striking in this connection is a theme that is repeatedly addressed in many different variations: that of the micro- and macro-historically relevant homecoming—to one's family, from the city to one's native village, from a foreign country to Luxembourg—in short, to a *status quo ante* that is seen as morally superior.

Two examples may illustrate how these texts guide dissident individuals back into the community and mobilize them for national purposes. In the story *Ruf der Heimat* ("Call of the Homeland"), published in 1935, Albert Elsen describes the fate of a child who, following the death of his foster mother, leaves the Luxembourgish village where he grew up. Twenty years later, in 1914, he is one of the German soldiers occupying Luxembourg. Falling seriously ill, he is taken in and cared for by his childhood sweetheart, of all people. At the moment of death, he acknowledges Luxembourg as his homeland, "which recalls its most distant children and leaves them no peace until they have returned" (Elsen 1935, 96). In 1939, Adolf Weis published *Der nächtliche Pilger* ("The Nocturnal Pilgrim"), a story with a similar ideological timbre, in which an offender is accepted back into his former village community after his release. Since the events take place during the Octave of Our Lady,[15] he even finds his way back into the bosom of the Church.

Integrative utopian narratives such as these reach an unprecedented peak in 1939, as the international situation is rapidly deteriorating; it is unsurprising that not only individuals but also entire (fringe) groups are now addressed and symbolically recruited for the upcoming "spiritual national defense."[16] One example is the play *Vu mengem Dueref gong ech hier* (1939) ("From My Village I Came Here") by André Schoder. The piece features two emigrants who return to their village on the centennial of Luxembourg's independence, after a lengthy spell working as farm laborers in the United States.[17] Another publication that is revealing in this context is *Dohém. E klengt Spill aus schwe'rer Zeit* ("Home: A Little Play from Hard Times") by Adolf Weis. There, again on the day of the centennial, a Luxembourger volunteer returns from the Spanish Civil War. Back home, not only is he fully rehabilitated, but he even distinguishes himself as a leader of the future resistance, thanks to military skills acquired in the Battles of the Ebro and Teruel. The blueprint presented by the author displays remarkable resolve: the events of the crisis-ridden year 1938—the *Anschluss* (annexation) of Austria and the Sudeten crisis—have brought the immediate prospect of a pan-European conflict into view. While, on the eve of war, diplomacy still (half-heartedly) trusts in the binding force of international treaties and the Hitler regime's recognition of Luxembourg's neutrality, the play contrasts the precarious security situation with a utopian scenario of self-directed militant action (Lieb 2022). In this vein, with Camille Hubert's return from the Spanish Civil War, Grégoire takes Adolf Weis's embryonic figure of thought—of continuity between involvement in Spain and a campaign in the service of a free Luxembourg—and develops it into the pivotal point of his *Europäische Suite*. Nor is Grégoire content to let his protagonist's return from Spain suffice; with Camille's efforts to reach Luxembourg after the end of World War II, Grégoire portrays a second homecoming—granted, one that is prevented, but no less symbolically relevant.

The *Cäsur der Entscheidung* indirectly provides information about what could have motivated that second homecoming. In that piece, Grégoire describes his own return from Mauthausen as a contribution to the body of faith that is Roman Catholicism and to the fight against the religion's decline:

> Through reflection, my homecoming thus evolved into repentance that drives a man to salvation. Everyone's salvation begins with my salvation, which becomes yours before it shall become [another's]. Its tenor is: return to the abundance of Roman Catholicism and to a complete rejection of all compromises with one's neighbor who is lukewarm. (Grégoire 1946, 233)

When trying to categorize Luxembourg's conservative/Roman Catholic literature of the 1930s, as well as the personal accounts published after the war of returnees from resettlement, prisons, and concentration camps, the concept of *nostos* may prove useful, along with its corollaries, *anabasis* and *katabasis*. *Nostos,* familiar from the Homeric epics, especially the *Odyssey,* denotes the Achaeans' return from the Trojan War, as well as homecoming epics as a literary genre (Bonifazi 2009). Incidentally, the late-17th-century coinage 'nostalgia' also derives from the term.[18] The appeal of ancient terminology in discussing 20th-century wars is highlighted by historical events such as the Siberian *anabasis* ('deployment') of the Czechoslovak Legions (1918–1920),[19] but also by texts such as Rudolf Borchardt's *Anabasis* (addressed by Jan Andres in his chapter in this volume), and by historical research such as Kenneth Estes's monograph *A European Anabasis,* which studies foreign units in the ranks of the *Wehrmacht* and the *Waffen-SS* (2015). Moreover, several publications (Clauss 2008; Martiny 2010; Gardner and Murnaghan 2014; Riley 2019) have convincingly demonstrated that including the *nostos* category in the study of modern literature and film can promote new understanding.

Along the same vein, Camille Hubert's physically and psychologically traumatic experiences both in Spain and in Nazi Germany, and later in the Soviet occupation zone, suggest that *katabasis* may prove a useful analytical tool as well;

katabasis often precedes *nostos,* especially in its connotation of a descent (originally a descent by Odysseus, Orpheus, and other mythological figures) into the underworld (Frost and Laing 2012). Exploiting the hermeneutic potential of *katabasis* may prove particularly profitable, given that literary studies (e.g., Falconer 2005, 63–112, 224–31) have expanded the term's range of meaning to include spaces featuring the experience of violence—from Auschwitz, to the wars in Afghanistan and Iraq, and to the 9/11 attacks—as contemporary concepts of hell.

Taking a closer look at the above-mentioned Luxembourgish literary output with *nostos* in mind might help to bring (seemingly) disparate texts together in a thematically coherent body of work, reveal strong rhizomatic links, and thus assist in gaining interesting insights. Such an undertaking would be all the more fruitful, given that, even on cursory inspection, it is apparent that a specific feature of Luxembourgish *nostoi* entails interweaving the theme of homecoming with a multitude of politically and ideologically topical discourses. For example, in the play *Vu mengem Dueref gong ech hier,* the Grand Duchy's apologia that it is the best, most peaceful, and most freedom-loving country, is intertwined with a harsh condemnation of both emigration and US materialism. *Dohém* by Adolf Weis, meanwhile, combines praise of Luxembourg as a land of 'proper' freedom with a condemnation of atheism. *Europäische Suite,* for its part, interweaves its protagonists' experiences with unwavering Roman Catholicism and virulent anti-communism, and draws its discursive consistency precisely from such amalgamations.

Biographical Aside 2: Between Luxocentrism and European Integration

The beginnings of Grégoire's political activity can be traced back to the 1930s, when he supported his publishing director, Jean Origer, as leader of the Party of the Right by taking charge of the party organization. However, his actual career as a politician began in 1946, when he was elected as Deputy for the *Chrëschtlech-Sozial Vollekspartei* (Christian Social People's Party, or "CSV"). From 1952 to 1962, he served as General Secretary. Partly overlapping this timeline, from 1959 to 1969, he also held various ministerial posts, including the Arts and Culture, Education, Civil Service, and Foreign Affairs portfolios. From 1969 to 1974, he was President—and afterwards Honorary President—of the Chamber of Deputies.

Of particular interest in this context is his membership of the Council of Europe, from 1956 onwards. In that capacity, he played an active part in the work of European unification. Bearing in mind that, as suggested earlier, Grégoire regarded life and writing largely as a single continuum, this involvement repeatedly found its way into his publications. While *Die Gnadenstunde des Abend-landes* and *Rot sind die Reiter der Apokalypse* map the breakup of the anti-Hitler coalition and the animosity of the Cold War, the tracts *Europa zwischen Angst und Hoffnung* (1970) ("Europe Between Fear and Hope") and *Der Übergang des Abendlandes* (1977) ("The Transition of the Occident") coincide with disarmament policy and the *Ostpolitik* of the late 1960s and the 1970s (Stöver 2017, 381–409). Both as a Roman Catholic writer and as a Christian conservative politician, Grégoire was probably keen not to abandon the 'East' completely, but rather to *include* it within the scope of the theological virtues of faith, hope, and charity. A monologue by Camille Hubert in the final chapter of *Europäische Suite*, in which the topos of the 'East' is combined with that of martyrdom, suggests this position:

> But we, who still believe and love amidst the inhumanity of hatred […] know that no bars and no walls are able to hold us, […] we already live beyond all restraints and soar towards eternal freedom, held and borne up. […] The East has gloriously integrated into the whole. And, whole and united, the West, transformed in its salvation and saved in its transformation, rejoices as it thunders the *Te Deum* aloft to us. (Grégoire 1952, 186)

As we come to the end of this analysis, it is worth taking a closer look at that passage, which denounces the ambivalence of the 'East' as a place of terror and desire, of well-established Luxembourgish (state) ideologemes, and of persistent Western European stereotypes—all at the same time. The political content of the rhetorical figure of the *Te Deum* can be gauged if one considers that it is still performed in the capital's cathedral[20] on Luxembourg's national holiday (i.e., on the sovereign's birthday[21]). In this context, the military element contained within the semantic spectrum of the *Te Deum* is especially significant; since the Baroque era, this has taken concrete form in the hymn being performed at victory celebrations. The famous *Te Deum*, H. 146, by Marc-Antoine Charpentier, composed on the occasion of the Battle of Steenkerke (1692);[22] George Frideric Handel's *Utrecht Te Deum*, HWV 278, marking the end of the War of the Spanish Succession (1713); and the same composer's *Dettingen Te Deum*, HWV 283, reflecting the victory of Austro-British troops at Dettingen (1743), are just a few examples of the close links between warfare and liturgy (Heinz 2010).

This nexus is also incorporated, albeit in an over-coded form, in the passage from *Europäische Suite* quoted above, which implies the notion—deeply rooted in public perception—of the 'East' as Europe's 'problem area,' requiring Western leadership and, if necessary, even military intervention. This view was still partly present during the Yugoslav Wars and in the run-up to the EU's eastward expansion. In *Rot sind die Reiter der Apokalypse,* Grégoire also involves the Grand Duchy in this eminently power-political discourse by invoking the medieval Holy Roman Emperors from the House of Luxembourg[23] as cultural heroes and pioneers of the European movement, who would have incorporated Czechs and Slovaks into the Holy Roman Empire. The 'return' of these territories would not only restore the lost unity of the 'West'; the imagined element of a cultural mission in the 'East' also lends Luxembourg the semblance of imperial prestige and allows the country, which notoriously struggles with its small dimensions (Linden 1999), to outgrow itself symbolically. In keeping with the previously outlined notion of the Grand Duchy's exceptional significance in the history of salvation, the figuration of a greater Luxembourg is part of a national self-image that consistently transforms geopolitical deficits into a superior (moral) capacity. That applies, if not in territorial terms, then at least—and even more so—in terms of civilization. Against this backdrop, it is quite unsurprising that Grégoire tacitly claims for Luxembourg the leading role in a united Europe.

Translated from German by Delphine Lettau

Notes

1. Accordingly, the sequence "de l'État à la nation" is seen as a fundamental paradigm of Luxembourg's history; cf. Trausch 1989. For the history of events, cf. Pauly 2011, 66–72.

2. Typical examples from recent years include Siggy Koenig's novel *Zakopane* (2020) and Jemp Schuster's extensive family saga *Bluttséffer* ("Blood Guzzlers") (2020) and *Ouereschléffer* ("Ear Pinchers") (2021). In the latter, World War II marks the transition between the two volumes.

3. 'Obligatory books' applied to three books (at least one of which had to be by a Luxembourgish writer) that needed to be purchased each year to maintain membership in *Der Freundeskreis.* The 'obligatory books' series may have been launched by Grégoire's story *Die Entdeckung des Giano Coricio* ("The Discovery of Giano Coricio") (1949), although the volume has no number. In 1951, *Der spanische Wirbel* and *Der deutsche Totentanz* were jointly added to the series as the third volume. In 1952, *Das russische Gespensterballett* became number six. Over the following three decades, the publisher repeatedly included publications by its 'in-house author' Grégoire in the series: *Die Geschichte der Filmkunst* (1955) ("The History of Cinematography"), *Kleine Spiele um den grossen Spieler* (1962) ("Little Plays around the Great Player"), *Mein Buch der Tausend Sprüche* (1969) ("My book of a thousand sayings"), *Der Übergang des Abendlandes* (1977) ("The transition of the Occident"), and, to conclude the series, *Luxemburgs Kulturentfaltung im neunzehnten Jahrhundert* (1981) ("Luxembourg's Cultural

Development in the Nineteenth Century"). Grégoire provided further evidence of his close links to the *Freundeskreis* (as well as of his personal intellectual authority) by writing the prefaces for other authors' books on several occasions.

4. Translations from non-English sources are from Delphine Lettau.

5. Given the sources currently available, the precise context in which this statement was made remains unclear. It was printed in *Luxemburger Wort* on April 17, 1937 without explanation, but with the Roman Catholic newspaper's typical polemical thrust in its dealings with left-wing politicians.

6. In the autumn of 1938, the International Brigades were disbanded by Spanish Prime Minister Juan Negrín and given a ceremonial send-off in Barcelona. However, some 2,000 fighters, including roughly a dozen volunteers from Luxembourg, remained in Spain and took part in the defense of Catalonia in January 1939. They only left the country after the Franco regime was officially recognized by France and the UK in March 1939.

7. For example, Camille Hubert voices an unexpectedly harsh opinion on conservative clerical forces in Luxembourg who openly sympathize with the putschists "because they wield incense and palm fronds to dispel the smell of the blood of those who have been massacred" (Grégoire 1951, 23).

8. To date, there has been no attempt at a biography of Grégoire that would even come close to meeting scholarly criteria. Moreover, since his papers remain inaccessible, no such publication is to be expected in the future. The key biographical data on which these remarks are based were painstakingly filtered out of the (emphatically hagiographical) Festschrift "Pierre Grégoire Seen Through the Eyes of His Friends" (*Pierre Grégoire gesehen mit den Augen seiner Freunde*, Heiderscheid and Hoffmann 1982), which was presented to him on his 75th birthday.

9. Large numbers of such pins (*Spéngelen*, in Luxembourgish) were distributed to the population during the 1939 centennial celebrations (cf. Endnote 17). In August 1940, when Luxembourg was assigned to the *Gau Moselland* and thus de facto annexed by the German Reich, many people expressed their protest by wearing similar pins showing the Red Lion, the likeness of Grand Duchess Charlotte, and other patriotic symbols. This act of passive resistance was to go down in Luxembourg's history as the "The War of the Pins" (*Spéngelskrich*). On November 22, 1940, the *Gauleiter* issued a decree ordering the destruction of all artifacts associated with the centennial. Some families consider it a privilege to have managed to save one or the other object and to have preserved it to this day.

10. The selectivity of Grégoire's criticism of communist crimes mainly manifests itself in the fact that he focuses almost exclusively on (high-ranking) members of the Roman Catholic clergy. Christian Orthodox (and even more so Islamic) Eastern Europe remains largely beyond the scope of his empathy. This gap quintessentially corresponds to the West's traditional unease toward Orthodox or Islamic theology, which is seen as

incapable of modernization; an attitude still present in Samuel P. Huntington's *Clash of Civilizations* (1996).

11. The cult is analogous to the veneration, deeply rooted in Luxembourg, of Our Lady of Consolation/the Comforter of the Afflicted (*Consolatrix Afflictorum*), patron saint of Luxembourg City since 1624, and of the country as a whole since 1678. For the associated Octave of Our Lady, cf. Endnote 15 below.

12. For some years now, the museum's management has been attempting to modernize the institution architecturally on the one hand, and refocus its activities on the other, from concentrating exclusively on the history of the Luxembourg Resistance to placing them in a supranational context of human rights, tolerance, and the promotion of democracy. On that point, cf. Thomas 2010.

13. The continuing validity of Lemberg's study, which is now almost 40 years old, was recently demonstrated by Schlupp 2019, using the example of Wallachia.

14. One particularity of Luxembourg's pre-war constructions of self is that state independence is always related to material, cultural, and moral achievements, so it is underpinned by argument: that Luxembourg deserves to be independent and remain so because it has its own language and culture, because Luxembourgers are peaceful and hard-working, etc. Only the country's liberation after World War II (and its abandonment of neutrality in favor of NATO membership) would lead to sovereignty being perceived as a non-negotiable status that no longer requires justification.

15. The Octave of Our Lady, which has been celebrated since the 17th century and is perceived as forging a sense of national identity, is the most important event in the Roman Catholic festival calendar in Luxembourg (cf. Kmec 2014).

16. In 1938, this was the slogan with which the literary and cultural magazine *Les Cahiers luxembourgeois* ("The Luxembourgish Revue") called on everyone involved in cultural life to speak out and actively support the Grand Duchy's independence (cf. Pétin 1938).

17. The centennial of Luxembourg's independence, celebrated at great expense in all the country's cantons from April to September 1939, included events such as parades, concerts, exhibitions, and the erection of monuments large and small. Numerous fictional and documentary publications appeared to mark the occasion. The celebrations were intended to demonstrate, especially to neighboring Germany, that the Grand Duchy had both the will and the ability to maintain its sovereignty. On this topic, cf., e.g., Wey 1989 and Staus 2000.

18. The term 'nostalgia' was coined by the Alsatian physician Johannes Hofer, who in his *Dissertatio Medica de ΝΟΣΤΑΛΓΙΑ, oder Heimwehe* ("Dissertatio Medica de ΝΟΣΤΑΛΓΙΑ, or Homesickness", Basel 1668) blended the two Greek words *nostos* (return) and *algos* (mourning) to describe the psychopathological condition of a Swiss mercenary far from home. For a literary analysis of the link between *nostos* and nostalgia, cf. Gerschmann 1975 and Pache 2008.

19. The *anabasis* of the Czechoslovak Legions was the protracted evacuation across Siberia of Czech and Slovak volunteer units fighting in Russia on the side of the Entente during World War I, and subsequently involved in the Russian Civil War. For the history of the legions, cf. Bullock 2009.

20. On the role of the *Te Deum* in an ethnically and culturally pluralistic society, long perceived as problematic in progressive circles, cf. Huss 2008. In 2013, the traditional *Te Deum* was for the first time preceded by an interfaith prayer. Since 2014, a civil ceremony has been held in the capital's Philharmonic Hall on the morning of June 23, with the traditional *Te Deum* in the cathedral being moved to the afternoon. Since the morning ceremony is the more prestigious of the two, the *Te Deum* has lost some of its former significance.

21. Since 1962, for reasons linked to the climate, the national holiday has been celebrated on June 23, regardless of the respective sovereign's actual birthday.

22. In 1954, Charpentier's composition embarked on a remarkable secular/civil career by being chosen as the Eurovision melody.

23. This refers to Henry VII, Charles IV, and Sigismund; cf. Pauly 2011, 34–44, who describes the activities of these emperors in a chapter headed "The Age of the Luxembourgers in Europe" (*Das Zeitalter der Luxemburger in Europa*). That medieval dynasty's exceptional and continuing contribution to forging the country's identity is conveyed by the Luxembourg government's website *LuXembourg—Let's make it happen*. The site introduces the three rulers under the headline "At the Helm of the Holy Roman Empire: The History of the Germanic Emperors of the Luxembourg Dynasty. Luxembourgers Holding the Reins of the Holy Empire." (Cf. LuXembourg: Let's Make it Happen).

References

Berg, Angela. 2005. *Die Internationalen Brigaden im Spanischen Bürgerkrieg, 1936–1939*. Essen: Klartext.

Bonifazi, Anna. 2009. "Inquiring into Nostos and Its Cognates." *American Journal of Philology* 130, no. 4 (Winter): 481–510.

Bullock, David. 2009. *The Czech Legion, 1914–20*. Oxford: Osprey.

Clauss, James J. 2008. "Hercules Unchained: Contaminatio, Nostos, Katabasis, and the Surreal." *Arethusa* 41, no. 1: 51–66.

Collado Seidel, Carlos. 2006. *Der Spanische Bürgerkrieg: Geschichte eines europäischen Konflikts*. München: C. H. Beck.

Conter, Claude D., Daniela Lieb, Marc Limpach, Sandra Schmit, Jeff Schmitz, and Josiane Weber. 2020. *Luxemburg und der Zweite Weltkrieg: Der literarisch-intellektuelle Diskurs zwischen Machtergreifung und Epuration*. Mersch: Centre national de littérature.

Elsen, Albert. 1935. "Ruf der Heimat." *Luxemburger Marienkalender* 54: 93–96.

Estes, Kenneth. 2015. *A European Anabasis: Western European Volunteers in the German Army and SS, 1940–45.* Solihull: Helion and Co.

Falconer, Rachel. 2005. *Hell in Contemporary Literature: Western Descent Narratives since 1945.* Edinburgh: Edinburgh University Press.

Frost, Warwick, and Jennifer Laing. 2012. "Travel as Hell: Exploring the Katabatic Structure of Travel Literature." *Literature & Aesthetics* 22, no. 1: 215–33.

Gardner, Hunter, and Sheila Murnaghan, eds. 2014. *Odyssean Identities in Modern Cultures: The Journey Home.* Columbus: Ohio State University Press.

Gerschmann, Karl-Heinz. 1975. "Johannes Hofers Dissertation 'De Nostalgia.'" *Archiv für Begriffsgeschichte* 19: 83–88.

Grégoire, Pierre. 1946. *Die Cäsur der Entscheidung: Gefängnisse und Konzentrationslager 1940–1945.* Luxembourg: Sankt-Paulus-Druckerei.

———. 1950a. *Die Gnadenstunde des Abendlandes.* Luxembourg: Sankt-Paulus-Druckerei.

———. 1950b. *Rot sind die Reiter der Apokalypse.* Luxembourg: Sankt-Paulus-Druckerei.

———. 1951. *Europäische Suite: Ein Roman in drei Teilen. Der spanische Wirbel. Der deutsche Totentanz.* Luxembourg: Der Freundeskreis.

———. 1952. *Europäische Suite: 3. Teil. Das russische Gespensterballett.* Luxembourg: Der Freundeskreis.

———. 1969. *Mein Buch der Tausend Sprüche.* Luxemburg: Der Freundeskreis.

Heiderscheid, André, and Fernand Hoffmann, eds. 1982. *Pierre Grégoire gesehen mit den Augen seiner Freunde.* Luxembourg: St-Paul.

Heinz, Andreas. 2010. *Lebendiges Erbe: Beiträge zur abendländischen Liturgie- und Frömmigkeitsgeschichte.* Tübingen and Basel: Franke.

Huss, Jean. 2008. "Te Deum oder integrativer Nationalfeiertag?" *Forum für Politik, Gesellschaft und Kultur* 33, no. 281 (November): 52–53.

Kmec, Sonja. 2014. "Die Muttergottesoktave im Wandel der Zeit." In *Luxemburg, eine Stadt in Europa: Schlaglichter auf mehr als 1000 Jahre europäische Stadtgeschichte,* edited by Marie-Paule Jungblut, Michel Pauly, and Heinz Reif, 270–84. Chemnitz: Germagz.

Langewiesche, Dieter. 2000. *Nation, Nationalismus, Nationalstaat in Deutschland und Europa.* Munich: Beck.

———. 2019. *Der gewaltsame Lehrer: Europas Kriege in der Moderne.* Munich: Beck.

Lemberg, Hans. 1985. "Zur Entstehung des Osteuropabegriffs im 19. Jahrhundert: Vom 'Norden' zum 'Osten' Europas." *Jahrbücher für Geschichte Osteuropas. Neue Folge* 33, no. 1: 48–91.

Lieb, Daniela. 2022. "Der 'Spueniekämpfer' in Adolf Weis' Theaterstück *Dohém*." *Hémecht: Zeitschrift für Luxemburger Geschichte* 74, no. 3: 331–45.

Linden, André. 1999. "'Un beau PETIT pays?': Bilder und Diskurse um das Luxemburg der fünfziger Jahre." In *Le Luxembourg des années 50: Une société de petite dimension entre tradition et modernité*, edited by Claude Wey, 197–243. Luxembourg: Musée d'histoire de la Ville de Luxembourg.

LuXembourg: Let's Make it Happen. n.d. "At the Helm of the Holy Roman Empire." Accessed August 19, 2022. https://luxembourg.public.lu/en/society-and-culture/history/helm-holy-roman-empire.html.

Martiny, Erik. 2010. "Modern Versions of Nostos and Katabasis: A Survey of Homeric Hypertexts in Recent Anglophone Poetry." *Anglia: Journal for English Philology* 127, no. 3: 474–85.

Milchner, Hans Jürgen. 2004. *Nachfolge Jesu und Imitatio Christi: Die theologische Entfaltung der Nachfolgethematik seit den Anfängen der Christenheit bis in die Zeit der devotio moderna.* Münster: Lit.

Pache, Corinne Ondine. 2008. "'That's What I'll Remember': Louise Glück's Odyssey from Nostos to Nostalgia." *Classical and Modern Literature* 28, no. 2: 1–14.

Pauly, Michel. 2011. *Geschichte Luxemburgs.* Munich: Beck.

Peporté, Pit, Sonja Kmec, Benoît Majerus, and Nicolas Margue. 2010. *Inventing Luxembourg: Representations of the Past, Space and Language from the Nineteenth to the Twenty-First Century.* Leiden: Brill.

Pétin, Jean. 1938. "Geistige Landesverteidigung: Lieux de Luxembourg." *Les Cahiers luxembourgeois* 15, no. 8: 907–10.

Riley, Kathleen. 2019. "'The Forewarned Journey Back': *Katabasis* as *Nostos* in the Poetry of Seamus Heaney." In *Seamus Heaney and the Classics: Bann Valley Muses*, edited by Stephen Harrison, Fiona Macintosh, and Helen Eastman, 205–22. New York: Oxford University Press.

Schaller, Helmut. 2002. *Der Nationalsozialismus und die Slawische Welt.* Regensburg: Pustet.

Schlupp, Ana-Maria. 2019. *Die Walachei: Zur Herausbildung eines literarischen Topos.* Bielefeld: Transcript.

Schoder, André. 1939. *Vu mengem Dueref gong ech hier: Patriotescht Stéck an 3 Akten mat letzeburger Vollèks- an Hémechtslidder.* Letzeburg: Worré-Mertens.

Staus, Yvan. 2000. *La Célébration du centenaire de l'indépendance du Grand-Duché de Luxembourg en 1939 dans sa signification historique.* Mémoire hist., UFR.

Stöver, Bernd. 2017. *Der Kalte Krieg: Geschichte eines radikalen Zeitalters.* Munich: Beck.

Subotić, Yelena. 2019. *Yellow Star, Red Star: Holocaust Remembrance after Communism.* Ithaca: Cornell University Press.

Thomas, Bernard. 2010. "Bruchstellen: Chronik des Escher Resistenzmuseum." *Forum für Politik, Gesellschaft und Kultur* 35, no. 299 (September): 12–18.

Trausch, Gilbert. 1989. *Le Luxembourg: Émergence d'un État et d'une nation.* Anvers: Fonds Mercator.

Wagner, Moritz. 2016. "'Die Perser! Die Perser kommen…': Zur Aktualisierung eines Barbaren-Topos in der deutschen Exilliteratur." *Colloquium Helveticum: Schweizer Hefte für Allgemeine und Vergleichende Literaturwissenschaft* 46, no. 5: 135–56.

Wehenkel, Henri. 1985. *Der antifaschistische Widerstand in Luxemburg: Dokumente und Materialien.* Luxembourg: COPÉ.

———. 1997. *D'Spueniekämpfer: Volontaires de la Guerre d'Espagne, partis du Luxembourg.* Dudelange: Centre de documentation sur les migrations humaines.

———. 2012. "Loi-muselière (1937)." In *Lieux de mémoire au Luxembourg II: Jeux d'echelles,* edited by Sonja Kmec and Pit Peporté, 31–36. Luxembourg: St.-Paul.

Weis, Adolf. 1939a. "Der nächtliche Pilger." *Luxemburger Marienkalender*: 113–15.

———. 1939b. *Dohém: E klengt Stéck aus schwe'rer Zäit.* Letzeburg: n.p.

Wey, Claude. 1989. "Le Centenaire de l'Indépendance et sa commémoration en 1939." *Hémecht: Zeitschrift für Luxemburger Geschichte* 41, no. 1: 29–53.

Figures

Fig 1. Devotional image of the *Christus cardiophorus*, 1906. Diocesan Archives of Luxembourg (DAL), Théophile Walin Bequest 172_0307.

Fig 2. Pins (*Spéngelen*, in Luxembourgish) with national symbols, 1939. Archives communales de Sanem. Photograph: Christof Weber.

Fig 3. *Musée National de la Résistance* in Esch-sur-Alzette (2008). Photograph: Frank Schroeder.

Fig 4. Cover of *Rot sind die Reiter der Apokalypse* by an unnamed graphic artist.

WRITING UNDER/ AGAINST OCCUPATION: STRATEGIES OF RESISTANCE AND PROPAGANDA

Introduction to Part 3

JEANNE E. GLESENER

Part three takes a closer look at occupied territories as an intercultural contact zone and the devices used to implement cultural policy and propagandist discourses.

Opening this part is **Stefan Laffin**'s chapter on the role of US-American writers and war correspondents as cultural brokers, their mission to frame narratives of the war, and their attempts to translate the modes and practices of occupation for the US-American readership. Laffin underlines how literary representations of the Allied occupation of Italy were instrumentalized in establishing the discursive horizon for a 'good' occupation. The chapter shows how novels such as the very popular *A Bell for Adano* (1944) by John Hersey, who served among the Allied troops in Sicily, had shaped the morale and reputation of the Allied administration before any official accounts or histories of the Allied occupation had emerged, and how such works also, to some extent, participated in codifying the narrative of the 'good occupation.' Laffin insists that the literary output portraying the very first weeks of the Allied occupation shaped not only the later historical understanding of that period but also even the perspective at the time. Consequently, when assessing whether Allied military rule over Italian territory was either a liberation or an occupation, this literature must be viewed specifically against the backdrop of interpretations that existed when it was published. Depending on the perspective, paternalistic notions with colonial overtones emerge, revealing the occupied territory as a gendered space; as Laffin explains, the Italian people are feminized when they are portrayed as being in need of rescue.

Following from how writers were instrumental in crafting frames of reception for the war, the next chapter illustrates how cultural policies were used to enhance collaborations with the occupying powers, especially when the latter confronted difficulties in establishing effective propagandist support in the contact zone. By examining the cases of the Protectorate of Bohemia and Moravia and the Territory of the German Military Commander in Serbia, where the implementation of Nazi Germany's cultural policy beyond a narrow circle of conservative and far-right-wing intellectuals proved difficult, **Aleksandar Momčilović** takes a look at the organization and promotion of literary competitions. The latter were led by the collaboration authorities and intended to include the wider population, as well as to mobilize support 'from below' in the process of 'normalizing' the occupation. Looking at texts written mostly by lay authors, the chapter reconstructs the ways in which they, as spokespersons of that part of the population willing to cooperate, experienced occupation. Momčilović's description of literary life under duress also reveals the instrumentalization of an institutional device—the literary competition—as a system to legitimize and control the literary field. He also points out the limitations that are imposed on the literary imagination when literary quality cedes way to ideological fidelity to 'acceptable' literary themes, particularly where the topics of nationalism, religion, ruralism, rebirth, family, and hard manual labor served to link National Socialist ideology with the occupied populations' everyday existence. Not unlike the other cultural spaces of occupation analyzed in the book, literary competitions, it turns out, are a privileged medium for discerning the shaping of new sets of values, conflicting moralities, and identity discourses in a situation of controlled literary aesthetics.

Broadening the investigation into the impact of war and occupation on the literary field, and pointing out the role of linguistic and cultural transfer for enhanced understanding of the contact zones of war and occupation, **Joanna Rzepa** examines the translation and circulation of texts from occupied Poland in Britain, both during World War II and in the early years of Poland's Soviet occupation. Her chapter focuses on the dynamic relationship between British publishers and the Polish government-in-exile in London and shows how important an element publishing was to the war effort for the Polish government. The publications that the Polish government sponsored included literary texts based on real-life events that directly spoke about Poland's Nazi occupation (e.g., Aleksander Kaminski's *Stones for the Rampart*, Jerzy Andrzejewski's *Roll Call*), and autobiographical writings that addressed the Soviet invasion of the country (e.g., Irish-born Zoe Zajdler's *The Dark Side of the Moon* and *My Name is Million*). The chapter highlights to what extent publishing was considered an important tool in ideological warfare and explains how propaganda departments and cultural diplomacy vied for the attention of British readers by means of translations and publishing campaigns, alongside enlisting the support and endorsement of British authors, well-known politicians, and public intellectuals to recommend these texts to the British audience. Rzepa persuasively reconstructs the challenges faced by the Polish authorities and authors who, as cross-cultural brokers who were aware of the public's distrust for atrocity propaganda, needed to strike the right tone to convey the experience of extreme deprivation and unimaginable violence in a way that was understandable and, more importantly, believable to a readership exempt from this experience.

The last chapter in this part looks at processes of cultural translation strategies, intercultural communication, and the role of cross-cultural knowledge brokers in the post-war German–American contact zone. In 1946, when Allied reeducation programs caused resentment and irritation among post-war German society, the German–American journalist Margret Boveri wrote *Amerikafibel für erwachsene Deutsche* (1946) ("American Primer for Grown-up Germans"). It quickly achieved mass circulation among the four occupied zones. As a foreign correspondent and one of the most influential go-betweens in the European and trans-Atlantic literary field from the late 1930s to the 1960s, Boveri was ideally placed to write a primer aimed at helping her fellow Germans better understand the US-American liberators. Rather than focusing exclusively on the current situation, however, Boveri also drew upon historical, cultural, climatological, and characterological reasoning to explain the US-Americans' non-Europeanness. In her interpretive reading of Boveri's primer, **Sandra Schell** brings to the fore the pronounced ambiguities of the book: highlighting its literariness by outlining aesthetic techniques and discursive strategies, she shows the line it walks between encouraging transcultural communication and fostering ethnopluralist narratives of German (or, at least, European) supremacy. Despite this ambivalence, Schell argues, cultural brokers such as Boveri were crucial in influencing post-war European identity constructions.

CHAPTER 8

Setting the Stage for an Immediate Historicization?

Early Sense-Making of the Allied Occupation of Italy between Fictionalized Accounts, War Novels, and Propaganda (1943–1947)

STEFAN LAFFIN

Charlie, Bizzy, and I, all different in approach, all agree that A Bell [John Hersey's *A Bell for Adano*, New York 1944] is a drip. It's really bad. Sure, it gives some idea about military government, just as Eddie Guest, writing about an orchard in bloom, […] must give some vague idea of what an orchard is about. But the book is naïve, wrongly cued, and malicious about Patton, and so oversimplified, for our worst headaches don't come from the military but from the civilians and our own Hq. But that's too hard and subtle and non-dramatic to write about. Does War and Peace have a devil and an angel? […] No great novel is done in terms of black and white. Write A Bell off, please.[1]

This damning review of John Hersey's *A Bell for Adano* came, in some respect, straight from the horse's mouth. Allied Civil Affairs Officer (CAO) Maurice F. Neufeld wrote this scathing criticism to his wife in April 1944, some two months after the novel—centered on a fictional CAO—was published (Hersey 1944).[2] Neufeld's assessment is notable insofar as he vehemently criticized a book that sang the praise of local Allied, specifically US-American, CAOs working in Southern Italian cities and towns. Hersey used Major Victor Joppolo, the novel's protagonist, to offer a portrayal of a purportedly good US-American occupation. To get this message across, he conceived of the CAOs as good-hearted individuals, at times diametrically opposed to the cynical and brutal behavior by military authorities. The terms of the publication of Hersey's novel were likewise striking given the swift manner in which it came about.

Hersey was part of the Allied troops going ashore in Licata, a city at the Southern coast of Sicily that played a crucial role in the logistics of the invasion of Sicily (Morison 2002). The place fell quickly into the hands of the invading Allied soldiers, and it was there that CAO George McCaffrey established his first headquarters for some days. Licata was also the first city where Allied military courts duly functioned (Allied Commission 1945, 11). McCaffrey would rise to ill fame, as he was the main culprit in committing a massacre a few days later in a city nearby, in which he shot numerous Italian civilians (Patti 2013, 74; Mangiameli 2012). This, as much as the Allied military courts, points already to the fact that the Allied arrival was as much about the aspect of liberation as it was about establishing an occupation defined by clear hierarchies between the Allied occupiers and the occupied Sicilians, all with an eye toward providing stability so as not to impede the war effort.

The Italian case is, in general, noteworthy for two reasons. It marked the first instance in which British and US-American troops occupied territory together in Europe, on top of which this territory belonged to a (soon-to-be former) Axis member.[3] The alleged 'novelty' of occupying foreign territory—when, in fact, only the program to train and prepare prospective CAOs back in the United States was new (Carruthers 2018), but not the phenomenon of occupation itself (as shrewd contemporary observers noted [cf. Gabriel 1943])—was also the reason why prominent writers such as John Steinbeck sought to participate in the Italian campaign. Yet what makes the Italian example likewise striking are the poles of liberation and occupation between which both the campaign and the occupation oscillated: while it was, on the one side, a liberation from Fascist rule and exposure to Nazi terror, it was not a liberation from daily needs, be those hunger, housing, clothing, or medicine. With the Allied arrival, neither did a "reign of plenty" (as the Allied head of military government would call it) set in, nor did a 'sparkling moment' of liberation eventuate over the coming weeks (Allied Commission 1945, 12).[4] What rather gained a foothold was not so much a liberation itself as did a new occupation, this time by the Allies. Allied rule was deemed necessary for military reasons (i.e., to further the war effort and guarantee order in the rear area), as well as for political ones. After all, Fascist Italy had spent the three years before the Allied invasion fighting alongside its Axis partners; democratizing Italy was considered opportune, if not outright necessary, both for preventing future conflicts and also for stipulating the terms of US post-war dominance.

Before any official accounts or histories of the Allied occupation would emerge, novels such as, most famously, *A Bell for Adano* had already provided a glance into how the Allied administration would be remembered and historicized. The act of liberation, which the Allied propaganda in its countless leaflets had promised and that was noticeable and tangible whenever Allied soldiers entered Southern Italian villages, therefore found its expression in how Hersey's novel was configured. The myth of the USA, in particular, would have entered these villages and to joyfully welcome them exceeded the mere aspect of liberation as it also meant to participate in the victory of those who actually fought (Fascist) Italy (Gallerano 1997: 459). While the military organization was not always perfect (in John Hersey's novel, the figure of General Marvin, modeled after George Patton, was not depicted in all-too-positive terms…), Hersey was out to describe the good-hearted, selfless nature of the US-American individual who would find his way into the hearts of the people he administered, and who would establish a benign, noble occupation. In this idealized version of the military government, the word 'occupation' would hardly do justice to the jolly cooperation between Italians and US-Americans in their common quest to handle daily life under such conditions of turmoil. The task at hand was no less than building an entire post-war world out of the ruins of World War II. While the Allied war propaganda had already established this discursive horizon, novels in the second half of the 1940s continued emphasizing the role of morally decent individuals in a world that was morally decayed.

Against this backdrop, Maurice Neufeld should actually have appreciated Hersey's novel. Neufeld was, by all means, a political-progressive liberal, arguing for the implementation of far-reaching policies in Italy to effect extensive social and political change. As a CAO working right in the thick of the Allied occupation, he technically 'should' have felt flattered by Hersey's account. Neufeld—as was Major Frank D. Toscani, on whom the figure of the novel's protagonist was based—was part of the team of civilians-turned-soldiers who worked at the headquarters of military government within George Patton's army. The head of this unit was Charles Poletti, a New York politician who advanced to becoming one of the poster boys for the morally decent Allied occupation efforts; the "Charlie" in the prefacing quote refers to Poletti. It was this Poletti who had allowed Hersey to participate in staff meetings of the CAOs in Palermo and then organized transport for him so that he could observe the work of a local CAO in the field in Licata (Mercuri 1992, 63–64).

The opening quote shows, however, that Neufeld did not take kindly the plot—or main thrust—of Hersey's novel. The crux, in a way, concerned the novel's 'character.' Neufeld called the book's depiction of the military government "oversimplified," the true nature of it "too hard and subtle and non-dramatic to write about."[5] In this sense, it seems that the CAO considered Hersey's writing at face value, or rather: Neufeld believed that the novel's task was to convey a realistic notion of the military government—rather than to take literary licenses, which novels are wont to take, and that *A Bell for Adano* obviously did.

The vision of what war novels and different shades of writing about the Allied occupation of Italy should accomplish touches right upon the argument of this chapter. It deals with the sense-making, if you will, of the Allied occupation of

Italy, through literary production. Of course, the lines here are especially blurry, given that sense-making texts ranged from war dispatches and travelogues, to novels, diary entries, or poems—just to name the most common examples. Oftentimes, such texts shared elements of more than one genre anyway. While reflecting upon these texts, this chapter also takes, whenever considered opportune, into account Italian discourses and the liberation paradigm. This paradigm involves considering the Allied arrival in Sicily (where the campaign and, hence, also occupation of Italy began) as a liberation from the claws of Fascism and Nazism, rather than highlighting the dynamics of the Allied occupation, which oftentimes spawned more sinister corollaries than the positive momentum of liberation would suggest (Laffin 2020; Patti 2013). As liberation was also a key term for the Italian resistance movement, the word in itself as much as the years from 1943 to 1945 also found manifold expressions in Italian literary production. Here, especially the experiences of the partisan fight against Nazi Germany and Fascists in Italy were processed and narrated. It helped supporting the evolution of a memory discourse that established the theme of the 'good Italian' (Focardi 2013, especially 33–76) and that was needed to establish a new political culture. The antifascist movements' "group memory became the center of the Italian memory discourse of World War II," as Guido Bartolini has recently emphasized (Bartolini 2021: 23). These memories, however, predominantly reflected experiences of Northern and Central Italy, whereas the Southern histories, and ways in which the Allies figured in these histories, were neglected for the first decades of the Italian Republic.

Rather than adopting a literary criticism perspective, this chapter will take a historical perspective in its reflections upon some early occupation literature (for an elaboration of this term, see the introduction to this volume), most prominently John Hersey's novel.

What bearing did literature about the Allied occupation have on both contemporary and historical understanding? How did the literary output portray the very first weeks of the occupation, considering the (ambiguous) dichotomy between liberation and occupation? In what ways was literature then 'used' and employed by the occupiers—meaning not just US-American novelists such as John Hersey, but also Allied personnel such as Maurice Neufeld?

After the first part of this chapter discusses how literature played into the making of the 'good occupation,' the second part will pay closer attention to the literary productions themselves, before finally turning to some remarks regarding how this interpretation relates to experiences in Germany and France. I argue that occupation and liberation, each, figure prominently in these different representations, and I outline how literary texts that emerged contemporarily on the Italian case served goals that were ultimately political and propagandistic.

"I have been a lucky man, for it has been my fortune to be in the midst of great events": US Efforts to Establish the 'Good Occupation' Paradigm

John Hersey was, by no means, the only writer engaged with reporting from the war zone. For instance, it was with the section-opening quote above that the famous journalist Herbert L. Matthews described his training as a war correspondent (Matthews 1946, 5). Part of his education—he would call his experiences in Abyssinia, Spain, India, and elsewhere "courses"—was also the fact that he took part in Allied landings in Southern Italy in July and September 1943. Meanwhile, Ernie Pyle was perhaps the most famous—and certainly, among soldiers in the European theater, the most popular—writer who also published books on his experiences; namely, collections of his newspaper columns, in book form (Pyle 1943, 1944). The US government was keen to have these 'journalist-writers' reporting from the theater of war (to use a hybrid term that captures the dual role many of these people assumed). John Hersey's work marks an exemplar in this regard, as the plot of his novel exhibits a very close linkage between his journalistic war dispatches and his subsequent novel. In a way, the contributions of these journalist-writers served a multifaceted purpose: they showcased transparency, set the record straight, and left a record for posterity as to how democracies prevailed in World War II by means of their virtues. In quite similar fashion, the attendant press coverage of the war and occupation in Italy corroborated this aim as the affirmative articles in *The New York Times*, for instance, would prove.

In other fields, too, the Allies had an interest in displaying moral superiority and the virtues of democracy, to which end they took great care in showing respect for occupied territories' cultural goods; such an attitude was intended to suggest that democracy was a worthy victor in the field of culture, too. For example, teams were established for the task of assessing Italian archival records and ensuring their protection (Bell and Jenkinson 1947), and the Allies' established the Monuments, Fine Arts, and Archives Program to similar ends. It is not for nothing that one of the more than two dozen sub-commissions of the Allied (Control) Commission, the main organizational body to administer the occupation after its establishment in November 1943, dealt with fine arts.[6] Relatedly, similar to war correspondents being sent to the battle zones to write, the US Department of War also instituted a program for artists, and the War Department Art Advisory Committee, from 1942 onwards, discussed which artists were to be sent, and for what purposes, to the battle zones. Painter George Biddle was one of its most devoted members; he wrote to President Roosevelt that he believed those sent to Italy "have here the greatest opportunity that has ever been offered to a group of artists to record the full impact of War." Being more than simply "news-gatherers," they would have to "give a deeply, passionately felt, profoundly reflective interpretation of the spirit and essence of War."[7]

What the Department of War anticipated from people like Biddle or Hersey was to translate what they observed in Sicily by means of their paintings or newspaper columns. In Biddle's words, what this truly meant was to "report, report always. The rest can come later."[8] (Incidentally, Biddle 'later'—as in, already in 1944—turned his experiences into a book, too (Biddle 1944).) These writers and artists were expected, basically, to introduce their US readership to the occupation, this allegedly new phenomenon whose undertaking had stirred up so much political debate in Washington in the preceding years. Most notably absent in the news coverage and in more elaborated publications later on, though, was the question of the *legitimization* of the war through these dispatches. Here, one might contemplate the assertion of political scientist Lance Bennett, who argued that war coverage, in its explanation of a war, usually does not go beyond the interpretive framework predefined by the political debate within the country where its audience lives (Bennett 1990). The same, it could be added, holds true with regard to the occupation of Sicily, which the interested public sought to study closely, given its first-time character in the timeline of this war: that is, US soldiers of World War II now actively involved in the practice of occupation. The heading for Herbert L. Matthews' *The New York Times* article—"We Test a Plan for Governing Europe"—already alluded to the fact that not only was the first real, practical implementation of occupation policies and practices observable in Italy (Matthews 1943), but rather that this occupation marked the launching ramp for the beginning of the post-war period, with US eyes already set on intervening deeper into Europe's affairs than in the decades before.

In particular, paintings, photographs, newspaper columns, and eventually books would establish the discursive horizon of a good occupation; that is, they would serve to shed light on the practices of morally decent soldiers. Robert Capa's famous imagery of the Sicilian Campaign might be the best-known example of the effort to create a narrative of friendly relations between US-Americans and Sicilians. In terms of literary production, the prevailing opinion was, "Books are weapons in the war of ideas," as the banner of the Council on Books in Wartime would have it (Carruthers 2014, 1091). Guided by friendly occupiers who arrived with noble intentions—"to bring light to the heathen," as one critical voice would flippantly remark (quoted in Fainsod 1948, 27)—Italy would embark upon its quest toward democracy, supported by CAOs who would exemplify this liberal, democratic world through their actions. This was how John Hersey conceived of Major Joppolo in his book. Accordingly, a review in the *New York Post* considered Hersey's novel as

> the finest tract for democracy produced by the war—fiction or non-fiction. In
> fact, because it is such well-contrived and well-executed fiction it has infinitely

> greater appeal and power than the dozens of sober studies of democracy that have
> appeared these last few years. (Halper 1944, 6)

John Hersey was himself acutely aware of this quality, setting the inherently good CAO against the turmoil provoked by war, but also against his own military superiors.

This aim to cast the Allied occupation in a good light was also part of the reason why aspects such as black marketing, coerced sexual relations (from prostitution to rape), corruption, or other atrocities committed in the theater of war found little way into contemporary columns and books. This fact can not only be reduced to issues of censorship. Rather, Hersey's novel, more than any other text, established and codified the narrative of the good occupation (Carruthers 2014). In other words, part of the logic behind the novel was "to proactively shape the civic model for the occupation as such," as Robert S. C. Gordon has put it (Gordon 2018, 10). Then again, Gordon has also pointed to the fact that there is sort of a darker theme of occupation to be found in *A Bell of Adano*, "a hint of reality hanging over this near-utopia of benign rule" (Gordon 2018, 16). This dimension, however, the presence of the mafia, the profiteering from the occupation by means of engaging in the black market, sexual violence, bombed houses, and many more aspects clearly take a backseat compared to the respectable character of the occupation, as embodied by Major Joppolo.

The paternalistic (in some ways also colonial) notions underlying the relationships of Allied personnel and Italian civilians have been emphasized by historical research (Buchanan 2008) and the gendered dimensions of the occupation and its representations rendered problematic (Escolar 2019). Also contemporarily, occupation was not simply seen as an idle undertaking. In the words of critics such as US Secretary of the Interior Harold Ickes, occupation oozed forms of imperialism and therefore, by definition, could not be a decent endeavor. Given this background, active efforts were required to cast occupation in a good light, as Susan Carruthers convincingly argues in her seminal monograph on this issue (Carruthers 2016).

War correspondents, novelists, or artists could render valuable services in this regard. They would historicize the first encounter between the Allies and the Sicilians, thereby laying down the terms of the noble occupiers, as well as preconfiguring future encounters with respect to the liberation of, for instance, Northern Italy or France. This was especially crucial because the actual evidence in the field showed a different picture, when food rations, to just name one example, were usually lowered whenever Allied soldiers liberated Italian villages. Theoretically speaking, novels would frame the reception of war and occupation in US public opinion, with their choice of focus (in their reporting) already being the biggest influence on how events would be interpreted (Reese, Gandy Jr., and Grant 2001). Reporting from the war scene, these correspondents would act as cultural brokers, translating the modes and practices of occupation for the US audience. That this could go both ways, and only gained in relevance for future occupations, is apparent in Sandra Schell's chapter in this volume. What is more, artists were part of a wider effort to teach and set an example of democracy. In this way, culture, and particularly the arts, should offer an ideal of a less militaristic society, so that British, US-American, but also German exile artists were constantly employed to instill a new culture, or rather mentality, in defeated nations and peoples (Feigel 2016).

War correspondents were only one group of potential brokers who were needed, however, both with regard to public opinion on the home front as well as in the constant negotiation of the shifting meanings of occupation. Italian-American soldiers would, in this sense, also be a fascinating group to study (Fusi 2018), as would be translators, who interpreted the occupiers' utterances both literally and figuratively (Schirbock 2017). Due to the manifold migratory links between the two countries, in addition to the fact that the US conceived of Italy as naïve and a rather 'friendly' enemy in contrast to Germany or Japan, this cross-cultural contact was usually imagined to be full of harmony. Contemporary Allied literature doubled down on this motif to bring home the notion of an occupation that allegedly assumed the character of a peaceful coexistence.

This overarching objective was yet another reason (besides the adventurous nature of journalist-writers not to miss "the chance of a lifetime and the chance of a century") why prestigious writers and artists were chosen for the task.[9] As an established painter, Biddle would need no introduction to the US audience, for instance. The same is true for John Hersey, who was, by the mid-1940s, already an established journalist and novelist (Gordon 2018, 11). What set him apart from other war correspondents, such as John Steinbeck or Ernest Hemingway—other than the literary output and accolades of these latter two—was his fairly young age, not even having turned 30 when *A Bell for Adano* was published. He was part of a group of writers who sought to gain first-hand experiences from the war theaters to collect material: material they could first turn into columns for the newspapers and magazines with which they were affiliated, before, eventually, also drawing from these experiences and observations as the basis for their more fictionalized book publications. What these writers shared was a penchant for adventurism, for enriching their war stories by immersing themselves in the situations they described, and, hence, for bringing the war home successfully to a US audience. Thus, in more than one way, time—and timing—was of the essence, since most political and military Allied decision-makers expected the Italian campaign to be short-lived.

"Above all you see a thing succeeding and it looks like the future": Novels' Contributions to Building an Early Post-war World

John Hersey wrote this euphoric line in his most elaborate article on the Allied Military Government of Occupied Territories (AMGOT) for *Life* (Hersey 1943, 30). The "thing succeeding" was precisely the occupation, in US imaginations, with the CAO in Licata (who was at the heart of Hersey's article for the magazine) running things to everybody's satisfaction. Not only was the encounter between Allied soldiers and Italian civilians a positive one; daily life under occupation was indeed portrayed as a collaborative endeavor.

On a more structural level, and abstracting from the individual case of *A Bell for Adano*, at least three qualities of Allied novels about the occupation can be identified, which are important to consider while reflecting upon the issue at hand. The *first* pertains to the authors. A great part of them had not been writers in the first place, but instead came to Italy as war correspondents—although the precise relationship between these two roles must be examined in each individual case. For instance, while established novelists such as John Steinbeck made their way to Italy to experience the horrors of war firsthand, find inspiration for new material, and heed the patriotic battle call with what they were best qualified to do (i.e., reporting on the war in factual-yet-striking fashion for US civilians), others were simply war correspondents or enlisted soldiers who would go on to turn their observations and columns into wholesale novels. Steinbeck, for his part, had already offered his services to a higher cause by publishing *The Moon is Down*, a novel that tells the story of a Northern European town occupied by a hostile army (Steinbeck 1942). Even without directly naming it, it was abundantly clear to contemporaries that the book was about the German occupation of Norway. This propaganda novel aspired to bolster public morale regarding the 'rightfulness' of the Allied war effort and was meant as a support of people who were living under Nazi occupation in Europe. In much the same fashion, the novels by other war correspondents served similar motives, although their target audience was as much the US home front as it was the people living under occupational regimes.

The rather superficial distinction between different types (or groups) of professional authors obviously leaves a whole other group of text-producers from the Allied occupation of Italy out in the cold: texts produced by escaped prisoners of war, CAOs, or higher-ups in the military hierarchy also flooded the book market, sometimes decades after the war had ended (Hill and Hill 1982; Lessa 1985; Lewis 1978; Miller 1989)—but in these latter sorts of texts, the borders between source, fiction, and authoritative account became blurred. As such, given the lack of serious, impartial scholarship studying the Allied occupation of Italy for the first three decades after World War II, texts by on-site personnel were initially cherished by historians as 'neutral' accounts, or at least as 'unproblematic' sources. The treatment of Norman A. Lewis's unreliable account of the situation in occupied Italy marks a striking case in point in terms of how historians have dealt with historical accounts that were deeply augmented by fictional elements before scholarship then moved on to deconstruct the narratives established by authors such as Lewis.[10]

The *second* important quality of novels about the Allied occupation concerns their content. Given that some of these novels were published immediately after the war ended—as a matter of fact, some of them while the fighting was still going on, as was the case with Hersey's book—they served as more than just fictionalized stories of the Allied occupation. In fact, however fictionalized these writings were, they were nonetheless the first chance for a US audience to gain insights into the inner workings of the occupation and which sorts of problems and situations soldiers actually faced in Europe. In many ways, these novels also informed readers about daily life under the occupation. This latter point is especially true for authors such as John Hersey or Ernie Pyle, who based their novels on the war columns they had written as somewhat objective accounts of what they witnessed during their time in Italy. Many themes the authors highlighted revolved around the problems the Allies faced in their task of administering occupied territories and societies, with issues such as food provisioning, black marketeering, and prostitution being most prevalent. As has already been emphasized, however, these themes remained rather vague in most novels and often marked only the backdrop against which the heroic individual soldier could rise. In other words, the solution of these problems, rather than the problems themselves, took center stage in the novels.

In contrast, and perhaps not surprisingly, the problematic, 'darker' issues of the occupation constituted the focal points of Italian literature—and Italian neorealist cinema, too—whenever the Allied occupation was dealt with. The center of attention was usually on the resistance movement, though, which almost became a sort of civil religion for the immediate postwar years, as Tommaso Baris has pointed out (Baris 2008). Victimhood as a central factor to gain political legitimacy and indeed capacity to act was part of the reason why the Italian resistance became such a strong focus in this negotiation of public memory (Forlenza 2012). Set against this official discourse, Elsa Morante's diary provides ample evidence of how aware other novelists were of the cynical dimension these Italians dealings with the past entailed (Baldasso 2022, 1).

Once the Allied occupation then found entry into literary depictions, the theme of victimhood was often reinforced. Here, the lack of food, clothing, or housing constituted the frame for a gloomy depiction of the Allied occupation. The scenery in Naples, in particular, provided the setting for horrific depictions of the occupation, often resorting to mythical, phantasmagorical imaginings of life under the new occupiers (see also Mamatsashvili, and Momčilović in this volume for more information on how cities figured into occupation narration). Curzio Malaparte's *La pelle* might be the most remarkable example in that regard (Malaparte 1949), even though the author was actually out to criticize the direction the established politics of memory took by pointing to a world full of moral decay. In some ways, he therefore denied any legitimate ground for a moral rebirth after World War II, for which only the resistance could serve as appropriate pillar given Italy's fascist past (see also Baldasso 2022, 172–97).

The novels, *third*, became efficacious insofar as they conditioned the view on both the occupied people and the occupiers. Not only did they inform about their subject matter at hand but also, if read as historical sources, they provided insights into the general zeitgeist, along with cultural representations and clichés that were rampant at the time of their production and publication. In this way, the accounts yield a similar result to what H. Stuart Hughes has argued was a lasting impression for US soldiers upon entering Italy via its allegedly backwards south:

> These impressions, added to the mediocre record of the Italian armed forces, seemed to confirm the prejudices that Americans already entertained: that the Italians were a dark, dirty, and ignorant people, corrupt, thieving, and cowardly. And so the American soldiers usually behaved with arrogance and tactlessness— if not outright brutality—toward the 'Eyeties' they frankly considered their inferiors. (Hughes 1968, 11)

John Hersey's novel succumbed to the same logic. Yet it also offered a solution, or rather fresh perspective, with a committed CAO trying to help Sicilians to transcend their (stereotyped) character. Eric Linklater's novel *Private Angelo* played into this cultural stereotyping as well; the Scottish writer and military historian was tasked to produce 'instant histories' of the war, as the British War Office Public Relations Department, which commissioned this work, would call them. Linklater characterized Private Angelo as a character devoid of many stereotypically 'masculine' qualities—lacking courage, fighting skill, and so on—yet gifted with virtues such as love, innocence, and beauty. This characterization was, in turn, how the Allies imagined Italy as a country, where it was upon the 'manly' US soldier to kiss the idle beauty (i.e., Italy) awake and offer her a redemptive future. In a fine irony, Linklater put proper words into Private Angelo's mouth when he had him say: "I hope you will not liberate us out of existence" with respect to, particularly, the US efforts (Linklater 1946, 142–143). Highlighting dichotomies was certainly possible in these novels, even though they generally succumbed to the idea of displaying the encounter between Italians and the Allies as a jolly affair (Plain 2017).

Perpetuating the Moment of Liberation and Euphemizing the Occupation

Literary representations on both the Italian as well as the Allied side played a role in articulating the Allied presence in Sicily either as a liberation or an occupation. The liberating moment was often overemphasized. It was also suggested that the liberation was more than just a sweeping moment but indeed a rupture with the (Fascist) past, a watershed after which this very past would have evaporated and a fresh start would be looming on the horizon (Bartolini 2021). Historiography, to some extent, has contributed to this phenomenon: when (at times) 'liberation' is described as the moral act undertaken by the Italian resistance movement, it somehow logically follows to discount the Allied experiences, especially in Southern Italy. Highlighting the Allied occupation indeed would only puncture the carefully woven web of the Italian memory discourse. This was especially true for the immediate years after 1943 and after the war had ended two years later. Accordingly, historian Tony Judt identified the years until 1948 as those in which "Europe's postwar memory was moulded" (Judt 1992: 86). By the end of the decade, however, Sicilian writer Leonardo Sciascia described the scenery when the Allies entered local villages:

> It was July 14 [1943]. In the afternoon, the news spread that the Americans were arriving. The mayor, the archpriest, and an interpreter set out to meet them. [...] [F]ive soldiers with a long rifle lowered suddenly burst into the square, undecided. They saw, in front of a half-open door, a few men in uniform and moved confidently. The Carabinieri found their rifles pointed at them without yet realizing that the Americans had finally arrived. Their guns dangled in the hands of one of the patrolmen. A round of applause roared. A voice called for cigarettes, and the American corporal felt the pockets of the Carabinieri brigadier, pulled out a pack of Africas, and threw it to the spectators [...] [T]he party had begun.[11] (Gordon 2018, 12)

The cigarettes, together with chocolate, and flowers decorating Allied vehicles, all of them prominent symbols for Italian–American interactions, figure prominently in this account. In addition, here they come not as a gift from the soldiers but instead are taken from the Carabinieri—a gesture intended to signal the breakdown of the old authority and to suggest that the Allies would side with the Italian people in the clash with state authority, given that the Carabinieri had been a trusted police formation for the Fascists in power.

So, while on the one hand, literature served to mark the precise moment of liberation, even more so in Italian accounts, it was especially once this snapshot was 'taken' and the occupation established—with all its sinister corollaries, such as shortages of food, clothing, and medicine, black markets, prostitution, venereal disease, and so on—that literature served the purpose of justifying and also explaining the occupation. It was here where John Hersey's *A Bell for Adano* came particularly in handy for Allied authorities.

In a place like Licata (Adano) with its some 30,000 people officially living there, military government meant two things: an institutional act and a practical one. The occupation was established by means of posting the first proclamation that announced it. Yet this proclamation meant little on the scene in the following weeks. It was rather the practices of the CAOs that set the precedent; in other words, the actions in the field defined the Allied occupation, not so much the directives, proclamations, and General Orders that were issued over the coming weeks and months. Directives simply meant little if they could not be translated into concrete practices in the field. In this context, the CAOs became the face of the Allied occupation, as they had full governing powers, especially in remote towns and villages, where transport and communication were not often available (neither to the Italians *nor* to the Allies themselves). All this, naturally, made the local Allied Military Government of Occupied Territories representative, Frank Toscani, such a convenient figure that John Hersey could transform him into 'Major Joppolo' and craft his story around an individual CAO.

The US military obviously had these legitimacy and popularity concerns in mind when they allowed Hersey to accompany US troops in their quest to invade and govern Sicily in July 1943. Substantial reflections on what he could observe in Licata appeared in *Life* in August 1943. The piece was called "AMGOT at Work" and was accompanied by a photo reportage by the famous Robert Capa, who provided one of the iconic pictures of the war and occupation as imagined by the US-Americans: a moment of cooperation between Italians and US-Americans. The photo showed an elder Sicilian pointing out something to a young GI who stooped over so that he was at eye level with the Sicilian. The article and caption went on to mention that the Allies would learn in this way about the exact routes the German had taken in their retreat from the invading Allies. The underlying pattern of hierarchization and stereotyping that said cooperation entailed were simply swept aside.

The CAOs, as described by Hersey, often and especially in smaller villages became a part of the local social structure, to the point of mingling with the people over whom they were tasked to rule. This also involved sexual relations, which were strictly forbidden but in reality were practiced constantly. The depiction of Joppolo's affair had, in this way, real-life consequences; Frank Toscani (the inspiration for the novel's protagonist) sued Hersey for his portrayal in the novel, as his wife filed for divorce back home in the United States after learning about her husband's extramarital activity. These sexualized depictions of the Allied occupation and the relations between occupiers and occupied were also reminiscent of what Marisa Escolar defines as the "Gendered Redemption of World War II" in Italy, arguing that the US-American occupiers were sketched as male saviors rescuing Italian women—and rescuing a feminized Italy—from their downfall (Escolar 2019). Novels such as Hersey's were, hence, offering a deeply sexualized rendition of the Allied occupation, which established gendered hierarchies for the post-war world.

This post-war world also seemed to be the backdrop against which Hersey wrote his novel. Hersey spent time observing Frank Toscani in his daily practices navigating the manifold challenges of occupation in July 1943. After a mere week, he returned to the United States, and he came up with *A Bell for Adano* after three weeks of writing in "angry haste" (Carruthers 2014, 1090). In early 1944, the novel got published and made massive waves right away. It was turned into a motion picture a year later, with rising actor John Hodiak playing the lead. The rapid progression from Hersey's stay in Sicily and the intimate access he had there to occupation personnel, to the swift recording of his observations and his ability to turn them quickly into a novel, and eventually the instant prominence that the book acquired for political and propagandistic purposes, all suggest that the novel emerged at an opportune time. It was indeed very much welcomed and solicited by those politicians who saw occupation as a decisively good endeavor to convert former enemies into friends.

Hersey turned Licata into Adano and Major Toscani into the novel's protagonist Major Joppolo. It was basically an artistic elaboration of the columns Hersey had written for the magazines *Life* and *Time*. With the novel's ill-concealed shots at George Patton (the general of the US Army in the invasion of Sicily) and Lord Rennell (the head of the AMGOT), *A Bell for Adano* set out to establish relative fame and glory for the otherwise-unknown CAOs, on their own in remote villages and local societies that they did not know how to govern. Accordingly, in one of the earlier scenes in the novel, Major Joppolo tears apart his instructions and manuals and solely relies on his own notes, titled "Notes to Joppolo from Joppolo," which basically came down to the motto: "When plans fall down, improvise…" (Hersey 1943, 14). Singing the praises of CAOs during the occupation as oftentimes the only visible and inherently good actors of the military government performing the occupation, Hersey struck a chord with the political sphere. After all, much of the military and political debate concerning the need to occupy liberated and conquered territories revolved around the quality of this very military government-Ament, and the extent to which CAOs should actually intervene in foreign affairs.[12]

The novel was probably also popular because it did not prominently display the real problems of the Allied occupation: the shortage and provision of food or the health situation. Instead, it focused on the eponymous "Bell for Adano." This bell symbolized Italy's traditions, and the search for a new one would mean the restoration of a kind of normalcy, while also moving on to the future. At the same time, a distancing from the Fascist regime was implied, as the Fascists had taken the bell to melt it for its gold. In other words, with the quest for a bell taking precedence over more dire matters such as food, a spiritual and moral re-awakening was just as needed as day-to-day survival was—or so Hersey seemed to imply.

> The Major [Joppolo] said: "You say you've come to advise me. Then tell me, what does this town need the most right now?" This time the fat Craxi got there first: "To eat," he said, "much to eat." Cacopardo said: "It needs a bell more than anything." Craxi said: "Foolishness, a bell. More than anything, to eat is necessary." Cacopardo said: "The town needs its bell back. You can always eat. [...] The bell was of our spirit. It was of our history." (Hersey 1944, 19)

The story of the bell was an artistic liberty Hersey took, as this was one of the instances that was not based on his observations as a war correspondent. The search for the bell constituted the leitmotif of the novel. In this respect, Robert S. C. Gordon has already remarked that "culture and liberty nourish as much as food and money" in this depiction of the occupation (Gordon 2018, 17). And one may add that culture and liberty carried decidedly US definitions, as the triumphal march of US culture across post-war Italy would evidence. What is more, the symbolism the bell offers was in line with Italian views that advocated for a return of conditions before Fascism, thereby interpreting the fascist rule as a mere interruption of an otherwise morally decent political culture, as most famously outlaid by philosopher Benedetto Croce.

John Hersey sought to address basically two audiences with depictions such as those offered in *A Bell for Adano*. One involved the domestic public: as alluded to, there were fierce debates in Washington about the spirit and purpose of the character of World War II occupations. Many politicians and commentators alike saw no less than an imperialistic notion inscribed in the military government. Literary characters such as Major Joppolo, thus, would offer a deeply idealized version of US-Americans as noble and benevolent occupiers. The second target group for Hersey's novel were the occupied people themselves, who would find themselves being governed by the Allies, come future times. *A Bell for Adano*, in this way, conditioned people elsewhere to see *future* liberations, and the occupation that went hand in hand with them, as a rather good deal for civilians.

At the time of its publication, Hersey's novel offered just the right dose of what the US public needed. Probably not so much for its prose or style as for its contemporary relevance, Hersey was awarded the Pulitzer Prize in 1945, which was announced on May 8, 1945, the day of liberation (Gordon 2018, 15). The fact that this symbolic date was chosen for the announcement supported the narrative that *A Bell for Adano* offered: that the US-Americans' arrival was meant to be a liberation, which was not false per se. Yet this aspect of liberation superseded memories and interpretations of occupation, meaning the rather unpleasant events that were also unleashed, or at least did not cease, with the Allied arrival: epidemics, lack of food, housing, clothing, medicine, and so on. Leonardo Sciascia's recollection of the events only corroborated this officially sanctioned memory, one that was also helpful for many Italians, as this version of the narrative saved them from having to answer the question of why they were occupied in the first place—a question whose answer would have involved investigating the personal and institutional Fascist past. In other words, the country's eagerness to forget its Fascist memory lent yet another reason why the US version of a liberation was celebrated, especially given its conformity with the Italian emphasis on the resistance movement. The quarreling then rather involved the question whether the Allies or the partisans were the principal protagonists of the liberation. Connected to this question, which rather played out in the field of a politics of memory than in historiographical discourse, was also the role of the USA in postwar Italy in general. Literary representations, such as Domenico Rea's *Gesù, fate luce* ("Jesus, shed light"), only began in the mid-1950s to emphasize the horrors of the Allied occupation, when these works painted gruesome scenes of dead civilians, soldiers, and horses lying all over the islands, who needed to be buried quickly to prevent epidemic outbreaks (Rea 1950). It was at the same time, however, that 'America' became an ever more important topos for Italian postwar politics and reorientation (Forlenza 2019: 68–101).

It bears emphasizing here that Hersey was not so much interested in what AMGOT actually accomplished on the ground. Rather, he offered a version of events in which the redemptive quality of occupation could turn the US presence into something positive. While writing against old narratives—here, the notion that any hierarchical group who rules over another is always bad—writers obviously also establish *new* narratives. In Hersey's case, this new narrative was the 'good occupation,' and Italians soon published their own novels in which they either presented themselves as having gained legitimacy and agency through their participation in the resistance movement or as being in dire need of the occupiers' guidance—thereby presenting themselves a victimized nation that had been devoid of all agency in the 1920s and 1930s, betrayed by Fascism and threatened by Nazism. This was the same lack of agency and scope of action that Eric Linklater so adamantly ironized in *Private Angelo*. Now it was on the US-Americans to instill agency in the Italians and to lend a helping hand. Questions of personal guilt and war guilt, then, ceased to demand answers.

Whereas the Allied occupation of Italy aimed to be a liberation, as Italy was deemed worth saving (not least because of its scenic beauty), the Allied occupation of Germany was imagined differently (for the intricacies of this case, see also Bogdal's chapter in this volume). Politically speaking, in the case of Germany, it was not a question of whether a full-fledged military occupation was necessary or not. Consequently, in terms of literary output, the occupation of Germany by the Allies could not be portrayed as one of cooperation between the occupied and the occupiers. What rather took center stage in such accounts was a shroud of gloom, under which occupation's sinister corollaries became acknowledged more overtly, especially since US audiences took a more distant emotional stance toward the principal war enemy than they had to Italy, where quite many had recent ancestry. The black market, disease, and crime figured prominently now in literary collections, such as Kay Boyle's *The Smoking Mountain: Stories of Postwar Germany* (1951).

Boyle was asked by an editor at *The New Yorker* to come up with accounts of the occupation. This resulted in stories that conceived of the occupation now as a dark sphere, in which espionage, betrayal, and similar phenomena were paramount. Here, the occupied (German) society was imagined as one in which simply *everyone*—occupiers and occupied alike—was bound to suffer. Clearly, the distinctly positive spin that the literature about (and from) Italy gave to the post-war experience did not shine through in these narrations. Other creatives, such as Margaret Bourke-White—who had also been among the journalist-writers who reported directly from the Italian theater of war (Bourke-White 1944; Bond 1992, 86)—supported this perspective on the occupation. Naturally, in occupation accounts, the respective contexts loom large. Hence, whereas in Italy, the Allied encounter with the occupied people started off with exchanges of flowers, chocolate, and cigarettes (or so the popular portrayals went), Bourke-White published her *Dear Fatherland, Rest Quietly* collection under the impressions that Buchenwald had left on her, after she arrived at the camp together with George Patton in April 1945 (Bourke-White 1946). Ultimately, the notion of overtly jolly encounters between occupiers and occupied in post-war Germany was simply a tough sell for a US public so used to war propaganda that had juxtaposed the dangers emanating from Nazi Germany and Fascist Italy, with the latter being rather belittled than taken seriously as principal enemy (an attitude that public opinion surveys also corroborated (Gallup 1972)).

Conclusion

When Jean-Paul Sartre published his *Paris Under the Occupation*, he was still actively processing the German occupational regime in Paris (Sartre 1998 [1944]). He too, albeit under different circumstances than with the Italians under the Allied occupation, referred to the agency and room for maneuver that civilians could enjoy under occupational regimes. But while the Allies' administration of Italy would actively encourage the Italians to take matters into their own hands (even though it was clear that a US-American path toward democracy and modernity was to be followed), Sartre wrangled with the accusation presented by British and US commentators: namely, that the French, allegedly, did not exhibit much will to fight the German occupiers. What this charge implied, however, was that the French technically did have agency, whereas the Italians—as satirized in Eric Linklater's *Private Angelo*—ostensibly had none and could only hope to find a decent moral beacon in the real-life counterparts of figures like Victor Joppolo from *A Bell for Adano*.

In his reflections, Sartre mentioned something that, for most of the literature on occupation discussed here, holds true as well: "The occupation was a *daily affair*," and the "occupation was an immense social phenomenon that affected" millions of people (Sartre 1998 [1944], 2, emphasis in the original). It is this sort of banality, the everyday occurrence and performance of the occupation—with its specific rules and practices—that mattered most, not only in the novels but also in other texts arising out of the occupation. Because the occupied society was truly that: it consisted of occupiers and occupied, and of these parties' countless, asymmetrical interactions, defined by the rule of one group over another, no matter how favorable this occupation was meant to be imagined and presented.

Literary representations of Italy's occupation by the Allies, therefore, fulfilled various functions, whether written as contemporary first-hand accounts or in retrospect. They documented and thereby ascribed sense to the everyday life of the occupation in question. More than just casting them as time-bound documents and historical sources, this chapter has emphasized that they actually offer a rarely explored dimension of the occupation's inherent dynamics. Long before the history of everyday life (*Alltagsgeschichte*) would gain traction in historiography, and while the official histories and first books about the Allied occupation of Italy only reverted to a recapitulation of political decision-making processes in London and Washington, these novels provided fresh insights into the scenery on the field, however fictionalized these insights were. The fuzzy demarcation between war correspondents and novelists, between war dispatches and essays or novels, helped give these texts the appearance of being proper historical sources on the occupation itself. This, partly, also explains why Norman Lewis' *Naples '44* was cherished by historians as a viable source, although it is clearly a very fanciful account of the occupation.

The conditions and objectives of writing, then, only become that much more important to investigate. Because in the end, literature about the Allied occupation of Italy, about *any* occupation, truly became—and aspired to be—a site of negotiation, which was constantly contested and shifting (see also Buschmeier's chapter in this volume). Such literature broke down established narratives, such as in the case of Sartre's essay, which was, more than anything else, an intellectual intervention to set the record straight. At the same time, such works created and substantiated new narratives, as in the case of the good occupiers of John Hersey's *A Bell for Adano*. What must be further expounded, and that I have only hinted at occasionally, is, at least from a historian's perspective, the social profile of those producing literary texts under occupational regimes. The fact has already been pointed out that many of these works issued from a sphere where the boundaries between war correspondent, novelist, essayist, and so on were rather fluid. Beyond that, however—and Sartre as an intellectual is a case in point—looms also the question of who was actually able to write on the side of the occupied people. This question refers to a context in which many people in Southern Italy could chronicle and reflect on their experience only in hindsight, as they had to spend the occupation itself worrying about their daily survival, and at a time in which the public memory already heavily emphasized Northern experiences of the war. The question of who was able to write also carries very literal implications when we consider that Sicily or Calabria had illiteracy rates of more than 50 percent at the time of the occupation.[13]

For Southern Italy, it could therefore be argued that people had to rely on Allied literature that sought to establish the theme of a 'good occupation.' Much like the occupier took the Italian pupil by the hand to walk together toward democracy and modernity (or so the self-imaginations went), US-American authors also set the agenda in terms of how the occupation—albeit not the Italian resistance—would be processed and remembered. Italians, for the most part, would all too willingly take this extended hand, not least since a 'good occupation' allowed them to glance over the fact that some Italians had a tainted, Fascist past. Only in later years, Italian literature, and here specifically novels set in Naples, would show a gloomy side of the Allied occupation—but by then, the paradigm of the good occupation was already well established. In public memory, thus, 'occupation' soon became associated with German military rule in World War II, whereas Allied occupations, if at all considered as such in the immediate postwar years in Italy, operated under the 'liberation' paradigm. Novels—long before official historiographies could do so—framed the Allied administration in Italy in precisely this way.

While no 'liberation' was meant for Germany, in Italy 'liberation' took on a decisively paternalistic notion, feminizing the Italian people, who were deemed in need of saving (Escolar 2019). In this way, John Hersey's *A Bell for Adano* constituted a prime example that paved the way for future sparkling moments of liberation, by conditioning audiences' impressions of the first encounter between the US-American occupiers and the occupied civilians they would meet in the near future.

Notes

1. Library of Congress (LoC), Manuscript Division, Maurice Neufeld Papers, Box 6, Folder 1. Correspondence, 1919–1990, Family, Neufeld, Hinda Cohen (wife), April–June 1944. Maurice Neufeld to Hinda Neufeld, April 17, 1944.
   I would like to thank the editors and the peer reviewers for the thoughtful comments and constructive criticisms.
2. A month earlier, Neufeld aired his grievances about Hersey's novel in similarly heavy words to his wife. See, for this, Carruthers 2014, 1106. This article uses *A Bell for Adano* as a focal point for the analysis of the US-American endeavor to turn occupation into a decisively good enterprise. For her seminal book on this, see Carruthers 2016. Both Carruthers (2014) and Gordon (2018) have explored the themes, backgrounds, and reception of *A Bell for Adano* in much more detail than I can offer here.
3. The fascist regime toppled two weeks after the Allied invasion, and in September 1943 an armistice was declared. The full turnabout happened in October 1943, when Italy declared war on its former ally, Nazi Germany. See, in general, Ellwood 1985.
4. The recent research on the Allied occupation has highlighted the idiosyncrasies of the Allied occupation. See for instance Patti (2013), Williams (2013) and my own monograph on the topic Laffin (2024).
5. LoC, Manuscript Division, Maurice Neufeld Papers, Box 6, Folder 1. Correspondence, 1919–1990, Family, Neufeld, Hinda Cohen (wife), April–June 1944. Maurice Neufeld to Hinda Neufeld, April 17, 1944.
6. It would drop 'Control' in early 1944 to display a less authoritative occupation semantically as well.
7. LoC, George Biddle Papers, Box 19, War Department Art Advisory Committee, Organization, 1943. George Biddle to Franklin D. Roosevelt, February 13, 1943.
8. LoC, George Biddle Papers, Box 19, War Department Art Advisory Committee, Organization, 1943. George Biddle to Reeves Lowenthal, September 1, 1943.
9. LoC, George Biddle Papers, Box 19, War Department Art Advisory Committee, Organization, 1943. George Biddle to Edith Halpert, February 23, 1943.

10. See in this regard especially the works of Gallerano (1985), Chianese (2004), and Gribaudi (2005). These works provided a detailed interpretation of Southern experiences after 1943 and revised many of the myths found in Lewis' elaborations.

11. Original full quote (quoted after Sciascia [1949] 2012, 1243–44)): "Eravamo al 14 luglio. Nel pomeriggio si diffuse la notizia che gli americani arrivavano. Il podestà, l'arciprete e un interprete si avviarono ad incontrarli. La popolazione in attesa si preoccupò di bruciare, ciascuno nella sua casa, tessere, ritratti di Mussolini, opuscoli di propaganda. Dagli occhielli i distintivi scivolarono nelle fogne. Ma gli americani ancora non venivano […] cinque soldati con un lungo fucile abbassato sbucarono improvvisamente nella piazza, indecisi. Videro, davanti una porta semiaperta, qualche uomo in divisa e si mossero sicuri. I carabinieri si trovarono puntati addosso i fucili senza ancora capire che gli americani erano finalmente arrivati. Le loro pistole penzolarono nelle mani di uno della pattuglia. Un applauso scrosciò. Una voce chiese sigarette; e il caporale americano tastò le tasche del brigadiere dei carabinieri, ne tirò fuori un pacchetto di Africa e lo lanciò agli spettatori […] la festa era cominciata."

12. The opening of the Army School of Military Government in 1942 provoked these fierce debates. See, for instance: US Provost Marshal General's Bureau, Hoover Institution Archives, Box 1. Memorandum of Secretary of War Henry L. Stimson for President Roosevelt, November 1942.

13. See: Daniel Lerner Collection, Hoover Institution Archives, Box 22, Folder 2. Italian Basic Handbook. Part I. Internal Organisation and Policy, 48.

References

Allied Commission. 1945. *A Review of Allied Military Government and of The Allied Commission in Italy, July 10, 1943 D-Day Sicily to May 2, 1945, German Surrender in Italy.* Rome: Public Relations Branch, Allied Commission, U.S. Army.

Baldasso, Franco. 2022. *Against Redemption: Democracy, Memory, and Literature in Post-Fascist Italy.* New York: Fordham University Press.

Baris, Tommaso. 2008. "Amnesie, conflitti e politiche della memoria". In *Gli Italiani in guerra: Conflitti, identità, memorie dal Risorgimento ai nostri giorni, Vol. IV, Subvolume 2: Il Ventennio fascista: la seconda guerra mondiale,* edited by Mario Isnenghi and Giulia Albanese, 721–33. Turin: UTET.

Bartolini, Guido. 2021. *The Italian Literature of the Axis War: Memories of Self-absolution and the Quest for Responsibility.* London: Palgrave Macmillan.

Bell, H. E., and Hilary Jenkinson. 1947. *Italian Archives During the War and at Its Close.* London: H. M. Stationary Office.

Bennett, W. Lance. 1990. "Toward a Theory of Press–State Relations in the U. S." *Journal of Communication* 40: 103–25.

Biddle, George 1944. *Artist at War*. New York: The Viking Press.

Bond, Randall I. 1992. "Traveler to Arcadia: Margaret Bourke-White in Italy, 1943–1944." *The Courier* 27, no. 1: 85–110.

Bourke-White, Margarete. 1944. *They Called It "Purple Heart Valley."* New York: Simon & Schuster.

———. 1946. *Deutschland: April 1945 (Dear Fatherland, Rest Quietly)*. New York: Simon and Schuster.

Boyle, Kay. 1951. *The Smoking Mountain: Stories of postwar Germany*. New York: McGraw-Hill.

Buchanan, Andrew. 2008. "'Good Morning, Pupil!': American Representations of Italienness and the Occupation of Italy, 1943–1945." *Journal of Contemporary History* 43, no. 2: 217–240.

Carruthers, Susan L. 2014. "'Produce More Joppolos': John Hersey's A Bell for Adano and the Making of the 'Good Occupation.'" *The Journal of American History* 100, no. 4: 1086–1113.

———. 2016. *The Good Occupation: American Soldiers and the Hazards of Peace*. Cambridge, MA: Harvard University Press.

———. 2018. "Preoccupied: Wartime Training for Post-War Occupation in the United States, 1940–45." In *Transforming Occupation in the Western Zones of Germany: Politics, Everyday Life and Social Interactions, 1945–55*, edited by Camilo Erlichman and Christopher Knowles, 25–42. London: Bloomsbury.

Chianese, Gloria. 2004. *Quando uscimmo dai rifugi: Il mezzogiorno tra guerra e dopoguerra 1943–1946*. Rome: Carocci.

Ellwood, David W. 1985. *Italy, 1943–1945: The Politics of Liberation*. Leicester: Leicester University Press.

Escolar, Marisa. 2019. *Allied Encounters: The Gendered Redemption of World War II Italy*. New York: Fordham University Press.

Fainsod, Merle. 1948. "The Development of American Military Government Policy during World War II." In *American Experiences in Military Government in World War II*, edited by Carl J. Friedrich and Associates, 23–51. New York: Rinehart and Company.

Feigel, Lara. 2016. *The Bitter Taste of Victory: Life, Love and Art in the Ruins of the Reich*. London: Bloomsbury.

Focardi, Filippo. 2013. *Il cattivo tedesco e il bravo italiano: La rimozione delle colpe della seconda guerra mondiale*. Rome: Laterza & Figli.

Forlenza, Rosario. 2012. "Sacrificial Memory and Political Legitimacy in Postwar Italy: Reliving and Remembering World War II." *History and Memory* 24, no. 2: 73–116.

———. 2019. *On the Edge of Democracy: Italy, 1943–1948*. Oxford: Oxford University Press.

Fusi, Francesco. 2018. "Le visits home dei soldati italo-americani durante la Campagna d'Italia (1943–1945): Tra turismo di guerra, homecoming e diaspora tourism." *Diacronie. Studi di Storia Contemporanea* 36, no. 4: 1–23.

Gabriel, Ralph H. 1943. "American Experience with Military Government." *The American Political Science Review* 37, no. 3: 417–38.

Gallerano, Nicola. 1997. "L'arrivo degli alleati". In *I luoghi della memoria: Strutture ed eventi dell'Italia unita*, edited by Mario Isenghi, 455–65. Rome: Laterza & Figli.

———, ed.. 1985. *L'Altro Dopoguerra: Roma e il Sud 1943–1945*. Milan: Angeli.

Gallup, George H. 1972. *The Gallup Poll: Public Opinion, 1935–1971*. New York: Random House.

Gordon, Robert S. C. 2018. "Adano: Sicily, Occupation Literature, and the American Century." *ISLG Bulletin. The Annual Newsletter of the Italian Studies Library Group* 17: 1–23.

Gribaudi, Gabriella. 2005. *Guerra totale: Tra bombe alleate e violenze naziste*. Turin: Bollati Boringhieri.

Halper, Sam. 1944. "Book Review: A Bell for Adano by John Hersey." *New York Post*, April 20, 1944. Quoted in: National Archives and Records Administration, College Park, Maryland, Record Group 331, 10100-101-14, Box 3632, Press Comments & Opinions (Confidential), March-August 1944. Digest of Public Opinion on Allied Military Government. Prepared by the Analysis Branch, News Division, War Department Bureau of Public Relations, p. 6.

Hersey, John. 1943. "AMGOT at Work." *Life*, August 23, 1943: 30–31.

———. 1944. *A Bell for Adano*. New York: Alfred A. Knopf.

Hill, Robert M. and Elizabeth Craig Hill. 1982. *In the Wake of War: Memoirs of an Alabama Military Government Officer in World War II Italy*. Tuscaloosa: University of Alabama Press.

Hughes, Henry Stuart. 1968. *The United States and Italy*. Rev. ed. New York: Norton.

Judt, Tony. 1992. "The Past is Another Country: Myth and Memory in Postwar Europe." *Daedalus* 121, no. 4: 83–118.

Laffin, Stefan. 2020. "Occupied Naples and the Politics of Food in World War II." In *War and the City: The Urban Context of Conflict and Mass Destruction*, edited by Tim Keogh, 139–66. Paderborn: Ferdinand Schöningh.

———. 2024. *Unter alliierter Besatzung: Das lange Ende des Krieges in Süditalien, 1943–1947*. Berlin: De Gruyter.

Lessa, William A. 1985. *Spearhead Governatore: Remembrances of the Campaign in Italy*. Malibu: Undena Publications.

Lewis, Norman. 1978. *Naples '44: An Intelligence Officer in the Italian Labyrinth*. London: Collins.

Linklater, Eric. 1946. *Private Angelo*. London: Jonathan Cape.

Malaparte, Curzio. 1949. *La pelle*. Milan: Aria d'Italia.

Mangiameli, Rosario. 2012. "Le stragi americane e tedesche in Sicilia nel 1943." *Polosud. Semestrale di Studi Storici* 1, no. 2: 141–78.

Matthews, Herbert L. 1943. "We Test a Plan for Governing Europe." *The New York Times*, August 22, 1943.

———. 1946. *The Education of a Correspondent*. New York: Harcourt Brace & Company.

Mercuri, Lamberto, ed. 1992. *Charles Poletti. "Governatore" d'Italia (1943–1945)*. Foggia: Bastogi.

Miller, John. 1989. *Friends and Romans: On the Run in Wartime Italy*. London: Grafton.

Morison, Samuel Eliot. 2002. *Sicily—Salerno—Anzio: January 1943—June 1944*. Urbana: University of Illinois Press.

Patti, Manoela. 2013. *La Sicilia e gli Alleati: Tra occupazione e liberazione*. Rome: Donzelli.

Plain, Gill. 2017. "Eric Linklater, Private Angelo (1946)." *Studies in Scottish Literature* 43, no 2: 200–2.

Pyle, Ernie. 1943. *Here is Your War*. New York: Henry Holt and Company.

———. 1944. *Brave Men*. New York: Henry Holt and Company.

Rea, Domenico. 1950. *Gesù, fate luce*. Milan: Mondadori.

Reese, Stephen D., Oscar H. Gandy Jr., and August E. Grant, eds. 2001. *Framing Public Life: Perspectives on Media and Our Understanding of the Social World*. London: Routledge.

Sartre, Jean-Paul. 1998. "Paris under the Occupation." *Sartre Studies International* 4, no. 2: 1–15 [first published as "Paris sous l'occupation." La France Libre, November 15, 1944].

Schirbock, Byron. 2017. "Translating Occupation: Interpreters and German Authorities in Occupied France, 1940–1944." *Francia. Forschungen zur westeuropäischen Geschichte* 44: 383–92.

Sciascia, Leonardo. [1949] 2012. "Una kermesse." In *Leonardo Sciascia, Opere*, edited by Paolo Squillacioti, 1240–46. Milan: Adelphi.

Steinbeck, John. 1942. *The Moon Is Down*. New York: Viking Press.

Williams, Isobel. 2013. *Allies and Italians under Occupation: Sicily and Southern Italy, 1943–45*. Basingstoke: Palgrave Macmillan.

CHAPTER 9

Literature from Below

Literary Competitions in Serbia (1941–1945) and in the Protectorate of Bohemia and Moravia (1939–1945)

ALEKSANDAR MOMČILOVIĆ

The Protectorate of Bohemia and Moravia was established in March 1939, after two significant events marked the end of the Czechoslovak state. The first was the German violation of the Munich Agreement of 1938, which recognized Germany's claims to territories with a majority-German population in the so-called Sudetenland; the second was the declaration of the independence of Slovakia in March 1939. Although undoubtedly a collaborationist creation, formally led by the appointed President Emil Hácha, the Protectorate provided a kind of limited cultural autonomy for the Czechs and intended to gain broader popular support. Nazi Germany's cultural policy aimed primarily to pacify the Czech population and ensure uninterrupted industrial production (Mohn 2018, 31). Yet, during the six years of German control of this territory, the cultural policy changed, eventually including plans to assimilate a portion of Czechs with enough 'Aryan blood,' and becoming increasingly repressive, with extensive censorship and brutal purges, especially after World War II began.

Unlike the Protectorate of Bohemia and Moravia, which had formed as a result of coercive diplomacy, the (German) Territory of the Military Commander in Serbia was established as a consequence of the military conflict and the forceful dismantling of Yugoslavia by the Axis powers. After satisfying the territorial claims of Hungary, Bulgaria, and Italy, and after the establishment of the puppet state on the territory of Croatia, Nazi Germany established an administrative unit that included central Serbia and most parts of the Banat region (the northern part of today's Serbia) with a significant German-speaking minority. The first administration, the so-called 'Commissioner Government' (*Komesarska uprava*), lasted only a few months and was set to establish a bureaucratic apparatus but was quickly replaced due to its incompetence. The second administration, appointed soon after, was the so-called 'Government of National Salvation' (*Vlada narodnog spasa*), led by Prime Minister Milan Nedić, whose proclaimed cultural task was returning to "old Serbian values" and rejecting the Yugoslav idea.

Unlike their neighbors—the Independent State of Croatia and the Slovak State—Czechs and Serbs under German occupation did not appear as 'independent' states. Thus, the collaborationist administrations in those territories found it more challenging to legitimize their apparatus as an outcome of the people's will. Support from below—that is, broad popular support, or at least the appearance of it—was therefore vital for both administrations. Culture was of particular use for this kind of social mobilization because, in the absence of any political and economic sovereignty, it was only through the organization of cultural life that the occupying society could attempt to legitimize its image—and one especially insightful strategy for legitimizing the occupational and cultural policy (as well as for overcoming the lack of mass support) was the organization and promotion of literary competitions. These competitions, conducted by the collaboration authorities, incentivized participation by means of prizes; in this way, the broader population was not only included in but also *encouraged* to join in the process of 'normalizing' the occupation.

This chapter aims to reconstruct how the occupation was legitimized by 'ordinary people' willing to cooperate with the occupiers, and how the occupation authorities directed this legitimization by awarding simultaneously well-known and lesser-known writers. Various themes that were covered—from pastoral depictions of village life to the daily life of sanitation workers—served as a link between the National Socialist ideology and the occupied populations' everyday existence. The set of commonplaces that characterized the prize-winning literary texts demonstrates the boundaries of socially acceptable imagination in the daily life under the occupation. Despite the differences between the two territories with respect to their local literary traditions, national mythologies, and the intensity of repression, in both cases, published fictional accounts tended to reconcile the occupation with patriotic sentiment, presenting it as the will of the majority.

For opportunistic reasons, the Nazis allowed more cultural autonomy in the Protectorate than in Serbia (especially in the first two years of the Protectorate's existence). Because of this, cultural life in the former was much livelier and more diverse. Accordingly, more literary competitions were held there (i.e., several times a year), and more prizes were awarded there than in occupied Serbia. For instance, in addition to 'thematic' contests and those organized by publishing houses, some national prizes for established writers were founded as well, and some of the existing prizes continued to be awarded (Mohn 2017, 32–41).

By contrast, in Serbia, the majority of the competitions were held only in 1943–1944 and were organized by a fascist weekly magazine, *Srpski narod* ("Serbian People"), under the patronage of Milan Nedić and his ministers. A handful of smaller contests were also organized, such as: the competition by the Academic Theater (*Akademsko pozorište*) in 1942, for a play with the subject "exclusively from the Serbian environment" (Anonymous 1942, 5);[1] the competition of the 'Serbian Labor Union' (*Srpska zajednica rada*), for plays "imbued with a national understanding of life and work" (Anonymous 1943a, 4); and the competition of a comedy theater in 1943 (Anonymous 1943c, 4). That said, no awards in Serbia for established writers could be tracked down.

Literary competitions and prizes provide remarkable insight into what new national literatures would have looked like in the new European order—or, specifically, how occupation authorities and their intellectual apologists saw these national literatures within the new European artistic landscape. Together with unknown authors who were affirmed through competitions, the collaborationist administrations in both occupied areas also republished works by classical authors and tried to rethink their canonical works—which had been valuable for the cultural memory and identity of those countries—in a new, Nazi-approved context. Fundamental works of Czech and Serbian culture, starting from their folk traditions, were interpreted in the spirit of the European New Order. Amidst this literary climate, awarded texts and their authors depict both continuities and discontinuities with the previous literary tradition, pointing toward relevant and obscure authors, themes, forms, and values, and lumping together affirmed authors with novice ones. While the organization of these competitions and prizes showcases the broader workings of the literary-critical universe under the Nazi occupation, it can also reveal some of the specific differences in practice between the literary policy that Nazi Germany implemented within its own borders versus that within the occupied territories.

In Nazi Germany, literary criticism was practically banned. In a speech delivered at the end of November 1936, Joseph Goebbels condemned literary criticism "in its past form": "The reporting of art should not be concerned with values, but should confine itself to description" (Mosse 1968, 162). The task of the *art observer*, then, was only to elaborate on predetermined positions on the given subject, because the critical and analytical approach was understood as a criticism of the regime itself (Kater 2019, 23-4). Instead of critiquing a work, a new type of reviewer should present and *describe* it, and "the people" are the ones who give the final judgment. (In practice, such ideas did not truly mean what "the people" liked but rather what the construct conceived of as a 'nation' under Nazi occupation *should* like.)

Probably the most distinctive feature of the Nazi cultural policy was its condemnation of the modernist tradition and all the literature written by authors whose origins or activism did not fit into their vision of society, such as Jews, Communists, and Anti-Fascists. Nazis were not particularly successful in producing their own art, the art that would celebrate their successes, idols, and ideology, and that would be created according to their aesthetic ideals. Instead, their strategy was mainly based on the re-interpretation of old works (mainly from the 19th century) in which they could read some of their ideas and whose conservative literary form corresponded to their aesthetic standards (Kater 2019, 1–53). The written and unwritten rules they enforced primarily concerned prescribed themes that were desirable to cover; thus most of the literature put into circulation built upon the late-19th-century literary trend of *Heimatkunst*, writing about folk-rural themes "decorated with the swastika and inflated with the racial philosophy of the Nazis" (Bradley 1944, 106). This trend had started in the last years of the Weimar Republic, when "more kitschy agrarian-based novels were published than ever before about Germany as the home of simple, yet trusty peasants" (Kater 2019, 8). In addition to themes of the distant and ambiguously defined past, and fairy-tale-like stories about simple, healthy, and strong peasants, Nazi literary culture encouraged ancestor idolization, motifs related to the soil and the earth, the cult of the mother and fertility, the family, etc. As the war intensified and was increasingly felt at home, books that described direct experiences and heroism from the front also began to be published (Kater 2019, 66–77).

Literature was of less importance to the Nazis than other artistic media (such as film). Partly, this cultural bias was due to literature's lower mobilization potential, but it was also due in part, simply, to the personal affinities of the Nazi leaders. Still, the Nazis strived to overcome the problem of the lack of 'authentic' and effective Nazi literature by organizing competitions and awarding prizes to stimulate new, primarily young authors (Kater 2019, 123–24). Given that German authors were expected to express the Nazi worldview (including German racial superiority), it is unsurprising why some have characterized these authors' works as "simply uninteresting," due to the lack of any quality "that makes them compelling enough to spend your time with them" (Gilman 2009, 230). The present analysis will exclude authors and texts in the German language, primarily because the cultural life of Germans played out under somewhat different rules, as German-speaking authors were more easily integrated into already existing Nazi institutions.

Texts written by non-German authors, however, exhibit more complicated relations. Even though it functioned as a mixture of racist theories and opportunistic improvised practice, in which different Slavic groups were treated differently depending on German war interests, Nazi policy was ultimately steeped in anti-Slavic sentiment (Connelly 1999). Therefore, the poetics of Slavic authors in the occupied territories that did not get their puppet states—these authors being members of the category of 'sub-humans' (*Untermenschen*)—could not be the same as the German Nazi authors, members of the 'Aryan race.' The self-understanding of the Czech and Serbian authors about their place in the European New Order could lend insight into the Nazis' practice toward the Slavs and how the latter's national mythologies were refashioned to align with a regime whose ideology was directly opposed to them: if Nazi theory denigrated Slavs, what could have been a consistent ideological answer by a Slavic fascist?

Radical, brutal, and violent social change was somehow meant to be rendered 'symbolic' for all parties involved in the war. However, since the war havoc had invalidated the old system of signs and symbols, it was important for the occupying administrations to give this conflict a new meaning. This struggle of ideas was perhaps most clearly projected onto fiction, because it is fiction that defines, in a way, the boundaries of the possible and the imaginable in a society—that is, not only what patterns of imagining are desirable but also, simultaneously, what kind of society these patterns of imagining imply. The fact that meaning was closely controlled under Nazi rule implied that summaries and interpretations of the texts might have been more useful means of promoting cultural values than (or at least as important as) the full literary works themselves. Descriptions indicated the 'meaning' to which each text was reduced and thus simplified the 'moral' of the text to (potential) readers. For instance, none of the awarded texts in occupied Serbia has been published in book form: the only edition that could be tracked down of the novel *Dva života* ("Two Lives") by Vojin Puljević, awarded in the competition of the weekly *Srpski narod* in 1943, is a 1970 private edition published by Puljević's sister as the fulfillment of the author's testament (Puljević 1970). Instead, only selected passages, text descriptions (involving straightforward suggestions as to how the text should be interpreted and what values should be attributed to it), and the authors' biographies were published in newspapers at the time, apparently serving a more important propaganda function than the texts themselves.

Organizing the literary public sphere shared by known and novice writers reveals much more about society-building under the occupation than does analysis of the process of canonizing already known authors, as the former reveals how new values were attempted to be created. Meanwhile, the publication and re-interpretation of canonical authors' works demonstrate the new values of these newly occupied societies, along with the elements of the local tradition that the new society hoped to build upon. Nonetheless, it is only through the attempt to affirm *new* authors, books, and themes that one can complete the picture of value-building.

Literary life during the occupation in Serbia has been little explored by literary historians to date. A voluminous yearbook of cultural life under occupation was compiled by literary historian Bojan Đorđević, in which he presents a detailed list of all texts devoted to culture in all relevant daily and weekly magazines that were published during the occupation (Đorđević 2001). Aleksandar Stojanović, in his book about the so-called Serbian civil/cultural plan of the Government of Milan Nedić (i.e., the collaborationist government's program on the organization of every facet of life in peacetime conditions), touches on literary life, but not in detail (Stojanović 2012). Radomir Konstantinović analyzed some aspects of literary life under the occupation in the philosophical book *The Philosophy of Parochialism* (2021; originally published in Serbian as *Filosofija palanke*, 1969), focusing on what he considered the ideological basis of cultural life under the occupation—the so-called Serbian Nazism (Konstantinović 2004).

By contrast, culture in the Protectorate of Bohemia and Moravia is a more thoroughly researched topic. Jiří Doležal touched upon literature in his monograph on culture during the Protectorate, including the fields of publishing, education, and film (Doležal 1996). Volker Mohn lays out a very detailed analysis of the cultural life in the Protectorate in his doctoral dissertation, published as a book; he surveyed the Nazi cultural policy in the Protectorate, focusing on how it was conceived at the very top of Nazi Germany and what its implementation looked like (Mohn 2018). Beyond these sources, as part of the project of the Institute for Czech Literature of the Czech Academy of Sciences, "Literature under the Protectorate of Bohemia and Moravia (1939–1945)," several articles and collections were published, leading up to the voluminous *Dějiny české literatury v protektorátu Čechy a Morava* ("History of Czech Literature in the Protectorate of Bohemia and Moravia"), edited by Pavel Janoušek (Janoušek 2022). These and other researchers of the culture in the Protectorate explored the essential themes, motives, authors, context of cultural policy, etc. Alena Šidáková Fialová mapped out the main trends of mainstream Czech literature, especially prose, finding that the literature of the time was dominated by psychological fiction, stories about life in small towns, an unusually significant number of texts dedicated to Prague, historical prose, and the thematization of rural life (Šidáková Fialová 2021, 182–88). Finally, Volker Mohn provided a detailed overview of the literary competitions and prizes in Bohemia and Moravia, in the 2017 volume edited by Lucie Antoníšková, *Zatemněno: Česká literatura a kultura v protektorátu* ("Darkened: Czech Literature and Culture in the Protectorate"). However, he stopped at a detailed description of the organization and context of these contests, leaving out the literary analysis. For him, literary contests were "carrots" in the carrot-and-stick dynamics of Nazi Germany's cultural policy in the Protectorate, offering incentives for those willing to fit into the cultural establishment (Mohn 2017, 30–44).

Nationalism

A general framework of literary life in both occupied territories was nationalism. Yet the collaborationist bureaucracies had to take care to appropriate nationalism in a way that would not endanger the politics of the Nazi powers; active participation in the occupation administrations was to be presented as a patriotic act.

Before the outbreak of World War II, the cultural 'autonomy' provided by the German occupation administration in the Protectorate had seemed relatively mild to all those who were not under the direct blow of the National Socialist regime. Nazi propaganda promoted its cultural policy as a period of flourishing Czech culture (Mohn 2018, 17–20). In general, Nazis' attitude toward Czechs was much more favorable than toward Serbs, as Nazis seemed to place Czechs higher in the hierarchy of races than most of the other Slavic nations, deeming most Czechs to exhibit enough 'desired' racial qualities that would make them eligible for long-term assimilation and Germanization (Novotný 2021, 488–98). A 'tacit agreement' of allowing *national* cultural activities, thus, facilitated easier control and exploitation of the territories of Bohemia and Moravia with less resistance.

In the first years of occupation, the nationalist sentiment in the Protectorate was, on the one hand, a defiance of Germany and its attempts to Germanize the population and the culture. On the other, the way that this nationalist sentiment was officially practiced did not threaten the Reich's political, economic, and military needs. Limited cultural autonomy facilitated a collaborationist, self-legitimizing narrative, based on the claim that the new national policy "saves the people" (Mohn 2018, 45–57). The situation would eventually change, first with the beginning of the war, and then after Reinhard Heydrich, appointed Deputy Reich Protector, began to govern the territory. Finally, at the beginning of 1943, the Czech authors, especially younger ones, were expected to enlighten the whole Czech nation in the spirit of great Germany (Mohn 2017, 42–43).

In occupied Serbia, the situation with nationalism was slightly different. Since Serbia's occupation had resulted from a war conflict, the pre-war era's extreme right-wing intellectuals, conservatives, and fascists were immediately appointed as part of the local Nazi administration. Thus, the fascist version of Serbian nationalism immediately became official and completely fit in with the National Socialist ideology. Therefore, it is no wonder that more *manifestly* nationalist texts were awarded in occupied Serbia than in occupied Czechia, as Serbian cultural life was stricter and was expected to be more focused on connecting national sentiments with the Reich's military goals.

This fascist nationalism had another vital role: the opposition to Yugoslavism. The occupation and dismemberment of Yugoslavia by the Axis Powers were easier to explain as consequences of the decadent Yugoslav elite, who had ostensibly worked to the detriment of Serbia and had chosen the wrong side of history by opposing German domination. According to this view, decadent elites, at the expense of foreign powers (mainly Great Britain)—by deciding to terminate the signed agreement on Yugoslavia's accession to the Tripartite Pact—committed an act of treason and sealed Yugoslavia's suicide (Gregorić 1942).[2]

In fact, interwar decadence is the theme of the aforementioned novel by Vojin Puljević. The book's conclusion is dominated by a scene wherein the Yugoslav flag replaces the Serbian one, thus implying the end of Serbian statehood and the death of Steva, a man who represents the old Serbian virtues. In contrast, Ivan, a man of the new, decadent era, becomes a minister in the newly formed government. The new elites have wasted the decades-long struggle of the "Serbian peasant" for freedom, culture, literacy, and state-building. How Puljević thematizes World War I, one of the principal events for Serbian national sentiment, speaks to his type of Nazi-eligible nationalism. Although World War I is a significant formative experience for Steva, the narrator avoids giving the enemy of the Serbian army a name, mainly addressing the opposing forces as, simply, "the enemy"; Germans are only mentioned in passing, along with Bulgarians, Italians, and others (Puljević 1970, 180–200).

Another award-winning novel in the same contest, *Gresi otaca* ("Sins of the Fathers") by Borislav Paunković, deals with the theme of the interwar period's decadence. Namely, post-World War I brings to Belgrade a new spirit, rhythm, and "fashion," from and defined by the West; the acceptance of this spirit eventually leads to the "collapse of an environment" (Anonymous 1943d, 11).

Most of the awarded texts in occupied Serbia seem to be aligned with this form of Serbian nationalism that Radomir Konstantinović labels 'Serbian Nazism.' According to him, the poetics of Serbian Nazism was based on the principles of individual self-sacrifice, absolute rationalism (hence the rejection of aestheticism), and "realism" as opposed to "abstraction" (Konstantinović 2004, 309–11). Konstantinović does not see 'Serbian Nazism' as imported from Germany, but rather as part of the local intellectual tradition (Konstantinović 2004, 301). Those already belonging to the intellectual milieu of Serbian Nazism were in charge of leading the cultural policy under the occupation and even organizing literary competitions. For instance, the five-member jury of *Srpski narod*'s literary competition for poetry was headed by the critically acclaimed, interwar, avant-garde-poet-turned-fascist-apologist Svetislav Stefanović (Anonymous 1943c, 10).

Czech collaborationists were not much different regarding their view on the importance of breaking from continuity with the previous governments. While Serbian Nazi apologists interpreted the demonstrations on March 27, 1941, against the accession to the Tripartite Pact as being due to meddling by Western foreign powers intent on leading Serbia astray, Czech collaborationists, like Emanuel Moravec (later the Minister of Education in the Protectorate and the chairman of the Board of Trustees for the Education of Youth, a Czech fascist youth organization), were disappointed by the West's surrender of Czechoslovak interests in the Munich Agreement: "Perhaps one day we will thank the West for relieving us of our obligations to it. They must forgive us for taking our affiliation with the German Empire very seriously in the future!" (Moravec 1941, 360). The authorities in the Protectorate of Bohemia and Moravia and in Serbia shared a similar nationalist framework, seeing the highest interests of their nations in the choice to subordinate to the 'superior' Germany, which was viewed as spiritually and militarily capable of leading them on the right path. However, all this being said, the theme of breaking with the previous system was not equally significant in Czech literary works awarded at contests compared to in occupied Serbia, did not appear frequently, and the link between the ideological assumptions of the occupation regime and the awarded texts was much looser.

Religion

Most of the award-winning literary texts in occupied Serbia, in some way, capture the Kosovo myth, an essential victimizing narrative of Serbian nationalism. Even though it has not been a unified narrative with identical political meaning from its inception in the folk tradition to the present day, its main elements could be summed up as the mythical representation of the Battle of Kosovo in 1389, in which the Serbian feudal rulers lost the battle against the Ottoman Sultan Murat I. In the oral tradition, the aftermath of this event is interpreted as the point when Serbia's statehood was lost, with Serbia falling under Ottoman occupation. The myth presents the leader of the Serbian feudal forces, Prince Lazar, who was referred to as *Car Lazar* ("Emperor Lazar"), as a Christian martyr who fell in the fight for the Kingdom of Heaven and thus provided the Serbs with a heavenly kingdom, instead of an earthly one. The particular religious character of this myth is accorded to the fact that the battle took place on the day of St. Vitus. The cultural policy of the collaborationist Government of National Salvation firmly relied on the ahistorical reading of the epic oral tradition, identifying itself with the myth's patriarchal feudal values. Although the award-winning texts did not always refer directly to the historical events and the shape they took in the oral tradition, they kept reiterating a set of commonplaces that seemed to parallel the myth. Namely, they suggested that World War II was a similarly great tragedy for Serbia that threatened to jeopardize its statehood (implying that Yugoslavia and the decadent interwar period had led to this, not that the German occupation had) and that the struggle that was ahead of Serbia was a struggle for spiritual rebirth (or, in the discourse of the Kosovo myth, the battle for the Kingdom of Heaven). This was most evidently presented in the third-place poem of the *Srpski narod* magazine contest in 1943, wherein the hardships of the Serbian people in World War II were introduced in the manner of Christian martyrs' torment and compared to the resurrecting figure of Jesus Christ (Sušić 1943, 11).

One essential religious figure in the literary-religious corpus in occupied Serbia was the character of St. Sava, the 13th-century founder and first archbishop of the Serbian autocephalous church. Serbian fascist nationalism from the late 1930s saw the embodiment of true feudal, medieval values in St. Sava. In this type of ideological reading, St. Sava was seen as the ideologue of a specific *Serbian path* base, a combination of nationalism and the Eastern Orthodox clericalism (opposed to Roman Catholicism and Judaism). The official ideology of the occupation authorities was sometimes referred to as *svetosavlje* or *svetosavski nacionalizam* ("St. Sava's nationalism"). They extensively promoted his cult, and fictionalized biographies of St. Sava were a frequent theme of school essays and competitions. For instance, in the youth literary contest of the *Srpski narod* magazine, first place went to the author of a fictionalized biography, *Putevi Svetog Save* ("St. Sava's Paths") (Anonymous 1943e, 12, 1943f, 10).

Although religious authors (mainly Catholic) were part of the cultural mainstream of the Protectorate also, religious motives were not as significant among award-winning authors there. In Czech texts awarded during the Protectorate, God and religion were mentioned as part of the traditional patriarchal system, or as spiritual meditations on the overall calamity in which the world finds itself. Thus, in Metoděj Jahn's memoir, called *Jarní píseň: chlapecké vzpomínky* (1940) ("The Spring Song: Boyhood Memories"), awarded the National Award for Art (*Národní cena za umění*)[3] in 1940, the author describes unfortunate circumstances as 'God's will'/'providence,' while priests, the church, and religious holidays are part of everyday life in the countryside. The same holds for another laureate, Jan Vojtěch Sedlák's novel *Věnec jeřabinový* (1938) ("The Rowanberry Wreath"), wherein the influence of the church and religious customs on the daily life of peasants was described even more clearly in several extended scenes of funerals, weddings, and masses. Religious-conservative elements became mainstream during the so-called Second Czechoslovak Republic (i.e., the period from signing to violating the Munich Agreement), when other Catholic authors, such as Jan Zahradníček and Jan Čep, were decorated with the same award.

Catholic-conservative authors in the Protectorate received special attention, starting from the beginning of the war, when the occupation introduced additional coercive measures (Mohn 2017, 35). However, not all the Catholic authors followed a unified political line because clerical nationalism, as a state ideology, did not dominate literary life in the same way as in occupied Serbia. For example, some of the Czech religious poetry collections expressed a pessimistic image of life surrounded by the brutal world, as in Vilém Závada's *Hradní věž* (1940) ("The Castle Tower"), in which religion serves as a consolation in a world plagued by war chaos—for instance, the verses: "Paradise lost is behind us/Hell burning is behind us/The kingdom of God is before us" (Závada 1940, 82). Yet this type of pessimistic poetry could only be published in the early stages of the war; the cultural policy became more and more strictly focused on achieving the war goals of the Axis powers, especially after 1942 and 1943. As such, the new poetry was not allowed to fall into individualism and pessimism but rather was expected to display the inner strengths of faith and enthusiasm (Piorecká 2021, 483).

Rebirth

Another critical issue for building the national myths in general and for the poetics of most pastoral/ruralist authors is the entanglement of fertility, regeneration, moral rebirth, and national revival. This is encapsulated in an award-winning short nationalist poem from 1943, *Pesma za Srbiju* ("A Poem for Serbia"), where Serbia was personified as the mother figure who is life-giving but also larger than life. The country was described in terms of several natural attributes, such as rivers, meadows, lakes, and flowers. It concludes with a stanza explaining that the mother (i.e., Serbia), is currently mourning, but a revival—or, more precisely, a rebirth—is being prepared. As in most of the poems, short stories, and accompanying texts published in *Srpski narod*, this poem implies that the national revival will take place within the framework of the new Europe, where *the new Serbia* has its place (Filipović 1943, 11).

In the cultural life of both occupied territories, in fact, the countryside had a unique role as a place of moral rebirth. It signified the return to the old times, a return to nature, and a rejection of the modern way of life that brings only misfortune, vice, and decadence. For instance, in the memoir *Jarní píseň: chlapecké vzpomínky* ("The Spring Song: Boyhood Memories"), as well as in the novel *Věnec jeřabinový* ("The Rowanberry Wreath"), the village way of life has a regenerative effect on the characters. The first book follows the narrator as an ailing child sent to the countryside to be healed and strengthened. The countryside has a restorative impact, not only by its nature, clean air, and water but also by the peasants' way of life: existing in harmony with the land; demonstrating humility, diligence, and dedication to their work; and appreciating the fruits of nature (Jahn 1941). In the other book, sinister things come from the city, threatening the village's inner peace, such as the eviction letter for the protagonist's best friend, which brings unrest. Also, between scenes of action and dialogue, the protagonist takes walks through the forest among the birds and the stream's murmur, and these walks are presented as regenerative rituals (Sedlák 1938). Although the plot in these works is set in a specific time (often in the past), these books do not convey any sense of precisely when that is. For instance, the accounts from *Jarní píseň* and *Věnec jeřabinový* most likely take place a few decades apart. Still, we learn little about exactly when; time passes only by the change of day and night and the change of seasons, which implies a cyclical understanding of time—a kind of timelessness.

While the ruralist presumptions of the countryside as the place of moral and physical regeneration and as the nation's place of birth faded over time in the Protectorate, in occupied Serbia they were part of the official ideology all the time. The convenience of advocating for ruralism as a legitimizing ideology for the political and literary establishment in occupied Serbia was reinforced on the level of the language; the word *zemlja* can be used in Serbian interchangeably to denote 'land,' 'country' (as in countryside), 'soil,' and 'nation.'

The award-winning play *Marija Paleologova* ("Maria Palaiologina") by Slobodan M. Isaković, staged under the title *Dušanovo jutro* ("Dušan's Morning"), encapsulates almost all the ideological commonplaces of the Nedić regime. The play thematizes the medieval past and affirms a new, "healthy" Serbia (as opposed to dead Yugoslavia), which originates from the countryside (embodied in Dušan, whose court is in the countryside) and that fights against foreign scheming. Set in the 14th century, the play deals with the historical conflict between the Serbian king Stefan Dečanski and his son Dušan the Mighty, presenting it as an upshot of the conspiracy of Stefan's wife, the Byzantine princess Maria Palaiologina. She wants the Serbian throne for her son Simeon Siniša (also a son of Stefan) instead of for Dušan (Stefan's son with another wife). While Stefan is an aged and blind Serbian king with almost no political agency whatsoever, Maria is presented as a manipulative wife and a foreigner who wants to introduce foreign rule over Serbia, which the Byzantine army is willing to help her to accomplish. Dušan, for his part, is determined to preserve peace in the country and prevent a civil war between the noblemen who support him and the noblemen who support his father; he is so conciliatory, however, that some noblemen condemn him for this quality and even abandon him. Eventually, due to a series of incidents from the opposing side, Dušan decides to go into what was presented as an *imposed* civil war (Isaković 2010, 89–165). Maria portrays the Serbian nobility as savage and peasant, while seeing Byzantium as a cultural and civilizational alternative. Dušan and his nobles, on the other hand, affirm their peasantry: "He, a peasant, will wear the imperial crown" (Isaković 2010, 105), says one of Dušan's most faithful noblemen.

Although an allegorical reading of the play under the German occupation might equate the German occupier with Byzantium (a foreign power that wants to abolish Serbia's independence), the author, jury members, and other contemporaries interpreted it differently. It was not Germany, the foreign power, menacing Serbia's independence, but the "Judeo-Bolshevist" ideology:

> With it [the play], I wanted, in addition to depicting life at the court of Stefan
> Dečanski, to point out a turning point in our history, similar to this one now, in

which youth, with its sense of the future and mission of the state, defeated the scheming of others. (Anonymous 1944, 20)

The foreign intrigues that Isaković alludes to primarily refer to the "Bolsheviks," who were perceived by Nedić's government as the main political and military threat; along with the Jews, communists were considered the main "conspirators" undermining the unity of Serbia. It is implied several times in the play that Serbia's internal revival will come from the countryside, where Dušan's palace is located, not from the Byzantine *civilization*. Moreover, the site of the court of medieval Serbian rulers in the 14th century, Nerodimlje, is renamed Porodimlje. The name change bears progenitive implications, for, in contrast to Nerodimlje (which might be roughly translated as 'Barrenborough'), with undertones of barrenness, Porodimlje (roughly translated as 'Birthborough') implies fertility (Isaković 2010, 89–165).

All the other texts awarded in occupied Serbia were almost entirely dedicated to rural themes. The treatment of city life (i.e., 'civilization') often shows the decadence that urban life brings to society. In the aforementioned novel *Dva života* ("Two Lives"), a positive portrayal of Steva's upbringing affirms the peasant life filled with hard work, modesty, and sacrifice. It highlights the role of the peasant way of thinking in the foundation of independent Serbia toward the end of the 19th century, while it criticizes the complacency and selfishness of Ivan—a man of the city brought up in Yugoslavia (Puljević 1970). The author described it as "the novel of a peasant who gets an education and gets ahead of himself with his homeland and Serbian society" (Anonymous 1943c, 10). Similarly, the short story *Na splavu* ("On a Raft") takes place in a village where raftsman Drago is in love with Mara. The plot begins with her father's request that she go to the city to study and work. This decision brings unfortunate events for Drago, Mara, and the whole village; things return to good only when Mara returns home. It was the city that brought misfortune (Đurić 1943a, 10–11, 1943b, 10–11).

Regarding Czech literature under the Protectorate, it is interesting that the cultural policy of Nazi Germany was built upon the already existing tradition in Czech interwar literature: the literary movement of ruralism (*ruralismus*). Some authors consider Czech ruralism a 'version' of the German literary movement *Heimatkunst* from the turn of the 20th century, whose representatives treated rural and small-town themes, promoting 'healthy' German life, and opposed urbanization and modernization. The significance of ruralism diminished even during the Protectorate, and it was completely rejected after the war. This trend is evident in the analysis of selected works, with some critics dismissing its central premise that the 'return to the countryside' fosters moral regeneration in the nation (Holeček 2019, 508–9). The 1939 laureate of *Státní cena za literaturu*

(The State Award for Literature), Jan Vojtěch Sedlák's *Věnec jeřabinový* (1938) ("The Rowanberry Wreath") was an entirely ruralist novel. The story of turbulent events in the affluent rural family Melen and the conflict between the father and his son who decides to marry a girl of whom the former disapproves was primarily praised for its lyrical elements and underlying values. Literary critic Vladimír Hellmuth-Brauner wrote in 1939:

> There are few novels of recent times that can create something so truly national, that capture the depths of our national instincts, the unconscious rhythm of our national soul, that can be recognized in one dramatic abbreviation of a person who passes inaudibly through the plot and yet carries the great treasures of the race, its pain, and its great victory. (Hellmuth-Brauner 1939, 299)

Despite fading influence, ruralist literary works continued to be published in the following years, such as *Písně za pluhem* ("Songs Behind the Plough"), the collection of selected poetry from 1940 sent to the 'Liberal Country Teaching Competition' (*Svobodné učení selské*). The set of values that the editor of the collection presents in the preface does not differ much from what was propagated as the highest cultural value by the regime of Milan Nedić in occupied Serbia or, for that matter, in Nazi Germany:

> The rural environment of peasant work and faith, with all the customs, traditions, and festivals of the seasons and the Christian year, has always been a fertile ground for folk poetry, expressing a deep Christian and moral feeling, the strength of family tradition and family togetherness, the fervor of religious and amorous feeling, a deep sense of justice and goodness. (Škvor 1940, 8)

It is worth noting, however, that despite the attempts by Nazi theoreticians to frame ruralism exclusively in the context of *Blut und Boden* (blood and soil) ideology, the poetic and ideological principles of ruralism did not aspire to include the entire organization of life that would have corresponded to the Nazi one (Holeček 2019, 512–13). To this could be added the fact that some of the authors of ruralist pieces died fighting Nazism, such as Karel Dvořáček, the holder of *Národní cena za umění* (The National Award for Art) for the novel *Pole kráčí do hor* (1941) ("The Field Walks into the Mountains"). Regardless, among Serbian and Czech ruralists alike, there is undoubtedly a vital link among the terms of the state, the village, and the country. This does not necessarily mean that they all built upon the theory of blood and soil, but they were indeed in tune with it. Nevertheless, the causes of the declining influence of ruralism in the Protectorate can be sought in literary reasons: exhaustion of form and content. Additionally, one reason may also be that Nazi Germany did not plan for the territory of the Protectorate, at least in the near future, to be an agricultural area but an industrial one. Nazi literary policy in the Protectorate was not limited to ruralism, although this would be in line with their ideological assumptions.

Finally, the city/village dichotomy seems to be a common theme in literatures of military occupation, regardless of their ideological attachment to ruralism. Atinati Mamatsashvili notes that both authors as disparate as an anti-Soviet, Georgian writer who experienced Soviet rule after 1921 and a German antifascist exile writer treated the *city* under the occupation as a vile and hostile place (see Mamatsashvili's chapter, this volume).

Family

The land is directly connected to the family because the family is the living, biological, embodiment of continuity from ancient times to the present day. At the beginning of *Věnec jeřabinový* ("The Rowanberry Wreath"), the eldest member of the Melen family is in poor health and worried about the estate's future because he has two sons, both of whom want to stay on the estate. He categorically refuses to divide the property because the property is not to be separated but rather increased. He leaves everything to the older son and sends the younger one to school (Sedlák 1938). In other words, his concerns for his family are shaped by his concerns for the property: how the son will get married, whether this son will be able to maintain the household, and the like.

The family theme, in a way, encompasses all of the enumerated motifs—nationalism, religion, and ruralism—because the way that family life is presented in almost all works is inseparable from the rural way of life. In a time of great turmoil and unprecedented industrial death and suffering, only the family and the 'backyard' are a place of security. The family is, of course, patriarchal; things are decided based on age, the oldest male being the one who decides everything. Suppose a character leaves the family and disrespects family values. In that case, she/he is doomed, as in the 1940 novel *Moudrý Engelbert* ("The Wise Engelbert"), wherein a couple's premarital adventures lead them to the moral abyss (John 1942).

A similar atmosphere was described in Serbian texts, too, as it is encapsulated in the short story *Smrt srpskog domaćina* ("Death of a Serbian Householder"), about an old peasant who has been ill for a long time but one day starts feeling better. He understands this as a sign of his imminent death and begins to sort things out—visiting the yard and the country estate and giving instructions to family and friends on how to prepare him for death. The householder is at the center of events: a sage who foresees death, takes care of the family, and believes in God (Ilić 1943, 12–13). Again, as in *Věnec jeřabinový*, the householder's concern for the family amounts to his concern for the future of the household, what it will look like, and whether it will be able to continue to exist. Indicative enough, the one who obediently fulfills his requirements is the female figure of a daughter-in-law, who corresponds to the ideal patriarchal image of a woman.

Labor

Another emerging theme in the literary contests is the cult of labor, particularly relevant for the Protectorate, the industrialized occupied territory that was a significant supplier of weapons. In general, manual labor was associated with the rural way of life, the cultivation of the land, and the hard-working farmers: a peasant who worked hard in the fields, tamed nature, made bread, etc. However, the literary competition organized by the National Trade Union Employees' Headquarters (*Národní odborová ústředna zaměstnanecká*, or NOÚZ) seems to be a particularly interesting counter-example. NOÚZ was a kind of union founded in 1939 after the disbandment of all pre-occupation trade unions into one organization, under the control of the occupation authorities. Over time, the activities of NOÚZ became more and more controlled, with purges of unreliable personnel due to strikes and potential production disruptions. Yet this did not prevent the organization of NOÚZ's first illegal resistance groups in 1943, in the beginning mainly by social-democratic activists and pre-war trade unionists (Růžička 1963, 15–16).

Primarily due to the advanced production of weapons developed on the territory of Czechoslovakia, the policy of Nazi Germany toward Czechs was relatively mild compared to its policy toward some other Slavic groups, among whom were the Serbs. As such, the majority of Czechs continued their daily lives in a relatively settled manner, as long as the labor force was exploited and fulfilled its tasks (Connelly 1999). Perhaps for this reason, the Nazi institutions were more lenient toward the Czech workers and paid particular attention to gaining their support, or at least avoiding active resistance. Even in the later stages of the war, when the initially limited cultural autonomy faded away with ever-increasing coercive measures, Germans, not wanting to risk the stable production of weapons, kept organizing cultural events aimed at Czech workers (Mohn 2018, 32). Nazi Germany's propaganda and concessions to Czech workers were extraordinarily significant. Such an attitude opened up the space for the kind of subversion that could not have been imagined in occupied Serbia.

As part of its cultural activities, NOÚZ organized a literary competition in 1941 for workers to write about their own experiences under the slogan *Z práce a o práci českého dělníka* ("From and about the Work of the Czech Worker").

Needless to say, the commonality to all works awarded in this competition was a glorification of labor. František Erik Šaman's awarded novel *Moje ruce* ("My Hands") follows the toiling metalworker Štěpán Hora, an enthusiastic laborer who had both hands amputated after an accident and who slowly returns to a normal life, refusing pity and mercy. The novel abounds with episodes from the shop floor and living conditions in working-class homes. Yet what makes it particularly compelling is a quote by Romain Rolland chosen as the prefacing quote: "there is only one heroism in the world: to see the world as it is, and to love it" (Šaman 1942). Although this quote may refer to the naturalist depiction of workers' lives, full of unapologetic but poignant descriptions, Rolland's years-long anti-fascist activism introduces reasons for reading it as a provocative hint.

Even more interesting is the case of Karel Vokáč, whose cycle of poems was awarded in the same competition. Two years later, in 1944, this collection was adjusted and extended for another cycle, *Z domoviny* ("From the Homeland"). While the first cycle captured "the worker's being and inwardness in their various forms and tremors, utilizing imagery that is intimately fervent and almost visionary," the second cycle introduces elements of nature, the village, and the peasantry, showing that "Vokáč's industrial worker, however, remains closely connected to the region and nature of his native countryside" (Vokáč 1944). The earliest stamp on the second edition indicates April 5, 1944 as the date of release, when Vokáč had already been imprisoned for his underground activities. Vladimír Thiele, another poet who was awarded in the same competition, left testimony about Vokáč's last weeks in the penitentiary. He conveys a letter that Vokáč secretly sent from his prison cell to the poet Jaroslav Seifert, asking him to alert some of the well-known German editors to put in a good word with the public prosecutor for his cycle *Utkáno z dýmu* ("Woven of Smoke") (Thiele 1946, 773–82). Karel Vokáč was executed a few months later, in July 1944.

Unlike ruralist authors who were marginalized entirely after the end of World War II and the coming to power of the Communist Party, most of the award-winning works from NOÚZ's competition had been integrated into the new literary life. Yet another awardee, Alfred Technik, continued his career as a writer and journalist after the war, working for Czechoslovak Radio (*Československý rozhlas*), writing reportage, screenplays, and books. His documentary work *Muži pod Prahou* ("Men Under Prague")—a series of loosely connected reportage pieces with lyrical descriptions of workers in the Prague sewer[4]– was used as the basis for a 1947 film of the same name.

In a sense, the diversity of entries in the NOÚZ literary competition encapsulates the complexity of literary life in the Protectorate. Although, on the thematic level, many of the award-winning texts fit into Nazi Germany's demands for Czechs, from whom they found it vital to extract an uninterrupted supply of weapons, some of the contest entries, at the same time, demonstrate diverse strategies of resistance. Such literary works should be seen as vital components of the broader resistance strategy employed by 'ordinary people' in the Protectorate. Kateřina Piorecká demonstrates how unnamed clerks sabotaged the attempts by the Nazi bureaucratic apparatus to centralize and tighten control of the literary public sphere. The detailed lists and records of cultural workers were filled with intentional omissions of the facts that could have compromised the authors, thus providing the occupier with a distorted picture (Piorecká 2021, 469–98).

Finally, what emerges as a striking detail when it comes to literary competitions in both of the territories is that there is almost no openly antisemitic content among the award-winning texts. For instance, there were no stereotypical Jewish characters or tirades against the Jewish–Bolshevik–Masonic conspiracy, content that was otherwise common in pulp fiction, pamphlets, newspapers, or popular entertaining magazines such as Czech *Ejhle!* ("Look!") or Serbian *Bodljikavo prase* ("Porcupine"). Yet this conspicuous absence of such content should not obscure the fact that antisemitism was, all the same, a feature of the cultural life in both occupied territories: authors of Jewish descent were persecuted, censored, and banned from publishing and participating in cultural life.

Conclusion

Themes of nationalism, religion, ruralism, rebirth, family, and hard manual labor occur repeatedly in most texts that won awards in the literary competitions of occupied Bohemia and Moravia, and Serbia. Despite the territories' differences in the treatment of these themes, these themes were mainly in tune with the demands and needs of the National Socialist regime. Hence, the themes of the contests show a glimpse of daily life as it would have ultimately been organized had Nazi Germany won the war. For instance, occupied Serbia would have been focused on providing agricultural goods, while occupied Czechia would have probably been the manufacturing heart of the new Europe.

In the Protectorate—based on the context, range of values, and themes—it can be seen that literary competitions were organized with the idea of 'normalizing' the occupation and encouraging cultural production. As many awards were aimed at established authors, literary contests and prizes were clearly intended to 'distill' existing trends within Czech literature and encourage those that were not in conflict with Germany's war goals; this strategy was an attempt to rearrange the hierarchy of values within the literary system.

By contrast, in Serbia, awards aimed at established authors could not be tracked down, so it can be assumed that the cultural policy in occupied Serbia carried the intention of a more fundamental change. The cultural policy in Serbia was stricter, not only because the occupation was a result of the conflict but also because the occupied territory had a more active armed resistance. Literary contests there were organized only in the second phase of the war, and the awarded works show a much narrower thematic range. The collaborationist authorities in Serbia made more transparent the connection between the extreme right-wing clerical-nationalist tradition and the attempt to establish an entirely new literary life. The set of values exhibited in occupied Serbian literature was constrained to spreading the ruralist, anti-modernist attitudes and medieval feudal values, thus fitting the Serbian literary tradition into the framework of the new Europe—a Europe that would be led by a developed, industrial Germany, and where Serbia would be assigned the role of an agricultural producer.

Notes

1. Translations from non-English sources are my own.
2. The curiosity is that Gregorić's book "The Suicide of Yugoslavia" (*Samoubistvo Jugoslavije*) was published in the Protectorate in the Czech translation in 1944.
3. After 1941, "The State Award for Literature" (*Státní cena za literaturu*) was renamed to *Národní cena za umění* ("The National Award for Art") (Mohn 2017, 35).
4. A lengthy episode of Technik's documentary work depicts the daily lives of Prague's ratcatchers getting rid of vermin. Although there is no implied antisemitism throughout the text, a detailed description of the mass capture and destruction of rats and mice leaves an ominous impression on the modern reader because of the frequent comparison of Jews and rats by the Nazis, as, for example, in the film "The Eternal Jew" (*Der ewige Jude*, 1940).

References

Anonymous. 1942. "Konkurs Akademskog pozorišta za dramsko delo." *Novo vreme*, July 14, 1942.

———. 1943a. "Dramski konkurs SZR." *Novo vreme*, February 3, 1943.

———. 1943b. "Dramski konkurs Ace Cvetkovića: Aca Cvetković daje tri nagrade za najbolju komediju, farsu ili skeč." *Novo vreme*, June 22, 1943.

———. 1943c. "Nagrađeni romani i drame na književnom konkursu 'Srpskog naroda.'" *Srpski narod*, December 4, 1943.

———. 1943d. "Pisac nagrađenog romana 'Gresi otaca.'" *Srpski narod*, December 18, 1943.

———. 1943e. "Značajan uspeh omladinskog književnog konkursa." *Srpski narod*, December 18, 1943.

———. 1943f. "Najbolji rad omladinskog književnog konkursa 'Putevi Svetog Save' od Ivanke Tasić." *Srpski narod*, December 25, 1943.

———. 1944. "'Imam jednu veru—Srbiju, jednu ljubav—Srbiju, jednu nadu—Srbiju': Slobodan Isaković, pisac nagrađene drame 'Marija Paleologova.'" *Srpski narod*, January 7, 1944.

Bradley, Lyman R. 1944. "Literary Trends under Hitler." *Science & Society* 8, no. 2: 104–14.

Connelly, John. 1999. "Nazis and Slavs: From Racial Theory to Racist Practice." *Central European History* 32, no. 1: 1–33.

Doležal, Jiří. 1996. *Česká kultura za protektorátu: školství, písemnictví, kinematografie.* Prague: Národní filmový archiv.

Đorđević, Bojan. 2001. *Letopis kulturnog života Srbije pod okupacijom 1941–1944.* Belgrade: Matica Srpska, Institut za književnost i umetnost.

Đurić, Dušan. 1943a. "Na splavu." *Srpski narod*, August 7, 1943.

———. 1943b. "Na splavu (nastavak iz prošlog broja)." *Srpski narod*, August 14, 1943.

Dvořáček, Karel. 1941. *Pole kráčí do hor: román.* Prague: Josef Lukasík.

Filipović, Veselin. 1943. "Pesma za Srbiju." *Srpski narod*, June 19, 1943.

Gilman, Sander L. 2009. Review of *Hitler's War Poets: Literature and Politics in the Third Reich*, by Jay W. Baird. *The American Historical Review* 114, no. 1: 230–31.

Gregorić, Danilo. 1942. *Samoubistvo Jugoslavije: poslednji čin jugoslovenske tragedije, drugo, nepromenjeno izdanje.* Belgrade: Izdavačko i prometno A.D. Jugoistok.

Hellmuth-Brauner, Vladimír. 1939. Review of *Věnec jeřabinový* (nakl. "Novina," edice "Hlasy země"), by Jan V. Sedlák. *Tak: kulturní i politický čtrnáctideník* 2, no. 19–20: 299–300.

Holeček, Lukáš. 2019. "Proměny 'venkovské prózy' v české literatuře let 1939–1945 orientace, návraty, perspektivy." *Česká literatura: časopis pro literární vědu* 67, no. 4: 497–523.

Ilić, Dragutin Jejo. 1943. "Smrt srpskog domaćina." *Srpski narod*, July 31, 1943.

Isaković, Slobodan. 2010. "Dušanovo jutro." In *Savremena Srpska drama 43*, edited by Miodrag Đukić, 89–165. Belgrade: Udruženje dramskih pisaca Srbije, Pozorište "Moderna Garaža."

Jahn, Metoděj. 1941. *Jarní píseň: chlapecké vzpomínky.* Prague: Miroslav Stejskal.

Janoušek, Pavel, ed. 2022. *Dějiny české literatury v protektorátu Čechy a Morava.* Prague: Academia, Ústav pro českou literaturu AV ČR.

John, Jaromír. 1942. *Moudrý Engelbert: láskyplný román.* Prague: Ústřední dělnické nakladatelství.

Kater, Michael Hans. 2019. *Culture in Nazi Germany.* New Haven: Yale University Press.

Konstantinović, Radomir. 2004. *Filosofija palanke.* Belgrade: Otkrovenje.

Mohn, Volker. 2017. "Literární ceny a soutěže jako nástroj německé kulturní politiky v Protektorátu Čechy a Morava." In *Zatemněno: Česká literatura a kultura v protektorátu*, edited by Lucie Antoníšková, 30–44. Prague: Academia.

———. 2018. *Nacistická kulturní politika v Protektorátu: Koncepce, praxe a reakce české strany*. Prague: Prostor.

Moravec, Emanuel. 1941. *V úloze mouřenína (československá tragedie r. 1938)*. Prague: Orbis.

Mosse, Georg L. 1968. *Nazi Culture: Intellectual, Cultural and Social Life in the Third Reich*. New York: Grosset & Dunlap.

Novotný, René. 2021. *Řešení české otázky: Nacistická rasová politika v protektorátu Čechy a Morava*. Prague: Nakladatelství Epocha.

Piorecká, Kateřina. 2021. "Prominentní, povolení, nežádoucí, zakázaní…: Seimy a evidence českých spisovatelů jako nástroj proměny struktury literárního pole za protektorátu." *Soudobé dějiny* 28, no. 2: 469–98.

Puljević, Vojin. 1970. *Dva života: roman našeg društva između I i II. svetskog rata*. Belgrade: n.p.

Růžička, Karel. 1963. *ROH v boji o rozšíření moci dělnické třídy (1945–1948)*. Prague: Práce.

Šaman, František Erik. 1942. *Moje ruce: román*. Prague: Ústřední dělnické nakladatelství.

Sedlák, Jan Vojtěch. 1938. *Věnec jeřabinový*. Prague: Novina.

Šidáková Fialová, Alena. 2021. "Kudy do protektorátní prózy: nejvýraznější tendence a díla." *Český jazyk a literatura* 71, no. 4: 182–88.

Škvor, Jiří, ed. 1940. *Písně za pluhem: výbor veršů ze soutěže Svobodného učení selského*. Prague: Novina.

Stojanović, Aleksandar. 2012. *Srpski civilni/kulturni plan Vlade Milana Nedića*. Belgrade: Institut za noviju istoriju Srbije.

Sušić, Veljko. 1943. "Molitva Hristu." *Srpski narod*, June 19, 1943.

Technik, Alfred. 1942. *Muži pod Prahou*. Prague: Ústřední dělnické nakladatelství.

Thiele, Vladimír. 1946. "Ták odchází chlap." In *Žaluji: pankrácká kalvarie, druhá část*, edited by Karel Rameš and Vladimír Thiele, 773–82. Prague: Orbis.

Vokáč, Karel. 1944. *Utkáno z dýmu*. Prague: Ústřední dělnické nakladatelství.

Závada, Vilém. 1940. *Hradní věž*. Prague: Melantrich.

CHAPTER 10

Translating Occupied Poland into English, 1939–1955

JOANNA RZEPA

Introduction

As Hilary Footitt has observed, "The business of war has seldom been a monolingual one. Whether we choose to notice it or not, the 'ground of war' is almost always a landscape marked deeply by languages" (2012, 229). The transnationalism of war and occupation requires communication across languages and, thus, requires translation. Paying close attention to linguistic and cultural transfer is crucial to a better understanding of the contact zones of war and occupation (Baker 2007).

Indeed, if World War II is considered from a translation-oriented perspective, one quickly realizes that language expertise played a strategic role both at the front (intelligence, counter-intelligence, diplomatic dispatches) and in occupied societies in general (communication with the occupiers, propaganda, and counter-propaganda disseminated in various languages). Translation was also a medium of communication within the large coalition of Allied countries. It allowed for the narratives of conflict to travel across languages and cultures, providing readers of Allied states with an opportunity to gain access to witness accounts of life under occupation.

This chapter's focus is specifically on English-language translations of Polish narratives of Nazi and Soviet occupation published in the United Kingdom between 1939 and 1955. Drawing on recent research in translation studies and book history (Bachleitner 2010; Rundle 2010), it discusses the state interventions that shaped wartime publishing and had a significant impact on the reception of translated books. It explores the position of translated texts on the British book market, interrogates the framing of translations through various paratexts (i.e., introductions, prefaces, forewords, epilogues), analyzes the textual construction of a witness voice, and, finally, evaluates the reception of translated texts among British readers through a study of reviews and debates that they generated.

Wartime Book Market, State Propaganda, and Translations

The impact of the war on the British book market was significant. As Iain Stevenson observes, "Publishers not only played a pivotal role in the war effort, but the war was also crucial in creating new conditions" (Stevenson 2010, 107). Changes in publishing assumed a global scale, leading to a significant international expansion of British and American publishers funded by state-sponsored institutions, such as the British Council and the International Book Association (Hench 2010). As wartime propaganda was dependent on printed matter, books were considered an important tool of ideological warfare or, in W. W. Norton's words, "weapons in the war of ideas" (Hench 2010, 45). The wartime home market was beset by problems that all publishers struggled to navigate, including paper rationing and shortages of labor, and—in the case of some, such as Longmans—the destruction of their warehouses and offices during the Blitz. When the Ministry of Supply appointed a paper controller, the publishers' quotas were reduced to 60 percent of their consumption in the previous year. This was further reduced to 37.5 percent in 1941 (Stevenson 2010, 115–17). Thus, while "the number of titles published annually in Britain dropped from 14,904 to 6,747," the demand for books remained high, given that alternative forms of entertainment, such as cinema or pubs, were severely restricted due to air raids and blackouts (Holman 2008, 25).

Throughout the war, various British publishers maintained close informal relations with the British Ministries of Information and Supply, as printing books that were deemed to be of propaganda value allowed publishers to increase their paper quotas. The government, in turn, benefited from this situation by having the opportunity to frame the narrative of the war in ways considered most beneficial to the war effort. The Ministry of Information worked with publishers such as Hutchinson, Faber, Collins, Odhams, and the Hogarth Press, who published titles that the government considered to be of ideological value, lending their imprints to prevent the public from viewing the material as state propaganda (Holman 2008, 98–100).

The political role of book publishing became even more important when, with the ongoing Nazi invasion of Europe, London became the headquarters of governments and royalty from Belgium, Czechoslovakia, France, Greece, Luxembourg, the Netherlands, Norway, Poland, and Yugoslavia. This unprecedented diplomatic development created a situation in which several governments with their own information and propaganda departments and cultural diplomacy attempted to vie for the attention of British readers by means of translation and publishing campaigns. Because the exiled governments did not have the resources to offer practical help to the populations of their Nazi-overrun states, much of their effort was directed at influencing the policies of the British and American governments instead. As Michael Conway points out, the exiled governments' existence was characterized by strong "bonds of dependence on the Allies," and they "could do or say nothing of significance either to the outside world or to their native lands without the approval of their British minders" (2001, 257–58).

The relations between the British government and the exiled governments were shaped through official diplomatic channels and networks, but they were also, to a great extent, informed by public opinion: "Official concern with public opinion and the state of national morale embraced a growing interest in reading and in the nature of people's responses not just to literature but also to published information and propaganda" (Holman 2008, 48). These responses were regularly monitored by the Mass-Observation project and reported to the British Ministry of Information, which could then design propaganda and publishing campaigns in response to the public mood at any given time (McLaine 1979). The exiled governments, with their own Ministries or Bureaus of Information, also recognized the importance of book publishing for drawing attention to their narratives of the war, or even for reframing the dominant narrative in British political discourse.

What was particularly important for all Allied governments who launched propaganda campaigns during World War II was to distance themselves from German propagandists and avoid "giving the impression that published material was subject to any form of central control" (Holman 2008, 99). This posed a number of difficulties, as maintaining high public morale and winning the ideological war were dependent on "channels through which particular messages or impressions might reach a designated audience" (Holman 2008, 99). These objectives, however, could be effectively achieved through the development of successful relationships with publishing houses that were willing to embrace covert sponsorship by governments—while these sponsorships led to the production of books that could not be attributed to the state.

War conditions brought to the fore issues related to the materiality of book publishing as well. As Hench observes, "books were among the most conspicuous victims of this vicious warfare. Millions were destroyed by air raids, ship sinkings, infantry actions, orchestrated book burnings, and civilian paper drives" (2010, 19). Printing presses in the countries overrun by the Nazis were either shut down or allowed to publish little other than German propaganda. In the case of Poland, the Nazis not only halted the production of new books but also carried out a deliberate destruction of public and private libraries. The Polish authorities and authors were thus completely dependent on British publishers and on the few Polish publishers who managed to relocate their firms to London before the outbreak of the war.

Translating Nazi-Occupied Poland

The Polish government-in-exile closely analyzed the British public's mood and attitudes when designing their translation and publishing campaign. The Polish Ministry of Information followed all the main British newspapers, and members of the Polish Research Centre (PRC), which was set up and sponsored by the Ministry, toured the country engaging in cultural diplomacy: delivering public lectures on topics related to Polish history, culture, society, and the political situation, and reporting back on the responses of their British audiences. The PRC's 1944 memorandum stipulated that "Polish propaganda has to be subtle," emphasizing "British society's general dislike of propaganda of any type." Careful attention was paid to the ways in which Polish speakers were perceived by British audiences. Speakers discussing the Nazi occupation of Poland were instructed to remain calm and composed and to "avoid any kind of affectation, sentimentality, or exaltation" (PRC Collection, 434/203).[1] This would ensure that they would come across as reliable and trustworthy witnesses. The same principles applied to printed material.

However, what made it particularly difficult to engage British readers with publications that were based on reports and witness accounts coming from occupied Poland was that British readers had a general distrust of anything they perceived as 'atrocity propaganda.' Namely, due to the legacy of propaganda narratives from World War I that had been subsequently exposed as misleading or entirely false (Kingsbury 2010), both the British and the American public approached reports of atrocities coming from occupied Europe with a big dose of skepticism. In 1942, journalism scholar Vernon McKenzie observed:

> I have been shocked and puzzled by the seeming callousness with which friends and acquaintances decline to accept reports from Nazi-held areas, even when they are based on unimpeachable evidence or on official proclamations and admissions in the Nazi-controlled press. (McKenzie 1942, 269)

Considering public reactions to atrocity stories, McKenzie concluded that, during World War II, these types of narratives were met mostly with indifference and hostility, as well as a refusal to engage with them critically. "Millions were so conditioned," McKenzie argues, "that when the day came when Hitler invaded Poland they could say, or at least feel, that they were 'fed up by horror reports,' or that 'one side is probably just as bad as the other'" (1942, 270).

For his part, Arthur Koestler, a Hungarian-born Jewish writer who worked at the British Ministry of Information from 1942, connected the public's mistrust of atrocity accounts to the perceived distance between British readers and the populations of Nazi-occupied states:

> [B]oth 'knowing' and 'believing' have varying degrees of intensity. […] Distance in space and time degrades intensity of awareness. So does magnitude. Seventeen is a figure which I know intimately like a friend; fifty billions is just a sound. A dog run over by a car upsets our emotional balance and digestion; a million Jews killed in Poland cause but a moderate uneasiness. (Koestler 1944, 30)

According to Koestler, the news coming from occupied Europe did not seem relatable enough to the British public, and it did not seem real. While people would see "films of Nazi tortures, of mass shootings, of underground conspiracy and self-sacrifice" and be moved by them, they would not "connect it with the realities of their normal plane of existence" (1944, 30).

Aware of these difficulties, the Polish government-in-exile developed its publishing campaign in a way that was designed to counter British readers' distrust of state-sponsored propaganda; their reluctance to become emotionally involved in material that appeared too foreign, distant, or peripheral; and their distrust of atrocity stories and any material that did not appear 'believable,' which could be viewed as state-controlled fear-mongering. The primary aim of the Polish government-in-exile's publishing campaign, then, was to present Poland's case and the Polish war effort as issues that were, in fact, close and relevant to the British reader—and to do this, the published texts had to appear both trustworthy and not too far removed (Rzepa 2019b). While the texts themselves carried indelible foreignness—dealing with Poland, a far-away country about which most of the British readership knew quite little—the Polish authorities tried to win British readers' trust by domesticating the translations through extratextual and material elements. Specifically, they domesticated these translations by means of paratexts (such as prefaces and introductions by British MPs and public intellectuals), imprints (i.e., commissioning British publishers to print selected translations), and distribution channels (e.g., inclusion in British publishers' catalogues).

Liberty Publications was one of the most important London-based imprints established by the Polish Socialist Party (*Polska Partia Socjalistyczna* (PPS)), and it was sponsored by the Polish government through the Polish Social Information Bureau. It published English-language pamphlets "dealing with different aspects of Polish life and with questions and problems concerning Poland" (Adam Ciołkosz Papers, 133/95). As the titles they printed had an explicit and open focus on Polish issues and were often based on underground reports brought from occupied Poland, the editors sought to secure an endorsement from well-known

British politicians and public figures, in the form of a preface or a foreword for each of their publications. Such an introductory paratext would typically be two or three paragraphs long and reaffirm the value and relevance of the publication. While the name of the pamphlet's author was in most cases suppressed, the name of the person who endorsed it featured prominently on the cover to generate trust and credibility in the eyes of British readers.

Liberty Publications managed to secure the endorsement of a number of British MPs, including Philip John Noel-Baker, future winner of the Nobel Peace Prize, who wrote a foreword to *Underground Poland Speaks* (1941); Vernon Bartlett, who introduced *Unknown Europe* (1942); Arthur Greenwood, who wrote a preface to *Towards a New Poland* (1942); Lord Wedgwood, who endorsed *Stop Them Now* (1942); and Jennie L. Adamson, who wrote a foreword to *Camp of Death* (1944). Both *Stop Them Now* and *Camp of Death* were based on intelligence reports produced by the Polish Underground Movement and witness accounts. They described the ongoing persecution and extermination of Polish Jews (*Stop Them Now*) and the camp of Auschwitz (*Camp of Death*). Accordingly, in their forewords, both Lord Wedgwood and Jennie L. Adamson emphasized the need to treat the accounts as credible sources of information on the developments in Nazi-occupied Poland. Wedgwood contended that "those who shut their eyes, who refuse to believe and seek to escape from thought of what is going on in Poland [...] are guilty" (*Stop Them Now* 1942, 3). His foreword was followed by an introduction penned by Szmul Zygielbojm, a Jewish refugee from Poland and member of the Central Committee of the Jewish Socialist Party "Bund" and of the Polish National Council in London. Zygielbojm urged the reader to accept the veracity of the reports: "I realise that the facts contained in [...] this booklet are so monstrous and inhuman that most normal persons would hesitate to believe them. And yet they are true and real [...]" (*Stop Them Now* 1942, 4). The facts to which Zygielbojm was referring included the eyewitness account of the gassings of Jews in the extermination camp of Chełmno (Kulmhof), which had started to operate in 1941 and was where the majority of Jews from the Łódź Ghetto were murdered. By giving British readers access to those early witness accounts, the editors of the pamphlet were attempting to draw attention to the fact that "the policy of the Germans is to wipe out entirely, not only the Jews in Poland, but the Jewish population of the whole of Europe"—and were urging their readership to intervene and find a means to prevent it (*Stop Them Now* 1942, back cover).

In a similar way, *Camp of Death* aimed to provide the British public with a narrative account of life in the concentration camp of Auschwitz. Based on the pamphlet *Obóz śmierci*, ("Death Camp") authored by Natalia Zarembina and clandestinely published in Poland in 1942 (Fleming 2014, 195–97), *Camp of*

Death reported on the situation in Auschwitz in 1941 and early 1942, before the mass exterminations of Jews began. However, the footnotes that the editors of the English translation attached to the text provide additional information about the ongoing mass murder. "Large transports of people," wrote the editors in the final footnote, "have been directed from the trains immediately to the gas chambers and killed there without registration on the camp-roll" (Zarembina 1944, 30). That said, the murder statistics provided in the pamphlet were lower than those in other underground reports arriving in London to which the editors would have had access. As Michael Fleming suggests, the editors "were very well aware of the sensibilities of their British audience and sought to establish credibility" by providing data that looked less shocking and more trustworthy (2014, 196). At the same time, the editors did incorporate some of the recent numbers, adding in a footnote that the estimated number of Jews killed in the camp by December 1943 amounted to 1 million.

The distribution of such pamphlets presented a challenge to Liberty Publications. While printing anonymous pamphlets that had a price on them (on average, they were sold for one to three pence and could thus be considered of commercial value) was relatively effective at the beginning of the war, it was increasingly difficult by 1944 to find a market for them. In September 1942, *Stop Them Now* was printed in 60,000 copies, most of which had been distributed by December 1944, when only 160 remained in stock. *Camp of Death*, on the other hand, was printed in 25,000 copies in July 1944 and did not sell well, even though it was advertised in the *Times Literary Supplement* and other outlets. Liberty Press still had 10,000 copies in stock by December 1944 (Adam Ciołkosz Papers, 133/95). They continued to advertise it throughout 1945, even after Auschwitz was liberated, changing the text of the advertisement accordingly: "Full story of the Concentration Camp in Oświęcim recently liberated" ("Other New Publications" 1945). Yet distribution and reception of the pamphlet remained hindered, which can be largely attributed to its perceived lack of credibility and to a simultaneous lack of interest in the subject matter among the target audience, who, by then, would have encountered numerous reports on liberated concentration and extermination camps in the daily press.

In December 1944, *The London Typographical Journal* published a first-page review of *Camp of Death* (Anonymous 1944), which, while endorsing it as a text that should be read, at the same time undermined its veracity. "So much horror has been described for us in the daily and weekly Press in its accounts of German concentration camps," the anonymous reviewer contended, that "we fear that repletion of the stories has given rise to suspicion. Is it true? we ask." Their response to this profoundly important question is to state that even if "only half [of *Camp of Death*] is true—nay a tenth—it is sufficient to outlaw those who gave the order to those who carried them out" (Anonymous 1944). While explicitly condemnatory of the crimes described in the pamphlet, the reviewer's words also draw attention to the possibility that readers might, in fact, be dealing with a piece of atrocity propaganda and that only a tenth of the account might be credible. The reliability of the text is undermined as the focus shifts from the crimes being described to the interrogation of the veracity of the source itself.

Thus, in the final years of the war, despite sustained attempts at a wide distribution of titles that aimed to give British readers insight into what was happening in Nazi-occupied Poland, Liberty Publications struggled to reach its target audience. In their correspondence with the booksellers W.H. Smith & Son in February 1945, the publishers emphasized that their publications, including *Camp of Death*, "deal(t) with subjects which are at the moment being widely discussed and upon which public interest is focussed"—but the response they received from W.H. Smith & Son was unequivocal: "pamphlets of this nature and price have very little chance of sales at our branches" (Adam Ciołkosz Papers, 133/111).

Apart from producing pamphlets based on underground reports, the Polish authorities also aimed to attract British readers' attention by translating and publishing fictionalized literary texts based on witness accounts. Two such texts, penned by established Polish writers Aleksander Kamiński and Jerzy Andrzejewski, were brought to London in April–July 1944 by Polish resistance officers who were airlifted from Poland in clandestine military operations code-named Wildhorn I, II, and III (Rzepa 2019a). Both Kamiński's *Kamienie na szaniec (Stones for the Rampart)* and Andrzejewski's *Apel (Roll Call)* (Andrzejewski 1945) are based on real-life events. The former tells the story of the scouts' contribution to the resistance movement in Nazi-occupied Warsaw; the latter recounts a disciplinary roll call held in Auschwitz in the autumn of 1941. When the texts were delivered to the Polish Ministry of Information, they were translated into English, and two renowned British critics and poets were invited to write introductions to them: T.S. Eliot was approached by Adam Żółtowski, director of the Polish Research Centre (PRC), and Percy Hugh Beverley Lyon, headmaster of Rugby School, was contacted by Jan Baliński-Jundziłł, deputy director of the PRC. Eliot's and Lyon's endorsements were seen as incredibly valuable, as both men were important public intellectuals and would be perceived as impartial and unbiased parties with no obvious connections to the Polish government-in-exile. Both Eliot and Lyon were informed that the texts "most authentically" came from Poland and were "sent by our [Polish] Underground Movement." In his letter to Eliot, Żółtowski admitted that his desire was that "the most outstanding British critic should testify that the publication is well worth reading," and Baliński-Jundziłł informed Lyon that "a foreword from (him) would be most gratifying to my countrymen, as well as being a very fine introduction to English readers." Both

Lyon and Eliot agreed to write the introductory texts, and Eliot explicitly refused to "take payment from the Polish Government for a service of this sort" (PRC Collection, 434/124 and 434/193).

In early 1945, *Stones for the Rampart* was published with Lyon's foreword. In his foreword, Lyon put emphasis on the book's credibility, highlighting that it is "no tale of fancy," but rather "a record, written on the spot by those whose lives stood in daily peril of torture and death" (Górecki 1945, 1). While *Roll Call*, on the other hand, seems to have been withdrawn from publication (as it never appeared in print with Eliot's preface), in Eliot's correspondence with the Polish Research Centre, he too emphasized the need to establish the credibility of the text: "I think there should be some statement about the origin of the manuscript, or some readers will presume it to be simply a brilliant piece of imaginative fiction" (PRC Collection, 434/124; Eliot 2017a). In both Lyon's and Eliot's view, the reception of the translations hinged on their being perceived as non-fictional texts. While the Polish authorities could provide assurances to that effect, such assurances, in the eyes of the British reader, could amount to glaring examples of foreign propaganda that should not be taken at face value. This double bind provided an almost insurmountable challenge that seriously hindered the dissemination of translated texts.

Because the reception of publications that were perceived as state-sponsored propaganda was hostile, Polish authorities began to emulate the work of the British Ministry of Information by commissioning established British firms to print covert translations of Polish books that had propaganda value. The advantage of such an arrangement was that books published by British publishers, such as Hutchinson or Allen & Unwin, had the appearance of ordinary commercial books. Both the British and the refugee governments recognized that, as Holman observed, "propaganda was most effective when least visible, that is, when it appeared to be produced and distributed by a trade publisher with no connection to the Government" (2008, 102). Therefore, the covers and title pages of such commissioned publications would not disclose the fact that they were government-sponsored. Rarely, trade publishers took on the cost of publishing books that they considered to have commercial potential, which was the case for Jan Karski's *Story of a Secret State*, whose American edition was issued by Houghton Mifflin in 1944 and the British edition by Hodder & Stoughton in 1945 (Karski 1944, 1945). Karski, who was a courier of the Polish underground state and during the war carried reports of Nazi atrocities from occupied Poland to London, had to agree to Hodder & Stoughton's demand that his book should take the form of a first-person narrative and speak of his personal experiences as a liaison officer and courier, must not include any overt propaganda, and should not to be advertised by the Polish government-in-exile. These precautions were taken by the publisher to ensure that the book would not be seen as yet another propaganda volume. They had significantly contributed to the book's popular success as it sold more than 15,000 copies in the first two weeks and was subsequently translated into other languages (Rzepa 2018). Yet such arrangements with trade publishers were incredibly rare. Most frequently, it was the Polish government-in-exile who took initiative and provided funding and resources to produce relevant publications.

In most cases, the title pages of government-commissioned publications did not include the name of the translator, instead attempting to pass for texts that had been originally written in English; by hiding their foreignness behind the British publishers' imprints, such publications could more easily attract British readers' attention. The only element of the title page that could give away the foreign nature of such books was the name of the author, and in some cases even this element was deliberately altered, suppressed, or anglicized. An example of such a publication is *Two Septembers: Warsaw 1939—London 1940*, published by Allen & Unwin in 1941 and written by Stephen Baley—whose real name was Stanisław Baliński.

Baliński was a Warsaw-born writer and poet who fled Poland in 1939 and settled in London, where he worked for the Polish Ministries of Information and Foreign Affairs. In *Two Septembers*, he recounts the Nazi invasion of Poland in 1939 and the Battle of Britain in 1940. Writing about the campaigns that the Nazis waged against Poland and Britain, as well as the contribution of the Polish pilots who fought for Britain, Baliński argues that Poland and Britain share important ideals. He contends that "the ideal linking Great Britain in her heroic and successful resistance with that distant country which now lies under the yoke of enslavement to Germany is the love of freedom" (Baley 1941, 14). It is the common values and the experience of Nazi assault highlighted on the title page and in the introduction to *Two Septembers* that bind London and Warsaw together, making the book appear immediately relevant to the British audience.

Yet this was not the only way in which Baliński aimed to appeal to the British reader: he insisted on publishing the book under the pseudonym "Stephen Bailey." So committed was he to this pseudonym, in fact, that when Allen & Unwin sent him a draft of the advertisement slip with his real name, Baliński immediately complained, urging the publisher to "take steps to put the matter right" and correct the proofs and any advertisement materials (Allen & Unwin Collection, 122/10). The name that in the end appeared on the title page was "Stephen Baley" (rather than "Bailey"). Thus, not only was the book a covert, government-sponsored translation that assumed the appearance of an ordinary commercial publication, but it also pretended to be authored by an English speaker, not a Pole (as Baliński's letters reveal, it was translated into English by a "Mr. Stevens").

The cost of producing such publications was understandably high, and in the case of *Two Septembers*, the Polish Ministry of Information had to provide Allen & Unwin with paper, agree to purchase 1,000 copies of the book plus any unsold stock of the remaining 4,000 copies six months after the date of publication, as well as agree for Allen & Unwin not to pay any royalties on sold copies (Allen & Unwin Collection, 122/10).

Ultimately, *Two Septembers* and other books published under similar conditions were virtually unattributable. Furthermore, the radical anglicization of the material and the textual forms of such books meant that the translators' presence had to be erased as well: the books had to pass for original English-language texts. Indeed, today the translators' names can be recovered only from the surviving archival material, such as correspondence with publishers or invoices for commissioned translations. Yet despite the sustained efforts to conceal the foreignness of books such as Baliński's *Two Septembers*, reaching a wide readership for those titles nonetheless proved nearly impossible due to an apparent lack of interest in the subject matter. Commenting on wartime trends in readers' preferences, the Acting Manager of the Times Book Club observed in 1940: "The international affairs market is not as strong as it was before the war. […] There was a curious lack of interest in Poland. We had two books on Poland and we haven't done anything with either of them. Finland—yes" ("Book Reading in War Time," File Report 46, 18). Publishers, booksellers, and librarians observed an increased demand for prose fiction and a significant decrease of interest in political books. As the bookseller Christina Foyle remarked, "people are perhaps a little weary of reading of Hitler and the future of Europe" ("Book Reading in War Time," File Report 46, 9). This weariness, it seems, led to readers' gradual disengagement with publications that aimed to enhance their intellectual and emotional investment in the fate of Nazi-occupied Poland.

Translating Soviet-Occupied Poland

As the Soviet invasion and subsequent occupation of Poland on September 17, 1939 were perceived in Britain with ambivalence, publishing texts that narrated the experiences of people living under the Soviet occupation was even more challenging than bringing out narratives of the Nazi occupation. The Red Army came to occupy about half of the country, taking more than 200,000 prisoners of war and deporting more than 1 million civilians from eastern Poland to the Soviet Union in 1940-41. While Stalin's move to occupy Poland did not come as a surprise for the British government, as Keith Sword observes, "British policymakers had considerable difficulty in knowing how to interpret [it], and how to react to it" (1991, 84). This resulted in a cautious tone within official government statements, along with ambiguous media coverage of the Nazi–Soviet collusion, all of which reflected the diplomatic concerns of alienating Moscow. The British public's understanding of the Soviet Union's actions at the start of World War II was characterized by a certain dose of optimism and repeated attempts to see them as justified by immediate political and military necessity. Analyzing the press coverage of those events, Claire Knight has concluded that "the popular press began to define Soviet distinctiveness as rooted in its intentions toward and subsequent actions in Poland, which were depicted as morally acceptable in contrast to those of Germany" (2013, 480). Thus, despite the Molotov–Ribbentrop Pact, the press framed Soviet actions as qualitatively distinct from Nazi Germany's and insisted on seeing them as halting Hitler's advance. With the exception of the Soviet invasion of Finland, which was compared by the press to the Nazi *Blitzkrieg*, Soviet actions tended to be seen in a positive light.

This kind of reporting generated much public sympathy for the Soviet Union, with "a large majority in favour of friendly relations with the Soviet Union" by April 1941 (Bell 1990, 35). The outpouring of support among the British public reached its culmination with the Nazi invasion of the Soviet Union and the Anglo-Soviet Treaty of July 12, 1941, which confirmed Russia's status as a British ally. The reporting of the Battles of Moscow and Stalingrad captured public attention, and "the Home Intelligence reports recorded widespread and often deeply felt admiration for the Soviet Union among the British people" (Bell 1990, 88).

The British government was intent on controlling "any anti-Soviet elements which might divide opinion in the country," to maintain good diplomatic relations with the Soviets (Bell 1990, 67). Thus, publications that might threaten those relations were censored, so as not to antagonize the new ally. That said, the positivity of the coverage of the Soviet Union's actions was not dictated by the nature of Soviet actions or intentions (which were overwhelmingly ambiguous); rather, the orchestrated Soviet and British propaganda efforts—and, as Knight points out, the press's simultaneous attempts to reassure the British public—were designed to maintain high morale at the home front, and to minimize the perception of the Soviet Union as a possible future threat (2013).

The complicated issue of Polish–Soviet relations, however, significantly challenged this framing of the public image of the Soviet Union and its contribution to the war effort. Since September 1939, the question of the future Polish–Soviet border was seen as a matter that would be increasingly difficult to solve, but the intervention of the British government led to the re-establishment of Polish–Soviet diplomatic relations in July 1941. These relations remained troubled by the question of the fate of Polish deportees to the Soviet Union. In this uneasy context, it was the discovery of the mass graves of Polish officers, whom the Red

Army had murdered in the forest of Katyń, that was the main cause of a deep diplomatic crisis in April 1943. Since German troops had made the discovery and Nazi-controlled media had been the first to publicize the massacre, the story was initially perceived in Britain as a piece of propaganda aimed at antagonizing the Allies. As the Polish authorities confirmed that thousands of Polish officers who were taken into Russia as prisoners of war were indeed missing, and Poland insisted that the International Red Cross should conduct an official investigation into the mass graves that the German troops had discovered, the Soviet government responded by breaking off all diplomatic relations with the Polish government on April 26, 1943. This rupture posed a serious problem for the British government, as the Katyń revelations could cause significant damage to Anglo–Soviet relations (Stanford 2005). To minimize the damage, the British Foreign Office advised "that the story should be treated as a German attempt to undermine allied solidarity, and that nothing was to be gained by going into the rights and wrongs of the matter" (Bell 1989, 75).

While the British government managed to preserve the central lines of its policy, which prioritized maintaining the Soviet alliance and downplaying the Katyń revelations, along with the accounts by deportees to Soviet forced labor camps, this policy was to the detriment of the public perception of the Polish government, as well as of the authors who attempted to bear witness to and publicize the experiences of Poles who survived imprisonment and deportation to the Soviet Union. This loss of credibility was so serious that, as Home Intelligence reports highlighted, the British public started to perceive the Polish government as "being pro-German" in their malicious allegations against the Soviet allies (Bell 1989, 81).

While the Polish authorities, during the war, prepared a collection of accounts from deportees to Soviet forced labor camps in the form of a "red book" that would detail Soviet crimes against Polish citizens, the book's publication was postponed until 1949 for diplomatic reasons (Zajdlerowa 1989, 2). Indeed, no such accounts were published in English translation until the end of the war. One of the first book-length publications to address this topic in English was Zoë Zajdler's *The Dark Side of the Moon* (published anonymously by Faber & Faber in 1946 with T. S. Eliot's prefatory note). Zajdler, who also published under the pseudonym of Martin Hare, was an Irish-born writer who moved to Warsaw with her Polish-born husband in the 1930s. Her 1940 book, *My Name is Million: The Experiences of an Englishwoman in Poland*, tells the story of how she escaped from Nazi- and Soviet-overrun Poland through Lithuania, Latvia, and Estonia, and how she and her husband were captured by the *Gestapo*. While Zajdler was soon freed and managed to make her way to London, where she made contact with the Polish government-in-exile, her husband's fate remained unknown. Since she was an established writer who had published several novels before the war and had her own literary agent, Spencer Curtis Brown, her contribution to the Polish government's publishing campaign was highly valued. On November 21, 1942, Michał Protasewicz, Head of Bureau VI of the Polish General Staff and responsible for intelligence, sent a coded cable message to Warsaw to Stefan Rowecki, leader of the Home Army (*Armia Krajowa*, the Polish underground movement), inquiring about Zajdler's husband and adding that his wife is "a writer [and] contributes greatly to our cause. Information about her husband would be a small favour" (Boxes Collection, SK36). The reply from Warsaw confirmed that Zajdler's husband was well and revealed that he was an active member of the Home Army. When this exchange was taking place, Zajdler was already working on her next book, *The Dark Side of the Moon*, which tells the story of the Soviet invasion and occupation of Poland, and the subsequent deportations of hundreds of thousands of Poles to forced labor camps (known as the Gulag; see Khlevniuk 2004) in Siberia.

Since Zajdler was an experienced writer and Polish–English translator, she would not have had problems translating the deportees' accounts and editing them into a longer narrative. Her approach to the translation and editorial work can be characterized as, on the one hand, meticulously researched and informative, and on the other, uniquely personal. Zajdler positioned herself on the side of the occupied and, since she was in Poland when the Soviet Army entered the country, included autobiographical elements that add a personal angle and authenticity to her narrative. Indeed, she explicitly stated: "I shall set down, too, as much as I can of the emotions and sensations which we lived while the events were taking shape" (1946, 41). In that sense, her book is an attempt to convey not only a factual narrative of the Soviet invasion and occupation of eastern Poland, but also the emotional impact of those events on those who experienced them first-hand.

However, since Zajdler was able to escape to England in 1940, the chapters that narrate subsequent events, including mass deportations of Polish citizens, required her to adopt a different approach. To establish and maintain credibility within these chapters, she chose to build them around extensive citations of deportees' testimonies, which she herself translated into English. She provided an account of the research she conducted, engaging with "many hundreds of first-hand accounts" as well as "narratives, letters, diaries and other written statements of many hundreds of persons included in the deportations" (1946, 57). Further to that, she collected stories and statements "in personal conversations sustained over whole days, and in at least one case over whole weeks, with other deported persons, who reached England after 1941" (1946, 57), and she made use of official government documents to contextualize the personal narratives (much of which material is now in the Polish Institute and Sikorski Museum

Archive). She strongly emphasized that "to all of this evidence, as received by me, not one word has been added and from it not one word (again, unless otherwise stated in the text) has been taken away" (1946, 57).

While Zajdler comes across as a thorough and confident editor and translator, she nevertheless drew the reader's attention to some of the challenges that she encountered when rendering the deportees' testimonies into English; her reflections touch on the crucial question of how to articulate experiences of extreme deprivation and violence in a way that will be understandable to readers who have nothing to compare them to and may indeed doubt their veracity. Addressing this question, she positioned herself as a mediator between the Polish deportees and English readers in an understanding that the latter's horizons of expectations would be substantially challenged by the testimonies included in *The Dark Side of the Moon*. For instance, in the chapter describing the train journeys that the deportees were forced to take, Zajdler reflected on the challenge of conveying the deportees' experiences to the British reader:

> The reader can be given facts. He cannot share the *experience*. He can read about the filth, but he cannot taste it in his throat and feel himself saturated by it, as these people did. He has smelt some unpleasant odours. [...] His experience is unlikely to go further than this. The atmosphere breathed in by the people in these cars, the condition of the floors, the stench that rose from them, beat off the walls, lay under the roof, filled their hair, skin, pores and lungs, even while he reads, he has no conception at all; and cannot have. One can enumerate the horrors. (Zajdler 1946, 69, emphasis in the orginal)

Appealing to "the mind and the heart of the reader," Zajdler emphasized the need to suspend one's skepticism and believe the first-hand accounts included in her book. "Once you have grasped that these things can happen," she argued, "you know that they happened to all of these people all of the time. That nobody was spared" (1946, 69). Her editorial commentary includes a linguistic reflection on the difficulties of translating the deportees' accounts and finding a language that will be capable of conveying them in English. For example, when introducing the narrative of a 15-year-old girl, Irena, who was first imprisoned and then deported to a penal settlement in Starodub, she remarked: "In the translating of this document, [...] I have felt an even profounder dissatisfaction than always before at the poverty of my own powers of evocation" (1946, 125). What Zajdler found particularly difficult to convey in English was the "fearful resignation" of deportees' accounts and the "gigantic implications [...] behind every utterance of the single word 'home'" (1946, 125). Such critical reflections on the task that she had undertaken are a powerful framing device for Zajdler's book, as they bring to the fore the editorial and translational difficulties that she encountered while editing the testimonial accounts. She consciously avoided appropriating the victims' voices, using punctuation to indicate clearly which passages constitute direct citations of the deportees' narratives.

At the same time, in the course of the book, she revealed the personal significance she felt in the task she had undertaken. As the reader learns in the first chapters, although Zajdler managed to escape when the German and Soviet armies invaded Poland in 1939, many of those "once dear to (her)" had "vanished in the Soviet Union" (1946, 112). In particular, she mentioned her father-in-law, who "died as a convict in the oblast of Novosibirsk in Siberia," where he was deported together with his daughter, son-in-law, and their two children. Engaging with numerous accounts of death in the camps, Zajdler tried to imagine her father-in-law's final moments, in a poignant passage that she ended with an emphasis on her hope that he might "have been reassured just before death by somebody" and that he might have died "not quite alone, not quite like a pariah dog" (1946, 113).

When Zajdler submitted the manuscript of her book to Faber & Faber in 1945, it drew the attention of T.S. Eliot, who wrote the preface to the book himself, though its publication was delayed until 1946. Zajdler delivered the last chapter of the book on June 28, 1945, but it did not appear in print until June 10, 1946. Eliot and co-directors at Faber were impressed by the book but perceived it as "very damaging to our Russian allies, and therefore a ticklish business" (2017b, 746). What Eliot saw as the strength of the book was "the comparative absence of atrocity stories," although he was cautious about the book's direct indictment of the Soviet government. He suggested that Faber put the book under "closest scrutiny" to ensure that, once it was published, its critics would not be able to "draw red herrings by magnifying the importance of minor errors of fact or interpretation" (Faber Archive). Furthermore, it was decided that the book would be published anonymously, for Zajdler was concerned about the safety of her husband, who was still in Poland; however, the book would also include a brief note by Helena Sikorska, wife of the Prime Minister Władysław Sikorski. Sikorska's note affirms that General Sikorski had "confidence in the author" and that she was "given access to official material and documents" (Zajdler 1946, 4). Thus, though the book was written by an English speaker and published by an established British firm (which would have made it appear less foreign and more relevant to the British reader), it was nevertheless presented as fully credible and trustworthy, since it was based on authentic documents. Furthermore, Eliot's preface emphasized that the book was written "as dispassionately and fairly as is possible," vouching for the author's unbiased treatment of the subject matter (Zajdler 1946, 5).

As one of the reviewers aptly observed, "Mr. Eliot's name has attracted to the book attention in wider circles than it might otherwise have won" (Degras 1947, 120).

Indeed, *The Dark Side of the Moon* did relatively well, selling almost 7,500 copies between its publication in June 1946 and June 1948 (Faber Archive). It received much publicity and was reviewed in many leading magazines, such as the *Times Literary Supplement*, *The Spectator*, and *International Affairs*. Reviewers considered Zajdler's work "one of the most affecting and important books published in many years" (Schwartz 1947, 602), and they emphasized the "strong and scrupulous sincerity" of the author, whose work makes "grim and melancholy reading" (Charques 1946, 363). At the same time, however, they drew attention to the problem of the author's credibility, noting that some readers might find it difficult to accept the truthfulness of the account, as "the brutality, callousness and suffering here described will seem incredible" (Schwartz 1947, 603).

Indeed, the question of credibility and its lack is a recurrent theme in the reception of narratives of the Soviet occupation of eastern Poland and the deportations of Poles to forced labor camps. Ada Halpern's *Liberation Russian Style*, which was published in English in 1945, was prefaced with a foreword by Eleanor Rathbone, a British MP and humanitarian activist. In her introduction, Rathbone emphasizes the credibility of Halpern as a first-hand witness who was deported from Lwów (now Lviv in Ukraine) to Kazakhstan, to be released in 1941. For Rathbone, Halpern's credibility as a witness and author is built around her lack of association with the Polish government-in-exile who "might be suspected of prejudice based on their dislike of the Soviet system and government" (Halpern 1945, v). It bears noting that, as Britain and the United States withdrew their recognition of the Polish government-in-exile under Stalin's pressure on July 5, 1945, the public's perception of any overt links to the Polish authorities would have had the chance of harming the author's image. Indeed, Halpern is presented as a believable witness because she is an independent writer whose account can be characterized by "clarity, simplicity, restraint, and apparent absence of bitterness or exaggeration" (Halpern 1946, v). Since the British public generally questioned the veracity of deportees' accounts (as a review of *The Dark Side of the Moon* pointed out, readers with little knowledge of the Soviet Union would have considered many first-hand accounts a work of fiction), it was important for such narratives to come across as believable at the textual level. To construct an image and voice of a believable witness, the author and translator had to adopt a style characterized by emotional restraint, sincere simplicity, and lack of explicitly articulated anti-Russian or anti-Soviet prejudice. Some authors went further and chose to address the reader directly, acknowledging their doubts and skepticism. In the opening pages of *Vanished without Trace*, Antoni Ekart, who spent eight years in Soviet camps, asks:

> How to explain to men and women in London or New York that there is slavery in
> Russia and that every year several million people who are victims of it die at their

> work from sheer exhaustion? Who would believe me in Stockholm or Paris when
> I say that torture is organized by the State, acting through Government Depart-
> ments staff by intelligent and educated people? (Ekart 1954, 10)

Despite the translators' and publishers' efforts to emphasize the veracity of Zajdler's, Ekart's, Halpern's, and others' accounts, the perceived lack of credibility
came to define the early reception of most accounts of the Soviet occupation of
eastern Poland in the eyes of the British public. Edward Crankshaw, a British
writer, journalist, and political commentator who specialized in Soviet affairs,
testified to this skepticism in his introduction to the English translation of Józef
Czapski's *The Inhuman Land*, which appeared in 1951. The book narrates Czapski's deportation to the camp in Gryazovets; his release in 1941 as a result of the
Sikorski–Mayski agreement; and his subsequent search for fellow Polish officers
from the camps of Starobelsk, Kozelsk, and Ostashkov, who—as Czapski later
found out—had been murdered by the Soviet army in Katyń. Introducing the
book to British readers, Crankshaw emphasizes its literary qualities, "enriched
by the artist's detachment and common sense" (Czapski 1951, 2–3). At the same
time, he remarks that the "real trouble is that people will not believe" Czapski
or other Polish authors (Czapski 1951, 4). This lack of belief and the refusal to
engage with the accounts of survivors of the Soviet camps are something that
Crankshaw ascribes to the wider political context and its pressures, but also to a
sense of guilt over the British government's political decisions at the Yalta Conference. He highlights the absurdity of the dominant opinion that claimed that
the British public should not believe what "Poles have to say about their sufferings at the hands of the Russians because, as victims, they are prejudiced witnesses," and he urges British readers to end the "mental boycott of the Polish
tragedy" (Czapski 1951, 4).

Conclusion

The drive to publish English translations of witness narratives and first-hand
accounts from those who had direct knowledge of life under the Nazi and Soviet occupations was one of the Polish government-in-exile's foremost priori-
ties in London. This task was by no means an easy one, as the wartime publishing market in Britain was shaped by political and material pressures, including
paper rationing, staff shortage, and state censorship. Just as importantly, it was
increasingly difficult to make material of foreign provenance appeal to the British readership. The public's distrust of atrocity propaganda hindered the reception of texts describing the Nazi occupation, particularly describing the ongoing

persecution of Polish Jews. The reception of titles narrating the experiences of the Soviet occupation was shaped by the political pressures of the Anglo-Soviet Agreement; namely, this agreement made it difficult for British publishers to bring out texts that were critical of the Soviet ally. Indeed, it was only with the onset of the Cold War that the testimonies of deportees to the Soviet forced labor camps were re-evaluated as trustworthy sources. The annotated bibliography *Books on Communism*, edited by R. N. Carew Hunt, which, after its publication in 1959, became one of the most important research sources for scholars of the Soviet Union, provided an extensive list of testimonies of those who had survived Soviet camps and prisons—and it included Czapski's, Ekart's, Halpern's, and Zajdler's books, among many others. It is worth bearing in mind, though, that the reassessment of these works was part of the larger Cold War propaganda project, sponsored by covert funding from the British Information Research Department (Smith 2010; Defty 2004). As Soviet Russia turned from a British ally into an enemy state, the reception of the testimonials that thematized the experiences of Polish deportees underwent a radical shift; these narratives were now treated as key sources for British anti-communist propaganda. Thus, texts that were initially met with skepticism and doubt, due to the political questions that they raised, came to be seen as early warnings that should have been heeded before it was too late.

Notes

1. Unless otherwise stated, all translations from the archival material held at the Polish Institute and Sikorski Museum (PISM) and the Polish Underground Movement Study Trust (PUMST) collections are my own.

Archival material

Adam Ciołkosz Papers, 133. Polish Underground Movement Study Trust (PUMST), London.

Allen & Unwin Collection, University of Reading Special Collections, Reading.

"Book Reading in War Time: Report on Material Obtained from Publishers, Book Clubs, Libraries and Booksellers," File Report 46, Mass-Observation Archive (MOA).

Boxes Collection, SK36. Polish Underground Movement Study Trust (PUMST), London.

Faber & Faber Archive, London.

Polish Research Centre (PRC) Collection, 434. Polish Institute and Sikorski Museum (PISM), London.

References

Andrzejewski, Jerzy. 1945. *Apel: Z Przedmową Andrzeja Pomiana*. London: Światpol.

Anonymous. 1944. "Concentration Camps." *The London Typographical Journal* 39, no. 132: 1.

Bachleitner, Norbert. 2010. "A Proposal to Include Book History in Translation Studies: Illustrated with German Translations of Scott and Flaubert." *Arcadia* 44, no. 2: 420–40.

Baker, Mona. 2007. "Reframing Conflict in Translation." *Social Semiotics* 17, no. 2: 151–69.

Baley, Stephen [Stanisław Baliński]. 1941. *Two Septembers: Warsaw 1939—London 1940: A Diary of Events*. London: George Allen & Unwin.

Bell, P. M. H. 1989. "Censorship, Propaganda and Public Opinion: The Case of the Katyn Graves, 1943." *Transactions of the Royal Historical Society* 39: 63–83.

———. 1990. *John Bull and the Bear: British Public Opinion, Foreign Policy and the Soviet Union 1941–1945*. London: Edward Arnold.

Charques, D. 1946. "Poles in Captivity." *Times Literary Supplement*, August 3, 1946: 363.

Conway, Michael. 2001. "Legacies of Exile: The Exile Governments in London during the Second World War and the Politics of Post-war Europe." In *Europe in Exile: European Exile Communities in Britain 1940–45*, edited by Michael Conway and José Gotovitch, 255–74. New York: Berghahn Books.

Czapski, Joseph. 1951. *The Inhuman Land*. Translated by Gerard Hopkins. London: Chatto & Windus.

Defty, Andrew. 2004. *Britain, America and Anti-Communist Propaganda 1945–53: The Information Research Department*. London: Routledge.

Degras, Jane. 1947. "Review of *The Dark Side of the Moon*." *International Affairs* 23, no. 1: 120–21.

Ekart, Antoni. 1954. *Vanished without Trace: The Story of Seven Years in Soviet Russia*. Translated by Egerton Sykes and E.S. Virpsha. London: Max Parrish.

Eliot, T. S. 2017a. "Preface to *Roll Call*." In *The Complete Prose of T.S. Eliot: The Critical Edition*. Vol. 6: The War Years, 1940–1946, edited by David Chinitz and Ronald Schuchard, 581–85. Baltimore: Johns Hopkins University Press.

———. 2017b. "Preface to *The Dark Side of the Moon* [by Zoe Zajdlerowa]." In *The Complete Prose of T.S. Eliot: The Critical Edition*. Vol. 6: The War Years, 1940–1946, edited by David E. Chinitz and Ronald Schuchard, 742–47. Baltimore: Johns Hopkins University Press.

Fleming, Michael. 2014. *Auschwitz, the Allies and Censorship of the Holocaust*. Cambridge: Cambridge University Press.

Footitt, Hilary. 2012. "Incorporating Languages into Histories of War: A Research Journey." *Translation Studies* 5, no. 2: 217–31.

Górecki, J. [Aleksander Kamiński]. 1945. *Stones of the Rampart: The Story of Two Lads in the Polish Underground Movement*, with a foreword by Percy Hugh Beverley Lyon. London: Polish Boy Scouts' and Girl Guides' Association.

Halpern, Ada. 1945. *Liberation—Russian Style*, with a foreword by Eleanor F. Rathbone. London: MaxLove Publishing.

Hench, John. 2010. *Books as Weapons: Propaganda, Publishing, and the Battle for Global Markets in the Era of World War II*. Ithaca, NY: Cornell University Press.

Holman, Valerie. 2008. *Print for Victory: Book Publishing in England, 1939–1945*. London: The British Library.

Hunt, R. N. Carew, ed. 1959. *Books on Communism: A Bibliography*. London: Ampersand.

Karski, Jan. 1944. *Story of a Secret State*. Boston: Houghton Mifflin.

———. 1945. *Story of a Secret State*. London: Hodder & Stoughton.

Khlevniuk, Oleg. 2004. *The History of the Gulag: From Collectivization to the Great Terror*. New Haven: Yale University Press.

Kingsbury, Celia Malone. 2010. *For Home and Country: World War 1 Propaganda on the Home Front*. Lincoln, NE: University of Nebraska Press.

Knight, Claire. 2013. "The Making of the Soviet Ally in British Wartime Popular Press." *Journalism Studies* 14, no. 4: 476–90.

Koestler, Arthur. 1944. "The Nightmare That Is a Reality." *The New York Times*, January 9, 1944: 5, 30.

McKenzie, Vernon. 1942. "Atrocities in World War II: What Can We Believe?" *Journalism Quarterly* 19, no. 3: 268–76.

McLaine, Ian. 1979. *Ministry of Morale: Home Front Morale and the Ministry of Information in World War II*. London: Allen & Unwin.

"Other New Publications." 1945. *Times Literary Supplement*, May 12, 1945: 227.

Rundle, Christopher. 2010. *Publishing Translations in Fascist Italy*. Bern: Peter Lang.

Rzepa, Joanna. 2018. "Translation, Conflict and the Politics of Memory: Jan Karski's *Story of a Secret State*." *Translation Studies* 11, no. 3: 315–32.

———. 2019a. "The 'Demonic Forces' at Auschwitz: T.S. Eliot Reads Jerzy Andrzejewski's *Roll Call*." *Modernism/modernity* 26, no. 2: 329–50.

———. 2019b. "Publishing 'Paper Bullets': Politics, Propaganda and Polish–English Translation in Wartime London." *Comparative Critical Studies* 16, no. 2–3: 217–35.

Schwartz, Harry. 1947. "Review of *The Dark Side of the Moon*." *Political Science Quarterly* 62, no. 4: 602–4.

Smith, James B. 2010. "The British Information Research Department and Cold War Propaganda Publishing." In *Pressing the Fight: Print, Propaganda, and the Cold War*, edited by Greg Barnhisel and Catherine Turner, 112–25. Amherst: University of Massachusetts Press.

Stanford, George. 2005. *Katyn and the Soviet Massacre of 1940: Truth, Justice and Memory*. London: Routledge.

Stevenson, Iain. 2010. *Book Makers: British Publishing in the Twentieth Century*. London: The British Library.

Stop Them Now: German Mass Murder of Jews in Poland. 1942. With a foreword by Lord Wedgwood. London: Liberty Publications.

Sword, Keith. 1991. "British Reactions to the Soviet Occupation of Eastern Poland in September 1939." *The Slavonic and East European Review* 69, no. 1: 81–101.

Zajdler, Zoe. 1940. *My Name is Million: The Experiences of an Englishwoman in Poland*. London: Faber & Faber.

———. 1946. *The Dark Side of the Moon*, with a preface by T. S. Eliot. London: Faber & Faber.

Zajdlerowa, Zoe. 1989. *The Dark Side of the Moon*. 2nd ed. Edited by John Coutouvidis and Thomas Lane. London: Harvester Wheatsheaf.

Zarembina, Natalia. 1944. *Camp of Death*. With a foreword by Jennie L. Adamson. London: Liberty Press.

CHAPTER 11

How to Handle the New Occupiers?

Margret Boveri's *Amerikafibel für erwachsene Deutsche: Ein Versuch, Unverstandenes zu erklären* (1946)

SANDRA SCHELL

In 1946, when the Allied reeducation programs caused resentment and irritation among post-war German society (Leßau 2020; Niethammer 1982), the American-German journalist Margret Boveri (1900–1975) published her *Amerikafibel für erwachsene Deutsche* ("American Primer for Grown-Up Germans"). Notwithstanding a paper shortage and Allied censorship (Hurwitz 1972; Gehring 1976; Koszyk 1986), the text, licensed by French and British military authorities (Streim 2002, 493), quickly achieved mass-circulation among the four occupied zones. Taking occupation-as-experience seriously, her entertaining *Versuch, Unverstandenes zu erklären* ("Attempt to Explain What Has Not Been Understood")—so the primer's subtitle—aimed to help her fellow Germans better understand the US-American liberators. Alfred Döblin, who approved the manuscript as censor for the French office of public education, attested Boveri's primer to be "a useful book." Written in an easily readable manner, it addresses

> the differences in character between Americans and Germans, the differences in thinking, their social forms, etc. (Author is the daughter of an American, was correspondent of the *Frankf[urter] Zeitung* in New York). The book never theorizes but gives practical examples. It aims to overcome resistance, clarify misunderstandings. Clever, much expertise, valuable.[1] (Döblin 1946)

In the following, I argue that Boveri's *Amerikafibel*, influenced by the author's own experiences, is purposefully written to suit specific needs for intercultural encounters in the post-war German–American contact zone of occupation. In further elaboration of this thesis, I emphasize that the book serves as a noteworthy example within the broader context of European literature of military occupation. To understand this from today's perspective requires some hermeneutic effort. Thus, the essayistic primer does not give clear instructions on the virulent question, *How to handle the new occupiers?*, but rather provides ambivalent attempts at cultural mediation and identity negotiation.

In line with recent 'relational' approaches on the circulation of knowledge in global intellectual history and sociology, I refer to Margret Boveri as an American-German cross-cultural 'go-between' (Raj 2016). The concept of go-betweens, intermediaries, knowledge or cultural brokers focuses on "the interaction between mobile figures and the cultures they encounter, examining the negotiations, inflections, and reconfigurations that result from this process" (Raj 2016, 43). In post-war history, and before, protagonists as diverse as Carl Zuckmayer (1946/1947 [2004]), John Dos Passos (1946), Hannah Arendt (1950), Ruth Benedict (1946),[2] Alfred Döblin (see Siess in this volume), Stig Dagerman (1947 [2011]), and Margret Boveri (1946) engaged as cross-cultural mediators, especially by explaining (in fictional and non-fictional texts) a given culture and its specificities (the US, Germany, Japan, etc.) to a given audience (a public readership, a military, a government, etc.) for whom that culture was unknown (and perceived as foreign). Unlike Zuckmayer, Döblin, Dos Passos, and Benedict, however, Boveri neither worked for nor wrote at the invitation of the Allied military government. Still, she understood the external stimulation provided by US reeducation measures as an influential source of change and development in post-war Germany's culture, politics, and society. For this reason, the *Amerikafibel* seems an exemplary text by which to illustrate the "crucial need for mediation, brokerage, and cross-cultural communication in establishing sustained exchange between disparate and different cultures" (Raj 2016, 40) on the one hand, and the position of strength that cross-cultural brokers negotiate from within the intercultural contact zone on the other.

At the time of its publication, Boveri's essayistic primer was largely hailed as a practical and appropriate introduction to US culture, which, *first*, I shall outline here before touching upon its later criticism. *Second*, by close reading, I show how Boveri promoted a national-conservative conceptualization of 'the American' that results in a highly ambiguous understanding of the US-occupation and the Allied reeducation program. In a *third* step, I tentatively outline how Boveri's personal experiences abroad and in Berlin during 1944–1945 shaped her ambivalent and skeptical attitude toward the United States—an attitude that, in the *Amerikafibel*, fostered a concept of the "*abendländisch* European unity of culture" (Conze 2010, 48; for a different conceptualization of *Abendland*/Occident in the post-war context, see Lieb in this volume).

Margret Boveri, the *Amerikafibel für erwachsene Deutsche* and its Polyphonic Reception

Born in 1900 as the daughter of German zoologist Theodor Boveri and American biologist Marcella O'Grady, Margret Boveri grew up in a highly educated cosmopolitan milieu in Germany; later studied German, English, history, and political science in Würzburg and Berlin; and earned her doctorate with a dissertation on British foreign policy, chaired by the historian Hermann Oncken, who later was forced by the Nazis to retire. In 1934, Boveri started her career as a journalist in the Foreign Affairs section of the *Berliner Tageblatt*. Along with the *Frankfurter Zeitung*, the *Berliner Tageblatt* was one of the still relatively liberal German newspapers after the so-called *Gleichschaltung*. As a journalist and writer, she traveled the world extensively.[3] In the late 1930s, then, when German–American bilateral relations deteriorated dramatically in the wake of Roosevelt's criticism of Nazism, the focus of German interest in the United States also shifted from questions of economic policy to those of foreign policy (Patel 2000, 371; Gassert 1997), which made Boveri's expertise increasingly sought after. After the Nazi authorities shut down the *Berliner Tageblatt* in 1939, she worked as a foreign correspondent for the *Frankfurter Zeitung* in Stockholm, New York, and Lisbon. During World War II, she therefore had access to various international and, most importantly, uncensored newspapers (Görtemaker 2005, 2006; Belke 2005, 133). Boveri translated newsflash, and some of the travel reports and autobiographic anecdotes that she also published at this time were later adapted for her *Amerikafibel*.

After the United States entered the war, she was interned as an 'enemy alien' in New York (Görtemaker 2005, 162–67)[4] before being returned at her own request to Europe. Returning to Berlin in 1944, she then worked as a freelance writer with the Nazi weekly *Das Reich*. As Erika Martens and Ingrid Belke have pointed out, Boveri did not explicitly write Nazi propaganda, but her articles were still tendentious. By addressing problems such as racial segregation or corruption, her reports tend to present a distorted image of the United States during World War II (Martens 1972, 194f.; Belke 2005, 135).

As one of the most influential female 'go-betweens' (Raj 2016) in the European and trans-Atlantic journalistic field from the 1930s to late 1940s, Boveri had her finger on the pulse: she repeatedly responded, with different intentions and in different genres, to various types and experiences of military occupation. Among her works that touched upon aspects of occupation, she published travel literature about the colonies of Malta, Sudan, and Algeria and the protectorates of Morocco and Tunisia (Boveri 1936, 1938); she applauded Mussolini's invasion of Abyssinia (Boveri 1936, 187); and reported as a foreign correspondent (mostly in newsflash) about World War II. In Berlin, she experienced the last months of the war, the liberation, and the capital's occupation by Russian and, subsequently, American military forces. Living under occupation meant, for Margret Boveri as for many others, finding herself "in a situation of accelerated historical change and social pressure" (Buschmeier and Glesener 2021, 3; see also Buschmeier in this volume). Accordingly, her diaristic letter of March 1945 reads: "I think that what will happen in Berlin will be symbolic for the whole, and, to that end, I came back to experience it" (Boveri 1968a, 50).[5] As a journalist, she not only wanted to experience the new encounters herself; she also wanted to mediate them on behalf of the readership of her diaristic circular letter, mostly addressed to family and friends.

With her 1946 *Amerikafibel*, Boveri was immediately reacting to the new situation of US-American occupation by aiming to help a broader, public readership better cope with the wishes and impositions of the US-American liberators and the latter's attempts at reeducating post-Nazi Germany (Boveri 1946, 9–11; Streim 1999, 2002). Soon after the end of World War II, the Allied occupation forces, especially the US-American, had started their (cultural-)political campaigns in democratizing and reeducating the former enemy nation to make of its citizens a democratic society and, subsequently, turn Germany into an ally in the emerging Cold War. Amidst the many-voiced discussion at the time about US cultural policies abroad and, on the other hand, the potential for an 'indigenous' transformation of Germany, 'reeducation' emerged as a term rich in associations and inspiration, albeit a controversial one. The term, often pejoratively translated as 'Umerziehung', soon became a pivotal point in post-Nazi Germany's political, academic, and literary debates (Gerund and Paul 2015, 9f.). While the US educational ventures abroad offered Germany's "de-anchored, collapsed society" (Doering-Manteuffel 1999, 36) possibilities for participation in a democratic future and orientation in how such a future could look, 'reeducation' was often reinterpreted in the German discourse and met with refusal, particularly as these efforts were widely perceived as a forced Americanization (Lüdtke, Marßolek, and von Saldern 1996, 26).

Margret Boveri, while acknowledging the status quo and highlighting the power asymmetry of occupation, contributed with her *Amerikafibel* to the reconstruction of national and cultural identities in post-war Germany. In her book, she warns her readers that the intercultural encounters in the post-war German–American contact zone run the risk of cultural misunderstanding. Not without her reasons, she calls for her fellow Germans to be considerate:

Being considerate is more important than showing ourselves in a good light. Impartiality and attentiveness: these are the qualities we should show to our guests. If we observe rather than react too emotionally, if we draw our conclusions from these observations, we will thwart the emergence of resentments, which are so

> obvious and so dangerous, and thereby might even get to know the American
> species opening up to us.[6] (Boveri 1946, 108)

As already alluded to ambiguously in its title and in passages like this, the whole book is marked by irony and semantic ambivalence. Picking up on the subtle anti-American undertones, historians thus far have been interpreting the literary primer as a provocative "pushback against reeducation" (Görtemaker 2005, 224; similar: Vogt 2006, 261–67) that chipped away at US cultural policy and contributed rather monumentally to cultural misunderstanding (Görtemaker 2005, 223–9; 2006; Hoenicke Moore 2005; contemporaneous: Fitzsimons 1948, 254).

Completely different, however, to today's voices was the euphoric, contemporaneous press echo.[7] Döblin was not the only one who hailed the book as an appropriate introduction to 'Americanness'; journalists from across the four occupation zones, and prominent figures such as Theodor Heuss, declared that Boveri had presented "an eminently clever introduction to the American world, based on keen observation" (FM 1947, 26),[8] which satisfied the "practical need for a deeper understanding of Americans" (Steinberg 1946, 5).[9] Against this background, however, it seems to me that reducing this ambiguous text to a one-sided interpretation fails to recognize the complexity of the historical situation—and how the book was carefully composed to facilitate the intercultural encounters that transpired under the auspices of reeducation in the German–American contact zone (even if this objective was not the cultural primer's sole raison d'être). Nevertheless, meeting the genre conventions of an essay, Boveri's explorations of the causes of cultural differences (and of misunderstandings) are not always argumentative but rather more subjective, associative, and even contradictory. In her preface, she explicitly declares her insights into US culture not to be "objective." Yet, she claims, thanks to her American mother, her perspective on the United States is rich with "emotions," which she finds necessary for writing an entertaining, yet also authentic and educational, book (Boveri 1946, 6–8).

The resulting ambiguities, ambivalences, and inconsistencies are particularly revealing to an eye trained in rhetoric and literary studies. Thus, they can be identified not only on the macro-level of the author's overarching line of reasoning, but also on the micro-level, especially in the way she recodes specific terms, such as 'race' or 'reeducation.' If we take seriously the impressions by contemporaneous readers of her *Amerikafibel*, it seems that Boveri moves about as a mobile figure in the newly opened post-war German–American contact zone, a fact that encouraged not only resentment and distrust, but also exchange and intercultural communication (Boveri 1946, 8). Hereby she became involved in the 'boundary work' as a cross-cultural mediator, work that was deemed necessary for the pending reformation of German identity.

It goes almost without saying that the continuity in Boveri's career as go-between both before and after 1945 merits explanation, especially in the light of the Allied denazification-measures.[10] Margret Boveri was never a member of the Nazi Party, nor was she naïvely opportunistic, but it is important to note that as a world-traveling author, journalist, and foreign correspondent, she was nevertheless a careerist in the Nazi period and willing to make compromises. After the liberation of Berlin, the uneven distribution of power among the different occupier nations, not to mention their respective power differentials in relation to occupied Germany, revealed the complex nature of the process of intermediation. Knowledge brokers became sought after in this multicultural contact zone, and in the very first months after World War II, Boveri's role as cross-cultural mediator became useful to the Allied reeducation program. While working on the *Amerikafibel*, she translated an American children's book into German (Webster 1947) and compiled a list of English and American novels published between 1941 and 1945 for the translation program of the Ullstein publishing house (Boveri 1968a, 209). Moving between languages "served thus not only a collective interest; it was also the way to have an audience and to be published" (Verschaffel et al. 2014, 1267). Given how her career was unbroken by the rupture in the sociohistorical context,[11] Boveri is an excellent subject of study for analyzing the astonishingly resilient value of argumentative and rhetorical 'resources,' even in cultures that undergo an extreme transition of power.

Boveri's National-Conservative Conceptualization of 'the American'

In the preface, dated New Year's Eve 1945, Boveri outlines how the *Amerikafibel* aims to satisfy the newly emerging needs of the post-war intercultural contact zone and its encounters: "The Americans have come to us on a permanent visit," she claims—and further observes: "And yet, they caused great astonishment, especially among those who had most eagerly hoped for and most joyfully welcomed their arrival. [...] Minds are confused and full of doubts" (Boveri 1946, 7f.).[12] As her fellow Germans of the time obviously lack basic knowledge about the US-Americans, the former have been in for a big disappointment. Yet Boveri promises help. Her essayistic primer, written for "household use," will contribute to the understanding between the two peoples ("für den täglichen deutschen Hausgebrauch im Verstehenlernen der kommenden Jahre," Boveri 1946, 8).

In her attempt to bridge these cultures, Boveri is emphatically concerned with a profound mediation that penetrates into the "historical contingency of American nature" (Boveri 1946, 7). Programmatically, she outlines her method:

> Understanding between peoples cannot be achieved by acknowledging what is
> common to all human beings. [...] Understanding between people emerges only
> when we recognize what is fundamentally different about other peoples and their
> distinct historical contingency, and this means recognizing even those character-
> istics that we find repugnant.[13] (Boveri 1946, 7)

Herein, she seems to fall into line with the concept of an 'inter-ethnic', 'ethnopluralist' understanding, which was intensively discussed in the 'Third Reich'
(Albrecht, Danneberg, and Skowronski 2020). Quite in contrast with the German post-war efforts to cultivate humanism, Boveri's ethnopluralist approach
to the cultural boundary work conflicts severely. From a cultural relativist and
anti-universalist perspective, she argues that "Americans are a new people. If the
word had not been so misused, I would say: a new race" (Boveri 1946, 7).[14] She
is convinced that US-Americans are the only people of emigrants in the world
(Boveri 1946, Chapter 1), such that the American people are—in contrast to European people—neither historically nor culturally grown. Due to this "ahistoric
state of emigration" (Boveri 1946, 14),[15] Americanness is no conglomeration
of diverse European characteristics. Instead, the tremendous "melting process"
(Boveri 1946, 38) has been transforming all US-bound immigrants into the unified American people (Boveri 1946, 33, 89).[16]

Over the course of six chapters, Boveri explains this key assumption: namely,
US-Americans' non-Europeanness (Boveri 1946, 30, 42, 83; Hahnemann 2010,
87; Streim 1999). The underlying, well-known metaphor of a melting pot (here
referring to the process of 'assimilating' from 'immigrant' to 'US-American') is,
according to her, fulfilled by two different-yet-interwoven processes—and herewith, Boveri gives the old topos a new twist. First, the US-American-to-be as-
similates by means of what she calls "reeducation at home" (Boveri 1946, 34)—
she herewith vaguely refers to some sort of 'reeducation process' that immigrants
undergo in the US. And this is now partially projected onto the Germans. Second, the new migrant is shaped by the American continent's distinct climate and
geography.

The chapter entitled *Conform or starve. Oder: Die Umerziehung zum neuen
Menschentyp* ("The Reeducation into the New Type of Person") deals with the
first process and simultaneously reveals Boveri's rhetorical effort to relieve her
concept of 'race', ideologically, of the connotations with which Nazi doctrine
once burdened the term. Instead of focusing on contemporaneous US-American
educational ventures—that is, the so-called 'reeducation' (as the chapter's title
might suggest)—Boveri explains how generations of European and Asian immigrants alike were transformed from their 'race of origin' into the new "Menschentyp," namely the US-American. For the fact that 'emigration of conviction'

marks the beginning of US history (Boveri 1946, 9, 13), she argues that freedom seems more important to US-Americans than primordial national loyalty—meaning that immigrants' loyalty to their cultures of origin is relinquished by 'assimilation' (Boveri 1946, 38). The unifying power, then, stems from the will to one's Americanization ("Amerikanisierungswillen[]", Boveri 1946, 25), which Boveri closely links to US exceptionalism. The suggestive power of the conviction that America is the best, the greatest, the most beautiful, and the freest of all countries (Boveri 1946, 25) is crucial for what Boveri coins the successful US 'reeducation at home.' That said, although Boveri analyzes different waves of immigration in US history, the chapter does not address how the Nazis' expansive imperialist policy confronted millions of European citizens with an enduring occupation—whose attendant experiences of persecution and obliteration could have given enough plausible reasons for European emigration to the US or elsewhere in the first place.

How does the process of 'reeducation at home' transform immigrants into US-Americans, though? According to Boveri, the US's widespread adoption of new technologies, taken together with capitalism, commercialization, and the so-called American dream, have accelerated the migrants' transformation by means of "assimilation through adjustment, suggestion, and education" (Boveri 1946, 32; Keyserling 1930, 85); the resulting "mechanized unification" (Boveri 1946, 82; 1941a, 1941b) secures the United States' national unity. This, in consequence, explains the US-American urge toward normalization and standardization—something her contemporaries in occupied Germany can see now so clearly in the bureaucratic side of denazification, particularly in the Allies' seeming obsession with questionnaires (Boveri 1946, Chapter 3). To this latter point, as Werner Sollors has pointed out, the *Amerikafibel* is a significant and, compared with Ernst von Salomon's *Der Fragebogen* (1951) ("The Questionnaire"), quite early example of how the denazification questionnaire—symbolic for Allied democratization programs—"provoked writers on both sides of the Atlantic to represent it in fiction and non-fiction" (Sollors 2018, 139).

In resonance with Sollors' note on the transatlantic popularity of the theme, I underscore the notion of entangled interaction within the distinctive context of Margret Boveri's *Amerikafibel*: while her fellow Germans might have thought that their "human sensibility could not easily be understood that way" (Sollors 2018, 152), Boveri tries to explain how all kinds of evaluation methods are pervasive in everyday life in the US and, therefore, deeply rooted within the country's mentality. In line with Theodor W. Adorno and other conservative cultural diagnosticians of her time, Boveri herewith alludes to Max Weber's theory of bureaucracy. These evaluation methods were, of course, nothing specifically American. On the contrary, questionnaires and bureaucracy in general also played an important part in the Nazi terror system of expropriation, deportation, and murder. In fact, in her diaristic letter, dated June 5, 1945, Boveri herself compared the denazification questionnaire to Nazi techniques (Boveri 1968a, 184f.).[17] Only a few months after the exposure of concentration camps, the *Amerikafibel*, in contrast, is devoid of any criticism of the Nazi atrocities (Hoenicke Moore 2005, 231; Streim 2002, 496). Nevertheless, by casting these evaluation methods as a common 'American' practice, Boveri is attempting here to refute the virulent claim that the questionnaire was specifically invented to discriminate against or even torture the defeated nation (Boveri 1946, 46).[18] However, Margret Boveri closed her own denazification questionnaire with the general critique: "I reject the system of *Fragebogen* and their application to Germans in general and to myself in particular, and I have filled this out only at the request of and out of friendship for Professor Welter" (Boveri quoted in Görtemaker 2005, 230f.).[19]

While Boveri is convinced that these evaluation methods are successful in US society, considering the post-war situation of US-American occupation, she contrastingly claims: "The reeducation at home has been completely successful. Unlike France and Great Britain, who both gathered experiences from their long history of colonization, the Americans have neither long nor extensive experiences in reeducating abroad"[20] (Boveri 1946, 34).

This passage is, again, quite ambiguous: while pointing toward the insecurities and maladroitness on both sides of the new German–American contact zone, it simultaneously offers strong comfort to those readers who are afraid that reeducation and denazification might have severe impacts, in that she paints the US-Americans as largely ineffective at the task. Here and elsewhere, her explanation dialectically oscillates between a patriotic negotiation of German identity and a relational understanding of 'the Americans,' whereat she sometimes goes even further, indicating and acknowledging the US-Americans' role-model function: "In some places in this book, reference has been made to American qualities that can be exemplary for us. However, adopting the good of another can only be fruitful for those who feel secure in their own"[21] (Boveri 1946, 108). But can the methods of 'reeducation at home' be fully projected onto and successful at transforming post-Nazi Germans?

Closely linked to this question is Boveri's conviction that the American continent's distinct climate, geography, and natural resources have produced the US-American character (Boveri 1946, 35f., 40f., 108; for the historic link between physiognomy and theories of climate see Zacharasiewicz 2010, 67–119). To support her line of reasoning, she draws upon historical, cultural, geopolitical, climatological, and characterological concepts by Carl Gustav Jung (Boveri 1946, 38), Sigmund Freud (Boveri 1946, 97), André Siegfried (Boveri 1946, 26, 29, 51, 95), Hermann von Keyserling (Boveri 1946, 79), and others. She also names Anglo-American authorities, such as William Faulkner, and she repeat-edly quotes, in both English and German, a particular passage from his novel *The Unvanquished*, which claims that the United States is "the land of violent sun, of intense alteration from snow to heat-stroke which has produced a race impervious to both" (Faulkner quoted in Boveri 1946, 36, 39, 57; 1960, 11; 1968a, 289; 1968b).

This affinity for quoting Faulkner is especially worth expanding upon. In his 1938 novel, Faulkner had realistically depicted the decline of old Southern aris-tocratic families and the rise of brutal and corrupt upstarts. Given that literary representation played a major role in negotiating democracy, *The Unvanquished* had already been subject to a translation ban by the US cultural affairs office (Gehring 1977, 263). Boveri, however, takes up the notion of an "impervious race" and recodes it ethnically.

Yet her argument is ambiguous and aligned with explicitly racist interpreta-tions: as the American soil has already shaped the "race" of Indigenous peoples, she claims it seems plausible to assume that, over a longer period, the "American race" has been developing similar character traits to "the Indians." She attempts to lend substance to her reasoning by giving a first-hand anecdote. At a concert in New York that she attended, she at once recognized intrinsically 'Indigenous' traits in the upper-class white women of the audience:

> In our conversation […], they had been lively, youthful. Now, relaxed, they were completely different faces […]: they resembled Indians sitting silently, almost ab-sently, around a campfire. […] One among them I will never forget. […] Only the wreath of colorful feathers was missing; then she would have been a very aristo-cratic, very imperious chief […]. Was she a descendant of the Pilgrims, on whose structure and substance the new continent had already been modeling itself for three hundred years?[22] (Boveri 1946, 38f.)

Comparable to the anthropological concept of participatory observation, Boveri often calls upon her experiences from across her many years of being a foreign correspondent in the United States—oftentimes with heavily anecdotal evidence. By means of first-hand experiences like these, she not only highlights her own privileged position as American-German go-between but also re-evaluates and articulates racial, cultural, national, historical, and geographical boundaries. In her process, the interactions between Boveri as a mobile figure and the cultures she encounters (German and US) tend to result in "negotiations, inflections, and reconfigurations" (Raj 2016, 43); and against the backdrop of post-Nazi Ger-many, it is particularly interesting how she recodes terms that were put into question on both sides of the German–American contact zone—such as 'race,' 'assimilation,' and 'reeducation.' Rather than focusing too explicitly on the postwar situation, she syncretistically makes use of ideas that had already been vigorously debated at the turn of the century and that later found their racist and antisemitic manifestations mainly by Nazi ideologues. For example, in contrast to the racist and antisemitic Nazi concept of the 'Aryan race,' Boveri seems to attempt to recode the term 'race' by alternatives, such as 'Völker' (peoples), 'Menschentyp' (type (of person)), and 'Spezien' (species), in the sense of ethnic groups that are not biologically fixed and are equally capable of assimilation (i.e., geistige Rasse),[23] as well as malleable to the forces of climate and geography. It is evident that a thorough examination in this context prompts further inquiries, particularly concerning the ambiguous semantics the author uses: do these terms appear interchangeably over the course of her *Amerikafibel*? In which contexts might Boveri favor one term over the other? Such questions are unfortunately outside the scope of the present analysis.

Falling partly in line with the defense strategy of the so-called 'Inner Emigration,'[24] among whose adherents the *Amerikafibel* resonated strongly, Boveri seems, at first glance, to address explicitly those who stayed in Germany during the so-called Third Reich. However, it is reasonable to assume that she deliberately makes use of semantic ambiguities in order to address different groups of readers at the same time. Which (political) interpretations are guaranteed, though, by these ambiguities, in correlation with which groups of readers? In the immediate post-war context of new entanglements (so my overall hypothesis runs), Margret Boveri herewith explores, in her primer, how to adapt her former convictions to—and how to interweave them with—the changed political situation, and thus also the convictions of many German contemporaries, which have now been put into question by the US-American reeducation program (Ash 1995; Weisbrod 2002).

The *Amerikafibel* in Light of Boveri's Personal Experiences Abroad

Previous studies on Margret Boveri's *Amerikafibel* have noticed that it bears essential similarities to her journalistic articles written before 1945. No previous study, however, has evaluated in detail the cross references, nor has it taken into account her diaristic chronicle in letters, *Tage des Überlebens. Berlin 1945* ("Days of Survival. Berlin 1945"), as relevant context for grasping Boveri's experiences. Hence, I sketch an overview of some preliminary findings regarding how her personal experiences abroad and in Berlin in 1944–1945 shaped Boveri's ambivalent attitude toward the United States: the precise attitude that, in the *Amerika-*

fibel, fostered a concept of the "*abendländisch* European unity of culture" (Conze 2010, 48) and allowed her to slip into the role of cultural liaison for the Germans.

As already mentioned, Boveri returned to Berlin in March 1944 (rather than remaining in Lisbon). By the beginning of 1945, she started to chronicle the events of the war in the form of several circular letters addressed to friends in Zurich. In 1968, she revised and commented on these diaristic letters for publication. In her comments, she explicitly hints at the difference between her own positions in 1945 and those she now holds in the mid-1960s: she acknowledges her former misjudgments and situates the letters within their historical context. This makes her *Tage des Überlebens* an interesting document, illustrative of and reflective regarding the politics of memory. Rereading her chronicle for publication in 1968, Boveri describes her ambivalent feelings:

> I was offended by the profusion of tomboyish expressions, by the hastily-made judgments about public figures, and I was frequently startled by the content—not of the startling events I had recorded, but of the alien image of a being that was myself.[25] (Boveri 1968a, 29f.)

Written from February to September 1945 (Boveri 1968a, 318) under Allied censorship (Boveri 1968a, 8)—and, as Boveri later acknowledges, in the language of the perpetrators—her circular letters strikingly detail the last months of the war, and the occupation by Russian and, subsequently, US military forces (Schaumann 2009, 104).

Boveri approached her experiences in 1945 Berlin almost as a war correspondent, serving as a bold go-between (for other examples and for an exploration of the 'adventure' aspect of occupation in general, see both Laffin's and Meid's chapter in this volume). As her colleague Christa Rotzoll remembers:

> I almost never have the courage to go outside. On the contrary, Boveri has just come out of a German tank that she wanted to inspect from the inside […]. She has looked around fearlessly, elated, almost intoxicated by all the horror that is to be witnessed. She wants to know, to hear, to smell, to observe it all. She is a journalist, a witness. The fact that she does not have to write anything now, as nothing would get printed, does not slow down her curiosity. I am very amazed.[26] (Rotzoll 1987, 118f.)

In her circular letters, Boveri illustrates how the occupation of Berlin opened different contact zones, which, after Germany's capitulation, "also led to exchange and permanent communication, transforming the military front into a selectively permeable membrane of contact" (Buschmeier and Glesener 2021, 2; see also

Buschmeier in this volume), mainly with Russian and US soldiers. While occupation became a "social process of everyday life" (Długoborski 1996 quoted in Buschmeier and Glesener 2021, 2) for Boveri, she likewise explicitly tells how the contact zone of occupied Berlin turned into a zone of fear, displacement, rape, and starvation for others among her fellow Germans. In her letter dated August 1945, Boveri reports how close friends have been dispossessed of their home by US officers, and she combines this event with an observation: the US-Americans' fear of lasting Nazi terror. Ridiculing these fears, she invalidates criticism confidently:

> All this confirmed to me again what I had already noticed while I was interned
> in the US, namely that the Americans have no idea about Germany and the Ger-
> mans. They never bothered to determine what National Socialism really is, nei-
> ther for bad nor for good. They have constructed an image of Germany that prob-
> ably only fully corresponds in terms of the concentration camps [...], and this is
> the image over which they are berating us now.[27] (Boveri 1968a, 263)

Boveri ascribes to the US occupiers a largely indifferent attitude about the 'true' fundamental core of German national identity, the core that lies deeper than the Nazi period. In her opinion, this attitude results from the US's ostensibly ancestral principle of emigration: namely, that one must 'conform or starve'[28]—an attitude that they now attempt to impose upon all their spheres of control (Boveri 1968a, 262–66).

While her chronicle in letters is a diaristic expression written under the immediate experience of occupation—that is, at a time when Americanization and the reeducation measures were seen as a threat by part of German society—her *Amerikafibel* is a literary response to the new reality of occupation: Boveri aims to tutor and advise her readers on how to interact self-assuredly as Germans in the newly opened intercultural contact zone. Her reassurance to Germans is, I hypothesize, closely linked to the fact that Allied liberators are viewed not so much as 'saviors' but as occupiers in both texts (i.e., her private circular letters and the *Amerikafibel*).

As Matthias Buschmeier and Jeanne E. Glesener have pointed out, the "enduring presence of military forces" required "political, administrative, and cultural actions that, to a certain degree, involved and depended upon parts of the occupied population" (Buschmeier and Glesener 2021, 3f.; see also Buschmeier's introduction in this volume). Boveri's ambivalences, both in her chronicle in letters and in her *Amerikafibel*, seem to locate her somewhere between resistance and collaboration. As Hermann Bausinger highlights, it had not even taken a bad relationship with the Americans to perceive them negatively as foreign rulers in post-war Germany. In turn, in great part—even among liberal and

pro-American voices—this perception promoted the reawakening of nationalistic thinking (Bausinger et al. 2011, 222f.).

Looking from a transhistorical perspective that extends into our present, it is
interesting to ask how the ambiguities of Boveri's rhetoric have led some to use
her words to promote the notion of Western-European supremacy, casting the liberators' reeducation efforts as 'dark pedagogy.' Indeed, extremist authors who are
often associated with the German New Right movement (Schrenck-Notzing 1965;
Weißmann 2005, 2012) have linked their particularly anti-American nationalist
views to Margret Boveri and her *Amerikafibel*. These authors pursue an anti-democratic political agenda, namely an agenda that promotes their own national-conservative and far-right positions of ethnopluralism and xenophobia (Weißmann
2005, 2012) while refuting the successes of democratization and liberalization by
Allied policy. Such positions are, however, not in accordance with Boveri's own,
as she made clear in her review of Schrenck-Notzing's (1965) *Charakterwäsche.
Die amerikanische Besatzung in Deutschland und ihre Folgen* ("Character Washing.
The American Occupation of Germany and Its Consequences").

I do not intend to reinstall Margret Boveri as a liberal, America-friendly dem-
ocrat. She was always a national-conservative intellectual with antidemocratic
tendencies, who was emphatic about her "wholehearted loyalty to her homeland" (Person 2005, 32). Her ultra-patriotism was highly influenced by historical
and philosophical concepts of Americanness by European thinkers and therefore situated in the discourse of the "*abendländisch* European unity of culture"
(Conze 2010, 48). In *Tage des Überlebens* and in the *Amerikafibel*, Boveri invokes
the memory of Spengler and Rilke, exponents of German occidental culture, to
aid in her fight against the "hardening of the soul" ("Seelenverhärtung", Boveri
1968a, 328f.) and to exhort the reader to remember this thread of German occidental culture, which for pre-Nazi Germany was of great importance. This conservative notion of a historically grown German, leastwise European, cultural
unity was supposed to immunize Germany against a forced Americanization—a
concept, incidentally, that Boveri did not associate strictly with the reeducation
measures. Nonetheless, compared to Spengler and others, her stance seems decidedly balanced. She follows, for example, Spengler's concept of 'cultures' as or-
ganisms and closed social entities that, while they do interact, do not influence
one another more than superficially, on account of their essential differences. In
contrast to Spengler, though, she does not use these observations to launch an
anti-American polemic. Instead, Margret Boveri draws on widespread topoi of
'modernism,' such as materialism, capitalism, mechanization, standardization,
naïve optimism, mass culture, and democracy, to differentiate US-American
from European culture, especially German culture—and yet seems to recode
these topoi with the aim of assuaging post-war resentments.

Conclusion

Margret Boveri's *Amerikafibel für erwachsene Deutsche* resonated strongly with and was recognized by its audience due its acknowledgment of the complex living conditions under US-occupation. With her essayistic primer, she aimed deliberately to meet the specific needs of the occupied society by speaking reassuringly to the fears of an audience who was eager for guidance in the process of identity negotiation under the new and challenging intercultural contact zone of US-occupation—and, as such, the ambiguous (and abstract) options Boveri offers were quite likely designed to suit this end.

What can we learn from this case study about occupation literature? When approached from a more general perspective, the example shows, *first*, that, whatever might be considered the 'successes' of reeducation efforts,[29] culture brokering authors (or: cross-cultural mediators, go-betweens) from both sides of the Atlantic seem to have played a crucial role. Not only in this case, knowledge brokering is often "an occasional, conjunctural, activity, not an essential part of the being of the persons considered," as Kapil Raj (2016, 50) acknowledges. In literary history, knowledge- and culture-brokering authors like the American-German journalist Boveri are active within different (political, intellectual, etc.) 'communities of practice' (Cox 2005) and across borders, whereby they facilitate the transfer and exchange of (cultural) knowledge from where it is abundant to where it is needed.

Second, literature of military occupation appears to engage in the process of negotiation, clarification, or the (re-)establishment of boundaries and demarcations. In sociology, this phenomenon is known as boundary work. As observed in Boveri's essayistic primer, boundary work is used to construct, advocate, attack, challenge, or reinforce various lines of demarcation, declaring out- and insiders. However, this does not imply that boundary work merely relies on the binary rhetorical framework of friends–enemies. Rather, the boundary work undertaken by cross-cultural mediators operates on multiple and entangled levels. What has been emphasized in relation to occupation literature as a genre can also be asserted here: boundary work under occupation, too, "escapes any easy dichotomy" (Buschmeier in this volume). Connected with different communities of practice, Boveri was active across several borders without necessarily erasing them; thereby, she configured her own hybrid—namely brokering, national, intercultural, journalistic, and artistic—position. Since she differentiated internally within a Western setting between occupiers (the United States) and occupied (Germany), she simultaneously reinforced, by implication, strong (external) boundaries with the Soviet Union. If we examine Boveri's *Amerikafibel* as an exemplar of occupation literature, it becomes evident that the genre not only mirrors "the proximity and interconnectedness of occupiers and the occupied" (Buschmeier in this volume). It further emphasizes that future research on occupation configurations (in historical or literary studies) need to embrace not only bi- but *multi*lateral perspectives.

In the broader context of European literature of military occupation, aesthetically and rhetorically composed texts like Margret Boveri's *Amerikafibel* open multiple reflective approaches to occupation, its hybridity, recognition (Felski 2008, 23–50), and power differentials. It is an exemplar of the power of literature (whether fictional or non-fictional) and its potential to utilize ambiguity as an aesthetic technique and as a discursive strategy, to facilitate a desired impact and reception. In turn, literature offers insight into the interconnectedness and complex layering of identity work under occupation regimes. For the fact that these ambiguities are highly time-bound, any retrospective reconstruction must take the interwoven cultural, historical, and contemporary contexts into account.

Notes

1. All translations of non-English sources are my own. Döblin 1946: "Ein nützliches Buch. Es behandelt, leicht geschrieben, die Charakterunterschiede zwischen Amerikanern und Deutschen, die Unterschiede des Denkens, ihrer Gesellschaftsformen etc. (Autorin ist Tochter einer Amerikanerin, war Korrespondentin der Frank[furter] Zeitung in New York). Das Buch theoretisiert nie, giebt ständig praktische Beispiele. Es will Widerstände aufheben, Missverständnisse klären. Klug, viel Sachkenntnis, wertvoll."

2. I thank Daniela Lieb for this suggestion. Although quite contrary at first glance, a comparison of texts by Margret Boveri and Ruth Benedict seems especially fruitful, considering a comparative and transnational perspective on US-American reeducation measures in their various aspects in Germany and Japan, as the interdisciplinary project "Reeducation Revisited," University of Erlangen-Nürnberg, has recently pursued it (https://www.reeducation.phil.fau.de/).

3. Margret Boveri traveled throughout Europe and to the United States. In 1935 and 1936, she went to the Mediterranean region on behalf of the *Berliner Tageblatt*: to Malta in June 1935, to Greece in October, and to Egypt and Sudan in early 1936. She reported on her travels in the *Berliner Tageblatt*, combining anecdotes with political analyses and with digressions on the histories of these countries. On behalf of the *Frankfurter Zeitung* and the *Atlantis-Verlag*, she traveled through Turkey and other countries of the Middle East in 1938 (Görtemaker 2005).

4. As a so-called enemy alien, Margret Boveri was arrested for ten days at Ellis Island and spent then about four months at Hotel Greenbrier (White Sulphur Springs, West Virginia) (Görtemaker 2005, 166).

5. Boveri 1968a, 50: "ich glaube, was sich in Berlin ereignen wird, wird symbolisch sein fürs Ganze, und dies mitzuerleben bin ich doch zurückgekommen."

6. Boveri 1946, 108: "An uns liegt es, aufmerksam zu sein. Das ist wichtiger als der Versuch, uns in einem guten Licht zu zeigen. Vorurteilslosigkeit und Achtsamkeit sind die Eigenschaften, die wir unseren Gästen gegenüber immer bereit haben sollten. Wenn wir nicht nur gefühlsmäßig reagieren, sondern beobachten, wenn wir aus den Beobachtungen Folgerungen ziehen, wird die Entstehung von Ressentiments, die so naheliegend und so gefährlich ist, verhindert bleiben, und wir werden vielleicht erreichen, die Spezies Amerikaner in ihrer Entfaltung wirklich kennenzulernen."

7. I am aware of 18 reviews in German newspapers and 1 critical in the American journal *The Review of Politics*.

8. FM 1947, 26: "Eine eminent klug und auf scharfer Beobachtung fußende Einführung in die amerikanische Welt, allerdings mehr für Fortgeschrittene als für Fibelleser."

9. Steinberg 1946, 5: Boveri addresses the "praktische Bedürfnis nach tieferem Verstehen der Amerikaner."

10. In the context of the Allied reeducation program, it is also interesting to note Margret Boveri's pejorative comments on the program itself (Boveri 1960), and her reading of Erik H. Erikson (Boveri 1968b, 361ff.; for Erikson in the context of reeducation see Ponten 2020).

11. To highlight Boveri's very specific position of go-between in the early post-war German–American contact zone, I have deliberately refrained from going into detail on her political-journalistic commitment after the publication of the *Amerikafibel* (see Görtemaker 2005).

12. Boveri 1946, 7f.: "Inzwischen sind jedenfalls die Amerikaner zu uns gekommen,—auf einen Dauer-Besuch. Und sie haben großes Erstaunen erregt, gerade bei denen, die ihr Kommen am sehnlichsten erhofft und am freudigsten begrüßt hatten. [...] Die Gemüter sind verwirrt und voller Zweifel."

13. Boveri 1946, 7: "Verständnis zwischen den Völkern entsteht nicht dadurch, daß [...] [man] erklärt: im Grunde sind wir die Gleichen, deshalb müssen wir miteinander auskommen. Verständnis kann erst dann entstehen, wenn das von Grund auf Andersartige am Gegenüber erkannt und in seinen Wurzeln begriffen wird, gerade auch das, was uns selbst an ihm zuwider ist."

14. Boveri 1946, 7: "In diesen Gesprächen fand ich, daß einige Grunderkenntnisse über die Amerikaner und ihr geschichtsbedingtes Wesen in Deutschland ganz fehlen, als erstes die Tatsache, daß die Amerikaner nicht Europäer sind, die zufällig ein paar Jahrzehnte oder Generationen auf einem anderen Kontinent verbrachten, im Grunde also dieselben Leute wie wir, nur mit einigen angenommenen Kolonialsitten und einem

größeren Reichtum, sondern daß die Amerikaner ein neues Volk sind. Wenn das Wort nicht so mißbraucht worden wäre, würde ich sagen: eine neue Rasse."

15. Boveri 1946, 14: "dem geschichtslosen Zustand der Emigration."

16. This argument can already be found in her article "Landschaft mit doppeltem Boden: Einfluß und Tarnung des amerikanischen Judentums" ("Landscape with False Bottom: Influence and Camouflage of the American Jewry"), published in the *Frankfurter Zeitung* in May 1943 (Boveri 1943). Boveri argues that, despite their attempts at assimilation, emigrated Jews resist the "transforming power of the great melting pot of America." For this reason, the "Jewish race" is perceived in the United States "as an alien body to a much greater degree than the primitive, good-natured Negro" (Boveri 1943). It is her only contribution with explicitly antisemitic content; however, it must also be mentioned that Boveri was indignant at the fact that the published version bore editorial interventions of an antisemitic nature (Streim 2002, 491).

17. Boveri 1968a, 184: "Da die neue Bürokratie und Fragebogenwirtschaft noch unendlich viel komplizierter ist als die der Nazis, gibt es aber auch um so vielfältigere Wege, ein Ziel zu erreichen. [...] Der Fragebogen, in den ich einen Blick tat, bezog sich vor allem auf Zugehörigkeit zur Partei, SS, SA, Frauenschaft usw."

18. Boveri 1946, 46: "Denn darüber sind sich die wenigsten Deutschen klar, daß der Fragebogen nicht als Tortur für die besiegte Nation eigens erfunden wurde, sondern daß jeder Amerikaner sich selbst tausendmal einem Fragebogen unterwirft, daß er über sich selbst nach den gültigen Fragebogenregeln die Summe zieht wie über uns die Angehörigen der Control Councils und des CIC. Der Fragebogen entscheidet in Amerika nicht nur über Schulung, Berufswahl und Fortkommen; er ist gleichzeitig in der Form des 'Quiz' ein nationaler Sport auf geistigem Gebiet [...]."

19. Boveri quoted in Görtemaker 2005, 230f.: "Ich lehne das System der Fragebogen und ihre Anwendung auf die Deutschen im allgemeinen und mich im Besonderen ab, und habe den vorliegenden nur auf die Bitte von und aus Freundschaft für Herrn Prof. Welter ausgefüllt."

20. Boveri 1946, 34: "Die Umerziehung im eigenen Land ist vollkommen gelungen. Im Umerziehen außerhalb, wie es die Franzosen und Engländer in ihren Kolonialgebieten seit Jahrhunderten betreiben, haben die Amerikaner keine lange und keine ausgedehnte Erfahrung."

21. Boveri 1946, 108: "In dieser Schrift wurde an manchen Stellen auf amerikanische Eigenschaften hingewiesen, die für uns vorbildlich sein können. Das Gute eines anderen zu übernehmen, kann aber nur für den fruchtbar werden, der sich im Eigenen sicher fühlt."

22. Boveri 1946, 38f.: "Da waren sie [...] sprühend, lebendig, jugendlich gewesen. Nun, in der Entspannung, waren sie ganz andere Gesichter: [...] Sie glichen Indianern, die schweigend, fast abwesend um ein Lagerfeuer sitzen [...]. Eine von ihnen wird mir unvergeßlich bleiben. [...] Es fehlte nur der Kranz bunter Federn; dann wäre sie ein

sehr aristokratisch, sehr herrschgewohnt wirkender Indianerhäuptling [...] gewesen. War sie vielleicht eine Nachfahrin der Pilger, an deren Struktur und Substanz der neue Kontinent nun schon dreihundert Jahre gemodelt hatte?"

23. In accordance with Oswald Spengler and others, Boveri's understanding of 'race' is neither biologically nor ethnically fixed. Instead of physical or ethnic characteristics, she rather considers mental (*geistige*) traits to be valid criteria for identifying 'races.' This is also the reason why 'races' can, according to Boveri, assimilate fully (for the broader context see Pöhl 2018).

24. Cf. Boveri's use of the term against the background of the so-called *Große Kontroverse* (i.e., the huge controversy unleashed by the polemic debates between Walter von Molo, Frank Thiess, and Thomas Mann on questions surrounding exile, specifically whether exiled writers had relinquished the right to shape Germany's post-Nazi future); and in her later writings, defending her own position during the Nazi regime: Boveri 1960, 292, 305f., 321; Berbig, Bock, and Kühn 2008.

25. Boveri 1968a, 29: "ich stieß mich an der Überfülle burschikoser Ausdrücke, an den vorschnell gefällten Urteilen über Personen des öffentlichen Lebens und erschrak nicht selten über den Inhalt—nicht vor dem, was ich an erschreckenden Ereignissen verzeichnet hatte, sondern vor dem fremden Bild eines Wesens, das ich selbst war."

26. Rotzoll 1987, 118f.: "auf die Straße traue ich mich fast nie. Sie [i.e., Boveri] hingegen kommt gerade aus einem deutschen Panzer, den sie mal von innen sehen wollte [...]. Sie hat sich furchtlos umgetan, beschwingt, schon fast berauscht von all dem, was es draußen auch an Grausen mitzukriegen gilt. Sie will das wissen, hören, riechen, sehen. Sie ist Journalistin, Zeugin. Daß sie im Augenblick nichts schreiben muß, daß nichts gedruckt würde, bremst ihre Neugier nicht. Ich staune sehr."

27. August 1, 1945: "Das alles bestätigt mir wieder von neuen, was mir während der Internierung in Amerika schon stark auffiel, daß die Amerikaner überhaupt keine Ahnung von Deutschland und den Deutschen haben. Sie haben sich nie die Mühe gemacht, festzustellen, was Nationalsozialismus wirklich ist, weder im Schlechten noch im Guten. Sie haben sich ein Bild konstruiert, das wohl nur in Sachen KZ einigermaßen der Wahrheit entspricht [...], und auf dieses Bild hauen sie jetzt ein" (Boveri 1968a, 263).

28. This principle has already been widely discussed in her problematic article: MB 1943; see Endnote 16.

29. This does not mean that all transfer actions must meet their target; failed attempts are part of the routine.

References

Albrecht, Andrea, Lutz Danneberg, and Alexandra Skowronski. 2020. "'Zwischenvölkisches Verstehen': Zur Ideologisierung der Wissenschaften zwischen 1933 und 1945." In *"Zwischenvölkische Aussprache": Internationaler Austausch in wissenschaftlichen Zeitschriften 1933–1945*, edited by Andrea Albrecht, Lutz Danneberg, Ralf Klausnitzer, and Kristina Mateescu, 39–82. Berlin: De Gruyter.

Arendt, Hannah. 1950. "The Aftermath of Nazi Rule: Report from Germany." *Commentary* 10: 324–53.

Ash, Mitchell G. 1995. "Verordnete Umbrüche—Konstruierte Kontinuität: Zur Entnazifizierung von Wissenschaftlern und Wissenschaften nach 1945." *Zeitschrift für Geschichtswissenschaft* 43, no. 10: 903–23.

Bausinger, Hermann, Hans-Otto Binder, Johanna Petersmann, and Uta Röck. 2011. "'Warum gab es dieses große Schweigen?': Podiumsgespräch am 8. Juli 2010 in der Volkshochschule Tübingen." In *Vom braunen Hemd zur weißen Weste? Vom Umgang mit der Vergangenheit in Tübingen nach 1945*, edited by Hans-Otto Binder, Martin Ulmer, Daniela Rathe, and Uta Röck, 219–35. Tübingen: Universitätsstadt Tübingen, Fachbereich Kultur.

Belke, Ingrid. 2005. "Auswandern oder bleiben? Die Publizistin Margret Boveri (1900–1975) im Dritten Reich." *Zeitschrift für Germanistik* 53: 118–37.

Benedict, Ruth. 1946. *The Chrysanthemum and the Sword: Patterns of Japanese Culture*. Boston: Houghton Mifflin.

Berbig, Roland, Tobias Bock, and Walter Kühn. 2008. "Vorwort." In *Margret Boveri und Ernst Jünger: Briefwechsel aus den Jahren 1946 bis 1973*, edited by Berbig, Bock, and Kühn, 7–30. Berlin: Landtverlag.

Boveri, Margret. 1936. *Das Weltgeschehen am Mittelmeer: Ein Buch über Inseln und Küsten, Politik und Strategie, Völker und Imperien*. Zürich: Atlantis.

———. 1938. *Vom Minarett zum Bohrturm: Eine politische Biographie Vorderasiens*. Zürich: Atlantis.

———. 1941a. "Test and Facts: Erkundungsfahrt im amerikanischen Erziehungswesen." *Frankfurter Zeitung*, January 2, 1941.

———. 1941b. "Genies nach Quoten: Begabtenauslese in den Vereinigten Staaten." *Frankfurter Zeitung*, March 18, 1941.

———. 1943. "Landschaft mit doppeltem Boden: Einfluß und Tarnung des amerikanischen Judentums." *Frankfurter Zeitung*, May 28, 1943.

———. 1946. *Amerikafibel für erwachsene Deutsche: Ein Versuch, Unverstandenes zu erklären*. Berlin: Minerva.

———. 1960. *Der Verrat im 20. Jahrhundert*. Vol. 4: "Verrat als Epidemie: Amerika: Fazit." Reinbek: Rowohlt.

———. 1965. "Viel Ressentiment gegen die Amerikaner: Review of Caspar von Schrenck-Notzing: *Charakterwäsche: Die amerikanische Besatzung in Deutschland und ihre Folgen*." *Frankfurter Allgemeine Zeitung*, December 31, 1965: 14.

———. 1968a. *Tage des Überlebens. Berlin 1945*. Munich: Piper.

———. 1968b. "Erik H. Erikson." *Merkur* 22, no. 240 (April): 361–71.

Buschmeier, Matthias, and Jeanne E. Glesener. 2021. "Call for Papers: European Literature of Military Occupation 1938–1955." Accessed March 20, 2022. https://mis.uni.lu/wp-content/uploads/sites/131/2021/04/CfP-European-Literatures-of-Military-Occupation-1938-53-April-2022.pdf.

Conze, Vanessa. 2010. "Zum Europäer bin ich in Amerika geworden": Zum Zusammenhang zwischen Europabewusstsein und biographischen Erfahrungen in der Bundesrepublik der Nachkriegszeit." In *Entscheidung für Europa: Erfahrungen, Zeitgeist und politische Herausforderungen*, edited by Volker Depkat and Piero S. Graglia, 43–60. Berlin: De Gruyter.

Cox, Andrew. 2005. "What are Communities of Practice? A Comparative Review of Four Seminal Works." *Journal of Information Science* 31, no. 6: 527–40.

Dagerman, Stig. [1947] 2011. *German Autumn*. Translated by Robin Fulton Macpherson. Minneapolis: Minnesota University Press.

Długoborski, Wacław. 1996. "Kollektive Reaktionen auf die deutsche Invasion und die Errichtung der NS-Besatzungsherrschaft." In *Anpassung, Kollaboration, Widerstand: Kollektive Reaktionen auf die Okkupation*, edited by Wolfgang Benz, 11–24. Berlin: Metropol.

Döblin, Alfred. 1946. *Gutachten über Margret Boveris Amerikafibel für erwachsene Deutsche*, September 7, 1946. Copy in DLA Marbach, A: Döblin.

Doering-Manteuffel, Anselm. 1999. *Wie westlich sind die Deutschen? Amerikanisierung und Westernisierung im 20. Jahrhundert*. Göttingen: Vandenhoeck & Ruprecht.

Dos Passos, John. 1946. *Tour of Duty*. Boston: Houghton Mifflin.

Felski, Rita. 2008. *Uses of Literature*. Malden, MA: Blackwell.

Fitzsimons, Mathew Arnold. 1948. "'The United States and World Order': Review of *Amerikafibel für erwachsene Deutsche*, by Margret Boveri." *The Review of Politics* 10, no. 2: 253–55.

FM. 1947. "Review of *Amerikafibel für erwachsene Deutsche* by Margret Boveri." *Heute*, May 1, 1947.

Gassert, Philipp. 1997. *Amerika im Dritten Reich: Ideologie, Propaganda und Volksmeinung 1933–1945*. Stuttgart: Steiner.

Gehring, Hansjörg. 1976. *Amerikanische Literaturpolitik in Deutschland 1945–1953: Ein Aspekt des Re-Education-Programms*. Stuttgart: Deutsche Verlagsanstalt.

———. 1977. "Literatur im Dienst der Politik: Zum Re-education-Programm der amerikanischen Militärregierung in Deutschland." In *Nachkriegsliteratur*, edited by Nicolas Born and Jürgen Manthey, 252–70. Reinbek: Rowohlt.

Gerund, Katharina, and Heike Paul. 2015. "Einleitung." In *Die amerikanische Reeducation-Politik nach 1945: Interdisziplinäre Perspektiven auf "America's Germany,"* edited by Gerund and Paul, 7–18. Bielefeld: Transcript.

Görtemaker, Heike B. 2005. *Ein deutsches Leben: Die Geschichte der Margret Boveri (1900–1975)*. Munich: Beck.

———. 2006. "Einleitung." In *Amerikafibel für erwachsene Deutsche: Ein Versuch, Unverstandenes zu erklären*, by Margret Boveri, 9–45. Berlin: Landtverlag.

Hahnemann, Andy. 2010. *Texturen des Globalen: Geopolitik und populäre Literatur in der Zwischenkriegszeit 1918–1939*. Heidelberg: Winter.

Hoenicke Moore, Michaela. 2005. "Heimat und Fremde: Das Verhältnis zu Amerika im journalistischen Werk von Margret Boveri und Dolf Sternberger." In *Demokratiewunder: Transatlantische Mittler und die kulturelle Öffnung Westdeutschlands 1945–1970*, edited by Arnd Bauerkämper, Konrad H. Jarausch, and Marcus M. Payk, 218–50. Göttingen: Vandenhoeck & Ruprecht.

Hoffmann, Torsten. 2021. "Ästhetischer Dünger: Strategien neurechter Literaturpolitik." *Deutsche Vierteljahrsschrift für Literaturwissenschaft und Geistesgeschichte* 95: 219–54.

Hurwitz, Harold. 1972. *Die Stunde Null der deutschen Presse: Die amerikanische Pressepolitik in Deutschland 1945–1949*. Cologne: Verlag Wissenschaft und Politik.

Keyserling, Hermann. 1930. *Amerika: Der Aufgang einer neuen Welt*. Berlin: Deutsche Verlagsanstalt.

Koszyk, Kurt. 1986. *Pressepolitik für Deutsche 1945–1949*. Berlin: Colloquium.

Leßau, Hanne. 2020. *Entnazifizierungsgeschichten: Die Auseinandersetzung mit der eigenen NS-Vergangenheit in der frühen Nachkriegszeit*. Göttingen: Wallstein.

Lüdtke, Alf, Inge Marßolek, and Adelheid von Saldern. 1996. "Einleitung." In *Amerikanisierung: Traum und Alptraum im Deutschland des 20. Jahrhunderts*, edited by Lüdtke, Marßolek, and von Saldern, 7–33. Stuttgart: Steiner.

Martens, Erika. 1972. *Zum Beispiel "Das Reich": Zur Phänomenologie der Presse im totalitären Regime*. Cologne: Verlag Wissenschaft und Politik.

Niethammer, Lutz. 1982. *Die Mitläuferfabrik: Die Entnazifizierung am Beispiel Bayerns*. Berlin: Dietz.

Patel, Kiran Klaus. 2000. "Amerika als Argument: Die Wahrnehmungen des New Deal am Anfang des 'Dritten Reichs.'" *Amerikastudien* 45, no. 3: 349–72.

Person, Jutta. 2005. "Das Gespenst des Patriotismus: Weltkriegs-Journalismus made in Germany: Die umstrittene Publizistin Margret Boveri wird mit ihren Aufzeichnungen zum Kriegsende 1945 wiederentdeckt: Ein Portrait." *Literaturen* 5: 29–33.

Pöhl, Friedrich. 2018. "Oswald Spenglers Rassebegriff im Kontext seiner Zeit: Boas, Chamberlain, Lenz, Rosenberg, Sombart." In *Oswald Spenglers Kulturmorphologie: Eine multiperspektivische Annäherung*, edited by Sebastian Fink and Robert Rollinger, 643–74. Wiesbaden: Springer VS.

Ponten, Frederic. 2020. "Die Identität des Feindes: Erik H. Erikson, Margaret Mead und die Erfindung der Reeducation." *Zeitschrift für Kulturwissenschaften* 2: 67–95.

Raj, Kapil. 2016. "Go-Betweens, Travelers, and Cultural Translators." In *A Companion to the History of Science,* edited by Bernard Lightman, 39–57. Chichester: Wiley Blackwell.

Rotzoll, Christa. 1987. *Frauen und Zeiten.* Stuttgart: Engelhorn.

Schaumann, Caroline. 2009. "'A Different Family Story': German Wartime Suffering in Women's Writing by Wibke Bruhns, Ute Scheub, and Christina von Braun." In *Germans as Victims in the Literary Fiction of the Berlin Republic,* edited by Stuart Taberner and Karina Berger, 102–17. Rochester: Camden House.

Schrenck-Notzing, Caspar von. 1965. *Charakterwäsche: Die amerikanische Besatzung in Deutschland und ihre Folgen.* Stuttgart: Seewald. [Latest edition: 2015. Graz: Ares.]

Sollors, Werner. 2018. "'Everybody Gets Fragebogened Sooner or Later': The Denazification Questionnaire as Cultural Text." *German Life and Letters* 71, no. 2: 139–53.

Steinberg, Heinz. 1946. "'Frankreich und Amerika': Review of *Amerikafibel für erwachsene Deutsche* by Margret Boveri." *Der Sonntag: Unabhängige Wochenzeitung für Kunst und modernes Leben,* December 1, 1946: 5.

Streim, Gregor. 1999. "Junge Völker und neue Technik: Zur Reisereportage im 'Dritten Reich', am Beispiel von Friedrich Sieburg, Heinrich Hauser und Margret Boveri." *Zeitschrift für Germanistik* 9, no. 2: 344–59.

———. 2002. "Berichterstatterin in den 'Landschaften des Verrats': Margret Boveris Amerika-Darstellungen aus der Kriegs- und Nachkriegszeit: Mit dem Briefwechsel zwischen Margret Boveri und Carl Zuckmayer." In *Zur Diskussion: Zuckmayers "Geheimreport" und andere Beiträge zur Zuckmayer-Forschung,* edited by Gunther Nickel, 475–510. Göttingen: Wallstein.

Verschaffel, Tom, Reine Meylaerts, Tessa Lobbes, Maud Gonne, and Lieven d'Hulst. 2014. "Towards a Multipolar Model of Cultural Mediators within Multicultural Spaces: Cultural Mediators in Belgium, 1830–1945." *Revue belge de philologie et d'histoire* 92, no. 4: 1255–75.

Vogt, Jochen. 2006. "Sooo hoch! Momentaufnahmen vom allmählichen Verschwinden der 'Statue genannt Liberty.'" In *Das Amerika der Autoren: Von Kafka bis 09/11,* edited by Jochen Vogt and Alexander Stephan, 249–78. Fink: München.

Webster, Jean. 1947. *Daddy Langbein: Mit Illustrationen der Verfasserin.* Translated by Margret Boveri. Berlin: Minerva.

Weisbrod, Bernd. 2002. "Dem wandelbaren Geist: Akademisches Ideal und wissenschaftliche Transformation in der Nachkriegszeit." In *Akademische Vergangenheitspolitik: Beiträge zur Wissenschaftskultur der Nachkriegszeit,* edited by Weisbrod, 11–35. Göttingen: Wallstein.

Weiß, Volker. 2017. *Die autoritäre Revolte: Die Neue Rechte und der Untergang des Abendlandes.* Stuttgart: Klett-Cotta.

Weißmann, Karlheinz. 2005. "Autorenportrait Margret Boveri." *Sezession* 9 (April): 2–7.

———. 2012. "Margret Boveri." In *Staatspolitisches Handbuch im Netz*. Vol. 3: "Vordenker," edited by Erik Lehnert and Karlheinz Weißmann. Schnellroda: Antaios. Last modified October 10, 2017. Accessed December 27, 2023, https://wiki.staatspolitik.de/index.php?title=Margret_Boveri.

Zacharasiewicz, Waldemar. 2010. *Imagology Revisited*. Amsterdam: Rodopi.

Zuckmayer, Carl. [1946/1947] 2004. *Deutschlandbericht für das Kriegsministerium der Vereinigten Staaten von Amerika*, edited by Gunther Nickel, Johanna Schrön, and Hans Wagener. Göttingen: Wallstein.

REMEMBERING OCCUPATION

Introduction to Part 4

JEANNE E. GLESENER

This part concentrates on the enduring presence of occupation as a literary topic and on the memory discourses that it sparks in post-war literature across different cultural contexts.

As a medium that participates in both the creation and the mediation of collective memory, and as a memory archive of sorts, the post-war novel offers itself for investigation to inquire after which sites of memory are produced and by whom. How are they fictionally staged and narratively structured? And how do they reject or, on the contrary, reactivate cultural-historical myths and discourse figures? **Klaus-Michael Bogdal** addresses these aspects of the post-war novel by contrasting *Die feurige Säule* (1953) ("The Pillar of Fire") by Rolf Bongs, a former *SS* officer, and *In der Erinnerung* (1998) ("In Memory") by the distinguished author Dieter Forte; both works are set in Düsseldorf under British occupation. Observing the engineering of the topoi of 'national disgrace,' historical-cultural supremacy, and the politicization of national memory in the aftermath of the Allied occupation of Germany after World War I leads Bogdal to revisit the pervasive afterlife of this specific commemorative discourse in literary remembrance. It transpires that depictions of everyday life under occupation were subjected to an officialized process of denial in early post-war narrative accounts. Written almost forty years apart, the novels diverge considerably in their respective strategies of remembrance and their interpretations of the very same occupation. Bogdal demonstrates that—while in earlier texts, occupation only registers on the margins and is superseded (in Bongs's case) by a withdrawal into abstractions of human agency from a metahistorical perspective (and thereby early post-war texts gloss over questions of guilt, responsibility, and Nazi crimes and their victims)—later novels (such as Forte's), by telling the story 'from below' and from different narrative perspectives, cast occupation as a liberation, as well as an indispensable transitional stage toward a new beginning.

The modalities of silencing or obliterating memory in societies under ideological control were particularly pernicious in territories where Soviet rule sought legitimation. **Benedikts Kalnačs'** chapter traces literary representations of Estonia's and Latvia's experiences under military occupation by Nazi and Soviet forces—representations that had long been tabooed in Baltic cultures, where the

Soviet master narrative of history, alongside the regime's strict censorship, precluded any attempts to give voice to the suffering endured by (and likewise to act against the institutionalized repression of the collective memory of) the Baltic peoples. Noting how exile literature in particular reached beyond the personal suffering of displacement toward representations of a shared and collective experience—thereby bearing the hallmarks of affective realism—storytelling and (by that same token) literature became a means of preserving collective memory. In the post-war novels *Ilze* (1959) and *Piecas dienas* (1976) ("Five Days"), written in exile, the Latvian writer Anšlavs Eglītis creates an atmosphere of fear and alienation in conveying how the experience of occupation has substantially changed the lives of ordinary people. In his turn, leading 20th-century Estonian novelist Jan Kross, in his late novel *Paigallend* (1998) (*Treading Air*, 2003), scrutinizes the occupation of his country through the eyes of a character on the margins of political events—a widespread strategy in the tradition of the European historical novel and one that was constantly explored in the representation of the period under totalitarian rule. As Kalnačs shows, the 'forbidden' memory of the suffering endured by the Baltic peoples thus, on the one hand, became the prerogative of exile literature and, on the other, generated specific narrative strategies that functioned as a sort of shorthand to encode counter-official collective memory. Against this, the controlled politics of memory must be understood not only as a feature of Soviet occupation, Kalnačs argues, but as a mechanism pertaining to the colonial power matrix that determined the fates of small European nations under Soviet rule.

Literature and literary representations of collective memory as substitutes for a lacking or deficient memory culture are also highlighted in **Meinolf Schumacher**'s chapter, through a new reading of the four-volume novel *Jahrestage* (1970–1983) (*Anniversaries*, 2018) by Uwe Johnson. *Jahrestage*, which bridges the epochal gap between World War II and the subsequent Soviet occupation, looks back from the perspective of 1967–1968 on the events in the German provinces of Mecklenburg and Pomerania since the end of the Weimar Republic. Narratives about the war's end and the Red Army's conquest are at the hidden center of this epic masterpiece. Thematically, Johnson's novel about Mecklenburg and Pomerania deals with how stereotypes of 'the Russians' resulted in mass exodus and an epidemic of suicide; land reform; forced resettlement; the expansion of the Gulag to the West through internment camps; and lastly the banning of the very name 'Pomerania' (a ban initiated by the occupying power), along with the consequences that this latter decision had on the geographic location of various days of remembrance in Mecklenburg. Schumacher's chapter highlights the structural complexity of this novel, elaborating on Johnson's technique of 'factual inventions' to illustrate how suppressed or forbidden memories are relayed and refracted through a variety of means and voices, and how the different forms of media that are incorporated within the book function as conduits of memory. Looking at the novel from a present-day perspective, Schumacher opens up new routes of interpretation by suggesting that the reader apply—as in the case of the Eastern European countries discussed in the previous chapter—a postcolonial perspective on the Sovietization of Eastern Germany by way of occupation.

CHAPTER 12

"It was over. Düsseldorf was dead"

Narratives of a Renewed Occupation

KLAUS-MICHAEL BOGDAL

A National Politics of Memory: The Occupations of the Rhineland

Soon after the end of the First World War and amid the revolution of 1919, Bertolt Brecht wrote a one-act play titled *Der Bettler oder Der tote Hund (The Beggar or the Dead Dog)*, in which a beggar and the emperor argue over the narrative dimension of history:

> BEGGAR. That's what it was like thirty-eight years ago. The corn perished in the sun, and before it was done for, the rain came down so thick that rats sprang up and devastated all the other fields. Then they came into the villages and took bites out of people. That food was the death of them.
> EMPEROR. I know nothing of that. It must be a fabrication like the rest. There's nothing about it in history.
> BEGGAR. There's no such thing as history.
> EMPEROR. And what about Alexander? And Caesar? And Napoleon?
> BEGGAR. Stories! Fairy tales! What Napoleon are you talking about? (Brecht 1968, 121)

At stake in this exchange is the question of who remembers what, why, and how. As Walter Benjamin would do later in his theses *Über den Begriff der Geschichte (On the Concept of History)* (Benjamin 2006, 406), Brecht confronts "the memory of the anonymous" with that of "the famous, the celebrated." This question is relevant, not least of all to depictions of the occupation of Germany by the victorious Allies following both World Wars: do these depictions contain stories of the kind told by the beggar, or are they instead a historiography as the emperor conceives of it?

Among the historical differences between the two post-war situations is that, unlike after the toppling of Nazi rule in 1945, a long-term occupation and sole administration by the Allied military was not an option following the surrender and collapse of the German Empire in 1918. Among the provisions of the Treaty of Versailles, signed by Germany on June 28, 1919 and ratified on January 10, 1920, was a temporally and spatially limited occupation by American, French, and British forces, whose ultimate withdrawal was made conditional on the payment of reparations that were defined in the Treaty reparations. The limited scope for action left to the German state by France and Britain in particular meant that the political right was not alone in perceiving the occupations of the Rhineland (1918–1930) and the Ruhr (1923–1925) as national humiliations.

Yet it was the status accorded to them by nationalist conservatives and the burgeoning National Socialists in the Weimar Republic that made the Treaty of Versailles and the occupation of the Rhineland so historically consequential. A flood of propagandistic depictions of so-called foreign rule and its economic, political, and cultural consequences washed over Germany and continued to do so even after the last Allied forces had returned home. Numerous monuments and countless liberation ceremonies ensured that the interpretation of these events as a national disgrace and humiliation were lodged deep in the collective memory (Cepl-Kaufmann 2009).

Two factors in particular were conducive to the success of a nationalist and far-right politics of memory. First, much was made of the fact that France stationed African and Arab colonial troops in Germany. *Schwarze Schmach* ("black disgrace") soon became a propagandistic catchphrase to which a German public, who was attuned not only to antisemitism but to all kinds of racism, eagerly responded. It also crops up in Hitler's *Mein Kampf*, which harks back to a tradition of anti-French nationalism in order to condemn France's use of these (to the racist imagination) 'uncivilized' troops as a betrayal of the white race. The 385 mixed-race children born to German women and French soldiers were branded "Rhineland bastards," suffering first discrimination and then, once the Nazis came to power in 1933, sterilization or murder (Pommerin 1979). Such racism, if not to the point of state-sanctioned destruction, resurfaced after 1945, when children were again born of unions between German women and occupying soldiers (Pommerin 1979; Maß 2006).

The second factor was the emergence of the so-called *Freikorps* ("free corps") in the occupied territories. These were effectively mercenary gangs consisting of demobilized officers and soldiers who deployed military force against socialist or Soviet regional governments (as in Bavaria), attempted coups against the legitimate government of the Weimar Republic, and did not shy away from political murder, as in the case of Walter Rathenau, the German foreign minister. In the Rhine and Ruhr occupation zones, the *Freikorps* were known, above all, for planting bombs. A cause célèbre of Nazi propaganda was that of Albert Leo

Schlageter, a college dropout from South Baden (Zwicker 2006; Sprenger 2008) who was condemned to death by a French military tribunal on May 9, 1923. In the face of widespread protest, he was executed on May 26, 1923 on the Golzheimer Heide in Düsseldorf. The conservative nationalist professors of Schlageter's alma mater, the University of Freiburg, marked his death with a memorial parade through the city, led by the university's rector, Hans Spemann, who later became a Nobel laureate. The political right maintained this tradition of regularly honoring Schlageter. In 1931, several key right-wing organizations—from the *Stahlhelm* (a veteran's organization), the DNVP (an antisemitic, conservative nationalist party), and student fraternities to the Nazi Party—gathered in Golzheim for the unveiling of a monument to Schlageter (Knauff 1995).

This highly successful politicization of national memory after the First World War was based on the idea that patriotic principles found expression not only by having participated in the war itself but by continuing the armed struggle even through defeat and occupation, always against the backdrop of treaties that were found unacceptable and the democratic republic that had to negotiate them. Most Weimar-era texts, whether fiction or non-fiction, participate directly in this politics of memory (Kiesel 2017). They radicalize the nationalist conception of history that had dominated the German Empire.[1] As before, the template was provided by the *Befreiungskriege* ("Wars of Liberation") against Napoleon. Then, in 1813, volunteer paramilitaries, conceiving of themselves as something apart from regular (conscript) forces, had assumed the name of *Freikorps* and taken part in the conflict; then as now, the guiding concern was the armed struggle to shake off foreign rule *following* military defeat and occupation. Ideologically, the Wars of Liberation no longer referred to the Holy Roman Empire of old, but instead were thought of as heralding a new German nation, as in Ernst Moritz Arndt's popular poem *Des Deutschen Vaterland* ("The German's Fatherland"):

> That is the German's fatherland,
> Where anger consumes Latin trumpery,
> Where every Frenchman is called enemy,
> Where every German is called friend—
> That is what should be!
> The whole of Germany is what it should be! (Arndt 1912, 126f.; translation adapted from Simpson 2006, 173)[2]

Following defeat by the same enemy in 1918, the narrative of a national struggle for survival was dramatized by recasting the occupation in racist terms as a "black disgrace" while being culturally situated in a spiritual continuity with the tragic-heroic exploits of the Nibelungs. The Rhineland provided a suitable location for doing so. Exceptions are Joseph Breitbach's novel *Die Wandlung der Susanne Dasseldorf* (1933) ("The Transformation of Susanne Dasseldorf") and, conceived on a larger epic scale, Lion Feuchtwanger's *Erfolg* (1930) ("Success").

In his autobiography *The Turning Point* (originally published in English in 1942), Klaus Mann recalls the massive propaganda in unconventional and, from a nationalist perspective, provocative terms:

> How much did I know about crucial issues like the occupation of the Rhine and Ruhr zones by the Allied armies? Only what I learned from the glaring posters displayed all over the city. I studied them carefully; for some of them carried grisly cartoons and captions arraigning the outrages ostensibly committed by coloured troops. I recollect in particular one rampant account to the effect that a single Moor had raped not only scores of virgins and children but, as a climax of depravity, a handsome mare, sole and treasured belonging of an upright Rhenish peasant tribe. This sordid fabrication haunted me for years, replacing in my mind certain images out of "Uncle Tom's Cabin". (Mann 1942, 58f.; cf. Mann 2006, 113)

Mann denies these tales of supposed "outrages" the higher historical purpose they were intended to convey, instead reducing them to their psychopathological core when he writes: "The exorbitant potency of the dark-skinned satyr beguiled my imagination, whereas the so-called 'national disgrace' utterly failed to impress me. A beautiful poem or painting seemed more significant to me than the 'black pollution' [*die schwarze Schmach*] of Düsseldorf" (Mann 1942, 59; cf. Mann 2006, 113f.).

The Renewed Occupation of Germany in 1945 and Literature

In thinking about the works of literature dealing with the renewed occupation of the Rhineland by the victorious Western Allies between 1945 and 1949, it strikes me that the first occupation, which began barely twenty-five years earlier, must have been fully present in memory. Contemporaries could not fail to be reminded of it by monuments and street names. Meanwhile Schlageter, who had been raised to the position of a Nazi martyr, had figured prominently in the education of young men at the time.

There are important parallels between the two occupations. Again, the Rhineland was occupied by American, French, and British troops, and again the Allied ranks contained a significant portion of Black soldiers from the US and troops from African colonies. These facts raise the question of whether the narratives of the 1920s were likewise revisited, whether they were challenged, or whether at least some of the stories now being told were altogether new. In a first attempt at an answer, I shall consider two novels set in Düsseldorf and the Rhineland: Rolf Bongs's *Die feurige Säule* ("The Pillar of Fire") and Dieter Forte's *In der Erinnerung* ("In Memory"). Bongs's novel was written under British occupation and published in 1953; Forte, who was ten when the occupation began, started work on a trilogy of novels entitled *Das Haus auf meinen Schultern* ("The House Upon My Shoulders") in the 1980s, of which *In der Erinnerung*, published in 1998, is the third volume. The number of novels and stories dealing with the period of occupation is remarkably small in the first post-war decades. This applies to all four zones of occupation; clearly, the subject was taboo not just in the Soviet zone and its successor, the German Democratic Republic. Indeed, denial of the occupation appears to be even deeper than that surrounding the aerial bombardment of Germany. In the late 1990s, when W. G. Sebald (Sebald 2003), a writer and Germanist living in England, criticized his German compatriots for failing to address the latter subject, heated controversy ensued.[3] Why this should have been so is another question to be addressed here.

One of the few exceptions—in several respects—is Leonhard Frank's novel *Die Jünger Jesu* (1949) ("The Disciples of Jesus"), which deals with the American occupation in Würzburg. Frank, who had returned to Germany from political exile, unreservedly describes the occupation as liberation from Nazi rule. Since he painted the concerted action of German anti-fascists and the military authorities against the perpetrators of dictatorship and terror in a positive light, Frank's novel was criticized for bringing Germany into disrepute. Why it made uncomfortable reading can be seen from the following excerpt: "The teacher suddenly stood up straight, as if he had just completed a thought. The German people had sunk deeply. It was a matter of national disgrace that a German should have to testify before an American Jew" (Frank 1949, 194f.).[4]

A marked contrast to Frank's somber view can be found in Wolfgang Graetz's picaresque memoir of a petty criminal in the immediate post-war years, published in 1966 under the title *Die Welt von unten* ("The World from Below"). From the perspective of the marginalized narrator, the occupation presents an opportunity for conducting illicit trade with American officers and soldiers, offering them—in exchange for their resources—entertainment, ranging from bars and music to prostitution. Graetz's protagonists have just scraped through the hell of war in one piece and now live for the moment. They think they have found a model in the American way of life:

> Inge drags plenty of Yanks in here, and when she stops dragging them in, then we'll just have to visit them ourselves, in the Red Cross Club at Café Moder, where

the basement is stacked high with crates, and afterwards we'll celebrate our amnesty, wallow in *jam* and *ham and eggs* and *ice cream* powder and *plum pudding*
and cigarettes and coffee, we'll smell and taste and slurp because we got through
it all alive, cover ourselves in chocolate and lick it all off and realize how good we
taste. (Graetz 1966, 188; italics denote English words used in the original)

A singular position is occupied by the best-selling autobiographical novel "The
Questionnaire" (*Der Fragebogen*, 1951), in which Ernst von Salomon describes
internment in an American detention facility as akin to imprisonment in a concentration camp. Salomon's inversion of the roles of victim and perpetrator was
welcomed by many Germans who were eager to deny and forget what had happened. A few years later, anarchy, self-interest, and the unwillingness to undergo
denazification are themes addressed in *Off Limits* (1955); this novel, wildly successful in its day and now all but forgotten, was the work of Hans Habe, a press
officer in the US army at the time (later, a widely published journalist and author). The year 1957, then, saw the translation of *Fräulein* (1956) into German
(*Fräulein. Roman eines deutschen Mädchens*) by James McGovern. The film version, directed by Henry Koster, appeared the following year (Brauerhoch 2006).

Few literary works deal with the Soviet occupation, though two much-read examples—most likely written decades after the events they describe—include *Uns
geht's ja noch gold* (1972) ("We're Still Having a Golden Time Of It") by Walter
Kempowski and *Russische Zone* (2011) ("Russian Zone") by Christoph Meckel.

A Life after Total Defeat

Following Germany's unconditional surrender on May 8, 1945, unlike after the
First World War, the Allied occupying forces did not limit themselves to dismantling the armed forces and placing the civil administration in the hands of
their own military; they intended to go even further in removing Nazi perpetrators from office and, where necessary, punish them. The chosen instrument was
'denazification,' a process that relied on written questionnaires. Its legal and political principles were to be derived from the Nuremberg Trials, in which pillars
of the regime—from the Nazi Party, the military, the civil administration, and
even the world of business—were tried. The question here concerns the extent to
which these attempts to keep Nazi elites from taking a leading role in the reconstruction of Germany are reflected in post-war German literature (Fischer 1999;
Peitsch 2009; Siebenpfeiffer 2004).

To the judicial reckoning, the American and British occupation authorities
added a set of 're-education' measures that had been developed in the war years

and first deployed in prisoner-of-war camps. Among the first of these measures to be implemented was ordering the population of the surrounding areas to take tours of such concentration camps as Buchenwald, Dachau, or Bergen-Belsen. In addition, the US Army ordered German civilians to exhume mass graves and re-bury the victims of the Nazi regime individually (Barnouw 1996, 52). So-called 'atrocity' films, dealing with the human rights abuses at concentration camps, were screened in many towns and villages; attendance was mandatory and en-forced (Barnouw 1996, 7). Again, however, it remains to be seen whether these measures left traces in literature.

An indication of how different the behavior of many Germans after the Sec-ond World War was from that during the previous occupation may be found in the book *Eclipse* by Alan Moorehead. Moorehead, a British journalist who ac-companied the Allied advance through Europe, notes that the Germans "had an immense sense, not of guilt, but of defeat. If a man's shop was entered and looted by Allied soldiers, he never dreamed of protesting. He expected it. And the rea-son for this was that he was afraid" (Moorehead 1945, 231). Drawing on contem-porary images, the historian Dagmar Barnouw offers a psychological explana-tion, based on the idea of a German *Sonderweg* ("special path") to modernity:

> [The Germans' own] images and Allied documentation of a broken Germany point to the characteristic *corruptio pessima optimi*, the devastating self-destruction which is common to many utopian communities and which is intimately related to their notorious self-separation from the rest of the world. The Nazi regime had brought about, in the eyes of many, a revolution into a utopian future that then promptly disintegrated into dystopia—a disintegration all the more explosive because of the extraordinary exclusiveness of that German "new order." (Barnouw 1996, 36)[5]

Yet some of the novels written soon after 1945 also reflect attitudes that do not share in this supposed *corruptio pessima optimi*. For instance, while the protago-nist of Walther Hollander's *Es wächst schon Gras darüber* (1947) ("Grass Is Al-ready Growing Over It") is still full of the desire to make amends, this does not extend as far as the Allied soldiers, whom he denies the status of victims: "I certainly do want to pay my share. But only to those who suffered. To yesterday's sufferers, that is. Not to the high-handed victors of today, dripping with moral-ity" (Hollander 1947, 415).

The concrete historic context of Bongs's and Forte's novels has a good deal to contribute to their understanding. The British Army of the Rhine made its head-quarters in Düsseldorf (thereby anticipating its status as the future capital of the state of North Rhine-Westphalia), billeting its personnel and their dependents largely in the barely damaged districts of Golzheim and Stockum (Matzerath

1997). Though determined by circumstance, this choice could not but establish a link with the first occupation of the Rhineland, Golzheim being the site of Schlageter's execution; the Nazis had gone on to develop the area as a model neighborhood, building in a self-consciously *Heimatstil* ("vernacular style") and naming it after the "martyred" *Freikorps* member. They pursued a similar development in Stockum under the name *Wilhelm-Gustloff-Siedlung*. Nearby, the Nazis had also planned to erect a so-called *Gauforum*, an administrative and assembly complex whose scale and architectural stylings were to be modeled on the party's rally grounds in Nuremberg. There certainly was no trace of guilt or fear when, in 1947, a demonstration was held in Düsseldorf against the requisitioning of residential quarters in these districts, which had been home to so many members of the local Nazi elite. It is true, however, that housing—like so much else—was in short supply following the German defeat. As seen through the eyes of a ten-year-old narrator, they form a leitmotif in Forte's *In der Erinnerung*.

Victor Gollancz, a Jewish-British publisher whose eyewitness account *In Darkest Germany* appeared in 1947, gives a drastic account of the residential privations. Convinced though he was of the Nazis' guilt and "unspeakable wickedness" (Gollancz 1947, 30), Gollancz pleaded for the humane treatment of "[t]he people in the cellars and bunkers of ruined Germany, and particularly the women and children" (Gollancz 1947, 27)—all the more so given the standards enjoyed by British officers:

> While millions of Germans are living four, seven, or nine to a hole, our officers' messes are at worst pleasantly comfortable, and such of the senior ones as I visited were, for the most part, quietly and discreetly luxurious. (Gollancz 1947, 198)

Gollancz noted, for instance, that "every C.C.G. officer receives, as a matter of right, 200 cigarettes, a box of matches, a piece of soap, and a fair amount of chocolate every week" (Gollancz 1947, 202). Such details play an important part in Forte's novel.[6] A critical factor in improving relations between the German population and the British and American occupying armies was the repeal of the so-called "fraternization ban" on July 14, 1945. Contacts between victors and vanquished were henceforth no longer subject to penalties.

Bongs's Depiction of a Disintegrated Community

Now largely forgotten, the writer Rolf Bongs (1907–1981) came to exercise considerable cultural influence in his native Düsseldorf after World War II.[7] Like many Germans, Bongs was silent about his own involvement in the Nazi regime.

As a member of the 5th *SS Totenkopf* regiment, he was responsible for the resettlement to the Reich of so-called *Volksdeutsche* ("ethnic Germans") living in the areas annexed by the Soviet Union following the Hitler–Stalin Pact. In 1942 he published *Harte herrliche Straße nach Westen* ("The Hard Glorious Road West"), a book about his experiences (Bongs 1942b).[8] Soon after the war, he was able to whitewash his CV, thanks to the fact that the commander-in-chief of the British military government declared an amnesty for members of the *Waffen-SS* (Rajewskaja-Perzynska 2009, 137). This is not, however, the place to discuss the character of Bongs, who seems to have been in a difficult personal situation throughout; unlike Agnieszka Rajewskaja-Perzynska, I would conclude that several sources point to his having homosexual tendencies, though Bongs was married with one child.[9] His book *Die feurige Säule* contains evidence of him being misogynist and places male friendships in the foreground.

The setting of much of the novel in question is Düsseldorf and the Rhineland. It spans the period from 1939 to 1946/1947 and is set among the industrialists of the Rhine-Ruhr region, whose circle includes art dealers and painters. Their patronage extends to the novel's main character, the writer Johannes Rossa. The plot leaps from the immediate pre-war era to the year 1944. The events of the intervening period are related analeptically, by flashbacks to the protagonist's marriage, his experiences at the front, his home leave, and the evacuation of his wife to Pomerania. Rossa is wounded fighting on the western front in July 1944 and succeeds in obtaining a discharge. Back in Düsseldorf, he is an eyewitness to the city's destruction and the end of the war. Under British occupation, he assumes a subordinate role in the black-market dealings of an old friend, the industrialist Wrete, who is now a large-scale racketeer. When Rossa's wife returns home after an arduous journey from the occupied East, they seek refuge in the rural idyll of a wine-growing town in the Palatinate. The local mayor, a former comrade-at-arms, is on good terms with the French occupiers and finds Rossa a job at the town hall. That is where he begins to write a novel, to be titled *Die Brücke über den Strom* ("The Bridge Over the Current").

Most of the story unfolds against the backdrop of occupation by British and French forces. Yet the fact that the occupation regulates all circumstances of life, from residence permits to housing and food rationing, registers only on the margins. Portrayals of the 'victors' in terms conditioned by nationalist enmity, an almost-defining feature of post-1918 texts dealing with the post-World War I occupation, are seldom even hinted at in Bongs's novel, even though, by 1953, the year his novel was published, such portrayals would have been quite possible. Nor is reference made to the cult of Schlageter, though Bongs, who spent his youth in the occupied Rhineland, would have been well aware of the events surrounding it.

The novel also contains no allusions to the fact that the Allies were instrumental in toppling the Nazi dictatorship; nor does the author seem to appreciate the democratic and liberal approach they took to rebuilding public administration, political parties, publishing and the press, and cultural institutions. Neither is there mention of steps toward bringing Nazi criminals to justice, nor of re-education measures.

Bongs's determination to extricate the recent past from political and structural history and to embed in a natural-historical continuum beyond human control is monomaniacal. On such a cosmic scale, dictatorship, war, and genocide are reframed as the normal course of history:

> Spring lifted itself out of winter with early, radiant force. Glowing, the sun ascended to the sky's loftier fields. The cherry trees were in bloom.[10] The barrels of the cannons were rusting, and deadly projectiles no longer fell from the clouds. The world was changing its face. The other sky was and remained gray thanks to the heavy blanket of clouds lying across it. It darkened the shine of the stars and the course of the heavens. Nobody knew what was happening. (Bongs 1953, 251)

Or, again: "One day, we shall give up killing. Continents shall arise from the unknown. Why should not such a change overcome the earth instead of fiery rain, floods, plagues, or war?" (Bongs 1953, 438). What to make of such murmurings of the future, of this "one day we shall give up killing"[11] uttered in 1945, at the *end* of an unprecedented slaughter of human beings, and in view of the fact that an alliance of states that governed quite differently than the Nazis has *succeeded* in ridding Europe of a criminal regime?

Traveling by train to Mainz, from the British zone to the French, Rossa meets a history professor who launches into speculation on the principles of world history and the remarkably short lifespan of empires, from Alexander the Great to Hitler. "The history of the world—it consists of the significant doings of half-mad men. I mean those great phenomena we are wont to call statesmen. They are our undoing. There ought to be a law against them" (Bongs 1953, 451). These are the same 'great men' who are adduced as the makers of history by the Emperor in Brecht's one-act play. Though Bongs may pathologize them as half-mad, the view of history as specifically the history *of leaders* is the same. No consideration is given to the victims. The narrator describes most of the novel's characters as passive and disoriented, as though none of them had taken an active part in events. Aside from Hitler—mentioned by name only once—and a few war profiteers, actors do not appear as endowed with agency or responsibility for events. This view is extended to the victors.

With the exception of its decisionism-tinted ending, the novel displays the dystopian traits, marked by an unspoken disillusionment, that Alan Moorehead had observed: "It was over. Düsseldorf was dead" (Bongs 1953, 29). The narrator imagines people to act like "numb, petrified animals" (Bongs 1953, 72), his land-lady's "soul" to be "consumed with avarice" (Bongs 1953, 81), and everybody to fall into isolation (Bongs 1953, 248). This motif of a disintegrating community[12] is picked up repeatedly, at greatest length in words that he put into the mouth of a pre-war friend of Rossa's, the Franco-German painter Machandel:

> I'm a Frenchman, Johannes, that's what I've remained. […] Let me tell you what I feel now. This country is beaten and crushed. Its people are like hungry animals snapping at each other for the last bite. You have fallen silent in the world. You are hated in spite of your weakness. Defeated as no other people has ever been. But what did not die is that heart, that wonderful heart that never stopped living, that never fell silent—not amid the uproar of the bombs, not amid the screams of the suffering, not beneath the loud voices of the powerful. This heart remained pure. A heart is strong, it is unassailable, and you can feel it in Paris, in Normandy, in the canals of Venice and the ruins of Rome, as in a peasant hut in Campania, in the Ukraine, in the fields of Westphalia, the woods of Thuringia, the heaths of Scotland. You have lost everything. Your heart reveals itself from the ruins. It belongs to no one, no one can grasp it. It chimes like a bell. (Bongs 1953, 391f.)

It is thus left to a representative of France—from the opposing side in the recent conflict and the long-despised enemy in wartime propaganda since the procla-mation of the German Empire in 1871—to give absolution for Germany's crimes, couched in such clichéd terms as "heart" and "bell." What is more, his declara-tion turns the blood-soaked battlefields of recent memory, from Normandy to Ukraine, back into sites of European cultural heritage.

Nazi crimes[13] are dealt with in the same manner as history at large, being put into perspective by comparisons. Even in this early novel, it can be seen how responsibility is delegated to a single person, to Hitler: "Back then, the Church pursued heretics by means of the fire and the rope, running its quarry to ground; yesterday, one man chased the Jews and had them put to death in such a way that nobody dared to hear, to count their dying screams, today…" (Bongs 1953, 437f.).

The attempt by a woman living in exile in Switzerland to retrieve her furni-ture, artworks, and household effects from Düsseldorf after the war is recounted with a curious mixture of disapproval, understanding, and malice. Although the woman is clearly Jewish, the fact is not explicitly mentioned, being instead im-plied by her having to reclaim her property from the neighbors who acquired it illicitly—that is, by looting her apartment. She refuses to accept payment by way of purchase or compensation. "The moving truck that Margarethe Herrem, with the assistance of the English authorities, finally had dispatched to Basel—which was no easy matter, taking days and weeks" (Bongs 1953, 352) is stolen along the way and never reaches its destination.

As for the denazification proceedings, they are regarded as an impertinence, a humiliation imposed by the victorious powers (Tüngel and Berndorff 2004). They foster a sense of victimhood—of having fallen victim not only to the "one man" but also to the occupation: "The age of the questionnaire, of the inquiry pursued with inquisitorial exactitude, oppressed him, the legacy of his strict forebears, his sense of right and wrong, made him appear before himself as burdened with guilt" (Bongs 1953, 420). The narrator, it appears, would rather see his guilt—criminal though it may be—treated as a matter of conscience. That the moral judgment of a former member of the *Waffen-SS* might be open to question is not an idea that seems to occur to the author. Instead, Rossa—and never mind his conscience—takes advantage of a former comrade-in-arms' offer to wash his hands the dirty way: "You need denazifying? I'll put you through the mill down in Landau, you'll come out whiter than pastry flour. Nothing can happen to you" (Bongs 1953, 463).

Whereas this passage at least acknowledges a corruptible officer of the French occupying army, the ubiquitous British military government remains strikingly faceless. Bongs mentions only such things as sirens and curfews or the scent of English cigarettes. Yet "fraternization," as practiced by the wife of an interned Nazi, is condemned as a twofold betrayal, a betrayal of both her husband and her German ethnicity:

> Frau Renthoff had come over from Duisburg; her husband was in an internment camp. No doubt she was reassured to know him thus secured. In the first, warlike period of the occupation, her dark-skinned[14] passion had drunk its fill, such that she could gladly dispense with her husband until talk of her enthusiasms had died down. (Bongs 1953, 405)

Bongs lacks the courage to confront the realities of life under Allied military administration. This palpable indifference also assumes the guise of indifference to the political. The British appear as strangers whose coming (as victors) was inevitable and who will, in due course, leave. They register only when they impinge on the narrator's own interests (as in the case of denazification) or in the form of the sexual appetites of a German woman whom he considers immoral.

When, in the late 1950s, Bongs's membership of the *Waffen-SS* was made public, he responded with a story titled *Monolog eines Betroffenen* ("Monologue of a Concerned Party"), the ambiguous title of which contains the author's attitude in a nutshell. In this story, Bongs writes: "For one and a half years, anonymous people have been sending my past to my home. Excellent photocopies of what I published back in the day. It doesn't make comfortable reading now. But then I ask myself whether the past has not long since become a subject for ridicule and been forgotten" (Bongs 1961, 24).

Forte's Praise of Anarchy

Dieter Forte's novel *In der Erinnerung* artfully interweaves the narrative perspectives of the adult narrator and the ten-year-old boy he once was (Bogdal 2002, 2015). The *Stunde Null* ("zero hour") is reinterpreted here in a manner that has little in common with the myth of the completely new start that led to Germany's post-war 'economic miracle.' With regard to relations between people, this transitional situation is neither better nor worse than those preceding or succeeding it—it is simply different. From its chaos, a distinct order is emerging. "As far as the people were concerned, laws and regulations no longer existed. That was now the basic law" (Forte 1999, 649). In his imagination, the "boy" transports himself into a pre-natal situation amid a ruined world, a situation that is still replete with future possibilities. "He lay in a narrow room, in a place without time, as if the world had not yet been created" (Forte 1999, 634). This zero hour lasts until the moment when its absolute presence is terminated by reentry into history on 'grand' scale. "Perhaps they felt as he did that a fissure was slowly opening up across the world, growing unstoppably and menacingly wider, dividing them into people who wanted to think only of the future and people living in the past" (Forte 1999, 785f.). Across this fissure, the narrator recalls experiences of suffering that the 'normalizations' of post-war society may have been able to push out of sight, but which it could never 'heal.'

A conciliatory tone predominates in the description of the occupation. "The Americans," who reached Düsseldorf before the British, "moved along the main street on their quiet rubber soles with guns brandished" (Forte 1999, 599). Unlike Bongs, in whose account of seeing the Allied troops marching nearly all emotion is absent, the narrator in Forte's novel draws attention to the discrepancy between Nazi propaganda and his own experience:

> There he was now, the implacable, deadly enemy bent on forcing them into submission, as they had said on the radio; who was going to make slaves of them, destined for a horrible death by starvation. Now these were the enemies, giving out chewing gum and chocolate, dozing in the sun, listening to music [...]. (Forte 1999, 600)

The 'hybrid' dress of the survivors signals the beginning of a new era beyond clear-cut ascriptions. The narrator's mother "owned a pair of brown American soldier's shoes, which a Black man had thrown her from a moving Jeep" (Forte

1999, 640) and two quilted jackets: one from German military stock, the other Russian. The father gathers even more garments that previously advertised the wearer as either friend or foe: "Underneath a German army greatcoat and a Canadian army jacket, there trembled a pair of American army trousers; he had saved his paratrooper's boots and sported a Bersaglieri hat whose broken feathers gave him a devil-may-care look" (Forte 1999, 640).

There is little here to suggest a dystopian worldview. The narrator decides to tell the story 'from below,' but the break with the perspective 'from above' is even more decisive than that made by Brecht. Although long passages are given over to descriptions of the suffering and want experienced by 'common folk,' their failure and their death, Forte's losers can summon up their remaining strength and achieve remarkable things without guidance 'from above': "Everywhere, one could see these new bonds forming between people who had met on the road; it was as though new tribes were being founded, little nations that stick together" (Forte 1999, 610). Theirs is a community of experience, one that has its own way of freeing itself from heteronomy and the shackles of dictatorship.

The "complete freedom" that Forte (Forte 1999, 649) repeatedly mentioned is not significantly impaired even by the military government of a conquering power. With sympathy, the narrator describes the emergence of an unusual, precarious order that makes chaos livable: "Feeding the population fell to the black market and protecting the neighborhoods to the gangs. The highest authority of state was the military police" (Forte 1999, 654). The society that now emerges "could no longer be grasped in the bourgeois categories of old" (Forte 1999, 654). Its new "estates" (*Stände*) were called "war dead, war widows, war orphans, prisoners of war, missing persons, the fallen, late returnees [i.e., prisoners of war detained long after hostilities had ceased], refugees, forced laborers, conscripts, concentration camp inmates, displaced persons" (Forte 1999, 654). In the meantime, the terms that Forte lists are categories of victims that are officially recognized, for example in proceedings or processes for reparation (*Wiedergutmachung*). The state official culture of remembrance has also honored individual groups of victims.

One day, the narrator's father recalls the first occupation of the Rhine. He is described as taking advantage of

> the experience of his youth, when the city had once before been occupied by several foreign military powers, and with the occupation army he negotiated exceedingly complicated business deals, of which it was never clear what they resulted in, if anything, and what was legal about them and what was not. (Forte 1999, 677)

What he passes on are these experiences, of use in the struggle for survival, and not the nationalist legends of liberation and the hate-filled accounts of the "black disgrace." Without dignifying Schlageter and the *Freikorps* by so much as a mention, the narrator offers a counternarrative to a nationalist thread of memory that continued into the post-war era.[15] The story in question, familiar to this day, is that of the "Robin Hood of Düsseldorf," a young man named Hubert Lange (1927–2010) who styled himself "Count Mocca of Tonelli." He was the best-known among the leaders of the various gangs that had carved up the city's ruined neighborhoods under the occupation.

> These were [the narrator explains] private armies that continued to make war—deserted German soldiers, Hitler Youth lying low after having been drafted into service with a grenade thrower in the last days of the war and who had now lost their homes, Belgian and Dutch SS men on the run, Russian prisoners of war who feared being sent back to Russia, where they would be shot for desertion [...]. (Forte 1999, 667)

Hubert Lange had turned to burglary and robbery in 1941 and kept up his career, at the head of his gang, after the German surrender. In 1946, he was arrested by the British military authorities and sentenced to death by a Military Government Court. The sentence was commuted to fifteen years' imprisonment, of which Lange served about six months.

Schlageter and "Count Mocca" have a good deal in common. Both formed a criminal gang after defeat in war and under military occupation, both were condemned to death by a military court in Düsseldorf, and both were admired as heroes for their daring exploits. Here, however, the similarities end. Schlageter was incorporated into official memorial culture, and the nationalist and Nazi right exploited the possibilities this offered to the fullest. Meanwhile, the legends surrounding Lange, a hero of the Düsseldorf suburbs and the small-time criminal milieu, remained on a local scale and were mostly transmitted by word of mouth. This last point is important to Forte, whose other novels in the trilogy also do much to preserve and revive the oral tradition of immigrants and 'common folk.' Schlageter, the son of peasants from Baden, was a mercenary who fought wherever he was sent. "Count Mocca," the legend goes, fought on familiar ground to ensure the survival of the nameless victims of war and Nazi rule.

Occasional reference is made to institutional cooperation between Germans and Allies, and to re-education measures:

> In rather strained German, an English officer was delivering a lecture on the new era that was lost in the noise made by children and concluded with a poem by Goethe that nobody understood. After he had taken his leave with a cordial "good luck" and "bye bye," it emerged that the school was completely lacking not only desks but also teachers, for they had all been Party members [...]. (Forte 1999, 708)

The account of relations with the occupying force is limited to a longish passage about the narrator's mother (Maria) and her employment as housekeeper to a senior British officer. This upper-class English household is run according to principles of both arrogance and generosity, with sociability governed by class distinctions. In this scheme, Germans of whatever educational background invariably assume the status of domestic servants. To the narrator's family, however, this is quite satisfactory, since as domestics they are in a position at least to feed and warm themselves in the kitchen of the 'big house' (Forte 1999, 809). The occupiers are portrayed in terms lacking all hatred or resentment, instead taking on an ironic tone in the description of the officer's conciliatory attitude and his wife's lack of interest in the events around her: "The Major, kindly man that he was and actuated by such noble ideas as 'democracy' and 'friendship between peoples,' wanted to make sure that everyone had a '*schön schön deutsch deutsch Weihnak*' [*sic*], and everyone spent Christmas Eve carrying out his order" (Forte 1999, 811). "The Major's brilliant idea" of making everybody "keep changing places" to "ensure that Germans and British should sit side by side" (Forte 1999, 812) leads to a succession of intercultural misunderstandings that find resolution in a convivial booze-up: "As though they had wanted to make up for all the parties missed over the years" (Forte 1999, 816).

During the first occupation, after 1918, such a party in which victors and vanquished mingled chaotically would have been considered a disgrace and a betrayal of Germany. To celebrate together was as unthinkable as reconciliation was in general. Celebrations in the inter-war period were ritualistic in nature and aggressive in tone, and they continued in that manner even after the occupying forces had left—all the better to uphold enmity even in peacetime.

Repression and Testimony: Two Forms of the Politics of Memory

Not only Nazi rule and the experiences of the front and of bombing quickly recede from memory in *Die feurige Säule*. The occupation, too, is only an indistinct presence. Such a turn away from history on a grand scale, of the type that had been ubiquitous in the propaganda of the 'Thousand-Year Reich,' tells of a lack of interest in the political future of one's own country. This withdrawal takes the shape of a retreat to a rural idyll—a retreat made possible, however, by an old comrade-in-arms… thereby unintentionally harking back to the murderous war regardless.

Forte's novel, written more than forty years after the time in which it is set, leaves no doubt that defeat and occupation also marked a liberation. And yet it does not play into the narrative, which dominates the work of such historians as Heinrich August Winkler,[16] of a society steadily making its way from difficult beginnings in a new and better direction. Forte considers different moments to mark watersheds and pursues a different politics of memory. Instead of assuming there to have been a continuum between the occupation and the founding of the Federal Republic of (West) Germany, Forte postulates a break between the years spent in a no-man's-land full of utopian potential on the one hand and, on the other, the return and revival of Nazi ideology and elites as impediments to democratization.

Translated from German by Joe Paul Kroll

Notes

1. One vivid treatment of the theme is Ferdinand Hodler's mural *Auszug deutscher Studenten in den Freiheitskrieg von 1813* ("Pullout of German Students into the War of Liberation in 1813") (1909) in the *auditorium maximum* of the University of Jena; another—more controversial—is Gerhart Hauptmann's *Festspiel in deutschen Reimen* ("Festival in German Rhymes") (1913). On this, see Bogdal 1999.
2. All translations of non-English sources are made by Joe Paul Kroll.
3. See Hage 2003, and Sauder 2012.
4. Unless otherwise indicated, citations from works published in German refer to the original page numbers; the quotations have been translated for this chapter.
5. Ahead of its discussion later in this essay, it may be pointed out that indications of such behavior can be found in Bongs's novel, whose title—*The Pillar of Fire*—alludes to the destruction of Sodom and Gomorrah. Rossa, like Lot in the Biblical story, finds refuge in a small town. By contrast, Forte tells of people whom the war has left physically and psychologically mutilated yet who have not lost hope.
6. Yet he does not take this as an opportunity to express envy toward the victors or resentment of them.
7. Anyone interested in this outsider in the world of German letters will find much reliable information in Agnieszka Rajewskaja-Perzynska's dissertation (Rajewskaja-Perzynska 2009).
8. Bongs 1942a. An abridged version was published under the title "A Village Resettles" (*Ein Dorf siedelt um*). In *Monolog eines Betroffenen* ("Monologue of a Concerned Party") Bongs offers an indirect and veiled attempt at coming to terms with questions of guilt and responsibility.
9. Besides biographical details, this is also suggested by a passage from *Monolog eines Betroffenen*: "The atmosphere was different in Berlin. There were people who thought

as I did. We could pick each other out by smell. I don't know how we did it, but we did. In all those years I never picked the wrong man. Even if he was wearing a party badge" (Bongs 1961, 21).

10. This may conceivably be an allusion to Alfred Andersch's "The Cherries of Freedom" (*Die Kirschen der Freiheit*), published by Frankfurter Verlags-Anstalt in 1952.

11. "One day, humankind must turn about on its terrible path of bloody human sacrifice. I believe it must be possible." (Bongs 1953, 453) Surely the narrator ought to be content to see the regime disappear and for the German people to "turn about."

12. The community-based ideology of Nazism does indeed seem to have been missed.

13. "You are twenty-two. You are guiltless. I am not. People of my age are compromised, compromised by the past" (Bongs 1961, 10). "I am tired of justifying myself. You understand, first the Americans came with their questionnaires, then the English, then the Germans. I answered all the questions with as much precision as I could muster. I was tired of lying. I had been lying for so long" (Bongs 1961, 10f.). "I am no murderer. I gassed no Jews and I murdered no mental patients" (Bongs 1961, 11).

14. The phrase is steeped in racism.

15. See, e.g., Johst 1933, and the idea of the *Werwolf* as a reincarnation of the *Freikorps*.

16. Winkler 2007, 2020.

References

Arndt, Ernst Moritz. 1912. "Des Deutschen Vaterland." In *Arndts Werke: Auswahl in zwölf Teilen*, edited by August Leffson and Wilhelm Steffens. Vol. 1: *Gedichte*, 126–27. Berlin: Bong.

Barnouw, Dagmar. 1996. *Germany 1945: Views of War and Violence*. Bloomington: Indiana University Press.

Benjamin, Walter. 2006. "Paralipomena to 'On the Concept of History.'" In *Selected Writings*, edited by Howard Eiland and Michael W. Jennings. Vol. 4: *1938–1940*, 401–11. Cambridge, MA: Belknap Press.

Bogdal, Klaus-Michael. 1999. "Germania tot in Breslau: Gerhart Hauptmanns 'Festspiel in deutschen Reimen.'" *Text und Kritik* 38, no. 142: 97–109.

———. 2002. "Erhofftes Wiedersehen: Dieter Fortes Romantrilogie 'Das Haus auf meinen Schultern.'" In *Literatur und Leben: Anthropologische Aspekte in der Kultur der Moderne*. Festschrift für Helmut Scheuer zum 60. Geburtstag, edited by Günter Helmes, Ariane Martin, Birgit Nübel, and Georg-Michael Schulz, 305–18. Tübingen: Narr Francke Attempto.

———. 2015. "Abbrechendes Todesatmen: Forte und das Gedächtnis der deutschen Literatur." *Sprache im technischen Zeitalter* 53, no. 215 (June): 265–72.

Bongs, Rolf. 1942a. *Ein Dorf siedelt um*, edited by Luftwaffenführungsstab. Berlin: Wiking.

———. 1942b. *Harte herrliche Strasse nach Westen.* Berlin: Wiking.

———. 1953. *Die feurige Säule.* Roman. Emsdetten: Lechte.

———. 1961. *Monolog eines Betroffenen.* Erzählung. Mit einem autobiographischen Nachwort. Stuttgart: Reclam.

Brauerhoch, Annette. 2006. *"Fräuleins" und GIs. Geschichte und Filmgeschichte.* Frankfurt: Stroemfeld.

Brecht, Bertolt. 1968. "The Beggar or The Dead Dog." Translated by Michael Hamburger. *The Drama Review* 12, no. 2 (Winter): 120–23.

Breitbach, Joseph. 1933. *Die Wandlung der Susanne Dasseldorf.* Berlin: Kiepenheuer.

Cepl-Kaufmann, Gertrude, ed. 2009. *Jahrtausendfeiern und Befreiungsfeiern im Rheinland: Zur politischen Festkultur 1925 und 1930.* Essen: Klartext.

Feuchtwanger, Lion. 1930. *Erfolg: Drei Jahre Geschichte einer Provinz.* Roman. Berlin: G. Kiepenheuer.

Fischer, Ludwig, ed. 1999. *"Dann waren die Sieger da.": Studien zur literarischen Kultur in Hamburg 1945–1950.* Hamburg: Dölling und Galitz.

Forte, Dieter. 1999. *Das Haus auf meinen Schultern.* Romantrilogie. Frankfurt a.M.: S. Fischer. [Contains the novels *Tagundnachtgleiche*, 599–619, and *In der Erinnerung*, 621–864.]

Frank, Leonhard. 1949. *Die Jünger Jesu.* Roman. Amsterdam: Querido.

Gollancz, Victor. 1947. *In Darkest Germany.* Hinsdale, IL: Henry Regnery Company.

Graetz, Wolfgang. 1966. *Die Welt von unten.* Frankfurt a.M.: Büchergilde Gutenberg.

Habe, Hans. 1955. *Off Limits: Roman von der Besatzung Deutschlands.* Munich: Desch.

Hage, Volker. 2003. *Zeugen der Zerstörung: Die Literaten und der Luftkrieg.* Essay und Gespräche. Frankfurt a.M.: S. Fischer.

Hollander, Walther von. 1947. *Es wächst schon Gras darüber.* Roman. Hamburg: Springer.

Johst, Hans. 1933. *Schlageter.* Drama. Munich: Albert Langen and Georg Müller.

Kempowski, Walter. 1972. *Uns geht's ja noch gold.* Roman. Munich: Hanser.

Kiesel, Helmuth. 2017. *Geschichte der deutschsprachigen Literatur 1918–1933.* Munich: C.H. Beck.

Knauff, Michael. 1995. "Das Schlageter-Nationaldenkmal auf der Golzheimer Heide in Düsseldorf." *Geschichte im Westen* 10, no. 2: 168–91.

Mann, Klaus. 1942. *The Turning Point: Thirty-Five Years in this Century.* London: Victor Gollancz LTD.

———. 2006. *Der Wendepunkt: Ein Lebensbericht.* Reinbek bei Hamburg: Rowohlt.

Maß, Sandra. 2006. *Zur Geschichte kolonialer Männlichkeit in Deutschland 1918–1964.* Cologne: Böhlau.

Matzerath, Horst. 1997. "Rheinische Großstädte nach dem Ende des Zweiten Weltkrieges: Notverwaltung oder Neubeginn?" In *Kriegsende und Neubeginn. Westdeutschland und Luxemburg zwischen 1944 und 1947,* edited by Kurt Düwell and Michael Matheus, 1–20. Stuttgart: Franz Steiner.

McGovern, James. 1956. *Fräulein*. New York: Crown.

———. 1957. *Fräulein: Roman eines deutschen Mädchens*. Munich: List.

Meckel, Christoph. 2011. *Russische Zone: Erinnerung an den Nachkrieg*. Lengwil: Libelle.

Moorehead, Alan. 1945. *Eclipse*. London: H. Hamilton.

Peitsch, Helmut. 2009. *Nachkriegsliteratur 1945–1989*. Göttingen: V&R Unipress.

Pommerin, Reiner. 1979. *Die Sterilisierung der Rheinlandbastarde: Das Schicksal einer farbigen deutschen Minderheit 1918–1937*. Düsseldorf: Droste.

Rajewska-Perzynska, Agnieszka. 2009. *Rolf Bongs: Dissoziation eines Schriftstellers im Spannungsfeld zwischen Selbststilisierung und Anpassung*. Frankfurt a.M.: Lang.

Salomon, Ernst von. 1951. *Der Fragebogen*. Hamburg: Rowohlt.

Sauder, Gerhard. 2012. "Literatur und Bombenkrieg—Kritik an der Sebald-These." In *Berührungen: Komparatistische Perspektiven auf die frühe deutsche Nachkriegsliteratur*, edited by Günter Butzer and Joachim Jacob, 231–39. Paderborn: Wilhelm Fink.

Sebald, W. G. 2003. *On the Natural History of Destruction*. New York: Random House.

Siebenpfeiffer, Hania, ed. 2004. *Krieg und Nachkrieg: Konfigurationen der deutschsprachigen Literatur (1940–1965)*. Berlin: Erich Schmidt.

Simpson, Patricia Anne. 2006. *The Erotics of War in German Romanticism*. Lewisburg, PA: Lewisburg Bucknell University Press.

Sprenger, Matthias. 2008. *Landsknechte auf dem Weg ins Dritte Reich? Zu Genese und Wandel des Freikorpsmythos*. Paderborn: F. Schöningh.

Tüngel, Richard, and Hans Rudolf Berndorff. 2004. *Stunde Null: Deutschland unter den Besatzungsmächten*. Reprint. Berlin: Mathes und Seitz. [Originally published as *Auf dem Bauche sollst du kriechen*. 1958.]

Winkler, Heinrich August. 2007. *Germany: The Long Road West*. Transl. by Alexander Sager. 2 vols. Oxford: Oxford University Press.

———. 2020. *Wie wir wurden, was wir sind: Eine kurze Geschichte der Deutschen*. Munich: C.H. Beck.

Zwicker, Stefan. 2006. „*Nationale Märtyrer:" Albert Leo Schlageter und Julius Fučík: Heldenkult, Propaganda und Erinnerungskultur*. Paderborn: F. Schöningh.

CHAPTER 13

Reflections on Twentieth-Century Military Occupations in Latvian and Estonian Novels[1]

BENEDIKTS KALNAČS

Introduction

In the fall of 1944, the Latvian writer Anšlavs Eglītis joined tens of thousands of refugees who decided to leave their homeland in fear of war and terror, escaping the advance of Soviet military forces. As it turned out later, for these people, this was the beginning of a long-term Western exile that lasted until the end of the Soviet occupation in the Baltic littoral in 1991. Many of those refugees never again saw their native countries, and this was also the case for Eglītis, who died in Napa, California in 1993. In his turn, the Estonian author Jaan Kross was arrested by the Soviet authorities in the city of Tartu in 1946 and sent in 1948 to a labor camp in Siberia, from which he returned home only in 1954. Subsequently, writing in Soviet Estonia, Kross had to take into account the existing Soviet censorship, which severely limited his possibilities for expressing his thoughts freely. One way of escaping these restrictions was to focus on Estonia-related historical personalities and events. Eglītis, on the other hand, due to his very limited contact with his homeland during the post-war period, mainly reflected on the experience of the Latvian exile community. Thus, both authors were forced by circumstance to take literary 'escape routes' rather than enjoying the freedom to tackle the most topical issues regarding the ongoing Soviet occupation of the Baltic states.

Nevertheless, as I shall argue in this chapter, even if both authors were living on different sides of the Iron Curtain, the burning issue for each of them remained the contemporary hardships of their compatriots in their respective native countries, a problem that they could only address indirectly (Kross) or about which they lacked sufficient material in order to detail the everyday realities of post-war life back home (Eglītis). Indeed, many Baltic authors whose works deal with the consequences of World War II in Eastern Europe constantly felt the long-lasting presence of Soviet power in the Baltic littoral, alongside painful memories of the Nazi occupation from the period 1941 to 1944.

My main focus in this chapter, therefore, is on the manner in which the above authors represent long-term Soviet and Nazi military occupations and their impacts in the Baltic littoral. I approach this task primarily through two case studies: one of the Latvian writer Anšlavs Eglītis (1906–1993), and one of the Estonian author Jaan Kross (1920–2007), who share much in common despite belonging to different generations. The three chosen texts were published between 1959 and 1998, but each provides an extended reflection on earlier events; accordingly, another focus of this chapter is the complexity of the historical experience of these Baltic authors and their compatriots.

In the following, I first approach the historical contexts of the Soviet and Nazi occupations within the Baltic littoral's larger historical experience. Second, I introduce readers to the biographies of Eglītis and Kross with regard to the specific contexts of their personality formation. In the third step, I discuss the conditions in Soviet Estonia and Latvia on the one hand, and in Western exile on the other, with particular attention to the specificities of exile literature that substantially shaped the two texts by Eglītis that this chapter explores. Fourth, I analyze Jaan Kross's literary oeuvre, specifically with the aim of showing how stylistic features of his prose that had already been developed during the Soviet era came to new light in one of his most important prose texts, a work accomplished in the 1990s that tackles 20th-century events. Finally, in this chapter's conclusion, I summarize specific contexts and features of the reception of the Soviet and Nazi military occupations of the Baltic littoral, as represented by literary texts.

The Historical Background: Military Occupation during World War II and its Aftermath in the Baltic States

Ian D. Armour notes: "A Western perspective can blind us to the fact that, just as an East European dispute was the trigger for the war, so Eastern Europe was the crucial battlefield of the conflict, especially once the Soviet Union was involved" (Armour 2021, 119). A reminder of some important turning points in the history of World War II helps to appreciate the accuracy of this observation. On September 22, 1939, a joint parade of the Nazi and Soviet militaries took place at Brest-Litovsk, a small town on the demarcation line agreed upon in the secret protocols of the Molotov–Ribbentrop Pact (Kramer 2014, 268). The parade was a celebration of what had happened in the preceding weeks, during which the two occupying powers invaded Poland and violently tore the country apart in accordance with their respective visions of establishing a new political world order at the expense of other European nations. By September 1939, when Hitler's troops seized the west of Poland, they had already annexed and occupied the territories of Austria and the Czech Republic, while the Soviet Union invaded Poland from the east. Stalin took further advantage of the situation and launched a military campaign against Finland in November 1939, known as the Winter War. In its next move, the Soviet Union then occupied the independent states of Estonia, Latvia, and Lithuania in June 1940. The two authors discussed in this chapter, Eglītis and Kross, both became direct witnesses of these events, and direct references to the fact of occupation appear in all novels discussed here. While Kross faced the decisive events in his native Estonia, Eglītis happened to experience the beginning of Soviet occupation not once, but twice. In June 1940, he was in Lithuania, where there were guest performances of a major Latvian theater company, the *Dailes* ("Art") theater. It was exactly at this point that the Soviet tanks crossed the Lithuanian border. Then, in the following days, as Latvian artists (including Eglītis) were returning home, the Soviet Union made further advances, and very soon Soviet military columns were seen on the streets of Riga, Latvia's capital.

The occupation and the war itself caused enormous suffering across the continent. Two of the Baltic countries—Estonia and Latvia—had just established their statehood in 1918, for the first time in history, signing treaties with Soviet Russia soon afterwards that should have secured their peaceful existence. Alas, Soviet Russia only held these promises for two decades; the occupation of Estonia and Latvia in 1940 not only meant their loss of independence but also imposed a foreign rule that lasted in these territories for the next fifty years.

The measures carried out in the Baltic countries after the 1940 occupation closely resembled methods that had already been implemented within the Soviet Union during the previous decade of Stalinist terror. As such, in this perspective, this earlier history is crucial to understand as well. In the 1930s, on the domestic front, Soviet ideology had been imposed rigorously and by every means. The social scientist Vita Zelče refers to the canonical book *Short History Course of the All-Union Communist Party* (published in 1938) that established the foundations of Soviet ideology. This publication became

> a weapon of tyrannical power, the sole version of history, which not only displaced other opinions but excluded their possibility altogether. History was presented as the triumph of right over wrong in all realms of life, thereby assuming the meaning of a mythical tale. [...] The new concept of Soviet history also established a wide range of deceit in facts, data, the inclusion or exclusion of events and people in history. (Zelče 2011, 34)

Prior to the war, when the notion of a socialist revolution spreading across the globe had to be (at least temporarily) abandoned, the efforts to establish Communism in one country led to drastic measures intended to eliminate the opponents of Soviet power through class struggle and political terror, and these measures were carried out in particular against non-Russian ethnic groups (Snyder 2010, 59–118). Efforts to hasten industrialization in the economically underdeveloped Soviet Union were carried out at the expense of peasants, who now became obligated to provide a sufficient food supply for the workers of large factories. However, while many of these factories were located in the Russian mainland, the most productive agricultural lands were in the Ukraine. Hence, in the early 1930s, as the Soviet authorities imposed unreachably high quotas for food supply, peasants lived under constant pressure and threat from Communist rulers. Bereft of any possibility to secure a sufficient livelihood of their own, millions of Ukrainian peasants starved as a result. In addition, Soviet policies pertaining to the countryside relied on mass deportations of relatively prosperous peasants (so-called kulaks), who—whether openly or (in most cases) indirectly—opposed the compulsory system of collective farming and were thus considered enemies of the ruling party. Many of these people were shot dead shortly after their arrest or died along the road, even before reaching the destination that the deportation plans had envisaged for them: concentration camps. The historian Timothy Snyder estimates that, prior to the war, "the chances that a Soviet citizen would be executed in the kulak action were about seven hundred times greater than the chances that a German citizen would be sentenced to death in Nazi Germany for any offense" (Snyder 2010, 87). The Soviet-imposed famine of the Ukrainian population became one of the first obvious cases of the policies of the state specifically targeting ethnic minorities. In 1937 and 1938, due to Stalin's exaggerated fear of treason, he purposefully directed mass destruction against minorities such as Ukrainians, Jews, Poles, Latvians, and others. The intellectual and economic elites of these ethnic groups, as well as peasants, were targeted under the guise of the class struggle, and, under the pretext of state security, the highest-educated individuals were exterminated.

In the aftermath, then, of the occupation of parts of Poland and the Baltic states, the Soviets exported the same earlier tactics of targeting intellectual elites, while the Nazis implemented them too:

> Hans Frank, citing Hitler, defined his job as the elimination of Poland's 'leadership elements'. NKVD [People's Commissariat for Internal Affairs] officers took their assignment to a logical extreme by consulting a Polish 'Who's Who' in order to define their targets. This was an attack on the very concept of modernity, or indeed the social embodiment of the Enlightenment in this part of the world. (Snyder 2010, 153)

It was against this backdrop that the Molotov–Ribbentrop Pact in August 1939 effectively sealed the further ambitions of the two most influential dictators of the time. Soon thereafter, in September 1939, the Kremlin posed an ultimatum first to Estonia, then in October to Latvia, and subsequently also to Lithuania, demanding "the immediate stationing of Soviet army, navy and air forces at strategic locations" (Kasekamp 2018, 114). The Red Army received orders to prepare to invade Estonia on September 29, and the Estonians caved to Soviet pressure the day before the scheduled invasion—a decision soon followed by their two Baltic neighbors. This attempted compromise, however, did not save them from the subsequent full-scale Soviet occupation in June 1940, when additional military troops occupied the Baltic states and local governments were forcefully overturned.

Immediately after the occupation, Soviet rulers in the Baltics put into practice the same tactics of governmental violence that they had already carried out in other parts of the Soviet Union. Previous political structures were dissolved and the Communist party rule imposed. "While undermining established institutions, this involved creating new organizations and institutions, mobilizing social and cultural support for the new regime and restructuring the educational system to control the socialization of the young" (Senn 2005, 21). This process is eloquently discussed in Eglītis's novel *Piecas dienas* ("Five Days"). The swift implementation of structural transformations included rigged elections and fake referenda, used as a pretext for legitimizing the occupation and for the subsequent formal incorporation of the Baltic states into the Soviet Union, accomplished at great speed in August 1940.

The Soviets also tried to clear some diplomatic and ideological ground in the West, explaining their position in an attempt to legitimize their policies. In August 1940, Ivan Maisky, the Soviet ambassador to Great Britain, "told the British foreign minister Lord Edward Halifax the story of peasant Ivan, whose horse, cow, and plough were underhandedly carried off during his illness" (Annus 2018, 142). When the ailing peasant unexpectedly recovered his health (so the story went), he immediately wanted his possessions back, and so he went to all three neighbors and accomplished this. From the Soviet perspective, this was indeed a parable of what had happened on the political stage. According to Russian historian Elena Zubkova, the idea that the Soviet Union needed the West to see the annexation of the three Baltic countries as a restoration of Russia's historical borders was expressed for the first time in 1940 by Molotov and thereafter used in interactions with Baltic governments and in Soviet foreign diplomacy (Annus 2018, 143).

The advance of Nazi forces in June 1941, then, led to the continuation of the two superpowers' bloody confrontation, which was now taking place in the territories of formerly independent Baltic countries. It was primarily due to the incredibly painful experience of earlier Soviet occupation that the later horrors of Nazi rule were relativized in people's memories and life stories (Kõresaar 2007, 39). The mental mapping of history in the Baltic countries thus took a different turn, if compared with some other European territories. The trauma of ongo-ing humiliation, linked to the occupation and war, and then perpetually rein-forced by the omnipresent Soviet rhetoric that continued for decades after World War II, became the most painful experience for thousands of Latvians and Esto-nians, both in homeland and in exile. Eglītis and Kross shared these feelings, and these feelings found expression in their novels.

The Two Authors

Both writers were born into intellectual families, and their fates illustrate well the complexity of Baltic history. The father of Anšlavs Eglītis was well-known Latvian author Viktors Eglītis (1877–1945), one of the first modernist writers of the early 20th century. The family became part of the first refugee crisis dur-ing the Great War, when advancing German forces had occupied western re-gions of Latvia (then part of the Russian Empire). The front line was established alongside the main waterway, the Daugava River, and remained there for more than two years. Many Latvians tried to escape. Eglītis's family fled to mainland Russia, returning only in 1918, when the independent republic of Latvia was proclaimed on November 18. Upon their return, the Communist terror of the first half of 1919 served as the family's introduction to what the Soviet regime would mean for the Latvian population. The period from 1918 to 1920 has been variously called "civil war," "war of independence," "war for liberty," and "strug-gle for freedom" by today's historians (Minins 2015, 49), but in any case, strong interference by foreign powers was present. The short-lived Communist rule of 1919 demonstrated the Communist authorities' complete inability to deal with social, economic, and cultural issues.

During the interwar period, Eglītis gradually established himself as one of the most prominent authors in the flourishing intellectual milieu of independ-ent Latvia. His books became extremely popular, and he was considered one of the principal representatives of a new generation of Latvian authors. In 1940, however, history once again took a different turn, and the Soviet occupation in-evitably brought earlier memories back to Eglītis's mind. Then, after surviving both Soviet and subsequent Nazi rule, Eglītis fled to Germany in the fall of 1944, where he stayed until 1949. He later moved to the United States and eventually settled down in California. Most of his post-war fiction traces daily life in the Latvian diaspora in the USA, but the novels discussed in this chapter display his burning interest in the fate of his occupied homeland.

The life of Jaan Kross, on the other hand, developed in a different direction. Kross studied at Tartu University's School of Law from 1938 to 1944. During these years, he was involved with the Estonian press from 1940 to 1941, worked as a secretary at the Tallinn City Bank from 1941 to 1943, and then in 1943 became a translator for the German army. After surviving Nazi imprisonment, he worked in Tartu as a lecturer at the School of Law from 1944 to 1946. Becoming a Soviet political prisoner then in 1946, he was deported in 1948 and worked in a coal mine and brick factory in the Komi Autonomous Soviet Socialist Republic (ASSR) and in the Krasnoyarsk Krai (Org 2009, 158).

Kross returned to Estonia in 1954 and settled down as a professional writer. From the late 1960s onward, Kross displayed special interest in the past, in his books dealing with well-known personalities from Estonian social and cultural history, such as Balthasar Russow, Johann Köler, Otto Wilhelm Masing, and Kristian Jaak Peterson. This approach provided an escape route and an opportunity for discussing Soviet realities in an indirect manner. Toward the end of his life, Kross was referred to as the grand old man of Estonian literature and especially recognized for his achievements in the genre of the historical novel (Salumets 2000a, 225); he was nominated several times for the Nobel Prize.

Literature in the Soviet Period and in Western Exile

The brief biographical overview above has already indicated that the post-war literary activities of Anšlavs Eglītis and Jaan Kross unfolded under mutually juxtaposed conditions. In the Soviet Union, which had incorporated both Latvia and Estonia, strict censorship did not allow authors to air their personal views. The imposed ideology was marked by attempts to rewrite national histories, and this was also true with regard to the interpretation of recent events. The official narrative concentrated on the Soviet people's victorious efforts during the war, now termed the Great Patriotic War. According to the Soviet interpretation, the most important battles had been fought by the Russian nation, and the Russian nation had also suffered most during that period. Timothy Snyder makes it clear that such an approach was even instrumental in silencing the true scale of the Holocaust: "The number of Jews killed by the Germans in the Soviet Union was a state secret" (Snyder 2010, 342). This silencing amounted to the loss of Holocaust memory in the USSR, as it was not accepted that any group had experienced a fate more terrible than the Russians' fate during the war. In the late 1940s, the Soviet authorities even launched a campaign against so-called Jewish cosmopolites accused of anti-Soviet views. At the same time and under the same pretext, other ethnic groups were targeted as well. Thus, the class struggle and attempted extermination of individuals presumed hostile to the Soviet state was yet again taking place and led to the mass deportations of ordinary people.

Even during the so-called thaw, when many Soviet deportees—among them Jaan Kross—had been allowed to return home, their activities, including literary output, were strictly censored. In this regard, there was no principal difference between Soviet republics, even if specific decisions were at least partially implemented by local institutions, such as the newly established Unions of Soviet writers; the chief premises, such as the question of any given person's reliability, were taken into account and applied similarly everywhere.

In Latvia in particular, two characteristic examples are provided by the campaigns directed against prose writers Visvaldis Lāms and Ēvalds Vilks (Eglāja-Kristsone 2018, 209–11). Lāms had been forcedly mobilized into the Nazi-led Latvian Legion, and he returned from the Soviet filtration camp only in 1946. In the late 1950s, in his novel *Kāvu blāzmā* (Lāms 1958) ("In the Glow of the Northern Lights"), Lāms touched upon some of this experience. The novel's serialized print run in the literary magazine *Karogs* was interrupted, and Lāms' literary output was completely banned for six years. In the case of Ēvalds Vilks, the main target of Soviet censorship was his story *Divpadsmit kilometric* ("Twelve Kilometers"), published in *Karogs* in 1963 (Vilks 1982), in which the author approached post-war Soviet policies critically, suggesting that all nations and responsible individuals ought to be equally blamed for the injustices and cruelties they committed (Eglāja-Kristsone 2018, 210–11). The publication was condemned, and the story republished in 1968 with numerous 'corrections' requested by the Soviet censorship office (Hiršs 1982, 430–35). This was a psychological blow from which the author never recovered. Overall, as these writers' experiences illustrate, any opposition to the official Soviet 'heroic' version of the war narrative, any alternative approach to the history of the Baltic countries, was hardly possible while, "in the Soviet Union and current day Russia the event [i.e., the Soviet occupation] was and still is interpreted as a gesture of protection from Nazi Germany" (Saro 2014, 343).

Contrary to the conditions in occupied Baltic states, Western exile provided considerably more possibilities for Baltic writers to express their views, an opportunity of which they also tried to make use. Even from afar, writers' mental response to the occupation and to the continued Soviet military presence in their homelands remained a constant issue that colored their stance (Rozītis 2005, 26). Even when focusing on individual experiences, many authors display a rather generalized approach to the pain experienced by the refugees—made no less acute by subsequent moves from post-war Germany (where most of the displaced persons initially settled) to other countries. Reaching beyond one's private experience in the process of mutually shared storytelling, as a means of preserving collective memory, could well be referred to as 'affective realism' (see Buschmeier's introduction to this volume).

Alongside reflections on their (new) immediate surroundings, exile authors were constantly concerned with the sense of lost time that accompanied the 'loss' of their homelands, along with the notion that this time must be recovered (Undusk 2006, 127). In the opinion of Indrek Tamm, "A displaced historian tends to compensate the lack of spatial coordinates by temporal ones" (Tamm 2006, 130). During the Soviet era, similar mechanisms were at work with regard even to the inner exile. For Jaan Kross, delving into Estonia's past thus provided the possibility of cutting across different layers of experience in historical perspective.

The exile experience is also where an important link to the notion of diaspora as an extreme form of a scattered nation can be noticed. In a distantly related context, Homi Bhabha (writing about India) refers to "[n]ationness as form of social and textual affiliation" (Bhabha [1994] 2004, 201). Exile authors' contribution to this topic was vitally important, and it had obvious, even if indirect, links to anti-colonial narratives elsewhere in the world (Laurušaite 2008, 177).

Characteristically enough, exile literature regarding the representation of the occupied homeland tended to intensify at historical moments that coincided with indications of potential change in Soviet society, such as the occasion of Stalin's death in 1953, when an atmosphere of so-called thaw was felt in Soviet countries. A response to this climate of hope might be observed in exile authors' works during the second half of the 1950s; perhaps they were seeking a dialogue, if not with the authorities, then at least with parts of the population in the Baltic countries. Of course, however marginal the true possibilities of such dialogues were—especially given the ban on all Western publications within the Soviet Union—exile writers nonetheless wanted to share their experience and opinion. This much is also true of Anšlavs Eglītis's post-war novels.

Anšlavs Eglītis

In the 1930s, Eglītis was considered one of the most important innovators of Latvian prose, focused on representing his contemporary intellectual and artistic milieu. During his refugee and exile years, however, he shifted his emphasis to social issues, closely following his compatriots' fate in everyday contexts. Eglītis was a direct witness, and the first Latvian author to provide a vivid and detailed representation, of the bombardment of Berlin that took place on February 3, 1945. Even if he remained outside the post-war camps for displaced persons in Germany, his knowledge of the conditions in these camps enabled Eglītis to provide some of the most profound insights into refugee life in his novel "The Lucky Ones" (*Laimīgie*) published in 1952. The somewhat ironic title corresponds to a viewpoint that Eglītis promoted: namely, that the Latvian community in exile should continue to be engaged in meaningful activities, despite the extraordinary circumstances in which refugees found themselves. Despite the difficulties they faced, their future prospects were much better than the prospects of those who had to live under Soviet occupation. Prominent literary critic Jānis Rudzītis underlined the vital importance of Eglītis's message, the latter being a highly ambitious modernist author who nevertheless recognized the necessity not only of caring about the aesthetic value of his own work but also of turning close attention to the sufferings of his compatriots (Rudzītis 1977, 441).

Throughout the subsequent decades, Eglītis was a rare example among exile authors of Baltic origin in that he was able to continue his literary career on a more-or-less professional basis, due to his ability to attract readers' attention and to remain sufficiently prolific. In some of his texts—even if these particular ones were relatively few—he dealt with his first-hand experience of the occupation of Latvia, as well as tried to gather material with regard to post-war conditions. While the people in occupied Latvia were completely denied foreign information channels, Baltic exiles did have access to Soviet sources, including Latvian and Estonian periodicals. Such 'local' knowledge was vital to exile writers, as were sporadic conversations with people who had first-hand experience of the ongoing regime of occupation.

Eglītis's novel *Ilze* (1959) is based on a personal story centered on his mother-in-law, who managed to escape to the West in the fall of 1956 during the short-lived political thaw in the Soviet Union. The novel follows the story of the family being split in half in Germany during the final months of World War II. While the characters Kurts Druja and his wife Benita move to California, they continue their efforts to contact Ilze, Kurts's mother, whom they had to leave behind in Eastern Prussia. Ilze, for her part, suddenly finds herself in the Soviet occupation zone and experiences the cruelty of Soviet officers and soldiers against the local Germans, as well as against the refugees. Ilze shares the fate of many her compatriots when she is forced to return to Soviet Latvia in 1945, and the main body of the text follows her experience in post-war Riga, which bears signs not only of Soviet occupation but also of colonization. As the Estonian researcher Epp Annus persuasively argues, the long-standing nature of Soviet military, economic, and cultural dominance ultimately created mechanisms of the colonial matrix of power that acquired characteristics beyond those of 'occupation' alone:

> If the occupation does not end by expelling the occupiers from the country, then the relationship of domination in the occupied areas acquires features of colonialism: the occupiers settle in the occupied territory, and their ideology starts to change how the occupied people relate to the world. The oppressed country can still be called an occupied country, yet the economic, social and cultural models at work become those of the colonial enterprise. (Annus 2012, 37)

While it is generally recognized that features of colonialism persisted in the relations between Western European empires and their colonies after World War II (Schulze-Englert 2013, 672), it is also important to recognize related patterns that have played out in the fates of small European nations under Soviet rule.

Coming back to the experience of the protagonist of Eglītis's novel, *Ilze*, we notice how, upon her return to Soviet Latvia, it immediately turns out that the family's former flat is now occupied by a high-ranking Soviet official, Comrade Belte, a Latvian who, following the political and ideological practice widespread at the time, had been ordered to the Baltic littoral from the Soviet Union. Ilze faces enormous problems in reintegrating under the changed conditions, starting with her uncertainty about how to re-establish her legal status. It is only with great difficulty and help from her local relatives that she finds a room in a communal apartment, housing being a prerequisite for legal registration. Yet re-establishing her legal status is only the beginning of her post-war challenges; she feels the impact of the Soviet authorities' new rules everywhere. In the novel's representation of post-war Riga, Eglītis manages to capture the terrifying atmosphere of fear and alienation that, by the second half of the 1940s, had completely changed lives of ordinary people. The feelings of uncertainty and misinformation that the novel communicates match the actual conditions.

Eglītis's novel specifically focuses on the neighborhood where he and his family stayed before the war. Being relatively close to the city center, its territory is bordered by Krišjāņa Valdemāra Street, Bruņinieku Street, and Marijas Street, although almost all of those streets had lost their former names by the late 1940s: these three came to be called Maxim Gorky Street, Red Army Street, and Suvorov Street instead. The change from honoring Krišjānis Valdemārs, one of the leading personalities of 19th-century Latvian romantic nationalism, to honoring the Russian author and ideological father of so-called socialist realism, Maxim Gorky, is an especially poignant reflection of how the communist state reinforced its ideological message. However, the street that was renamed for the tsarist general Suvorov is probably the most telling of these street-name changes, as it clearly indicates the principal overlap of the imperial Russian and Soviet narratives, with the latter becoming a direct continuation of the ambitions displayed by the former.

Eglītis's skill for portraying the psychological impact of the Soviet occupation is especially poignant in the plot complication through which he links the story of Ilze to that of Comrade Belte. When Ilze manages to be hired as a cleaner in her former apartment, she notices that Belte has kept the interior almost exactly as it was before, thereby indirectly honoring its former owners' tastes, despite the fact that Latvian aesthetics diverged greatly from what Comrade Belte would have known earlier in Soviet Russia. Even a small photograph of Ilze's son Kurts in an interwar Latvian army uniform still stands on one of the shelves. When Ilze decides to quit her job as a cleaner—because making regular visits to her former apartment turns out to be too painful—she takes her son's photo with her. Comrade Belte discovers this immediately upon her departure, and he presumes that he was being spied on. Imagining that he has been betrayed, his mind immediately begins to haunt him with scenes of the arrest and torture he fears he will face, and he dies by suicide that very day in an attempt to avoid detention by the Soviet authorities. His totally unfounded supposition eloquently conveys the overall aura of suspicion and constant surveillance that people endured under Soviet rule—even the authorities themselves.

With all people living under constant threat, it is unsurprising that the novel ends with Ilze leaving Soviet Latvia as soon as this unexpectedly becomes feasible; she is allowed to join her son and daughter-in-law abroad during the short-lived change in Soviet policies in the late 1950s.

Eglītis's later novel *Piecas dienas* ([1976] 1992) ("Five Days") also deals with the experience of occupation, which, in the preceding decades, had not lost its acute feeling of loss or trauma for him; in fact, *Piecas dienas* is partly a memoir, albeit in a disguised form. During the late 1930s, Anšlavs Eglītis worked in the press, and after the occupation, he kept a minor position at the popular magazine *Atpūta*, which, strangely enough, was allowed to continue its run during the first year of the Soviet occupation, a time when most other previous institutions were dismantled. Eglītis's activity as a journalist in 1940 and 1941 allowed him to observe the unfolding transformations at close range, even if this kind of collaboration-by-necessity became the source of his inner contradictions as well (see Schell in this volume).

A meeting serves as the novel's framework: that of Klaudijs Velks, the principal character living in Soviet Latvia, with foreign tourists who are allowed to visit the USSR in 1974. Velks's conversations with the exile Armands Pols, a friend from his youth, inspire the former to evaluate his own life and the situation in post-war Riga, where he had stayed for personal motives. Through this retrospective approach, large parts of the text deal with the societal transformations brought about by the mid-century's events—and directly experienced by Eglītis.

Piecas dienas' Klaudijs Velks is the son of a former factory director. His father's leadership had been very successful in the 1930s, but his father died soon after the Soviet occupation began, having been arrested and deported to Siberia. As his successor, the factory's former janitor, Žanis Gnēze, also a former member of the underground Communist party, is appointed by the Soviet authorities as the new director despite having no previous experience. After the war's end, Velks becomes Gnēze's deputy and stabilizes the production, while at the same time Velks also nurtures the idea of avenging his father's death—as he knows that

Gnēze was responsible for the fact that his family members' names ended up on a deportation list in 1941. The author delves into elaborate reflections upon whether or not Velks's revenge fantasies might be considered meaningful, and these reflections help the narrator to hold the plot together. These reflections are especially important as a narrative device, as they allow for introducing detailed descriptions of relevant past events, particularly those that depict the Communist takeover in 1940. One such reflective episode describes the arrival of the newly appointed factory director, Gnēze, who is met with near-unanimous rejection. However, those who dare to protest openly are soon subjected to repressions.

In *Piecas dienas*, Eglītis also colorfully portrays the first congress of the Union of Latvian Soviet writers, which took place in Riga on June 13–14, 1941, and he offers a harsh criticism of Soviet cultural policies. In the field of culture, the strong canon called 'socialist realism' had been imposed on Soviet writers and artists as early as 1932 and became omnipresent; it was also later imposed on the newly occupied territories (Günther 2018, 17–18), with the effect that, by the time the Union of Latvian Soviet writers was established in 1940, these Soviet principles already excluded any alternative thought or method (Briedis 2010). The new political rulers created a rigorous system for supervising, co-writing, and editing literary texts that should display their (party-approved) ideological value while at the same time suppressing any individual creativity. (The above cases of Visvaldis Lāms and Ēvalds Vilks are characteristic of the prevailing climate.) Such a complex undertaking was hardly comparable with the previous era of tsarist censorship, which had consisted of a single person looking at texts to catch potentially subversive content; the Soviet system was much more multi-layered and repressive (Berelis 1999, 107). For their ideological purposes, Soviet authorities enlisted well-known cultural personalities who agreed to cooperate with the regime; they provided these chosen literati with substantial resources in exchange for demanding that they promote the official ideology. Thus, for example, Andrejs Upīts, a well-known author and long-standing leftist (and oppositional) critic, suddenly acquired the status of the most powerful interpreter of literary activities (Vāvere 2001).

As it happened, one of the most tragic experiences for the Latvian population—the mass deportations of June 14, 1941—coincided with the last day of the first congress of Latvian Soviet writers. In his novel, Eglītis depicts the ideologically charged atmosphere of this congress, sharply satirizing the official speakers who had been recruited from the ranks of less talented Latvian authors, as well as from among officially invited guests from the Russian Federation and other Soviet republics. In fact, *Piecas dienas* is one of the most critical texts that Anšlavs Eglītis produced. He wrote this work after already being separated from his native country for more than three decades and with no realistic prospect of returning home under the conditions of the Cold War (which, ultimately, he never did). His father, Viktors Eglītis, who stayed behind, was arrested by the Soviet communist regime as early as the fall of 1944, and died before his trial was officially finished. Even the date and location of his death remain unclear, as does the place of his burial—presumably, a mass grave. Viktors Eglītis was officially rehabilitated only in 1991 in the independent Republic of Latvia. In this regard, one can see how Anšlavs Eglītis, in this semi-autobiographical novel wherein the protagonist's father has been murdered by the regime, is not just airing political resentments, but also finding an outlet for some of the personal traumas that the Soviet occupation wrought for him—much like how his novel *Ilze* bore the personal touch of being based on his mother-in-law's experience with the Soviet regime.

Literature in the Independent Baltic States after 1991: Jaan Kross

In the Baltic countries, it only became possible to tackle freely the issue of military occupation after the independent states were re-established in 1991. Important changes in society had already taken place in the preceding decade, as "there was an important movement of national awakening in the 1980s" that turned attention toward memory (Davoliūte 2012, 107). These swift changes provided new opportunities for writers, including for Jaan Kross, who had been negotiating Estonia throughout his career (Hasselblatt 2006, 686). However, only gradually was Kross able to tackle the more specific issue of Estonian statehood:

> [A]t the beginning of the 1980s, with the Estonians not being able even to dream of their own restored state, and all publications being rigidly watched by Soviet censorship, the notion of "nation" (*rahvus*) naturally excluded any shade of a "state" (*riik*) as a political entity. However, as we come to Kross' latest historical fiction which, as a matter of fact, reaches the threshold of the new independence and is partly written in Estonia as a restored sovereign state on the world map, a new light is shed on the entire cycle of Kross' historical narrative. (Talvet 2000, 164)

By the 1990s, Kross had already written numerous works of historical fiction, portraying characters in different historical circumstances while scrutinizing their willingness either to adapt themselves to the actual situation or to try to protest. His approach provided a continuation of an important tradition of the historical novel, already established in the early stages of romantic nationalism in the 19th century (Kaljundi, Laanes, and Pikkanen 2015). An important feature of Kross's fiction is the overlapping boundaries among different social strata that one usually presumes would occupy strictly divided living spaces. For instance, the Baltic German nobleman Timotheus von Bock, the protagonist of his novel *Keisri Hull* (1978) (*The Czar's Madman*, translated in 1992), provides a challenge not only to the Russian Tsar Alexander I but also to the social norms of his immediate surroundings, as, in 1817, he marries an Estonian peasant woman (Salumets 2000b, 178). From the author's point of view, it is important to tackle the shared fate of the Baltic community:

> For both, Baltic Germans and the Estonian population, were affected by the established-outsider relations they together formed. As unequal as they were, neither could escape the influence of the other. The result was a continuously changing and hybrid rather than fixed and monolithic identity. (Salumets 1998, 172)

Throughout his career, Kross's historical novels included indirect references to the Soviet reality. Later, he turned to semi-autobiographical fiction. In his novel *Wikmani poisid* (1988) ("The Wikman Boys"), Kross introduced an autobiographical character, Jaan Sirkel, to whom he also returned in his late novel *Paigallend* (1998) (*Treading Air*; translated in 2003), which brought together the different strands of his earlier literary activities. In this latter novel, Kross documents the occupation of the country through the eyes of a character on the margins of political events—a widespread strategy in the tradition of the European historical novel, according to Richard Maxwell (2009), which was also explored in literary representations of the totalitarianism period. The story told by Jaan Sirkel traces the novel's main character, Ullo Paerand, who experiences and reflects on various 20th-century political transformations in his country, with especially vivid descriptions of life in independent Estonia in the late 1930s, as well as of political maneuvers that led to the Soviet invasion and occupation in 1940.

Similar to what we find in his Latvian counterpart Eglītis's novels, the Estonian author is also able to demonstrate how well-known places change radically under occupation. Contrary to the perception of 19th-century romantic nationalism, which sought the origin of national movements in the countryside, Jaan Kross from the very beginning concentrated on urban life, looking at Estonia's towns and cities as a place where high culture would develop. *Paigallend* is a characteristic example of how "the Estonian capital Tallinn, the main place of action in Kross' novels, was itself magically transformed into a living character" (Talvet 2000, 158). In Tallinn, the density of urban life also helps Kross to describe a large variety of the population:

> Like a hero of a picaresque novel, Ullo moves through different spheres of Estonian society, providing the reader with an access both to the "outside" and the "inside"

of it and letting him see it from the changing time perspective, as the narrative develops from the first Estonian republic to the post-war years. (Talvet 2000, 167)

During the Soviet period, Kross had elaborated a specific technique of the first-person narrative that allowed him to split time and narration (cf. Bhabha [1994] 2004, 242). In the opinion of Lea Pild, this allowed him to express his views without inserting direct authorial judgments and, thereby, to circumvent Soviet censorship (Pild 2012, 11). "The main narrative vehicle which made Kross, from his first narratives, differ from others and gradually helped him to build up his original style was the use of interior monologue" (Talvet 2000, 158).

Meanwhile, the core of his narrative itself was often provided by the protagonist's conflict with institutions of power and their representatives, a model similar to that explored in Eglītis's *Piecas dienas*. It is important to point out here that the potential for revenge—which runs through the pages of Eglītis's novels—is reminiscent of a particular type of English Renaissance tragedy, of which Shakespeare's *Hamlet, Prince of Denmark* (1601) is the most prominent example. In fact, Estonian writers and theater-makers were constantly (in a more or less disguised form) making references to *Hamlet's* plot throughout the Soviet period (Kruuspere 2006). This paradigm is crucially important for Kross's historical novels as well: "Their nucleus was Hamlet's dilemma whether in an alienated, corrupt or totalitarian society an (intellectually or spiritually advanced) individual should rebel against injustice, or conform to the historical circumstances" (Talvet 2000, 156).

In *Paigallend*, Kross at times mingles his own experience with that of both Jaan Sirkel and Ullo Paerand. Ullo, the principal character, accidentally gets involved in the Estonian government structures of the late 1930s. Thus, he also becomes a direct witness of one of the chief turning points in Estonia's history: the forced surrender in June 1940 to the advance of Soviet tanks in the border city of Narva in northeast Estonia.

> Some time—maybe only half a minute—before the first vehicles left the other side and reached this side of the border, a slight easterly wind began to blow the strong and alien Russian petrol fumes in our direction. The drone of the vehicles approached us and could be felt in every cell of your body, the dust raised by the vehicles had not yet reached us, the boys of the border guard stood to attention—then [the Estonian Colonel Johan] Laidoner turned to his entourage. I was standing three paces behind, between us were Captains Jaakson and Hint with a gap between them, so I saw his mouth move and heard him clearly when he said: "Gentlemen, I hope that what we have built up over the last twenty years will, if needs be, hold out for another two hundred." (Kross [1998] 2003, 194–95)

At the same time, Ullo is also a poet, and Kross includes examples of Ullo's free-verse poetry in the text of the novel—the intellectual content and stylistic features of which resemble Kross's own post-war poetry. In fact, Kross had already started writing when he was still in the Soviet labor camp, and *Paigallend* features an almost-authentic description of his writings being tracked down at the time by the authorities, and the subsequent conversation with a Russian military official. As the narrator points out, during the conversation, the official expresses widespread beliefs that still drive some policy makers today:

> 'But right from the start in 1918, that republic [independent Estonia] was nothing more than an armed revolt against Soviet power. Your so-called War of Independence was a revolt against the Soviet Union. Leaders of such revolts have to be shot. Their class base has to be eradicated. Those elements operating under their influence have to be scattered. To the taiga, the tundra, the steppe, the desert. Whatever.'
> I asked: 'Does this all mean that everyone who exhibited loyalty to Estonia over the period of twenty years is a criminal?'
> 'But of course. Everyone. Each in his own individual way.' (Kross [1998] 2003, 162)

Note that, despite highly unfavorable conditions in his occupied homeland, Jaan Kross was among those who made a conscious choice to remain in the country in which he was born, in the belief that "if there is to be hope, we cannot afford to leave our 'home' or forget the stories of its past" (Salumets 1998, 171). Kross allows several of his novels' principal characters to follow the same pattern. Thomas Salumets elegantly summarizes one of the central episodes in *Paigallend*, wherein Ullo, toward the end of the war, together with his wife Maret

> are on their bikes en route from Tallinn to the west coast of Estonia. Like so many Estonians really did, they are fleeing the country from the invading Russians. As dawn breaks, it is still raining, they stop, and wonder if they are doing the right thing when, in Ullo's word, 'thousands are fleeing but a million have to stay'. They turn their bikes around and ride back to Tallinn. (Salumets 2000b, 178)

According to Estonian scholar Jüri Talvet, "if we were to speak of Kross as a writer of politically orientated historical fiction, politics should be understood in a fairly broad sense—as a vehicle of a nation's self-realization, as well as an active part of its culture" (Talvet 2000, 165). To this, I would add that Kross's is the voice of a humanist paying tribute to the suffering and hope of millions of people still living under the conditions of oppression, occupation, colonization, and war.

Conclusion

The novels of the two distinguished Baltic writers discussed here indicate numerous ethical dilemmas that merit close examination. At the same time, these novels should also be read—and in the early 2020s perhaps more so than ever before—as an honest and unsparing testimony of the oppression that the Baltic states suffered under their offensive military occupiers for more than half a century. The role of the Soviet Union, alongside the cruelty of the short-lived period of Nazi occupation, is, in this perspective, certainly not to be underestimated. In the words of Ian D. Armour:

> only a blinkered apologist for Soviet communism would deny that the Soviet Union had its own imperialist counter-vision, rooted partly in the commitment to defend communism and extend its sway if possible, but partly also in the Soviet conviction that the territories lost after 1918 should be gathered back under Moscow's control. (Armour 2021, 122)

Indeed, due to the merciless policies of the Stalinist era, dramatic changes in the occupied Baltic territories became an immediate reality. "In this new aggressive spirit, the governments employed violence and even terrorism against their perceived enemies" (Senn 2005, 21).

According to Jüri Talvet, "what is always rejected [in Kross's fiction], is the violent totalitarianism of any kind (both that of the Nazi Germany and the Stalinist Soviet Russia), the Western complex of superiority and arrogant negligence of the 'other'—especially, if the latter is 'smaller'" (Talvet 2000, 166). The 20th century provided Latvian and Estonian writers with painful first-hand experience of military occupation, on which, in an attempt to come to terms with the realities of the past, these authors reflected constantly; indeed, the exemplary texts explored above were produced across a period spanning about five decades. The works of the Latvian and Estonian writers discussed in this chapter might, in this context, be considered their expanded autobiographies, which, in an apt formulation by Estonian literary scholar Tiina Kirss, "comes to mean not only a maximal inclusiveness and interweaving of narratives from many sources and involving many characters, but the mirroring and measuring of the autobiographical story over and against these stories" (Kirss 2000, 276).

The textual richness of these novels thus serves as another testimony that "all cultures are involved in one another, none is single and pure, all are hybrid, heterogenous, extraordinarily differentiated, and unmonolithic" (Said [1993] 1994, xxv). It is therefore universally important—across time and across place—that we never neglect the opportunity to contemplate the complexity of human experience. Even, and perhaps especially, those human experiences that play out under the most unfavorable conditions.

Notes

1. This research is funded by the State research program *Letonika—Fostering a Latvian and European Society* Project VPP-LETONIKA-2022/3-0003 *Narrative, Form and Voice: Embeddedness of literature in culture and society.*

References

Annus, Epp. 2012. "The Problem of Soviet Colonialism in the Baltics." *Journal of Baltic Studies* 43, no. 1 (March): 21–45.

———. 2018. *Soviet Postcolonial Studies: A View from the Western Borderlands.* London: Routledge.

Armour, Ian D. 2021. *A History of Eastern Europe 1918 to the Present: Modernisation, Ideology and Nationality.* London: Bloomsbury Academic.

Berelis, Guntis. 1999. *Latviešu literatūras vēsture: No pirmajiem rakstiem līdz 1999. gadam.* Riga: Zvaigzne ABC.

Bhabha, Homi. [1994] 2004. *The Location of Culture.* London: Routledge.

Briedis, Raimonds. 2010. *Teksta cenzūras īsais kurss: prozas teksts un cenzūra padomju gados Latvijā.* Riga: LU Literatūras, folkloras un mākslas institūts.

Davoliūte, Violeta. 2012. "'We Are All Deportees': The Trauma of Displacement and the Consolidation of National Identity during the Popular Movement in Lithuania." In *Maps of Memory: Trauma, Identity and Exile in Deportation Memoirs from the Baltic States,* edited by Violeta Davoliūte and Tomas Balkelis, 107–36. Vilnius: Institute of Lithuanian Literature and Folklore.

Eglāja-Kristsone, Eva. 2018. "Reading Literary History through the Archives: The Case of the Latvian Literary Journal *Karogs*." In *The Literary Field under Communist Rule,* edited by Aušra Jurgutienė and Dalia Satkauskytė, 201–12. Boston: Academic Studies Press.

Eglītis, Anšlavs. 1952. *Laimīgie.* Bruklina: Grāmatu Draugs.

———. 1959. *Ilze.* Bruklina: Grāmatu Draugs.

———. [1976] 1992. *Piecas dienas.* Riga: Preses Nams.

Günther, Hans. 2018. "How Socialist Realism Was Exported to Eastern European Countries and How They Got Rid of It." In *Socialist Realism in Central and Eastern European Literatures: Institutions, Dynamics, Discourses,* edited by Evgeny Dobrenko and Natalia Jonsson-Skradol, 17–24. London: Anthem Press.

Hasselblatt, Cornelius. 2006. *Geschichte der estnischen Literatur*. Berlin: De Gruyter.

Hiršs, Harijs. 1982. "Komentāri: Divpadsmit kilometri." In Vilks, Ēvalds, *Kopoti raksti*, Vol. 2, edited by Harijs Hiršs, 430–35. Riga: Liesma.

Kaljundi, Linda, Eneken Laanes, and Ilona Pikkanen, eds. 2015. *Novels, Histories, Novel Nations: Historical Fiction and Cultural Memory in Finland and Estonia*. Helsinki: Finnish Literature Society SKS.

Kasekamp, Andres. 2018. *A History of the Baltic States*. 2nd ed. London: Palgrave.

Kirss, Tiina. 2000. "Playing the Fool in the Territory of Memory: Jaan Kross' Autobiographical Fictions of the Twentieth Century." *Journal of Baltic Studies* 31, no. 3 (Fall): 273–94.

Kõresaar, Ene. 2007. "The Remembrance Culture of the Second World War in Estonia as Presented in Post-Soviet Life Stories: On the Logic of Comparison between the Soviet and the Nazi Occupations." In *We Have Something in Common: The Baltic Memory*, edited by Anneli Mikhelev and Benedikts Kalnačs, 35–60. Tallinn: The Under and Tuglas Centre of the Estonian Academy of Sciences.

Kramer, Mark. 2014. "Stalin, Soviet Policy and the Establishment of a Communist Bloc in Eastern Europe, 1941–1948." In *Stalin and Europe: Imitation and Domination, 1928–1953*, edited by Timothy Snyder and Ray Brandon, 264–94. Oxford: OUP.

Kross, Jaan. 1988. *Wikmani poisid*. Tallinn: Eesti Raamat.

———. [1978] 1992. *The Czar's Madman*. Translated from the Estonian by George Kurman. London: The Harvill Press.

———. [1998] 2003. *Treading Air*. Translated from the Estonian by Eric Dickens. London: The Harvill Press.

Kruuspere, Piret. 2006. "Is It Ghosting? The Motifs and Allusions of *Hamlet* in Estonian Drama." In *Different Inputs—Same Output? Autonomy and Dependence of the Arts under Different Social-economic Conditions: The Estonian Example*, edited by Cornelius Hasselblatt, 35–47. Maastricht: Shaker.

Lāms, Visvaldis [1958] 1989. *Kāvu blāzmā*. Riga: Liesma.

Laurušaite, Laura. 2008. "The Lithuanian and Latvian Exile Novel: An Attempt at a Postcolonial Perspective." In *Back to Baltic Memory: Lost and Found in Literature 1940–1968*, edited by Eva Eglāja-Kristsone and Benedikts Kalnačs, 170–82. Rīga: LU Literatūras, folkloras un mākslas institūts.

Org, Andrus. 2009. "Kross, Jaan." In *300 Baltic Writers: Estonia, Latvia, Lithuania. A Reference Guide to Authors and Their Works*, edited by Eva Eglāja-Kristsone, Virginijus Gasiliūnas, and Anneli Mihkelev, 158–60. Vilnius: Institute of Lithuanian Literature and Folklore.

Maxwell, Richard. 2009. *The Historical Novel in Europe, 1650–1950*. Cambridge: Cambridge University Press.

Minins, Aldis. 2015. "Latvia, 1918–1920: A Civil War?" *Journal of Baltic Studies* 46, no. 1 (Spring): 49–63.

Pild, Lea. 2012. "Introduction from the Editor." In *Jaan Kross and Russian Culture. Acta Slavica Estonica II*, edited by Lea Pild, 9–14. Tartu: University of Tartu Press.

Rozītis, Juris. 2005. *Displaced Literature: Images of Time and Space in Latvian Novels Depicting the First Years of the Latvian Postwar Exile*. Stockholm: Stockholm University.

Rudzītis, Jānis. 1977. *Raksti*. Västerås: Ziemeļblāzma.

Said, Edward W. [1993] 1994. *Culture and Imperialism*. New York: Vintage Books.

Salumets, Thomas. 1998. "Escape Artists and Freedom's Children." *Interlitteraria* 3: 165–86.

———. 2000a. "Introduction." *Journal of Baltic Studies* 31, no. 3 (Fall): 225–36.

———. 2000b. "Jaan Kross: Negotiating Nation." *Interlitteraria* 5: 171–85.

Saro, Anneli. 2014. "Superimposed Soviet Colonialism: The Processing of Soviet Memories in Estonian Literature, Theatre and Film." In *(Post-)Colonialism across Europe: Transcultural History and National Memory*, edited by Dirk Göttsche and Axel Dunker, 343–58. Bielefeld: Aisthesis.

Schulze-Englert, Frank. 2013. "Irritating Europe." In *The Oxford Handbook of Postcolonial Studies*, edited by Graham Huggan, 669–91. Oxford: OUP.

Senn, Alfred Eric. 2005. "Baltic Battleground." In *The Hidden and Forbidden History of Latvia under the Soviet and Nazi Occupations, 1940–1991*. Symposium of the Commission of Historians of Latvia. Vol. 14, edited by Valters Nollendorfs and Erwin Oberländer, 17–32. Riga: Institute of the History of Latvia.

Snyder, Timothy. 2010. *Bloodlands: Europe between Hitler and Stalin*. New York: Basic Books.

Talvet, Jüri. 2000. "'Paigallend,' or the Building of Estonia in the Novels of Jaan Kross." *Interlitteraria* 5: 152–70.

Tamm, Marek. 2006. "Displaced History? A New 'Regime of Historicity' among the Baltic Historians in Exile (1940s–1960s)." *Storia della Storiografia* 69, no. 1: 129–45.

Undusk, Jaan. 2006. "History Writing in Exile and in the Homeland after World War II: Some Comparative Aspects." In *Different Inputs—Same Output? Autonomy and Dependence of the Arts under Different Social-economic Conditions: The Estonian Example*, edited by Cornelius Hasselblatt, 127–44. Maastricht: Shaker.

Vāvere, Vera. 2001. "Andrejs Upīts." In *Latviešu rakstnieku portreti: Laikmeta krustpunktos*, edited by Viktors Hausmanis, Benedikts Kalnačs, and Ieva Kalniņa, 229–82. Riga: Zinātne.

Vilks, Ēvalds. [1963] 1982. "Divpadsmit kilometri." In *Kopoti raksti* [= Collected Works], Vol. 2, edited by Harijs Hiršs, 263–336. Riga: Liesma.

Zelče, Vita. 2011. "Latvia and the Baltic in Russian Historiography." In *The Geopolitics of History in Latvian-Russian Relations*, edited by Nils Muižnieks, 31–58. Riga: Academic Press of the University of Latvia.

CHAPTER 14

Occupied by Comrades?

The Concealed Story of the Soviet Military Presence in Mecklenburg and Western Pomerania after 1945 in Uwe Johnson's *Jahrestage* (1970–1983)

MEINOLF SCHUMACHER

A literary work faces particular challenges if it is to portray a military occupation whose memory is associated with an imposed and an imposing censorship and silence. Archives are not available to the author. He can hardly interview contemporary witnesses. Nor can he expect his book to be read by the very people who could remember the events themselves. Of course, if one reads such a book with some temporal distance, the situation may have changed thoroughly: the former political taboo no longer exists, and the archives are open—however, most of the contemporary witnesses are no longer alive, nor is the author. Imagine next that the book can be purchased in any bookstore, even in the region where it was once forbidden. Even then, new difficulties arise: much historical and geographical background knowledge, which the author took for granted that his readers would know, is no longer present. On the other hand, in the meantime, anyone who wished to be informed of the facts of the occupation could simply reach for a specialized book—or the internet.

What, then, would be special ways of accessing such a work of literature today, and wherein lies its value? Can it be located within the framework of today's culture of remembrance? Is it accessible through a post-colonially informed reading? To approach the answers to such questions, a thorough analysis of the design of occupation as a literary theme is necessary.

Johnson's "Factual Inventions" from Mecklenburg and the Absence of Western Pomerania from *Anniversaries*

This chapter is about the novel *Jahrestage*, written by the German author Uwe Johnson (1934–1984) primarily in New York, NY, and in Sheerness, Kent. In the recently published complete English translation, *Anniversaries* (Johnson [1970–

1983] 2018, cited here as *JA*),[1] it runs to almost 1,700 pages. In the original, the four volumes—published in 1970, 1971, 1973, and 1983 by the West German publisher Suhrkamp (cited here as *JT*)—exceed a total of 1,800 pages. The extent to which the title *Jahrestage* reflects the book's structuring principle is somewhat lost in translation: it connotes not simply *Anniversaries* but also the individual days of a year, and it is these daily entries, covering the period of one year, that make up the novel.

From August 21, 1967 to August 20, 1968, the day before Warsaw Pact forces invaded Czechoslovakia, *Jahrestage* records the everyday life in New York City of Gesine Cresspahl, a German-born employee at an American bank, and her daughter Marie. It contains reflections on experiences of racism and crime in the United States, as well as on events in the world at large (notably the war in Vietnam), for which the principal source, often quoted at length, is *The New York Times*. Political events and Gesine's personal life converge with the advent of the Prague Spring, when her bank plans to send her to Prague to negotiate a major credit deal with the new Czechoslovakian leadership. While one thread of the novel follows these current events, another opens up a historical perspective, recalling Gesine Cresspahl's life, from her birth in March 1933 to her departure in July 1953 from the German Democratic Republic (GDR). The book thus also assumes the character of a(n East) German chronicle, recounting how the Nazi dictatorship took hold in a small town in Germany, followed by World War II, the Red Army occupation, and the takeover of society by Stalinism in the early years of the GDR. It is at this point that the *Jahrestage* of the original title indeed become *Anniversaries*, days on which particular events are remembered. For what is being recounted are not simply occurrences *From a Year in the Life of Gesine Cresspahl*, as the English subtitle would have it, but rather events from across the course of her life: *Aus dem Leben von Gesine Cresspahl*. This record of a year is interspersed with biographical elements recalling the protagonist's childhood and youth. Some of these recollections are channeled through diary-like notes purporting to be Gesine's own, tape recordings, or historical documents, while others are presented in the form of conversations with her daughter Marie or with the dead, and finally in the voice of a narrator whose name and the author's are the same (van Laak 2009, 275–90).

In crafting this novel, Johnson consulted historical sources (e.g., Eggert 1967 on the end of the war in the western Pomeranian town of Stralsund) and incorporated elements of his research into the fictional narrative about Gesine, her family (particularly her father, Heinrich), and her friends.[2] To this technique, Johnson himself gave the name of "factual inventions" (*tatsächliche Erfindungen*) (Johnson [1979] 1988, 79). As always when a literary narrative deals with historical events, it is not always easy to be aware of the level on which it is operating at a

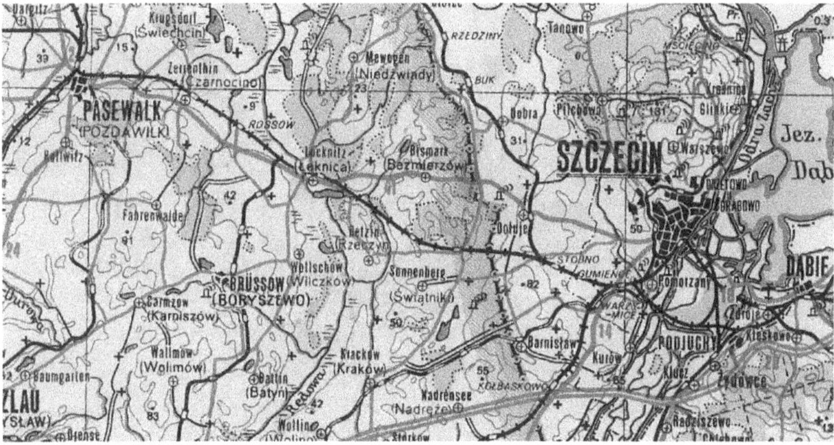

Figure 1. 'Szczecin' from the official *Mapa Polski* from 1947.

given moment: is it that of the reality of the historical events themselves or rather that of the fictional story whose background they form? This ambiguity need not be a disadvantage—for it is precisely out of this tension between historical truth and narrative invention that the novel, as a literary form of historical memory, places itself in its own right alongside the works of historical scholarship.

Just how freely Johnson compiles even his literary topography from the historical and geographical source material (Baker 1995; Fahlke 1992; Mecklenburg 1997, 336–409) may be illustrated by the following scene. It is Easter 1938, and Gesine and her parents, the cabinetmaker Heinrich Cresspahl (in the novel often simply called 'Cresspahl') and his wife Lisbeth, are visiting relatives in Podejuch (now Podjuchy), a suburb of Stettin (Szczecin).[3] Traveling by train from Pasewalk, they are reported to have "crossed the Pomeranian border between Grambow and Stöwen" (*JA* 1, 547; *JT* 2, 633). While there was no such thing as a "Pomeranian border" in that place and time, any confusion on the part of the reader cannot simply be resolved with reference to poetic license, which allows completely free invention: the matter is complicated by the fact that, today, there is indeed a border between the two villages of Grambow and Stöwen (today Polish Stobno) in western Pomerania, albeit one drawn in 1945—Poland's western border, as redrawn by the victorious Allied powers after World War II.

What, then, does this equation of the "Pomeranian border" with the Polish frontier signify, given that it occurs with reference to a period *before* the German invasion of Poland, the ultimate political and geographic result of which—the loss of Germany's eastern lands—it seems to anticipate?

At this point, it is worth giving some historical and geographical background. Pomerania was a province of Prussia until 1945, when it was wholly occupied

Fig. 2. Mecklenburg-Vorpommern. Charity stamps from 1945.

by Soviet troops and partitioned by the Allied governments. The eastern portion, known in German as *Hinterpommern*, was assigned to the reconstituted Polish state, while the western part, traditionally called *Vorpommern*, remained part of the Soviet occupation zone and thus, under international law, of Germany. Standing as an exception was the easternmost part of western Pomerania, around the provincial capital Stettin, which, after some uncertainty about its status, was also assigned to Poland and received the Polish name *Szczecin* (Aischmann 2008). The military government merged the larger part of western Pomerania—the portion within the Soviet zone, in which the GDR was established in 1949—with neighboring Mecklenburg, to form a new federal state or province known as Mecklenburg-Vorpommern. Although there were few historical links between the two parts, save for geographical proximity, the occupation established a political unit (Brunner 2006; Nochotowitsch 2009; see the postage stamps in Fig. 2) that was revived when Mecklenburg-Vorpommern became a constituent state of a unified Germany in 1990 (Müller 1999).

Meanwhile, the same Soviet authorities that had first established the state in 1945 ordered 'Vorpommern' to be struck from its name less than two years later. No official reason was given. Johnson's novel reflects these events thus:

> The revolutionary Red Army had even left them Mecklenburg as an autonomous province; the irritating addition, "-Vorpommern," had been removed by the law of March 1, 1947, so now they had less to say and really you had to chalk that up as a win for Mecklenburg. The province of Mecklenburg. *Land Mecklenburg.* (*JA* 2, 1268; *JT* 4, 1457f.)

Thereafter, a place called 'Pomerania' officially existed only in Poland, while the part that had remained German was forbidden from keeping the name. Such ancient Pomeranian cities as Stralsund, Greifswald, or Anklam now found themselves in the province of Mecklenburg—at least until a law passed by the GDR government on July 23, 1952 disestablished the constituent states and divided the country into smaller districts (*Bezirke*). 'Pomerania' remained a taboo term; 'Mecklenburg' less so, as Gesine explains to Marie: "You were only allowed to say 'Mecklenburg' in a linguistic or anthropological sense. Otherwise, it was now three districts: Rostock, Schwerin and Neubrandenburg" (*JA* 2, 1617; *JT* 4, 1837). A collateral loss that she particularly regrets is the abolition of the state flag: "Another piece of one's origins wiped out" (*JA* 2, 1617; *JT* 4, 1837). Yet the novel does not explicitly lament the fact that *Pomeranian* heritage, in particular, was wiped out: Johnson seems to have accepted the disappearance of a regional identity by order of the Soviet military government.[4] Only in the years immediately preceding the downfall of the East German regime (and thus after Johnson's death) did it once more become acceptable to use the name "Pomerania" in relation to historical events (Buske 1997, 77–83), whereas in contemporary contexts, this taboo remained in place for as long as the GDR existed. The lifting of this ban was greeted with widespread relief that "nobody any longer had to flinch at the mention of the word 'Pomerania' and cast anxious glances over their shoulder" (Müller-Waldeck 1991, 331); in the GDR, using the term meant being branded a revisionist and suffering the consequences. Given that a veil of silence lay over the region that had remained German within the historical territory of Pomerania, there was a certain logic to identifying the Polish frontier with that of Pomerania: after all, the official view—first of the Soviet authorities and then of the GDR—was that 'Pomerania' began only beyond the Polish frontier, with the Szczecin Voivodeship (now West Pomeranian Voivodeship).

Victors and Vanquished

That said, in *Anniversaries*, Johnson is not shy to discuss many other matters on which the GDR imposed silence, including the conduct of Soviet troops in the territories they had conquered and occupied.[5] This problem was not limited to German or formerly German lands. "Surviving the arrival of the Soviet army one way or another became something of a central and eastern European myth" (Piskorski 2013, 189).[6] Yet it was on crossing the Reich's old frontiers in East Prussia and Pomerania that the hatred felt by so many Red Army soldiers for the Germans erupted in a heightened degree of violence toward the civilian population and women in particular (Merridale 2006, 328–51; Naimark 1995, 69–83; Zeidler 1996, 135–67; see also Kopelew [1975] 1983, 91–138; Solschenizyn [1974] 1976).

In his novel, Johnson situates the Cresspahl family home in Jerichow, a fictitious town (not to be confused with the actual town of that name in Saxony-

Anhalt) on the northwestern edge of Mecklenburg, which, like the county seat of Gneez and the coastal resort of Rande, had initially fallen under British occupation (*JA* 1, 853–56; *JT* 2, 983–87) before being exchanged for a slice of Russian-occupied Berlin (*JA* 1, 866; *JT* 2, 998).[7] This setting not only allows the author to indulge in a counter-factual thought experiment—"If Jerichow had ended up in the West" (*JA* 2, 1075–79; *JT* 3, 1240–43);[8] it above all allows him to compare the policies pursued by the respective occupying forces. Moreover—at least initially—it leaves the much-described atrocities perpetrated by Soviet troops in the sphere of rumor, bolstered with fake images by Nazi propaganda (*JA* 2, 893; *JT* 3, 1030f.). Accordingly, what the novel describes are not the excesses of combat troops elated with victory and seeking their reward,[9] but the conduct of representatives of a military administration that is already firmly established.

Yet here, too, accounts and conversations that tell of women being raped increasingly shift from rumor to reality (*JA* 2, 924f., 953f, 976, 996; see also *JA* 1, 119; 2, 1410f.; *JT* 3, 1066, 1099f., 1126, 1148f.; see also *JT* 1, 140; 4, 1613). The narration sometimes works with misunderstandings taken up productively—for instance, when a Soviet soldier enters Otto Quade's hardware store to ask for a faucet. The soldier pronounces the German word *Wasserhahn* as *Wassergahn*, which is misunderstood by the shopkeeper's wife Bergie, who lives in fear of rape and has made herself look as unattractive as possible to escape soldiers' attentions. Bergie Quade takes *Wassergahn* to mean 'ins Wasser gehen,' that is, to go into the water—in other words, to drown herself, a last resort of many women who sought to avoid rape or found themselves overcome with shame:

> "Faucet," the soldier had said to Bergie Quade in his thick, *h*-less Russian accent: *Wassergahn* instead of *Wasserhahn*. Bergie—who, following the then-current advice, was dowdily dressed, with a filthy face and a rag smeared with chicken shit under her skirt—had answered, with typical Quadish presence of mind: *Wassergehn*? I'm not going into the water. Don't need to. Are you wanting to know who from around here's gone into the water? You mean drowned in the marsh, in the Baltic …? (*JA* 2, 896; *JT* 3, 1033; see Krappmann 2012, 248, 547f.; Michaelis 1983, 257f.)

Even the assurance offered by the town commandant of Jerichow "that he [the commandant] really meant it about the Red Army's chivalry toward women" (*JA* 2, 1025; *JT* 3, 1183) seems to convey the exact opposite (see Naimark 1995, 83–140).

Much like their American counterparts, the British military government had begun by confronting the German population with its share of the responsibility for Nazi crimes (Buschmeier 2022a, 324–30). This was done in part by means of photographs from the death camps, a tactic to which *Anniversaries* also refers (Zetzsche 1994, 256–70; see Brink 1998): "The means of administering the shock: a photograph the British took in the Bergen-Belsen concentration camp and printed in the newspaper they authorized in Lübeck after the war" (*JA* 1, 200; *JT* 1, 232). These images were intended to create an enduring sense of collective German guilt, and, in this, they appear to have been successful—certainly in the case of young Gesine Cresspahl (Mecklenburg 1997, 301–12; see *JA* 1, 739; *JT* 2, 851f.). In the novel, this appears to be confirmed by the author's voice, rather than by the protagonist's child self of 1945, at the point where Gesine recalls:

> It affected my group: I may have been twelve years old at the time, but I belong to a national group that massacred an excessive number of members of another group (to a child, even the spectacle of a single victim would have been excessive). (*JA* 1, 200; *JT* 1, 232)

In addition, residents of the British zone were forced to watch the removal of bodies from concentration camps and, in some cases, to assist in their burial:[10] "The British had made dead people public in Jerichow. They were the Nazis' prisoners from Neuengamme concentration camp, twelve miles southeast of Hamburg, along with its Mecklenburg branch camps, Boizenburg and Reiherhorst in Wöbbelin" (*JA* 2, 963; *JT* 3, 1111f.). The prisoners had been crammed into the ships *Cap Arcona*, *Thielbek*, and *Athen*, which sank under British fire (Emmerich 2005, 300–4). Many of the dead were washed ashore, and it was decided that they should be buried inland for political reasons and to make a point: "The MPs [military police] made the Germans leave their houses to look at the cargo as it was driven down Town Street to the cemetery at a walking pace" (*JA* 2, 966; *JT* 3, 1114).

> After the dirt had been shoveled onto the mass grave, the British fired a salute into the air. At the cemetery gate stood a sergeant, holding a box in front of him, and on this box he stamped the ration cards. Anyone who had not accepted the dead would not eat. (*JA* 2, 966; *JT* 3, 1115)

As soon as they took the reins of power, the Soviet authorities put an end to this "'shock' policy" (Kogon 1946, 328). In the novel, it was Pontiy, the commandant of Jerichow, who "stopped the education of the German people by means of the overland transport of bodies. This particular flotsam had to be collected in the cemeteries of the coastal villages, outside the territory under his command" (*JA* 2, 967; *JT* 3, 1116).

Since this was the actual policy of the occupying powers, the question arises: why did the Soviets put less faith in re-educating the Germans? One possible explanation is the Marxist theory of fascism, according to which National Socialism was the expression not of the German mentality (as Americans tended to believe), but of capitalist dictatorship over the proletariat, "as predictable symptoms of the decline of capitalism in its most highly developed phase, imperialism" (*JA* 1, 202; *JT* 1, 234). This allowed the Soviet occupying forces to take a comparatively lenient view of German guilt (Jähner 2019, 310), particularly when those concerned were not industrialists or great landowners (*Junker*), whose guilt required no further proof and who were swiftly expropriated. This fundamentally positive attitude on the part of the Soviets[11] is implied in the novel when the commandant expresses his surprise at the fact that the majority of the local population did not view or welcome the victory over Nazi Germany as a liberation. "During the first week, Pontiy asked his mayor: Why do the Germans see us, their liberators from the yoke of Fascism, and act like we're the devil?" (*JA* 2, 925; *JT* 3, 1068).

Heinrich Cresspahl, who had been installed as mayor of Jerichow by the British and was confirmed in office by the Soviets (*JA* 2, 902f.; *JT* 3, 1041f.) does not venture to answer this question, knowing as he does what the Germans really think of the Soviets: they take the Soviets to be *Untermenschen*, "subhumans" (*JA* 2, 925; *JT* 3, 1068). Nazi propaganda (see *JA* 2, 1562; *JT* 4, 1777) had applied this term not only to the Jews but also—at least since the attack on the Soviet Union and probably due to the notion of 'Jewish bolshevism'—to the 'Russians' (*JA* 1, 201; 2, 893; see also *JA* 2, 1562; *JT* 1, 234; 3, 1030; see also *JT* 4, 1777).[12] Although much effort was made to promote 'friendship' with the Soviet Union (*JA* 2, 1361; *JT* 4, 1559; on this see Behrends 2006), the legacy of widespread Russophobia long outlasted the war: the Soviets may have won, but the Germans felt vastly culturally superior. One aspect of this was the much-shared "rumor that the victors didn't know how to ride bikes" (*JA* 2, 895; *JT* 3, 1033), only how to steal them; a similar story was told with regard to clocks, which they were supposedly unable to wind, and so on (Karasek 1996, 45; Kempowski [1972] 1982, 79f.; Merridale 2006, 356). This disdain (see Volkmann 1994) was then transferred onto those who collaborated with the new occupying power—in the case of Jerichow, onto the mayor, who was tasked with implementing the commandant's (indeed often baffling) orders; the novel conveys this popular antipathy with expressions such as: "Soviets' accomplice," "Soviet lackey," "Russian lackey," "traitor," "Soviet lickspittle" (*JA* 2, 902, 907, 974f., 975; *JT* 3, 1040, 1046f., 1124f.).

Because the Red Army neither found itself broadly welcomed as a liberating force nor thought of itself as charged with the (re-)education of the German people, it was, as the novel suggests, concerned all the more with being respected as the victorious power. This was evident, for instance, in the order to erect a striking monument to the Soviet dead, "a field of honor," (*JA* 2, 988; *JT* 3, 1140) in Jerichow's market square, a place nobody could avoid passing: "So, the obelisk in the middle—marble, with a red star on top and tablets on all four sides" (*JA* 2, 989; *JT* 3, 1141). It was to serve as a visual reminder to all—and at all times—just *who* had won the war ("In other places there'd be an obelisk with a red star on it, lit up at night" [*JA* 2, 997; *JT* 3, 1150]). Reinhart Koselleck is surely correct in arguing that one purpose of these Soviet monuments in East Germany was "to continue writing the victors' history in such a way as to make them protectors of the vanquished" (Koselleck 1979, 266).

But an occupying force that is too insistent on its role as the "winner" ends up achieving nothing so much as the humiliation of the occupied, by constantly driving home the point that they are the losers. The child Gesine is amazed at the liberties the victors feel entitled to take solely on the strength of having won: "That's what winning means, Cresspahl?" (*JA* 2, 918; *JT* 3, 1059). Her father is unable to give a satisfactory answer to this question—and hence the novel gives none either.

The Occupation—"Not Fair"?

"I gather the Russian victors didn't behave well [*sollen nicht fair gewesen sein*]: she said" (*JA* 2, 892; *JT* 3, 1029). Today's readers may well ask just why the occupying Soviet forces *should* have behaved 'fairly' toward the people of Germany, in view of the immense destruction Germans had visited upon Soviet territories and their inhabitants—and all the more so since the skeptical question of whether war crimes had truly been perpetrated only by the SS rather than also the "official" *Wehrmacht* is explicitly put (*JA* 1, 801; *JT* 2, 923): "The SS does things like that./And not the army?"

That the countries occupied, pillaged, and often devastated by Nazi Germany should claim recompense after the war was no more surprising than that the victorious armies, before (and indeed irrespective of) any official agreements regarding reparations or damages (to be paid, respectively, by the state or by individuals), should begin to collect a part of their debt as the spoils of war—in short, as plunder, whether by order or for individual profit (Merridale 2006, 351–57). Among the official reparations demanded by the Soviet Union was the dismantling of industrial plants or railway tracks (*JA* 2, 1124, 1242, 1427; *JT* 4, 1409, 1429; 1631).[13] The alternative—converting East German companies into "Soviet joint-stock corporations"—at least preserved local jobs (*JA* 2, 1214; *JT* 4, 1398).

Finding comfortable billets is likely to be the first concern of any occupying army. Like the British in their zone (*JA* 2, 1006; *JT* 3, 1161f.), the Soviets too claimed entire neighborhoods to house military personnel. In Johnson's Jerichow, along the street known as "the Bäk," "a notice saying 'Requisitioned' was being nailed up on one house after another" (*JA* 2, 904; *JT* 3, 1044). The inhabitants were forced to vacate their houses with immediate effect, the neighborhood was fenced in, "and that was the last time this street was ever seen in Jerichow, to this day" (*JA* 2, 905; *JT* 3, 1044). Such segregated areas in which residential housing had been converted into barracks (see *JA* 2, 1008f.; *JT* 3, 1278) were typical of the Soviet military presence in the Eastern Bloc. Gesine later recalls what a waste of time she found it to spend six years learning Russian, when there was

> not a single Russian in the whole town we were allowed to talk to. They were housed behind high green fences, the officers didn't take public transportation, and when a private climbed over the slats looking for just a bottle of booze. (*JA* 1, 570; *JT* 2, 660)

Not all of the Soviet town commandant's orders could be so easily explained by reference to the exigencies of military administration. Order No. 2 required all residents "to turn in their radios, batteries, typewriters, telephones, microphones, cameras, etc. at Papenbrock's granary within three days." Moreover, "the following day, K.A. Pontiy's Order No. 4 demanded that all gold, silver, or platinum coins or bars, and all foreign currency, be handed in at the credit union, as well as documents pertaining to foreign assets" (*JA* 2, 907; *JT* 3, 1046). What may at first look like plausible reparations ("his commandant spoke of the many telephones and microscopes that Germany owed the Soviets;" *JA* 2, 921; *JT* 3, 1063) soon turns out to be a form of enrichment, one in which the boundary that separates reparation from plunder has dissolved. For the commandant "didn't hand over these precious objects to his country, but kept them for himself, traded them for liquor, handed them out to guests or underlings" (*JA* 2, 920; *JT* 3, 1062). When the teacher Dr. Kliefoth's coin collection is broken up and distributed, historic coins turn into a parallel currency of sorts in Jerichow (*JA* 2, 920; *JT* 3, 1062). The fact that plundering also occurred in the British zone is not denied, but these had been cases of "personal" initiative rather than official orders (*JA* 2, 1006; *JT* 3, 1161f.). Cresspahl makes it a point of honor not to do business with a "crook" of Pontiy's stamp. Yet the German side has petty crooks of its own (on the situation in the West, see Klaus-Michael Bogdal's chapter in the present volume). Johnson illustrates this in the character of Emil Knoop ("an ex-Nazi") who in 1947 rises to be "business king of Gneez" (*JA* 2, 1305; *JT* 4, 1497) by "assisting the S[oviet] M[ilitary] A[dministration] with liquidating various businesses" (*JA* 2, 1306; *JT* 4, 1499). "You could learn a lot from Knoop—all of it illegal, unfortunately" (*JA* 2, 1412; *JT* 4, 1615).

What was seen as particularly 'unfair' about the Soviets' behavior in their occupation zone is spelled out in an aside explaining that all citizens were ordered to surrender their valuables, "whether the owners had come by such property during the war or not, whether they'd followed the Nazis or shunned them" (*JA* 2, 920; *JT* 3, 1062). The problem was not even the loss of property so much as the absence of anything recognizable, in modern terms, as 'transitional justice' (see Brechtken, Bułhak, and Zarusky 2019). The second main complaint concerned the arbitrary nature of the Soviets' measures, denying those living under occupation the chance to recognize and follow a pattern in the demands made upon them.

> Cresspahl would have preferred it if the foreign commander had stolen the Germans' food out of hatred, as punishment, on his own account; he couldn't come to terms with the game Pontiy made of it, with his soulful *nichevos* [Russian for 'it doesn't matter'] and gentlemanly *shustko yednos* [Polish for 'whatever']. (*JA* 2, 957; *JT* 3, 1104)

In these aspects of their conduct, too, the occupying forces demonstrated above all that they had won the war.

Heinrich Cresspahl in Fünfeichen: The Soviet Special Camps

It is, thus, more or less by accident that Heinrich Cresspahl should one day be arrested. A drunken argument one night with the commandant, in which each had spoken of his own respective son's death in the war (*JA* 2, 1048; *JT* 3, 1209), may have been the trigger, but it can scarcely have been the official reason for Cresspahl being relieved of his duties as mayor (*JA* 2, 1047; *JT* 3, 1208). The officers who came to take him away on October 22, 1945 behaved decently enough. "Ever since then Cresspahl thought that an arrest wasn't seen as anything to be ashamed of in the Red Army, at most it was a bit of bad luck that could happen to anyone. Good luck, they wished him" (*JA* 2, 1054; *JT* 3, 1216).[14] Interrogation by the Soviet military tribunal in Schwerin left open both the nature of the investigation and its legal grounds (*JA* 2, 1056–59; *JT* 3, 1218–22). Soon enough, Cresspahl's "mistakes had been established, now he needed to recognize the crimes" (*JA* 2, 1058; *JT* 3, 1220). Though aware of his complicity by having done carpentry work for the Jerichow-North (Mariengabe) air base and thus contributing to the rearmament of Nazi Germany—a fact pointed out at the time by Lisbeth, his wife (*JA* 1, 408; *JT* 1, 470)—he refuses to accept the inference that this had made him guilty under the occupation: "he didn't want to follow them across the bridge to economic sabotage in Jerichow as a past and present Fascist. He wouldn't sign" (*JA* 2, 1058f.; *JT* 3, 1221). He is then imprisoned in a camp without even being certain: "Was that his sentence?" (*JA* 2, 1059; *JT* 3, 1221). His family receives no news of his whereabouts ("Marie, when the Soviets arrested someone he really and truly disappeared" (*JA* 2, 1088; *JT* 3, 1254)). Nor are former prisoners who might know something permitted to share information: "All had been strictly sworn to silence" (*JA* 2, 1111; *JT* 3, 1280).

Even after again being interrogated (probably in Schwerin) from December 1946 and being subject to severe physical abuse in the process (*JA* 2, 1114; *JT* 3, 1283f.), Cresspahl remains ignorant of any verdict against him. Toward the end of February 1947, he is again interned, this time in one of the notorious 'special camps' operated by the Soviets both in their German occupation zone and in the formerly German areas already officially under Polish civilian administration (e.g., in Landsberg an der Warthe; see Fricke 1990, 69–100; Greiner 2010; Landau and Heitzer 2021; Mironenko, Niethammer, and von Plato 1998; Reif-Spirek and Ritscher 1999). This is Special Camp No. 9 at Fünfeichen near Neubrandenburg (Baumann 1998; Jeske 2013, 2021; Krüger 1990). Whereas Special Camp No. 2 at Buchenwald (Weimar) was set up on the site of the former concentration camp, Fünfeichen had previously been a prisoner-of-war camp (Stalag II A Neubrandenburg) of the German army (*JA* 2, 1118; *JT* 3, 1288) in which many Soviet soldiers perished.

Johnson's account of Heinrich Cresspahl's imprisonment (*JA* 1112–27; *JT* 3, 1285–98; on this, see also Fernengel-Pflug 1992; Rütters 2007) displays several elements of literary stylization. First, there is the somewhat incongruous mock-idyll—a parody of the beginning of Thomas Mann's novella *Tristan* (1903)[15]—in which the camp is referred to as a "sanatorium" when, in fact, even those inmates who left it alive often did so with their health severely compromised:[16]

> Here lies Fünfeichen, the sanatorium! A long, brown, rectilinear building with its barracks and guardhouse, set in a spacious barren field abundantly equipped with muddy wooden walkways, barbed-wire passages, and squat watchtowers; behind its tar-paper roofs the mountains of Lindental and Tollense Lake tower heavenwards—evergreen, massy, cleft with wooded ravines—and prominent signs on the fence inform the nature lover in Russian and German and English: OFF-LIMITS. ENTRY FORBIDDEN. VIOLATORS WILL BE SHOT!
>
> Now as then the Red Army directs the establishment. Dressed in a belted tunic studded with medals and hanging far down over his baggy breeches, his head held high under the clay-colored cap, automatic rifle at the ready, the soldier herds the prisoner across the camp road. He is a man whom knowledge has hardened, holding his patients in his spell in his curt, reserved, preoccupied way, in amused amazement: all those individuals who, too weak to give and to follow laws unto themselves, put themselves into his hands, body and mind, that his severity may be a shield unto them. (*JA* 2, 1117f.; *JT* 3, 1287f.; see Johnson [1979] 1988, 83)[17]

Cresspahl's "transport" (*JA* 2, 1116; *JT* 3, 1285) there—on foot, naturally—is more than he can manage in his weakened state. He arrives only because younger and stronger men in his column more or less drag him along, which, one imagines, they are likely to have done out of a sympathetic concern that prisoners unable to walk would be shot (see *JA* 2, 1118; *JT* 3, 1288). His condition is reflected in his description of the path, a description combining fragments of memory with disjointed topographical details (Gerlach 1980, 147f.): having looked after geese and herded them past the Slavic fortress of Laschendorf in Malchow as a boy of six, the place evokes in him the legend of the "subterranean folk," the dwarves who live in "Wenches Hill, the old Wendish castle mound" and who

> were invisible when they walked out on Laschendorf farm in the daytime but a shepherd had once heard them cry *Give a hat, give a hat!* and he called for his hat and put it on and saw them standing in front of him, teeny little men with their three-corner hats, they jumped at him and scratched his eyes out and took his magic cap. The little folk in Wenches Hill made such lovely music, they say. (*JA* 2, 1117; *JT* 3,1287)

The description, written largely in Low German dialect, follows sometimes verbatim that given by the Mecklenburg folklorist Richard Wossidlo (1859–1939) (Scheuermann 1998, 174–75; see also Van Effelterre 2010).

A third element of literary stylization, alongside Johnson's reference to canonical literature (Thomas Mann's *Tristan*) and the popular legend (the story about Wenches Hill), is an exemplum of sorts contained within this account: while the march, on its way to Fünfeichen, is passing through Goldberg,

> [A]s the column rounded a corner one of the prisoners stepped out of it onto the sidewalk, grabbed a thoroughly startled housewife by the elbow, and made her keep walking with him, loudly marveling at their reunion:—Elli, my goodness, he cried in excitement. The scene had apparently been plausible enough for the Soviet guards; as they left town, they replaced the runaway with a civilian who happened to be digging in his garden. (*JA* 2, 1125; *JT* 3, 1296)

This would appear to be something of a migratory tale about the Red Army, told in a similar form by Max Frisch (Frisch [1950] 1976, 397f.). The gist in each case is that Soviet military tribunals have no interest in seeing justice done, operating instead on the assumption that something can be made to stick even to a man who was mistakenly imprisoned, who is then forced to acknowledge his (ostensible) guilt. Anybody is as good a camp inmate as anybody else.[18]

Johnson, however, problematizes the function of such cautionary tales, such as that of the Soviet soldiers arresting a man arbitrarily by referring here to a "yarn" (*Läuschen*) that "had been told a few too many times" (*JA* 2, 1125; *JT* 3, 1296), each time in a slightly different form. A *Läuschen*, in low German, is an anecdote (often humorous) of doubtful veracity (Herrmann-Winter 1999, 175), some famous examples in the Mecklenburg dialect having been published by Fritz Reuter in *Läuschen un Riemels* in 1853. The political implication of Cresspahl's story is clear, although whether it fits the facts of the case remains uncertain: "Eventually Cresspahl himself doubted he'd ever seen it happen" (*JA* 2, 1126; *JT* 3, 1297).

In the special circumstances of a camp under an occupation regime, the victorious power could afford to behave in a comparatively humane manner. This did not apply to its German helpers, their "hunting dogs" (*JA* 2, 1124; *JT* 3,1295), to whom Johnson refers as the "German kapos," using a term familiar from the Nazi camps (*JA* 2, 1119; *JT* 3, 1289; Rütters 2007, 75f.). The reference appears to be to members of the so-called camp police (Baumann 1998, 435f.), whose reign of terror over the inmates abated only occasionally, "When the Soviets had had ample time to observe what Germans are capable of doing to one another" (*JA* 2, 1124; *JT* 3, 1295). The novel does not explain who these kapos were or how they attained their position (Rütters 2007, 76); they are never referred to by their names. Instead, they are described as quashing any feelings of solidarity among the inmates and giving Heinrich Cresspahl a beating whose brutality is related matter-of-factly: "The wounds took until the following summer to heal; he could walk by early December" (*JA* 2, 1124; *JT* 3, 1295).

Johnson's account of Heinrich Cresspahl's spell in Fünfeichen and his awful experiences there ends with the remark: "Still, Cresspahl would have preferred a trial and sentence" (*JA* 2, 1127; *JT* 3, 1298). Whether he ever gets either and whether he even survives the camp are questions that readers, occasional hints notwithstanding (e.g., *JA* 2, 1126, 1155, 1165; *JT* 3, 1327, 1330, 1341f.), must wait more than 200 pages to see answered. Indeed, Johnson's early readers had to wait ten years between Volumes 3 and 4 while the author wrestled with writer's block. It may therefore have been all the greater a surprise to come across the bald statement: "In May 1948, Cresspahl lay stark naked in a water trough in Johnny Schlegel's flower garden" (*JA* 2, 1316; *JT* 4, 1510). After more than two and half years, he is free at last, having survived imprisonment and torture, although he "sure hadn't gotten out [...] intact," being instead "shattered" and "truly not a well man" (*JA* 2, 1321; *JT* 4, 1515f.).

Having been released in Schwerin, Cresspahl initially makes his way to the rural commune of his friend Johnny Schlegel, from where he is taken home in secret. His defining traits henceforth are compulsive washing and silence ("He never did [say anything about Schwerin]," *JA* 2, 1330; *JT* 4, 1524). He seldom leaves the house, can barely work, and his role as the novel's protagonist now finally passes to his daughter Gesine, soon to be joined by her daughter Marie. At last, he receives his sentence, passed according to Soviet criminal law (Fricke [1979] 1990, 106–10), on charges of "Espionage," "Sabotage against Business, Transportation, or Monetary Circulation, including to the benefit of earlier proprietors," and "Failure to Denounce Counterrevolutionary Crimes" (*JA* 2, 1328f.; *JT* 4, 1523f.). None of this has anything to do with working for the Nazis, let alone with war crimes—the purposes for which the Allied internment camps had officially been set up. And still hanging over his head was § 58, par. 10, under which "he faced imprisonment for saying anything about his life with the Soviets: Anti-Soviet Propaganda and Agitation" (*JA* 2, 1329; *JT* 4, 1523). It was, therefore, not just the trauma of the camp that made Cresspahl retreat into silence (as it did so many real-life inmates)—there was also the justified fear of being imprisoned again.

In view of this silence, which continued to be rigorously enforced by the GDR, it may be asked how Uwe Johnson would have learned of what happened in the Soviet special camps. His own father, Erich Johnson, who was arrested in Anklam in May 1945, does indeed seem to have initially been imprisoned in Fünfeichen before being deported to the USSR—probably to a Gulag in Belarus (Fahlke 1988, 236) or in Ukraine (Neumann 2000, 72); his ultimate fate is unknown. In *Anniversaries*, something similar happens to the student Dieter Lockenvitz's father (*JA* 2, 1511; *JT* 4, 1722). Someone who did, in fact, return from Fünfeichen was Johnson's uncle, Wilhelm Milding, who was a blacksmith in the Mecklenburg village of Recknitz and the head of the local Nazi Party. It was at his house that the Johnson family sought refuge along the course of its flight from Anklam in western Pomerania, where they sought to escape the advancing Red Army in April 1945. Yet contrary to much scholarly opinion (e.g., Neumann 2000, 75; Nöldechen 2008, 57f.), it seems doubtful whether Milding would have shared that many details with young Uwe. Even in the West, the Soviet special camps received fairly little publicity, and what did appear was usually given an anti-communist spin in a Cold War context (Niethammer 1998, 97).

This anti-communist air does not apply to one of the very few literary works to address the topic, the memoir *Der Wind weht nicht wohin er will* (Griese 1960). Its author, Friedrich Griese (1890–1975),[19] specialized in local, Mecklenburg subjects, allowed himself to be lauded by the Nazis as a poet of 'blood and soil' (Busch 1998, 36–81) and participated in official tours (*Dichterfahrten*) by German writers to recently conquered and occupied territories in Europe (Griese 1960, 15f., 37–40; see also Barbian 1995, 455–57). In retrospect, however, Griese does seem to have had a sense of guilt, particularly when considering his observations while on *Dichterfahrt* to the USSR in 1941, and the fact that Fünfeichen had originally been set up for Soviet prisoners of war: "and who could estimate how many thousands were imprisoned and died here" (Griese 1960, 177). He finds an element of poetic justice for both in his own internment (see Greiner 2010, 440f.), which means that the book, while drastic, does not judge the occupiers too harshly (thereby rendering it unsuitable for propaganda purposes in the Cold War). Griese was even able to do some clandestine writing in Fünfeichen, though he was not permitted to keep his notes upon his release from the camp (Griese 1960, 252f., 332). Instead, he tried afterwards "to gather the pieces of paper left behind in the camp in my memory" (Griese 1960, 282). The result, which appeared soon after his release and move to the West, combines childhood memoir with an ethnographic account of his native village (Lehsten bei Waren), in which the legend of the subterranean "little folk" also features (Griese 1947, 97–109). While Johnson has these creatures dwell in "the old Wendish castle mound" (*JA* 2, 1117; *JT* 3, 1287), Griese explicitly interprets the legend as memorializing the area's earlier Slavic ("Wendish") population, who had been displaced by the taller Germans (Griese 1947, 106f.). Since the little folk were said to be awaiting the chance to return ("The danger is mounting [...] War is coming." (Griese 1947, 109)), they were clearly meant to connote the 'Slavic' victors of 1945.[20] The subject of captivity, by contrast, is given only cursory treatment in this, his first book after his release (Griese 1947, 5–21, 254–56). Griese appears to have needed more than a decade before he could address his time in a special camp operated by the Soviet occupation forces.

The Subject of Occupation in *Anniversaries*: Between *Lagerliteratur* and the GDR's Founding Myth

Heinrich Cresspahl's internment in the Fünfeichen special camp under Soviet Occupation brings *Anniversaries* into the proximity of twentieth-century 'camp literature' (*Lagerliteratur*; see Fischer, Gronich, and Bednarska-Kociołek 2021) and specifically that of the Gulag (see Lachmann 2019). Yet the third volume, published in 1973, in which Cresspahl's tribulations begin, hardly ever figured in international discussions of Soviet camps, which reached a high point that year with the publication of Alexander Solzhenitsyn's *The Gulag Archipelago* and the author's subsequent expulsion from the USSR (e.g., Dutschke and Wilke 1975; Glucksmann [1974] 1976).[21] It would indeed seem that there have hitherto been no points of contact between scholarship on Johnson on the one hand and *Lagerliteratur* on the other, though both might stand to benefit.

A particularly relevant theme with regard to the subject of occupation is that of disappearance in the camps. It resonates throughout the countries of eastern and central Europe, where the NKVD always followed in the wake of the Red Army and carried off a part of the population to the Soviet Union. Research on the literature of the Nazi camps and the Holocaust brings into view ways of writing that often express themselves in intertextual references (e.g., references to Dante), which, in turn, are reflected upon (Fischer and Gronich 2021, 20–24). Accordingly, for instance, Johnson's parody of Thomas Mann, his reference to the legend of the dwarves, or his doubts as to the veracity of what has been related may all be understood as typical of the *Lagerliteratur* genre. The fact that, at the level of memory, the novel confronts recollections of National Socialism with no less detailed and harrowing depictions of Stalinism suggests familiarity with the theory of totalitarianism, developed by Johnson's friend Hannah Arendt (1906–1975).[22] According to Arendt, "the concentration camps are the most consequential institution of totalitarian rule" (Arendt [1951] 1958, 441). This idea could be said to be reflected in the central position that Johnson accords to Cresspahl's imprisonment in the Soviet camp. One also sees it reflected in the trumped-up charges and politically mandated sentences under a totalitarian legal system, for which Johnson accounts in two lists of victims in Mecklenburg, one list having come from the Nazi courts (*JA* 1, 821–24; *JT* 2, 945–50), the other of Stalinist victims (*JA* 2, 1574–78; *JT* 4, 1790–96).

This raises the question of the relationship between the Soviet occupation of part of Germany and the new communist state that was being set up under its aegis (Berbig 1993; Widmann 1991). Johnson himself spoke of "the birth of the GDR from the loins of the Red Army" (Neumann 2000, 706f.). But was this new state, as the phrase suggests, a logical consequence? And does it contribute to an understanding of the 1945–1949 period to have it point teleologically toward the establishment of the GDR—as that state's cultural policy would later insinuate?[23] Historians of the era find the situation to be less clear-cut. For one thing, Stalin had reasons for opposing the statehood of only a part of Germany—not least because he was interested in claiming reparations from Germany as a whole (Loth 1994). The small band of German communists who had survived Stalin's purges in the USSR (the "Ulbricht Group;" *JA* 1, 861; 2, 1177; *JT* 2, 993; 3, 1355) was, thus, not tasked with building socialism, as was later stated—they were, in fact, subject to the Red Army and its propaganda division (Ullrich 2021, 53–58). Yet they soon succeeded in seizing the reins of power (ibid. 70f.; Leonhard [1955] 1979) and suppressing any political forces that might have rivaled Stalinist communism. We cannot know how seriously to take Pontiy's response to Cresspahl's question "whether the commandant wanted a temporary or permanent fence" around his headquarters: "For e-v-ver, Meeyor" (*JA* 2, 921; *JT* 3, 1063).

However, in *Anniversaries*, the question is discussed, above all, with reference to the land reform measures of 1945 (on this see Bauerkämper 1996). As Gesine remarks:

> The Soviets were incomprehensible conquerors—they didn't introduce their own economic system in Mecklenburg. Not the big nationalized communal farms, their famous kolkhozes. They faithfully kept the agreement with their Allies, the Potsdam one, and took the land away from everyone who owned more than a hundred hectares, and of course from any Nazi leader. They did so earlier than promised, but did they do it in a Communist way? (*JA* 2, 1175f.; *JT* 3, 1353)

What is perhaps truly surprising is the very idea that the victors should want to implant their form of social and economic organization in the occupied territories. Military occupation is, by definition, a temporary arrangement; anything else would properly be called 'annexation' or 'colonization': one country brining another under its long-term control. Because it seemed pointless to break up large estates into smallholdings (*aufsiedeln*), only to merge them into large cooperative farms (*Landwirtschaftliche Produktionsgenossenschaften* (LPG)) modeled on the Soviet kolkhoz system, the population of Mecklenburg may have formed the impression that the victors would soon leave: "that didn't look like they were planning to stay" (*JA* 2, 1176; *JT* 3, 1353). Yet Mecklenburg soon saw its mistake, at the latest when agriculture was collectivized and the communists "after only six years, tried to take [their] gift back by converting the farms into Agricultural Production Cooperatives" (*JA* 2, 1620; *JT* 4, 1840).

Was this an about-face in policy, or had land been deliberately parceled up into infeasibly small plots and allocated to applicants lacking in agricultural know-how (see *JA* 2, 1216: "land lottery"; *JT* 4, 1401) to make a more convincing case for its subsequent collectivization (see *JA* 2, 1619f.; *JT* 4, 1839f.)? Whatever the case, Johnson recounts how a functioning alternative—the self-organized rural commune, organized along socialist principles of land reform laid down in the Weimar Republic—is destroyed and its charismatic leader, Cresspahl's friend Johnny Schlegel, sentenced to fifteen years' hard labor by a kangaroo court (*JA* 2, 1320f., 1596–1624; *JT* 4, 1514–16, 1814–44).

That any stirrings of socialist democracy (see *JA* 2, 1009; *JT* 3, 1164) should be nipped in the bud—in the nascent GDR as in eastern and central Europe as a whole—is reflected in the novel's present-day passages of 1967 and 1968, along with its depiction of the events unfolding in Czechoslovakia during the same timeframe. Much as German socialists' hopes were the first to be dashed by their purported comrades—the Soviet occupying forces—in 1945,[24] Czechoslovakian socialists find their illusions shattered by their 'friends,' the armies of the Warsaw

Pact who invade to suppress the Prague Spring. The novel ends with an entry dated August 20, 1968. The events of August 21 do not need to be recounted here, although they leave open the question of whether Gesine still boards her flight to Prague. In any case, for her and for Johnson's readers, the year of anniversaries is over.

After Reading *Anniversaries* Today: Current Issues and Perspectives

Looking across the temporal gulf that separates the present day from the writing of *Anniversaries*, it is striking how the change in the culture of memory described by German cultural studies scholar Aleida Assmann—a shift toward a culture that focuses on the relationship between perpetrators and victims rather than victors and vanquished (Assmann 2006, 62–116; see also Hofmann 2019, 201f.)—has not yet fully taken hold in this novel. It would be hard to find a work of contemporary German literature in which the words 'victors' and 'victory' appear with such frequency. Yet being on the losing side is no longer treated as a national humiliation, as it would have been after World War I. The terminology largely testifies to a recognition of power relations that Germany brought upon itself by pursuing a second World War. To borrow Assmann's terminology, the "loser's memory" has, by now, also assumed the character of a "perpetrator's memory" (Assmann 2006, 67). Military occupation by Allied forces, thus, does not seem an injustice, per se, even though its forms are still subject to criticism (see Schell and Laffin in the present volume).

As this chapter has shown, the Soviet occupation was criticized for its indifference to transitional justice and for its increasingly obvious intention of remaking state and society along Stalinist lines, in preparation for a quasi-colonial absorption into the Soviet sphere of influence. It therefore seems appropriate to apply a postcolonial perspective not only to the framing narrative set in New York (as suggested by Hofmann 2019) but also, as with other Eastern European countries, to the process of Sovietization in the wake of military conquest (see Kalnačs 2013 and in the present volume).[25] The people living under Soviet occupation are criticized for conforming more than necessary to the occupiers' actual or perceived wishes. For example, the "German kapos" in the Soviet special camps were infamous for practicing colonization of an extremely brutal kind, and even as a young student, Gesine realizes how ingrained the habits of 'colonized' thought have become when she is rewarded for denouncing Jean-Paul Sartre—a socialist writer, but a heterodox one—as a collaborator of sorts, noting that "this individual had published a book named *L'Être et le néant*, aka *Being and*

Nothingness, in Paris in 1943, under the Nazi-German occupation—enough for an A!" (*JA* 2, 1602; *JT* 4, 1820). In both cases, with respect to the conduct both of the occupiers and the occupied, the question is one of right or wrong conduct under conditions of military occupation, of the ethics of living in 'occupation societies' (Tönsmeyer 2015; see also Buschmeier in the present volume).

What happened under Soviet occupation in Mecklenburg and western Pomerania after 1945 is one of the major topics that Uwe Johnson's novel addresses. Given that the conduct of the Soviets in the conquered territories of Germany and Eastern Europe at large was one of the great taboos of the GDR, the book's subject matter is also one reason precisely why *Anniversaries* was banned throughout the Eastern Bloc. Yet, as this chapter has shown, the novel provided a literary substitute for the GDR's lacking culture of memory, particularly with respect to many aspects of the transition from the Soviet zone to the GDR— with one exception: in *Anniversaries*, the suppression of a Pomeranian identity, a policy mandated by the Soviet military authorities and continued under the GDR, goes unchallenged.

What reason might Johnson have had for following the official line in setting his novel entirely in Mecklenburg, while having Pomerania exist only as part of Poland? A clue may lie in Johnson's desire to "avoid the company of those calling for a revision of these outcomes of the war" (Fahlke 1988, 133; see also 239). At his time, Johnson was rightly concerned about being instrumentalized by the representatives of the expellees from the eastern German territories (*Vertriebenenverbände*). While some of them demanded the return of these territories to Germany (a position that West German politicians often supported because they wanted their votes), Polish communist politicians stirred up fear of this 'German revisionism' to present themselves as the only guarantors of a secure western Polish border.

Today the picture is completely different. Germany has recognized the border with Poland under international law. Both countries are members of the European Union and the North Atlantic Treaty Organization (NATO), which mutually respect their territorial integrity. In Germany, there is currently no political group calling for a revision of borders. And in Poland, though there is talk about reparations or about the dominance of the Germans in the European Union (EU), there is likewise no talk about the border. This state of affairs allows for a more 'relaxed' approach to the common history of areas such as Pomerania (or Silesia) that used to belong to Germany. Polish historians already practice this by including Vorpommern (even after 1945) as a matter of course in their studies of Pomerania (e.g., Piskorski 1999). These terms, of which Johnson was apparently afraid, no longer need to be treated as taboo.

However, the question of what happens to regional and national identities that find themselves an obstacle to the logic of an occupying power remains to be addressed.

Translated by Joe Paul Kroll

Notes

1. While the new translation by Damion Searls is excellent in itself, this chapter was written based on the German original, and the original page numbers are given in addition to those of the translation to make it easy for readers to work with both versions. I have occasionally taken the liberty of disagreeing with the translator's choices, for instance in rendering the German *Pommern* as the more familiar English *Pomerania(n)*, rather than retaining the German word as Searls does.

2. Numerous historical and ethnographic sources from Mecklenburg and Pomerania are cited in the commentary on *Jahrestage* by Helbig et al. (1999), whose usefulness to this essay is gratefully acknowledged.

3. Since this refers to a journey from 1938, the novel uses the German place names valid until 1945. I have included today's Polish names in parentheses.

4. This also applies, in part, to his own roots in western Pomerania (Kielmann 1993; Meyer-Gosau 2014; Neumann 2000, 30–47; Talarczyk 2020), regarding which Johnson expressed contradictory attitudes (Fahlke 1994, 14f.; Johnson [1977] 1992, 372).

5. See, e.g., de Bruyn [1992] 2000, 300: "For years afterwards, we would flinch at the very sound of Russian voices, and this fear died hard because we had known the Russians only as occupying soldiers who would control and confiscate, arrest citizens and dismantle infrastructure, and because there was a prohibition and writing and talking about the terrible things we had witnessed as the war came to an end. The trauma was not addressed, it was conserved."

6. Piskorski refers to Ondřej Trojan's film *Želary* (2003), based on a story ('Jozova Hanule') by Květa Legátová (1919–2012).

7. Christoph Meckel (1935–2020) remembers similar experiences when Erfurt was transferred from American to Soviet occupation (Meckel [2011] 2012).

8. This also allows Johnson to omit any descriptions of combat from the sections dealing with the war and its conclusion.

9. See Solschenizyn [1998] 2004, 108f.: "All were seized by the feeling of having earned a reward—even the highest officers, and the rank and file all the more so. They found what they were looking for and they drank. And they drank all the more to celebrate the encirclement of East Prussia."

10. Similarly, American troops forced Weimar residents to visit the recently liberated Buchenwald concentration camp (see Mann [1947] 1949, 481).

11. An attitude soon adopted by the Americans, the better to compete with Soviet efforts to win German hearts and minds amid the incipient Cold War. See Buschmeier 2022a, 329.

12. See Bienek [1982] 1985, 221; Kempowski [1972] 1982, 165. If the term *russische Untermenschen* ever appeared in the literature published in the GDR, it was placed in the mouths of Nazis; e.g., in Franz Fühmann's novella *Kameraden* (Fühmann [1955] 1990, 42).

13. That the Soviets wished to avoid scrutiny is evident from the case of Walter Kempowski (1929–2007), who would himself go on to become a writer. Kempowski and his brother were sentenced to twenty-five years' hard labor for espionage. They had passed bills of lading to the Americans, which showed that the Soviets were in breach of Allied agreements. This episode is discussed in his novels about Rostock under Soviet occupation (*Uns geht's ja noch gold*, [1972] 1982) and imprisonment (*Ein Kapitel für sich*, [1978] 1980). On relations between the two authors, see Johnson and Kempowski 2006.

14. This appears to be something of a topos in discussions of the Russian legal system: "In one of Gorky's stories, a prisoner is led away by two policemen, and both sides assure each other of their profoundest regret as one human to another." See Griese 1960, 93 and 247.

15. As Eugen Kogon (1903–1987) noted of the Nazi era: "There was no German who did not know of the existence of concentration camps; no German who would have mistaken them for sanatoria" (Kogon 1946, 331).

16. A comparable instance would be Imre Kertész's (1929–2016) novel *Fatelessness* (originally published in Hungarian in 1975), in which the author attempted to rewrite the story of Hans Castorp, the protagonist of Mann's *The Magic Mountain* (see Kertész 2022).

17. Cf. Mann's story: "Einfried, the sanatorium. A long, white, rectilinear building with a side wing, set in a spacious garden pleasingly equipped with grottoes, bowers, and little bark pavilions. Behind its slate roofs the mountains tower heavenwards, evergreen, massy, cleft with wooded ravines.

    Now as then, Dr. Leander directs the establishment. He wears a two-pronged black beard as curly and wiry as horsehair stuffing; his spectacle-lenses are thick, and glitter; he has the look of a man whom science has cooled and hardened and filled with silent, forbearing pessimism. And with this beard, these lenses, this look, and in his short, reserved, preoccupied way, he holds his patients in his spell: holds those sufferers who, too weak to be laws unto themselves, put themselves into his hands that his severity may be a shield unto them" (Mann [1903] 1922, 133).

18. The story may be read as an illustration of Hannah Arendt's claim, "Total domination, which strives to organize the infinite plurality and differentiation of human beings as if all of humanity were just one individual, is possible only if each and every person

can be reduced to a never-changing identity of reactions, so that each of these bundles of reactions can be exchanged at random for any other" (Arendt [1951] 1958, 438).

19. Even after the war, Griese continued for a time to be considered something akin to Mecklenburg's representative writer, much like Agnes Miegel was for East Prussia. After vehement objections made by the Germanist Karl Otto Conrady against the award of the Mecklenburg Prize for Culture to Griese in 1964 (see Conrady 1974, 215–26), the situation fell vacant in the public mind and gradually passed, after a fashion, to Uwe Johnson, whom most people today would think of as Mecklenburg's representative writer (and, by the same token, Siegfried Lenz rather than Agnes Miegel for East Prussia).

20. In *Anniversaries*, a (pseudo-)etymological link is established via "the language of the occupying power" (*JA* 1, 263; *JT* 1, 304), study of which was made compulsory in schools as soon as the Soviets took control: "In 1947 she was taking third-year Russian, still from Charlotte Pagels. The topic was the derivation of Mecklenburg words from the Slavic, a language group preceding Russian, well then. At the end Cresspahl raised her hand, with all the timidity this child had by then become known for, and asked permission to say something about Gneez. Maybe the name was derived from the Soviet [*sic*] word for 'nest,' *gnezdo*? An A in the roll book!" (*JA* 2, 1263; *JT* 4, 1452).

21. Writing to Hannah Arendt on January 25, 1974 (Arendt and Johnson 2004, 108–13), Johnson expressed his bafflement at this hype, noting that accounts by Yevgenia Ginzburg (*Journey into the Whirlwind*), Susanne Leonhard (*Gestohlenes Leben*), Margarete Buber-Neumann (*Under Two Dictators*), Wanda Brońska-Pampuch (*Ohne Maß und Ende*), and Erica Wallach (*Light at Midnight*) had long been known—as was Solzhenitsyn's own *One Day in the Life of Ivan Denisovich*. Johnson's preserved library contains copies of all these books.

22. "In its account of events in Mecklenburg, it seems that the book was initially meant to extend only as far as the end of the war. The decision to spin this strand further in time, into the establishment of the GDR, and the related decision to contrast the implementation of Nazi doctrines with the enforcement of Stalinism in Germany, was made only once Johnson had met Hannah Arendt and studied her theory of totalitarianism" (Neumann 2000, 836).

23. See Buschmeier 2022b, 122f., on Dieter Noll, *Die Abenteuer des Werner Holt: Roman einer Heimkehr* (1963).

24. See, e.g., *JA* 2, 893; *JT* 3,1030: "In Waren, an enemy of the Nazis known to the very end as the 'Red Pharmacist' had celebrated all night long with his liberators from the Soviet Union until they'd forced themselves on all the women in the house anyway and everyone in the family killed themselves with the poisonous medicine they hadn't been saving for such a purpose at all [...]." And Bertolt Brecht noted in 1948: "among the workers, i hear generally, the panic caused by the raping and plundering after berlin was overrun is still rippling below the surface three years later, in the working-class

quarters they had been looking forward to the liberators with desperate joy, arms outstretched, but the meeting turned into an assault which spared neither the seventy-year-olds nor the twelve-year-olds, and in public at that" (Brecht 1993, 400).

25. To her daughter Marie, who draws a connection between occupation and colonialism, Gesine replies: "Gesine, were the Soviets in your country more out of control than the British in India?—They behaved like occupiers. The country was theirs, they wielded the power, and along with the glory, they wanted to make sure they didn't get a raw deal" (*JA* 2, 1173; *JT* 3, 1350).

References

Aischmann, Bernd. 2008. *Mecklenburg-Vorpommern, die Stadt Stettin ausgenommen: Eine zeitgeschichtliche Betrachtung.* Schwerin: Helms.

Arendt, Hannah. [1951] 1958. *The Origins of Totalitarianism.* Cleveland, OH: Meridian Books.

———, and Uwe Johnson. 2004. *Der Briefwechsel 1967–1975*, edited by Eberhard Fahlke and Thomas Wild. Frankfurt am Main: Suhrkamp.

Assmann, Aleida. 2006. *Der lange Schatten der Vergangenheit: Erinnerungskultur und Geschichtspolitik.* Munich: Beck.

Baker, Gary Lee. 1995. "Die Poetisierung der Geschichte in Uwe Johnsons 'Jahrestage.'" In *Uwe Johnson zwischen Vormoderne und Postmoderne*, edited by Carsten Gansel and Nicolai Riedel, 143–51. Berlin: De Gruyter.

Barbian, Jan-Pieter. 1995. *Literaturpolitik im 'Dritten Reich': Institutionen, Kompetenzen, Betätigungsfelder.* Munich: dtv.

Bauerkämper, Arnd, ed. 1996. *'Junkerland in Bauernhand'? Durchführung, Auswirkungen und Stellenwert der Bodenreform in der Sowjetischen Besatzungszone.* Stuttgart: Steiner.

Baumann, Tobias. 1998. "Das Speziallager Nr. 9 Fünfeichen." In *Sowjetische Speziallager in Deutschland 1945 bis 1950*, edited by Sergej Mironenko, Lutz Niethammer, and Alexander von Plato. Vol. 1: Studien und Berichte, 426–44. Berlin: Akademie.

Behrends, Jan C. 2006. *Die erfundene Freundschaft: Propaganda für die Sowjetunion in Polen und in der DDR.* Cologne: Böhlau.

Berbig, Roland. 1993. "Eine Bürgerin der 'D.D.R.' namens Gesine Cresspahl erzählt: Beobachtungen zu der DDR in Uwe Johnsons 'Jahrestage.'" In *'Wo ich her bin…': Uwe Johnson in der D.D.R*, edited by Roland Berbig and Erdmut Wizisla, 320–51, 412–18. Berlin: Kontext.

Bienek, Horst. [1982] 1985. *Erde und Feuer: Roman.* Munich: dtv.

Brecht, Bertolt. [1948] 1993. *Journals, 1934–1955.* Translated by Hugh Rorrison. Edited by John Willett. London: Bloomsbury.

Brechtken, Magnus, Władysław Bułhak, and Jürgen Zarusky, eds. 2019. *Political and Transitional Justice in Germany, Poland and the Soviet Union from the 1930s to the 1950s*. Göttingen: Wallstein.

Brink, Cornelia. 1998. *Ikonen der Vernichtung: Zum öffentlichen Gebrauch von Fotografien aus nationalsozialistischen Konzentrationslagern nach 1945*. Berlin: Akademie.

Brunner, Detlev. 2006. *Der Schein der Souveränität: Landesregierung und Besatzungspolitik in Mecklenburg-Vorpommern 1945–1949*. Cologne: Böhlau.

Bruyn, Günter de. [1992] 2000. *Zwischenbilanz: Eine Jugend in Berlin*. 8th ed. Frankfurt am Main: Fischer.

Busch, Stefan. 1998. *'Und gestern, da hörte uns Deutschland': NS-Autoren in der Bundesrepublik. Kontinuität und Diskontinuität bei Friedrich Griese, Werner Beumelburg, Eberhard Wolfgang Möller und Kurt Ziesel*. Würzburg: Königshausen & Neumann.

Buschmeier, Matthias. 2022a. "The Absence of Productive Guilt in Shame and Disgrace: Misconceptions in and of German Memory Culture from 1945 to 2020." In *Guilt: A Force of Cultural Transformation*, edited by Katharina von Kellenbach and Matthias Buschmeier, 323–50. New York: Oxford University Press.

———. 2022b. "Moralisch verletzt—ideologisch geheilt: Zur Funktion des späten Heimkehrerromans für die DDR: Dieter Nolls 'Die Abenteuer des Werner Holt.'" In *Jugend ohne Sinn? Eine Spurensuche zu Sinnfragen der jungen Generation 1945–1949*, edited by Wolfgang Braungart, Gabriele Guerra, and Justus H. Ulbricht, 109–30. Göttingen: V&R unipress.

Buske, Norbert. 1997. *Pommern: Territorialstaat und Landesteil von Preußen*. Schwerin: Helms.

Conrady, Karl Otto. 1974. *Literatur und Germanistik als Herausforderung: Skizzen und Stellungnahmen*. Frankfurt am Main: Suhrkamp.

Dutschke, Rudi, and Manfred Wilke, eds. 1975. *Die Sowjetunion, Solschenizyn und die westliche Linke*. Reinbek: Rowohlt.

Eggert, Oskar. 1967. *Das Ende des Krieges und die Besatzungszeit in Stralsund und Umgebung: 1945–46*. Hamburg: Pommerscher Buchversand.

Emmerich, Wolfgang. 2005. "Dürfen die Deutschen ihre eigenen Opfer beklagen? Schiffsuntergänge 1945 bei Uwe Johnson, Walter Kempowski, Günter Grass, Tanja Dückers und Stefan Chwin." In *Danzig und der Ostseeraum: Sprache, Literatur, Publizistik*, edited by Holger Böning, Hans Wolf Jäger, Andrzej Kątny, and Marian Szczodrowski, 293–323. Bremen: edition lumière.

Fahlke, Eberhard, ed. 1988. *'Ich überlege mir die Geschichte': Uwe Johnson im Gespräch*. Frankfurt am Main: Suhrkamp.

———. 1992. "Heimat als geistige Landschaft: Uwe Johnson und Mecklenburg." In *Über Uwe Johnson*, edited by Raimund Fellinger, 311–33. Frankfurt am Main: Suhrkamp.

———. 1994. *Die Katze Erinnerung: Uwe Johnson—Eine Chronik in Briefen und Bildern*. Frankfurt am Main: Suhrkamp.

Fernengel-Pflug, Birgit. 1992. "Cresspahls Haftzeit im Konzentrationslager Fünfeichen und ihr realgeschichtlicher Hintergrund: Anmerkungen zu einem Kapitel in Uwe Johnsons 'Jahrestagen.'" *Internationales Uwe-Johnson-Forum* 2: 185–208.

Fischer, Saskia, and Mareike Gronich. 2021. "Was ist Lagerliteratur?—Schreibweisen, Zeugnisse, Didaktik." In *Lagerliteratur: Schreibweisen—Zeugnisse—Didaktik*, edited by Saskia Fischer, Mareike Gronich, and Joanna Bednarska-Kociołek, 9–40. Berlin: Peter Lang.

Fischer, Saskia, Mareike Gronich, and Joanna Bednarska-Kociołek, eds. 2021. *Lagerliteratur: Schreibweisen—Zeugnisse—Didaktik*. Berlin: Peter Lang.

Fricke, Karl Wilhelm. [1979] 1990. *Politik und Justiz in der DDR: Zur Geschichte der politischen Verfolgung 1945–1968. Bericht und Dokumentation*. 2nd ed. Cologne: Verlag Wissenschaft und Politik.

Frisch, Max. [1950] 1976. "Tagebuch 1946–1949." In *Gesammelte Werke in zeitlicher Folge*, edited by Hans Mayer. Vol. 2: 1944–1949, no. 2, 347–755. Frankfurt am Main: Suhrkamp.

Fühmann, Franz. [1955] 1990. "Kameraden." In *Erzählungen 1955–1975*. Edited by Ingrid Prignitz, 7–48. 4th ed. Rostock: Hinstorff.

Gerlach, Ingeborg. 1980. *Auf der Suche nach der verlorenen Identität: Studien zu Uwe Johnsons 'Jahrestagen'*. Königstein: Scriptor.

Glucksmann, André. [1974] 1976. *Köchin und Menschenfresser: Über die Beziehung zwischen Staat, Marxismus und Konzentrationslager*. Translated by Maren Sell and Jürgen Hoch. Berlin: Wagenbach.

Greiner, Bettina. 2010. *Verdrängter Terror: Geschichte und Wahrnehmung sowjetischer Speziallager in Deutschland*. Hamburg: Hamburger Edition.

Griese, Friedrich. 1947. *Die Dörfer der Jugend*. Kempen: Thomas-Verlag.

———. 1960. *Der Wind weht nicht wohin er will*. Düsseldorf: Diederichs.

Helbig, Holger, Klaus Kokol, Irmgard Müller, Dietrich Spaeth, and Ulrich Fries, eds. 1999. *Johnsons 'Jahrestage': Der Kommentar*. Accessed March 18, 2024, http://www.philfak.uni-rostock.de/institut/igerman/johnson/johnkomm/default.html.

Herrmann-Winter, Renate. 1999. *Plattdeutsch-hochdeutsches Wörterbuch für den mecklenburgisch-vorpommerschen Sprachraum*. 4th ed. Rostock: Hinstorff.

Hofmann, Michael. 2019. "Uwe Johnsons 'Jahrestage' als Text der Neuen Weltliteratur." *Johnson-Jahrbuch* 26: 193–213.

Jähner, Harald. 2019. *Wolfszeit: Deutschland und die Deutschen 1945–1955*. Berlin: Rowohlt.

Jeske, Natalja. 2013. *Lager in Neubrandenburg-Fünfeichen 1939–1948: Kriegsgefangenenlager der Wehrmacht, Repatriierungslager, Sowjetisches Speziallager*. Schwerin: Landeszentrale für politische Bildung Mecklenburg-Vorpommern.

———. 2021. "Neubrandenburg-Fünfeichen 1939–1948: Vom Stalag zum Speziallager." In *Zwischen Entnazifizierung und Besatzungspolitik: Die sowjetischen Speziallager*

1945–1950 im Kontext, edited by Julia Landau and Enrico Heitzer, 90–100. Göttingen: Wallstein.

Johnson, Uwe. 1970–1983. *Jahrestage: Aus dem Leben von Gesine Cresspahl*. Frankfurt am Main: Suhrkamp.

———. 1980. *Begleitumstände: Frankfurter Vorlesungen*. Frankfurt am Main: Suhrkamp.

———. [1979] 1988. "Lübeck habe ich ständig beobachtet." In *'Ich überlege mir die Geschichte': Uwe Johnson im Gespräch*, edited by Eberhard Fahlke, 79–85. Frankfurt am Main: Suhrkamp.

———. [1977] 1992. "Ich über mich." In *Über Uwe Johnson*, edited by Raimund Fellinger, 372–76. Frankfurt am Main: Suhrkamp.

———. [1970–1983] 2018. *Anniversaries: From a Year in the Life of Gesine Cresspahl*. Translated by Damion Searls. 2 vols. New York: New York Review Books.

———, and Walter Kempowski. 2006. *'Kaum beweisbare Ähnlichkeiten': Der Briefwechsel*, edited by Eberhard Fahlke and Gesine Treptow. Berlin: Transit.

Kalnačs, Benedikts. 2013. "Zur lettischen Literatur in der Sowjetzeit: Strategien des Widerstandes aus postkolonialer Perspektive." *Interlitteraria* 18: 534–44.

Karasek, Hellmuth. 1996. *Go West! Eine Biographie der fünfziger Jahre*. Hamburg: Hoffmann und Campe.

Kempowski, Walter. [1978] 1980. *Ein Kapitel für sich: Roman*. 3rd ed. Munich: dtv.

———. [1972] 1982. *Uns geht's ja noch gold: Roman einer Familie*. 10th ed. Munich: dtv.

Kertész, Imre. 2022. *Heimweh nach dem Tod: Arbeitstagebuch zur Entstehung des 'Romans eines Schicksallosen'*, edited and translated by Ingrid Krüger and Pál Kelemen. Hamburg: Rowohlt.

Kielmann, Peter. 1993. "Aber wohin ich in Wahrheit gehöre…" *Heimatkalender Anklam und Umgebung*, New Series 2: 80–87.

Kogon, Eugen. 1946. *Der SS-Staat: Das System der deutschen Konzentrationslager*. Frankfurt am Main: Verlag der Frankfurter Hefte.

Kopelew, Lew. [1975] 1983. *Aufbewahren für alle Zeit!* Translated by Heddy Pross-Weerth and Heinz-Dieter Mendel. 7th ed. Munich: dtv.

Koselleck, Reinhart. 1979. "Kriegerdenkmale als Identitätsstiftungen der Überlebenden." In *Poetik und Hermeneutik VIII: Identität*, edited by Odo Marquard and Karlheinz Stierle, 255–76. Munich: Fink.

Krappmann, Tamara. 2012. *Die Namen in Uwe Johnsons 'Jahrestagen'*. Göttingen: V&R unipress.

Krüger, Dieter, ed. 1990. *Fünfeichen 1945–1948: Briefe Betroffener und Hinterbliebener*. Neubrandenburg: Federchen.

Laak, Lothar van. 2009. *Medien und Medialität des Epischen in Literatur und Film des 20. Jahrhunderts: Bertolt Brecht—Uwe Johnson—Lars von Trier*. Munich: Fink.

Lachmann, Renate. 2019. *Lager und Literatur: Zeugnisse des GULAG*. Konstanz: Konstanz University Press.

Landau, Julia, and Enrico Heitzer, eds. 2021. *Zwischen Entnazifizierung und Besatzungs-politik: Die sowjetischen Speziallager 1945–1950 im Kontext*. Göttingen: Wallstein.

Leonhard, Wolfgang. [1955] 1979. *Die Revolution entläßt ihre Kinder*. Munich: Heyne.

Loth, Wilfried. 1994. *Stalins ungeliebtes Kind: Warum Moskau die DDR nicht wollte*. Berlin: Rowohlt.

Mann, Thomas. [1903] 1922. *Stories of Three Decades*. London: Secker and Warburg.

———. [1947] 1949. *Doctor Faustus: The Life of the German Composer Adrian Leverkühn, as Told by a Friend*. Translated by Helen Tracy Lowe-Porter. London: Secker and Warburg.

Meckel, Christoph. [2011] 2012. *Russische Zone: Erinnerung an den Nachkrieg*. 2nd ed. Lengwil: Libelle.

Mecklenburg, Norbert. 1997. *Die Erzählkunst Uwe Johnsons: 'Jahrestage' und andere Texte*. Frankfurt am Main: Suhrkamp.

Merridale, Catherine. 2006. *Iwans Krieg: Die Rote Armee 1939 bis 1945*. Translated by Hans Günter Holl. Frankfurt am Main: S. Fischer.

Meyer-Gosau, Frauke. 2014. *Versuch, eine Heimat zu finden: Eine Reise zu Uwe Johnson*. Munich: Beck.

Michaelis, Rolf. 1983. *Kleines Adreßbuch für Jerichow und New York: Ein Register zu Uwe Johnsons Roman 'Jahrestage'*. Frankfurt am Main: Suhrkamp.

Mironenko, Sergej, Lutz Niethammer, and Alexander von Plato, eds. 1998. *Sowjetische Speziallager in Deutschland 1945 bis 1950*. 2 vols. Berlin: Akademie.

Müller, Werner. 1999. "Die zwei Gründungen des Landes Mecklenburg-Vorpommern 1945 und 1990." In *Die DDR—Politik und Ideologie als Instrument*, edited by Heiner Timmermann, 523–40. Berlin: Duncker & Humblot.

Müller-Waldeck, Gunnar. 1991. "Gibt es eine pommersche Literatur?" In *Pommern: Geschichte—Kultur—Wissenschaft*. (1. Kolloquium zur Pommerschen Geschichte, 13. bis 15. November 1990), 331–36. Greifswald: Ernst-Moritz-Arndt-Universität.

Naimark, Norman M. 1995. *The Russians in Germany: A History of the Soviet Zone of Occupation, 1945–1949*. Cambridge: The Belknap Press of Harvard University Press.

Neumann, Bernd. 2000. *Uwe Johnson*. Berlin: Ullstein.

Niethammer, Lutz. 1998. "Alliierte Internierungslager in Deutschland nach 1945: Ein Vergleich und offene Fragen." In *Sowjetische Speziallager in Deutschland 1945 bis 1950*, edited by Sergej Mironenko, Lutz Niethammer, and Alexander von Plato. Vol. 1: Studien und Berichte, 97–116. Berlin: Akademie.

Nochotowitsch, Dina N. 2009. "Mecklenburg." In *SMAD-Handbuch: Die Sowjetische Militäradministration in Deutschland 1945–1949*, edited by Jan Foitzik and Tatjana W. Zarewskaja-Djakina, 534–41. Munich: Oldenbourg.

Nöldechen, Peter. 2008. *Neues Bilderbuch zu Uwe Johnsons Jerichow und Umgebung: Spurensuche im Mecklenburg von Gesine Cresspahl und Ingrid Babendererde*. Wismar: callidus.

Piskorski, Jan M., ed. 1999. *Pommern im Wandel der Zeiten*. Translated by Andreas Warnecke. Szczecin: Zamek Książąt Pomorskich.

———. 2013. *Die Verjagten: Flucht und Vertreibung im Europa des 20. Jahrhunderts*. Translated by Peter Oliver Loew. Munich: Siedler.

Reif-Spirek, Peter, and Bodo Ritscher, eds. 1999. *Speziallager in der SBZ: Gedenkstätten mit 'doppelter Vergangenheit'*. Berlin: Links.

Reuter, Fritz. 1853. *Läuschen un Riemels: Plattdeutsche Gedichte heiteren Inhalts in mecklenburgisch-vorpommerscher Mundart*. Treptow an der Tollense: Selbstverlag.

Rütters, Peter. 2007. "'Fünfeichen' als Gegenstand des Erzählens in Uwe Johnsons 'Jahrestagen': Ein erinnerungspolitischer Diskurs über sowjetische Speziallager?" *Johnson-Jahrbuch* 14: 65–83.

Scheuermann, Barbara. 1998. *Zur Funktion des Niederdeutschen im Werk Uwe Johnsons: 'in all de annin Saokn büssu hie nich me-i to Hus'.* Göttingen: Vandenhoeck & Ruprecht.

Solschenizyn, Alexander. [1974] 1976. *Ostpreußische Nächte: Eine Dichtung in Versen*. Translated by Nikolaus Ehlert. Darmstadt: Luchterhand.

———. [1998] 2004. *Schwenkitten '45*. Translated by Heddy Pross-Weerth and Fedor B. Poljakov. Munich: Langen Müller.

Talarczyk, Andrzej. 2020. "Pomeranus non cantat? Uwe Johnson i Pomorze. Topos utraconej (pierwszej) ojczyzny lub: skąd pochodzę, tego już nie ma." *Przegląd Zachodniopomorski* 64, no. 3: 27–48.

Tönsmeyer, Tatjana. 2015. "Besatzungsgesellschaften: Begriffliche und konzeptionelle Überlegungen zur Erfahrungsgeschichte des Alltags unter deutscher Besatzung im Zweiten Weltkrieg." Accessed March 18, 2024, http://docupedia.de/zg/toensmeyer_besatzungsgesellschaften_v1_de_2015.

Ullrich, Volker. 2021. *Acht Tage im Mai: Die letzte Woche des Dritten Reiches*. 6th ed. Munich: Beck.

Van Effelterre, Katrien. 2010. "Unterirdische." In *Enzyklopädie des Märchens*, edited by Rolf Wilhelm Brednich et al. Vol. 13: Suchen—Verführung, 1233–36. Berlin: De Gruyter.

Volkmann, Hans-Erich, ed. 1994. *Das Rußlandbild im Dritten Reich*. Cologne: Böhlau.

Widmann, Gudrun. 1991. *'Eine Art Information, in der Form von Erzählung': Die Darstellung der Vor- und Frühgeschichte der DDR in Uwe Johnsons 'Jahrestagen.'* Frankfurt am Main: Lang.

Zeidler, Manfred. 1996. *Kriegsende im Osten: Die Rote Armee und die Besetzung Deutschlands östlich von Oder und Neisse 1944/45*. Munich: Oldenbourg.

Zetzsche, Jürgen. 1994. *Die Erfindung photographischer Bilder im zeitgenössischen Erzählen: Zum Werk von Uwe Johnson und Jürgen Becker*. Heidelberg: Winter.

Figures

Fig. 1. 'Szczecin' from the official *Mapa Polski 1:500.000* (Warsaw: Wojskowy Instytut Geograficzny Sztabu Generalnego W.P. 1947), excerpt. Accessed March 18, 2024, http://maps.mapywig.org/m/WIG_maps/series/500K_post-WW2/MAPA_POLS-KI_1_500_000_SZCZECIN_1.jpg

Fig. 2. Mecklenburg-Vorpommern. Charity stamps commemorating land reform (inscription: "Junkerland in Bauernhand" (Junkers' land in peasant hands)). 6+14 (ploughman), 8+22 (peasant sowing), 12+28 (reaper) pfennigs, issued December 8, 1945. Michel catalog numbers: Deutschland/SBZ 23a, 24a, 25a. Source: Schumacher, collection, Bielefeld.

List of Contributors

Jan Andres is an associate professor (*Akademischer Oberrat*) of Literary Studies at Bielefeld University. He holds a Ph.D. in German Literature from the same institution, where he was also a member of the Special Research Area *The Political as Communicative Space in History* funded by the German Research Council. He is the author of *On Poetry Is Founded All the Security of Crowns* (2005) and has published extensively on various German conservative and right-wing writers as well as on Stefan George. His current research focuses on contemporary literature, the interplay between historiography and literature, and the relation between literature and politics.

Klaus-Michael Bogdal is a senior professor for Literature and its Theory at Bielefeld University. He has published well-received books on Heinrich von Kleist (1981) and on working-class literature (1991). His contributions to Foucault's historic discourse analyses (2007) have received widespread reception, both nationally and internationally. With the support of the prestigious OPUS MAGNUM fellowship from the Volkswagen Foundation, he wrote his book *Europe Discovers the Gypsies* (2011), which offers a detailed history of Antiziganism in Europe. This book has been translated into and published in several European languages, and it earned Bogdal the Leipzig Book Award for European Understanding in 2013.

Matthias Buschmeier is an associate professor (*Akademischer Direktor*) for German and Comparative Literature at Bielefeld University. He has published extensively on 18th- and 19th-century German and European Literature, as well as on questions of cultural theory. Matthias Buschmeier was co-convenor of the international research group "Felix Culpa? Guilt as Culturally Productive Force" at the Center for Interdisciplinary Research, Bielefeld. He is the editor of a special issue on Guilt and Culture of the *Journal for Cultural Poetics*. His coedited volume *Guilt: A Force of Cultural Transformation* was published with Oxford University Press in 2022. He is a member of the "Occupation Studies Research Network," hosted at Maastricht University.

Jeanne E. Glesener is an associate professor for Luxembourgish Literature at the University of Luxembourg. As a literary comparatist, she specializes in literary multilingualism, the aesthetics and reception of migration literature in Europe, literary historiography and small and minority literatures and their place in world literature. She is involved in collaborative research projects in the sociology of literature and in collaborative book projects such as *Trans-Culture: Migration and Literature in Europe since 1956* and *A Comparative History of Small and Minority Literatures in Europe*, both supervised by the Comparative History of Literature in European Languages Committee of the International Comparative Literature Association.

Benedikts Kalnačs is a senior researcher at the Institute of Literature, Folklore and Art, University of Latvia, Riga. He is a member of the publications committee for the Comparative History of Literature in European Languages (CHLEL) (2022–2024). Principal research areas are 19th- and 20th-century Latvian literature, comparative literature, and postcolonial studies. Publications include: *The Politics of Literary History: Literary Historiography in Russia, Latvia, the Czech Republic and Finland after 1990* (ed., with Liisa Steinby, Mikhail Oshukov, and Viola Parente-Čapková, forthcoming, Palgrave) and *A New History of Latvian Literature: The Long Nineteenth Century* (ed., with Pauls Daija, 2022, Peter Lang).

Stefan Laffin is a postdoctoral researcher (*Wissenschaftlicher Mitarbeiter*) in the Department of History at Leibniz University Hannover. He obtained his Ph.D. from Bielefeld University in 2021 with a dissertation on the Allied occupation of Southern Italy during and after World War II. He has received several fellowships to conduct research in Italy and the US. His dissertation won the Best Doctoral Thesis Award from the Bielefeld University Society. His current research interests include science policy, which led to his second book on the establishment of the German Study Center in Venice.

Daniela Lieb is a researcher at the National Literature Centre in Mersch, Luxembourg. She studied Japanese Studies, History, and Romanian Studies at the University of Cologne and Luxembourgish Studies at the University of Luxembourg. She co-authored the monographs *Luxembourg and World War I: Literary Histori(es)* (2014) and *Luxembourg and World War II: Literary and Intellectual Life from Hitler's Rise to Power to the Postwar Political Purges* (2020) and published numerous contributions covering the fields of the history of Luxembourgish literature, theater, dance, and circus.

Atinati Mamatsashvili is a professor of Comparative Literature at Ilia State University (Tbilisi). Her research focuses on literature and totalitarian regimes (Nazi and Soviet), French and Francophone literature, and antisemitism. Among her publications: *Déposséder-Dépossédé: Corps marginalisés, espaces déterritorialisés* (together with Blandine Landau), Tsafon—revue d'études juives du Nord, 84/2022; *Écrire une ville, habiter une ville: représentations spatiales des persécutions en Europe occupée (1940-1944)* (together with Helga Mitterbauer and Arvi Sepp), Cahiers de la Mémoire contemporaine, 2021; *Des écrivains face aux persécutions, au massacre de masse et au génocide* (together with Luba Jurgenson), Paris, Petra 2020.

Christopher Meid is currently an interim professor for Early Modern German Literature at the University of Osnabrück. He received his Ph.D. at the University of Freiburg in 2011 and qualified for professorship ('Habilitation') in 2019. From 2013 to 2015, he was a visiting scholar at the University of Oxford, and in 2019, he taught as a visiting professor at the Shanghai International Studies University. His research interests include travel literature and the relationship between politics and literature. In addition to numerous essays, he has written books on 18th-century German drama, on German travelogues about Greece, and, most recently, on political fiction of the Enlightenment.

Aleksandar Momčilović is preparing a Ph.D. thesis on the circulation of literary-theoretical knowledge within the Eastern Bloc. He received his MA from the Department of Anglophone Literatures and Cultures at Charles University in Prague. He specialized in Critical Theory and Cultural Studies. He also holds a BA in Comparative Literature and Literary Theory from the University of Belgrade. His academic interests include the theoretical underpinnings of world literature and the social and intellectual history of socialist countries, especially during the late Cold War.

Jeroen Olyslaegers is a distinguished Flemish novelist and playwright. His debut novel *Navel* was published in 1994. In 1996, he released the short story collection *Il faut manger*, and his novel *Open Like a Mouth* followed in 1999. In March 2009, Olyslaegers released a novel titled *We*. This is the first part of a satirical series of popular novels on memory and identity, each title of which begins with the letter W. In 2012, he then published *Winst*, about greed and the democratic deficit in the background of the art world. In August 2016, the third volume in the series, called *Wil*, was released; this latest novel offers an insight into Flemish collaboration during World War II. In 2014, Olyslaegers received the Ark Prize of the Free Word. He was also awarded the Fintro Literature Prize, the Confituur Bookstores' Prize, the Ferdinand Bordewijk Prize, and the Tzum Prize for the Best Literary Sentence of 2016.

Joanna Rzepa is senior lecturer in Literature in the Department of Literature, Film, and Theatre Studies at the University of Essex. Her research and teaching interests include comparative literature and cultural theory, modernism and twentieth-century literature, book history and print culture, literature and religion, cultural and intellectual history, literature and politics, cultural memory, Holocaust writing and testimony, and literary translation. Her monograph *Modernism and Theology: Rainer Maria Rilke, T. S. Eliot, Czesław Miłosz* was published with Palgrave Macmillan in 2021.

Sandra Schell is a Ph.D. candidate at Heidelberg University. Her doctoral thesis centers on the interrelation of German literature and the US *Reeducation*'s cultural politics (*c.*1940–1960s). During her Ph.D. and studies (German and English in Stuttgart, Bergen, and Heidelberg), she has been a recipient of scholarships by the Evangelisches Studienwerk. Conducting research on the '*völkisch*' author Börries v. Münchhausen and his literary commitment to Zionism (*Jahrbuch der deutschen Schillergesellschaft* 2021), she received her degree in 2020. Besides her research interest in 20th-century literature, and the relation between literature and politics, she publishes on Science Studies.

Meinolf Schumacher is a professor emeritus of German Literature at Bielefeld University. His research focuses on historical semantics and the literary history of guilt, compassion, and consolation. He published his book *Dirt of Sin and Purity of Heart* (1996) on impurity and purification as metaphors in Medieval Latin and German literature. In 2018 and 2019, he was an invited fellow of the international and interdisciplinary research group "Felix Culpa? Guilt as a Culturally Productive Force" at the Center for Interdisciplinary Research (ZiF) in Bielefeld.

Stefanie Siess is a Ph.D. candidate in History at Heidelberg University and at the School for Advanced Studies in the Social Sciences (EHESS) Paris. Currently completing a cotutelle, she works on her dissertation about Writing as an Intimate Act in Ego Documents from the French Zone of Occupation (1945–1955). In Heidelberg, she works as a research assistant and lecturer for the Chair of Contemporary History. Her research interests include writing as a social practice during wartime and occupation, ego documents and literature as historical sources, Franco-German relations and transfers, the history of everyday life, and the history of emotions and sensibilities.

www.ingramcontent.com/pod-product-compliance
Lightning Source LLC
Chambersburg PA
CBHW072242310326
42231CB00006B/164